Universal Grammar and Narrative Form

Sound and Meaning

The Roman Jakobson Series in Linguistics and Poetics

C. H. van Schooneveld, Series Editor

Universal Grammar and Narrative Form

David Herman

Duke University Press   Durham and London 1995

© 1995 Duke University Press
All rights reserved
Printed in the United States of America on acid-free paper ∞
Typeset in Minion by Keystone Typesetting, Inc.
Library of Congress Cataloging-in-Publication Data appear
on the last printed page of this book.

Contents

Acknowledgments

This study was possible only because I had the help of many people. Gerald Prince provided invaluable advice and assistance with the project from the start; I am grateful for his comments and criticisms and, more generally, for the exemplary excellence of his scholarship. I am also deeply indebted to Arkady Plotnitsky, first, for his polymathic expertise in areas of study informing this book, as well as many other areas the book either does not manage or does not attempt to incorporate, and, second, for the example of his unstinting intellectual integrity. I thank Vicki Mahaffey for her expertise on Joyce, Woolf, and modernism generally and for her long-standing advice, encouragement, and intellectual support. I am particularly grateful to Peter Steiner for his insights on Russian and Czech literary theory and linguistics, for relentless Central European irony, for continued advice and encouragement, and for letting me in on the secret of Belgian beer. I am also indebted to Michael Holquist and the other, anonymous reader for Duke University Press for their productive criticisms and suggestions. At the Press itself, Jean Brady, Sharon Parks, and Reynolds Smith, as well as freelance copyeditor Joe Brown, worked very hard to make this a better book, and I thank them for their gracious help.

Further, I am grateful for the insights, camaraderie, and support of many other friends and colleagues, all of whom contributed in one way or another to the completion of this project (whether they know it or not), but only some of whom I can name here: Eyal Amiran, Bruno Bosteels, Anna Botta, Michael Burri, Alison Byerly, Ortwin de Graef, Lubomír Doležel, Marian Eide, James English, Koen Geldof, Jay Grossman, Andrea Henderson, James Hicks, Steve Jensen, Laura Levine, Marjorie Levinson, Barbara Lonnquist, Jeff Masten, Nicholas Miller, James Morrison, Alexander Nehamas, Thomas Pavel, Nikola Petkovic, James Phelan, Ellen Prince, Marie-Laure Ryan, Susan Shelmerdine,

Craig Smith, Rei Terada, Jon Thompson, Craig White, and Walt Wolfram. I am also grateful to my students, who have taught me so much.

Most of all, however, my gratitude and appreciation go to my parents, Virginia and William Herman, for all their help; to my sister, Jennifer Cohen, for just the book I needed; and to Susan Moss, for the journey.

Earlier versions of parts of this book appeared in the following journals, and I am grateful for permission to draw on the same material here: *Česká Literatura* for "Pragmatika, Prag-matika, meta-pragmatika: Kontexty pragmatických kontexů" (1991); the *Journal of Literary Semantics* for "Meaning, Model-Theoretic Semantics and Model-Worlds" (1992); *Neophilologus* for "Pragmatics, Praguematics, Metapragmatics: Contextualizing Pragmatic Contexts" (1992); *Poetics* for "Towards a Pragmatics of Represented Discourse: Narrative, Speech and Context in Woolf's *Between the Acts*" (1993), by permission of Elsevier Science B.V., Amsterdam, The Netherlands; *boundary 2* for "Postmodernism as Secondary Grammar" (1993); *Semiotica* for "On the Semantic Status of Film: Subjectivity, Possible Worlds, Transcendental Semiotics" (1994), by permission of Mouton de Gruyter, a division of Walter de Gruyter & Co.; and the *James Joyce Quarterly* for " 'Sirens' after Schönberg" (1994).

Prefatory Note (On Translations and Citation Format)

Wherever possible, I have used existing translations of the texts discussed in this book. In some instances, however, I wished to preserve the nuances or richness—or at least the idiosyncrasies—of the original texts. As a result, I have sometimes provided my own translations of relevant texts and sometimes modified existing translations according to my own sense of fidelity to the original, all such modifications being duly noted in the text. Translated passages are enclosed in single quotes and placed immediately after the original version of those passages, which are enclosed in double quotes. In some of the end-notes, whose length I have sought to keep to a minimum, I refrained from translating (parts of) cited passages. In those cases I opted instead for direct citation of the original text in the original language or else short paraphrases supplemented here and there by quotations from the original.

Furthermore, since the arguments set forth here are in some respects histor-ical in nature—that is, since the study tries to establish grounds for making comparisons between developments in linguistics, literature, philosophy, and semiotics beginning around the turn of the century—I thought it important to indicate original dates of publication (in brackets) whenever citing texts either reissued or else translated at a later date. Thus "Carnap 1969 [1928]" refers to the 1969 translation of Rudolf Carnap's *The Logical Structure of the World*, which was originally published in 1928. For the sake of consistency I have used the brackets throughout, even where the difference between the original (bracketed) and subsequent (unbracketed) dates of publication is only a matter of a few years.

Finally, for the reader's convenience I sometimes cross-reference parts of the book treating the same idea or the same complex of ideas. For such internal references I use the following format, always set off in italic type: The first, boldface numeral refers to the chapter at issue, the second numeral to a particular section of that chapter, and the third and fourth numerals (where necessary) to the numbered subdivisions contained in some sections of the chapters. Thus *1.6.1* refers to chapter 1, section 6, subsection 1, and *0.2* refers to the introduction, section 2. Numerals unaccompanied by one in boldface specifying a chapter—for example, *4.2*—cross-reference sections and/or subsections contained in the current chapter.

Universal Grammar and Narrative Form

Introduction: The Project of Universal Grammar: Some Historical and Methodological Considerations

Distrust of grammar is the first requisite for philosophizing.—Ludwig Wittgenstein

1. The Scope and Aims of the Present Study

This book attempts to rethink some of the foundations, methods, and aims of narrative poetics. More precisely, studying the forms and techniques of representative early twentieth-century literary narratives as well as some later texts and artifacts, the book reevaluates the possibilities and limits of classical models for narratological research. The first phase of a project whose second phase is currently in progress,[1] *Universal Grammar and Narrative Form* focuses special attention on the conceptual underpinnings of narratology as classically conceived—underpinnings that supported the emergence, during the 1960s, of what Tzvetan Todorov baptized "la narratologie" in 1969 in his *Grammaire du "Décaméron."* By drawing on aspects of twentieth-century language theory that do not directly inform the earlier, structuralist models, the study seeks to enrich current narratological frameworks with key philosophico-linguistic concepts.

The concepts in question pertain to three areas of concern that emerged as separate dimensions of linguistic theory over the course of the present century. At issue, first, is *syntax* or the study of the structures of language, that is, "the principles according to which words can be combined to form larger meaningful units, and by which such larger units can be combined to form sentences" (Horrocks 1987: 24). Chapter 1 discusses concepts drawn from syntactic theory vis-à-vis the "Sirens" episode of James Joyce's *Ulysses* (1922). Second, we have *semantics* or the study of how linguistic expressions mean and refer, discussed in connection with Franz Kafka's *Der Prozeß* (*The Trial*) (1925) in chapter 2. The third area of concern is *pragmatics* or the study of how contexts license inferences about the meaning of utterances embedded in particular situations;

chapter 3 discusses ideas drawn from linguistic pragmatics in conjunction with Virginia Woolf's use of represented discourse in her novel *Between the Acts* (1941). (For further characterization of the syntax-semantics-pragmatics paradigm, see section 7 below.) Arguably, owing in part to the long-standing influence of Saussurean linguistics on Continental literary theory (Pavel 1989), classical narratology failed to accommodate crucial developments in syntactic, semantic, and pragmatic theory, many of which were advanced by researchers working outside the Saussurean tradition. Insofar as it explores the relevance of these developments for narratological inquiry, the present study can be viewed as a search for new tools for narrative theory.[2]

More than this, however, the book examines important links between twentieth-century literary experimentation and contemporaneous concerns in language theory. The aim throughout is to highlight modes of interface between science and art, theory and culture, philosophical analysis and narrative discourse. Using Joyce's *Ulysses*, Kafka's *Der Prozeß*, and Woolf's *Between the Acts* as case studies, the book argues that the formal profile of twentieth-century literary narratives links them with the modern resurgence of interest in the age-old tradition of universal grammars—a grammatical renaissance that began around the turn of the century. As we shall see later on in this introduction (secs. 4ff.), the rebirth of universal grammar was heralded by the publication of works like Gottlob Frege's *Begriffsschrift* (*Conceptual Notation*) (1879) and Edmund Husserl's *Logical Investigations* (1st ed., 1900–1901); these works anchored themselves in a long tradition of speculation on language and its power to inform us about the ultimate structure of reality. Read against the backdrop of the introduction, part I (chaps. 1–3) of this book suggests that, by examining widespread efforts to reinvigorate universal grammar earlier this century, we discover interesting affiliations between the narrative techniques of modernist texts and the analytic techniques simultaneously emergent in scientific (linguistic) and more broadly theoretical (logical, philosophical, semiotic) discourse.[3]

Part II (chaps. 4 and 5) tests the usefulness of grammatical theory for thinking about other cultural artifacts and problems; this "Extensions and Applications" section explores later twentieth-century cultural phenomena using the interpretation of universal grammar developed via Joyce, Kafka, and Woolf in part I. Thus chapter 4 extends the results of chapter 1, suggesting that, by modifying ideas drawn from syntactic theory, we can rethink the problem of citation in the discourses of postmodernism. Referring back to the analysis of Kafka in chapter 2, chapter 5 argues that ideas pertaining to semantic theory can help us redescribe modes of meaning in film. This chapter discusses the question of cinematic meaning through an interpretation of Peter Greenaway's 1989 film *The Cook, The Thief, His Wife and Her Lover*. Hence, part II seeks not only to consolidate and reinforce the arguments made in part I but also to suggest further applications of a linguistically enriched model for narrative theory.[4] The later chapters are intended to be blueprints for further research as much as self-contained analyses of quotation in postmodernism and meaning in film.

1.1. My working hypothesis, then, is that the modern-day rebirth of universal grammar can be used to help interpret contemporaneous innovations in narrative form, and vice versa. Over the course of the study, I therefore address two interlinked questions: first, whether familiarizing ourselves with ideas drawn from grammatical theory can also help us understand the form and functioning of (post)modernist narratives; second, whether study of twentieth-century narrative form can in turn illuminate the grammatical schemes emergent during the same era. Addressing the first question requires that we rethink standard periodizations and interpretations of modernism and, for that matter, postmodernism; addressing the second question requires that we rethink the functions typically imputed to literary discourse itself. More precisely, the second question centers on the capacity of literary narratives to inform—on the cognitive force of literary discourse vis-à-vis discourse commonly labeled theoretical by contrast.

In a manner that might be termed archaeological or genealogical (Foucault 1973 [1966], 1972 [1969]; Nietzsche 1968b [1887]), we shall work toward situating the texts under study in an entire network of language-theoretical discourses; in consequence, we shall be compelled to reassess the particular discursive formation, the episteme, that we have come to call *modernism*.[5] (The same holds mutatis mutandis for *postmodernism*.) As it turns out, although often aspiring to the putatively achronic, transcontextual profile of mythic forms (cf., e.g., Eliot 1975 [1923]), modernist literary narratives encode grammatical principles that began to be (re)fashioned by researchers in logic, linguistics, and philosophy around 1900. These texts everywhere display the signs of their times. Further, given that interpretation of the texts bears demonstrably on (emergent) methods for the analysis of language itself, we must come to grips with the cognitive dimensions of the narratives being considered—dimensions insufficiently emphasized in certain acceptations of terms like *literature* and *narrative*.[6] As we shall discover again and again over the course of this investigation, the materials under study are not merely *susceptible* of analysis via models drawn from linguistic theory; moreover they help recontextualize and so reframe the models themselves.

1.2. Hence, in the chapters that follow, universal grammar is sometimes the object and sometimes the method of description; universal grammar functions both as the *explanans* and as the *explanandum* of the present analysis.[7] Grammatical ideas provide a framework for understanding the formal profile of the texts under examination, but those ideas are also *what* narrative form is seen to enact, conjointly with surrounding theoretical discourses. A measure of circularity thus afflicts the argument. Debatably, however, this affliction represents not so much a logical defect as an indication of the complex, circuitous routes of exchange linking the various orders and domains of cultural production at issue. It is my purpose to trace some of these routes of exchange—to observe, but not necessarily police, the migration of language-theoretical concepts across the borders of disciplines, genres, and texts.

The first item of business, however, is to chronicle some of the adventures of universal grammar itself during its long and storied history. To be sure, I do not have space here to sketch anything resembling a complete synopsis of the grammatical theories that have evolved over the course of some two-and-a-half millenia of thinking about language. But we can rehearse some of the more important developments in the grammatical tradition, the point being to contextualize in the project of universal grammar as a whole innovations in twentieth-century narrative form in particular, and vice versa. In short, a genealogy of (universal) grammar is a necessary propaedeutic for the genealogy of universal grammar *and* narrative form that is to be conducted over the course of subsequent chapters.

2. (Universal) Grammar: Definitions and Traditions

R. H. Robins (1951) prefaces his account of ancient and medieval grammatical theory with a useful working definition of the term *grammar* itself. Historically, says Robins, "we may consider that, in the most general terms, grammatical study begins whenever in the stream of speech or the expanse of writing there are observed, and in some way systematized, similarities of form or patterns of arrangement, and these are partly at least correlated with the meanings or functions of the utterances in which they occur" (14). Robins also notes that, etymologically speaking, "the word 'γραμματική,' from which our 'grammar' is derived, is already found in quasi-technical use in Plato's dialogue *Cratylus*, and it is not unreasonable to assume that Socrates employed it in much the same sense. It was taken from the schoolroom. Boys were taught γραμματική, literally 'the art of writing,' when they learned to read and write" (1951: 12). To be sure, we should have to cover vast amounts of territory to move from these historico-intuitive characterizations of grammar to Noam Chomsky's definition of an *acceptable grammar* as a "finite mechanism capable of generating an infinite set of sentences"—that is, as a generative apparatus capable of giving "a precise specification of the (in general, infinite) list of sentences (strings of symbols) that are sentences of [the] language" in question (quoted in Gardies 1985 [1975]: 25–26). Here, I can give only a few indications of how the grammar of *grammar*, as it were, has evolved over time.

Note that, since its inception, grammar has been more or less intimately interinvolved with the theory of literary discourse. Thus, G. Behse (1974) observes that, in his Τέχνη γραμματική (*Art of Grammar*) of the first century B.C.E., Dionysius Thrax "definiert die Grammatik als die Wissenschaft, welche alle Probleme, die zur vollständigen Interpretation eines literarischen Werkes benötigt werden, behandelt. Grammatik ist also nach ihm Sprach- und Literaturwissenschaft" 'defines grammar as the science that treats all those problems pertaining to the complete interpretation of a literary work. Hence grammar is for him at once a science of language and also a science of literature' (846). In the Hellenistic period as a whole we find an "emphasis on literature . . . as against the study of current colloquial speech. Grammar had a practical purpose, to preserve good literary Greek . . . against decay from within and contamination from without" (Robins 1951: 39). Conversely, as Ernst Robert Curtius (1953 [1948]) puts it, "in Antiquity, the concept of the model Author was oriented upon a grammatical criterion, the criterion of correct speech" (250).

Significantly, grammar begins to attain the status of a theory of language, as opposed to a theory of literary usage, only after the infusion of philosophical discourse into the framework of grammatical analysis during the Middle Ages.[8] G. L. Bursill-Hall (1971) suggests that, after the "logicization of grammar" brought about by the introduction of Aristotelian philosophy into the West in the thirteenth century, "instead of grammar being studied as a key to knowledge of classical literature and the Bible, it became a branch of speculative philosophy, and grammar was now justified, not by illustration from classical literature, but by systems of logic and metaphysical theories of reality" (27). Similarly, Robins (1951) argues that, after the rediscovery of the philosophers of antiquity, medieval grammarians "sought, as the only sound method of research, to derive and justify rules of grammar from systems of logic and metaphysical theories about the nature of reality. . . . Now grammar was studied [both] as a means of reading Latin and as a branch of speculative philosophy, a key to understanding the nature and working of the human mind" (75).

In general, by the latter part of the medieval period, grammar "ist nicht mehr nur eine empirische und normative Hilfswissenschaft, sondern wird als autonome Wissenschaft aufgefaßt. Ihr wird als spekulativer Wissenschaft die Aufgabe zugewiesen, von der Wirklichkeit (res) aus, über die Verstandigtätigkeit (intellectus), die Verlautbarkeit im Wort (vox) rational verständlich zu machen" 'is no longer merely an empirical and normative auxiliary science; rather, it is construed as an autonomous science. To this speculative science is ascribed the task of making rationally comprehensible the expressibility in words [voice] of what passes from reality [thing] into the activity of the understanding [intellect]' (Behse 1974: 847). By the thirteenth century, in fact, speculative grammars constituted their own "literarisches Genus" 'literary genre' (847; cf. Burkhardt 1980: 87; Bursill-Hall 1971: 25–27). Such speculative grammars formed the privileged medium of medieval *Sprachwissenschaft*—a science of language whose scope was so broad as to include fields of study now divided up among logicians, linguists, and philosophers of language, among others (cf. Behse 1974).

2.1. I discuss the genre of speculative grammars in more detail in the next section. First, however, we need to highlight the more important features of the historical scenario just sketched. As we have seen, grammar starts to split off from literary theory and constitute itself *as* grammar in a quasi-modern sense—stipulating rules for the set of all (actual and possible) utterances—just when it attaches itself to the domain of philosophical analysis. As we might also put it—and to anticipate conclusions reached in chapter 1 in a more modern context—from the very start grammar has taken shape as *philosophical* grammar. In turn, however, philosophical grammar, whose principles are presumed to apply universally, across the entire domain of language use, is made possible by an inaugural bracketing of literary discourse from the corpus of utterances over which it ranges. Our guiding question then presents itself as follows: What are we to make of twentieth-century literary narratives whose form allows us to assimilate those texts to surrounding developments in philosophy and linguistics, for example, when all along the notions *literature, philosophy,* and *grammar* have functioned as profoundly interlinked (if not interdefined) concepts?

I reserve for subsequent chapters fuller discussion of questions about the historical interinvolvement of different modes of language-theoretical inquiry—modes of inquiry now divided up among different fields of study, including logic, literary theory, semiotics, linguistics, and the philosophy of language. But I can briefly outline the somewhat paradoxical profile assumed by (post)modernist narratives in this connection. What makes literary narratives "modern" or "postmodern," arguably, is the manner in which the design and interpretation of such texts restructure the relations between the discourses just mentioned. The narratives under study resist overrestrictive classifications as to genre, broadly construed; they feature (and self-consciously exploit) multiple connections with other discourses, other genres. Yet their polygeneric status, as it were, becomes detectable only amid the evolutionary patterns, the genealogical interconnections, of the discourses in which they are situated. Thus, the most radical formal innovations of (post)modern narratives curiously reattach those texts to an ancient research tradition—that is, the concepts and methods developed under the auspices of universal grammar.

True, the novelty of twentieth-century narrative form requires equally novel processing techniques. But at the same time, in interpreting the narrative techniques of the texts under study—in reading extraordinary forms of utterance designed to deautomatize traditional, ossified habits of reading—we are driven ever more deeply into the very oldest traditions for the study of language. This, perhaps, is the antinomy of universal grammar and narrative form.

3. On Grammars of a Higher Order

It will require the remainder of this study to work toward a more perspicuous characterization of grammar. Assume for the moment, however, that I have established at least a rudimentary conception of what grammar is and has been. My next task is to examine the second-order notions variously designated *general, philosophical,* or *universal* grammar. Intuitively, at least, the very locution *universal grammar* may seem like an oxymoron. Grammars are after all grounded in specific patterns of usage corresponding to particular languages. A speaker of English, say, begins to comprehend the grammar of German only by learning to recognize where the grammar specific to English interferes with, *differs from,* grammatical patterns required for acceptable constructions and interpretations of German sentences. By extension, it seems that the notion *grammar* must be defined differentially; at issue is the way the grammar of a given language contrasts with that of some other language(s). One might therefore venture that the grammar of *grammar* is analogous to the grammar of a group noun like *family,* which operates (in English) as a term designating a pattern of differences and resemblances situated in a vast network of other such patterns (Wittgenstein 1958 [1933–35], 1969). We can say *universal family* or *general family* only on pain of vacuousness or incoherence; does not the same stricture apply in the case of *grammar*?

There are conceptual grounds, and a wealth of historical precedents, for answering the previous question in the negative. The *Oxford English Dictionary*, for example, defines *general grammar* as "the science which analyses those distinctions in thought which it is the purpose of grammatical forms more or less completely to render in expression, and which aims to furnish a scheme of classification capable of including all the grammatical categories recognized in actual languages" (cf. Aarsleff 1982: 105ff., 165ff.). Witold Marciszewski (1988) offers a more precise statement of the grounds for talk about grammars of a higher order:

> A grammar, in the sense of grammatical theory, can be said to be universal if and only if the following holds: either (i) it can be used for the description of any language whatever in the stead of a respective particular grammar, or (ii) it is able to provide each particular grammar with a basic conceptual apparatus to be used in the construction of this grammar. Obviously, the latter alternative is more realistic, but the former can be used to define the limit to be approximated. Individual grammars which pretend to be universal in the sense of item (i) may be compared with each other as to the degree of approximation in satisfying this condition; the more inclusive is the class of particular grammars which are replaceable by the "more general" grammar in question, the more this grammar approximates the upper limit of universality. (87)

One might make a case for the view that grammars designed to meet the second of Marciszewski's two conditions have in fact been elaborated under the name of speculative, philosophical, and rational grammars, whereas *universal grammar* and *general grammar* are headings more appropriately applied to grammars designed to meet the first of Marciszewski's two conditions.[9] Here, however, I follow Marciszewski in using the term *universal grammar* to designate grammars constructed to meet either condition i or condition ii—or both i and ii.

3.1. Of more immediate concern is how, historically, efforts to design grammars of the sort meeting condition ii have been used to *justify* universal grammars of the sort meeting condition i. Less elliptically, my focus is on possible difficulties deriving from collapsing together Marciszewski's two conditions— that is, grammatical rules applicable to all possible languages and a conceptual apparatus for the construction of all possible grammars—under the single rubric *universal grammar*. Universal grammars traditionally ground in (postulated) structures of the world and of the mind itself the "conceptual apparatus" used to account for the grammar of a given particular language. In turn, that conceptual apparatus furnishes a theoretical basis for grammar in general. Higher-order grammars have thereby sought to confer universality of scope—a priori validity for all languages—on principles valid with respect to the structures and functions of the particular empirical language serving as the exemplary source or model corpus, so to speak.

Take, for example, the *grammatica speculativa* (speculative grammar) developed by medieval grammarians such as Thomas of Erfurt (1972 [ca. 1300–1310]; cf. Heidegger 1978 [1915]). Robins (1951) describes how the speculative grammarians or "Modistae" of the thirteenth and fourteenth centuries (so named because most speculative grammars were given the title *De modis significandi*) founded "grammatical rules . . . on extra-linguistic premises, the 'laws of thought' or the 'nature of things,' which are the concern of the philosopher. . . . Since grammar was now held to have its basis outside language itself, we can understand the claim of the Modistae that there is a universal grammatical structure inherent in all languages, and that the rules of grammar are quite independent, as rules, of the particular language in which they happen to find realization" (78–79). Tzvetan Todorov (1969)—significantly, in the act of proposing what was at that time only a newly emerging science, "la narratologie" (10; see secs. 4ff. below)—recounts the Modistic project in somewhat greater detail:

> Dans leurs 'grammaires spéculatives,' les modistes postulent l'existence de trois classes de 'modes': modi essendi, intelligendi, et significandi. La première classe correspond à la structure de l'univers; la seconde, à celle de la pensée; la troisième, à celle de la langue. Les modes de la langue sont les mêmes partout parce qu'ils représentent les modes de la pensée; ceux-ci le sont aussi parce qu'ils représentent ceux de l'univers. Autrement dit, les modes de la langue imitent, par l'intermédiaire de la pensée, les modes de l'univers. (15)

In their "speculative grammars," the modistae postulate the existence of three classes of "modes": modes of being, knowing, and signifying. The first class corresponds to the structure of the universe; the second, to that of thought; the third, to that of language. The modes of language are the same everywhere [i.e., the same in all languages] because they represent the modes of thought; and the latter are also the same because they represent those of the universe. Put otherwise, the modes of language imitate, through the medium of thought, the modes of the universe.

In support of Todorov's interpretation, Bursill-Hall (1971) points out that the term *speculative* is used by the Modistae "in the sense that language mirrors the 'reality' which, according to medieval metaphysics, underlies the phenomena of the physical world" (31). Bursill-Hall also remarks that we find in Modistic theory "a complete interdependence between language on the one hand and the structure of things on the other; this is central to Modistic grammatical theory, with the human mind, with its ability to perceive, signify and interpret these things in language, acting as the link" (73).[10]

In short, universal grammar of the speculative stripe "est universelle non seulement parce qu'elle est répandue dans toutes les langues de l'univers, mais parce qu'elle coïncide avec la structure de l'univers lui-même" 'is universal not only because its scope includes all the languages of the universe, but also because it coincides with the structure of the universe itself' (Todorov 1969: 15)—one subdomain of the universe being of course the domain of the human mind. The *vox-intellectus-res* correlation thus functions as an axiom within the system of speculative grammar. The structures of language, the mind, and the world are simply postulated to be exact analogues of one another, such that each term of the correlation can be mapped transparently and without interference into any of the other terms.

3.2. Note that this correlation rests on an initial, more or less surreptitious deduction of cognitive and ontological structures from the structures of language. Granted, Chomsky (1966a) suggests that the axioms of universal grammars formulated within the tradition of "Cartesian linguistics" can be reduced to those subtending a *vox-intellectus* correlation alone; Chomsky thus seeks to avoid the dubious ontological commitments introduced by the inclusion of *res* among the postulates of universal grammar. As he puts it, "The central doctrine of Cartesian linguistics is that the general features of grammatical structure are common to all languages and reflect certain fundamental properties of the mind. . . . Such universal conditions are not learned; rather, they provide the organizing principles that make language learning possible, that must exist if data is to lead to knowledge" (59–60). One might point out that Chomsky's historical interpretation, which has been disputed at length by Hans Aarsleff (1982: 101–19), serves his own eventual interpretation of linguistics itself as a branch of cognitive psychology. And the fact remains that the Modistae *did* attempt to incorporate ontological dimensions in their speculative grammars.

My larger point, however, is that, in talking about a *surreptitious* deduction of cognitive and ontological structures from the structures of language in this connection, we find ourselves face to face with something approximating the idea of *subreption* developed by Immanuel Kant in his first *Critique* and in earlier, precritical writings as well. Depending on the context in which the term is used, *subreption* generally indicates for Kant faulty inferences (specifically, claims over- or underextended in scope) obtained by way of illicit premises masking themselves as valid ones in otherwise sound arguments (cf. Frege's statement of the requirements for a genuine *Begriffsschrift*, as discussed in sec. *5.2* below. Subreptic inferences are a source of what Kant called "dialectical error," which occurs whenever reason leads the understanding astray, past the limits of what can really be known: for example, when a merely regulative idea ("infinity") poses as an idea amenable to and comprehensible by a finite human understanding.[11] Arguably, the speculative grammarians' "deduction" of cognitive and ontological structures from grammatical ones can be construed as a classically subreptic type of inference. The subreption occurs just when language L masks itself as language L_1, L_2, . . . L_n, such that the grammatical patterns, (onto)logical features, and *Weltanschauungen* bound up with L are universalized across all actual and possible languages.

Researchers such as Benjamin Lee Whorf (1956) and Willard V. O. Quine (1960) *also* argue for the preeminent role played by language in shaping operations of thought and conceptions of reality. Thus, Whorf discusses "far-reaching [behavioral] compulsion from large-scale patterning of grammatical categories, such as plurality, gender and similar classifications. . . . A category such as number (singular vs. plural) is an attempted interpretation of a whole larger order of experience, virtually of the world or of nature; it attempts to say how experience is to be segmented, what experience is to be called 'one' and what 'several' " (1956: 137). Quine, for his part, advances the famous thesis of the indeterminacy of translation, whereby "manuals for translating one language into another can be set up in divergent ways, all compatible with the totality of speech dispositions, yet incompatable with one another" (1960: 27; cf. 73–79). What Quine calls "empirically unconditioned variation" in speakers' and hearers' "conceptual schemes" (26; but contrast Davidson 1973–74 and Rorty 1972, 1982) gives scope to differences of meaning between utterances that are prima facie semantically equivalent, although in actual fact untranslatable into each other. But the point is that both Whorf and Quine avoid subreptic argumentation by stressing the *relativity* of conceptual predispositions and ontological commitments—the variability of the meanings commonly attributed to objects, events, and situations—across different languages or even among different users of the same language. By contrast, extrapolating from the structure of the particular language(s) on which their grammars are based, speculative grammarians typically presumed to make claims both about the operations of the mind as such and about the nature of things in general.

As a result, charges of a kind of grandiose parochialism have been leveled all along at Modistic speculative grammars. The accusation is that so-called universal grammars are but illicit extensions of the grammar of a particular language—notably, Greek and/or Latin—into a fictitious domain of grammar in general or grammar as such. For example, Thomas of Erfurt (1972 [ca. 1300–1310]) follows Dionysus Thrax and Priscian by appealing to the notion *parts of speech* (*pars orationis*)—noun, pronoun, verb, adjective, etc.—in the construction of his speculative grammar (155ff.). Yet we find no real anticipation of, let alone any attempt to correct for, problems introduced by the use of a parts-of-speech scheme for both synthetic or inflected languages (Greek, Latin, or German) and analytic or uninflected languages (French, Spanish, or English; cf. sec. *1.5.1.3* below).[12] To list just one potential problem, prepositions in analytic languages assume, at least to some extent, the functions of the case markings in synthetic or inflected languages, in which by contrast prepositions merely supplement syntactic functions already indicated by inflections. To the extent that we cannot set down rules that hold for the role of prepositions in both analytic and synthetic languages—let alone rules for all parts of speech in all possible and actual languages whatsoever—the notion of a "universal grammar" of prepositions seems absurd on its face.

3.3. The degree to which speculative and, later, general grammarians like Antoine Arnauld and Claude Lancelot (1972 [1660]) are guilty of such hypergeneralizing habits of analysis is perhaps subject to dispute. Chomsky (1966a), for one, argues for a relatively tolerant interpretation of general grammars modeled within the tradition of Cartesian linguistics:

> What is assumed [by the Port-Royal Grammar of Arnauld and Lancelot and writings of the Encyclopedist Du Marsais] is the existence of a uniform set of relations into which words can enter, in any language, these corresponding to the exigencies of thought. The philosophical grammarians do not try to show that all languages literally have case systems, that they use inflectional devices to express these relations. On the contrary, they repeatedly stress that a case system is only one device for expressing these relations. . . . It is important to realize that the use of the names of classical cases for languages with no inflections implies only a belief in the

uniformity of grammatical relations involved, a belief that deep structures are fundamentally the same across languages, although the means for their expression may be quite diverse. (45; cf. Lyons 1991: 110–45)[13]

Be that as it may, Robins (1951) locates at the source of grammatical theory a tendency on the part of ancient Greek theorists to project onto all possible languages the grammatical structures of their own language (18–19, 72ff.). Thus, in the *Categories,* Aristotle (1938) makes constant appeal to Greek grammar both in characterizing the various ontological categories ("Substance [Οὐσία] in the truest and strictest, the primary sense of the term, is that which is neither asserted of nor can be found in a subject" [2a, p. 19]) and, strikingly, as a rich source of examples of permissible modes of predication ("You may call a man 'learned in grammar.' And, therefore, his species and genus, that is to say, man and animal, you may also call 'learned in grammar' " [3a, p. 25; cf. 1a, p. 15; 10a, p. 73; 11a, p. 79; 14a, p. 99]). Aristotle's attempted projection of the logic of a language into the language of logic is paradigmatic for all subsequent higher-order grammars. In Otto Jespersen's formulation (1965 [1924]), universal and speculative grammarians have "tried to eliminate from a language everything that was not strictly conformable to the rules of logic, and to measure everything by the canon of their so-called general or philosophical grammar. Unfortunately they were too often under the delusion that Latin grammar was the perfect model of logical consistency, and they therefore laboured to find in every language the distinctions recognized in Latin" (46).[14]

Indeed, even in Kant, who otherwise takes great pains to safeguard himself against the subreptic types of inference that he had identified (see sec. 3.2 above), we find continued evidence of an unwarranted extension of the grammar of a particular language into the domain of a general or universal grammar presumed to be valid across all languages. For Mirella Capozzi (1987), "The question is: how is it possible that, if [as Kant's remarks on logic seem to suggest] logic precedes universal grammar and, *a fortiori,* is independent of the grammars of natural languages, both Kant's universal grammar and logic so openly borrow from the grammar of one particular natural language, i.e. Latin?" (105). Although we cannot enter into an analysis of Kant's logical writings here, we need to address the more general question raised by Kant's participation in the larger tradition of speculative or universal grammar. The question is whether Kant, and those who came before and after him, *could* have avoided founding the notion *universal grammar* on inferences of the subreptic type.

3.4. As already suggested, historically universal grammarians have relied on a model grammar accounting for an exemplary corpus (e.g., Latin or Greek); they have sought to work outward from the de facto structures of an empirically given language to principles and categories presumed to be applicable de jure to language in general and as such. To different degrees, then, they have been forced to come to grips with what Oswald Ducrot and Tzvetan Todorov (1979 [1972]) describe as the dilemma between philosophical and empirical grammar:

> A *general grammar* aims at enunciating certain principles that govern all languages and provide the basic explanation of their uses. It thus represents an attempt to define the general phenomenon of language (*langage*), of which the individual languages are particular cases. . . . [General grammar] marks, at least in intention, the end of the privilege accorded in preceding centuries to Latin grammar, which had tended to become the model for all grammar: general grammar is no more Latin than it is French or German; rather it transcends all language systems. . . . On the other hand, general grammarians avoided the dilemma, seemingly insurmountable until their time, of a purely philosophical and purely empirical grammar. . . . although grounded in logic, [the rules of general grammar] were not condemned merely to repeat it: they expressed its possible transparency through the material of human communication. (4, 6)

Of special concern to us here is the aim of (certain) higher-order grammars to highlight the "possible transparency [of logic] through the material conditions of human communication." After exploring arguments that it is impossible (in fact and in principle) to map the principles of logic into the circumstances of communication and so furnish what might be termed a *material calculus* (sec. 4), I synopsize three influential models for reconciling calculation with communication. These models include the Universal Characteristic proposed by Gottfried Wilhem Leibniz late in the seventeenth century and Gottlob Frege's and Edmund Husserl's (very different) attempts to revive the Leibnizian Characteristic late in the nineteenth and early twentieth centuries (sec. 5). Having surveyed the three models, I then examine how the construct *narrative grammar,* along with the narrative discourse under study, bears important connections to proposals for a material calculus (sec. 6). In turn, I work toward framing a hypothesis that, during the present century, narrative discourse has acquired the (paradoxical) status of a universal idiom (sec. 7)—a status once conferred on ancient Greek by Aristotle and on Latin by Leibniz and Kant.

4. Universal Grammar and the Concept of a Material Calculus

First, then, we need to examine in somewhat more detail Ducrot and Todorov's opposition between the principles of logic and the material conditions for communication. In this connection, Jean-Louis Gardies (1985 [1975]) has supplied a powerful diagnosis of the whole history of attempts to fashion universal or, in Gardies's scheme, rational grammars. According to Gardies, such higher-order grammars have evolved as part of a (futile) effort to construct a formalized language endowed with all the characteristics of a natural language. Yet, as Gardies suggests, the function of a formalized or symbolic language is to *calculate* by means of consistent rules of formation and transformation, which are designed to preclude contradictions and antinomies in the more complex formulae (i.e., strings of symbols) realized in the language (43ff.; cf. secs. 1.6ff below). For example, a formalized language will be so designed as to disallow homonyms; acceptable in natural language contexts, homonyms involve two or more terms sharing equivalent forms but endowed with different syntactic functions and performing distinct semantic roles. Take the term *strike* in the strings "The baseball players might *strike* this summer" and "The pitcher threw the batter a *strike*." A formalized language like Frege's *Begriffsschrift*, for example, aims to circumvent antinomies made possible by the ambiguity of terms like *strike* in these contexts (sec. 5.2).

By contrast, the primary function of natural language is to *communicate,* and language viewed as a means for communication aspires not to pure consistency in its design but rather to universal applicability in its use—to the highest possible degree of usability. Language as a vehicle for communication aims most of all at flexibility and intelligibility; it features modes of expression whose meaning is underdetermined by the forms of the expression themselves but that are for that reason more easily adapted to constantly changing communicative contexts. Hence the importance of deictic terms (*I, here, this*), for example, in natural-language contexts (Bar-Hillel 1954; Green 1989: 17–25).

To this extent, language viewed as an instrument for calculation cannot be reconciled with language viewed as a vehicle for communication. For example, Gardies (1985 [1975]) remarks that, "insofar as Indo-European languages frequently violate type distinctions,[15] such distinctions are of no interest to grammarians, whose concern is not to refine a logical tool but to account for the structures of languages as they are" (47). For "the universality of colloquial language" consists precisely in those features of its grammar that allow "a speaker to speak *about* the very language *in* which he is speaking" (48; cf.

Jakobson 1960: 356; and Jakobson 1971d [1957]: 131). As Gardies goes on to say, "It is very unlikely that natural languages could have any interest in adopting distinctions which in formalized languages serve to make these languages operational, in view of the fact that, in order to become operational in this way, natural languages would have to renounce their flexibility and that universality which remains the essential property of a good system of communication" (56; cf. Morris 1938: 11–12). The conclusion: that "the attempt to combine in one language the advantages of universality with those of non-contradiction seems . . . to be necessarily condemned to failure" (49).[16]

In short, when faced with the entire history of (doomed) attempts to effect just such a combination of calculative with communicative functions in a single language-theoretical framework, and in the wake of efforts to model a grammar that, because purely rational, would yield the same *vox-intellectus-res* correlation that underwrote the great speculative grammars of the Middle Ages,

> We are led . . . to the consideration of the goal or goals of language. . . . The *basic* goal of language in all known civilisations—whether it is functioning to address another person, in an order, a prayer, in advice, or in the giving of instructions—seems to be that of communication. . . . [But] onto [the] function of fixing messages which is peculiar to written languages, another function has increasingly come to graft itself—a function which was almost totally unknown to Greek civilisation, which has its beginning during the first thousand years A.D. in the Indian and Arab civilisations and which has become increasingly widespread in the West ever since the Middle Ages. Written language serves not only to communicate but also as a means of calculation. . . . The characteristic feature of a calculus . . . is precisely that it substitutes operations on signs for reasonings about what the speaker has in mind. . . . Historically, then, we have two functions [of language]—universality and operational reliability—which, as we saw above, cannot be combined. (Gardies 1985 [1975]: 49–54)

Insofar as higher-order grammarians have sought to combine universality with operational reliability to produce logico-grammatical schemes for modeling a jointly calculative and communicative language, the history of universal grammar is in part the history of efforts to construct what can be called a *material calculus*. At issue is a calculus designed to enjoy, on the one hand, all the economy and explicitness of a properly algorithmic device—a mechanism for generating strings of symbols explicitly marked according to their logico-semantic functions and so assessed for nonsensicality and/or absurdity without appeal to intuition. On the other hand, the calculus in question must also enjoy universal applicability; its scope must be wholly unrestricted with respect to use, its algorithmic mechanisms grounded in what Ducrot and Todorov term "the material conditions of human communication."

4.1. As we have seen, Gardies argues for the impossibility, in principle, of any such communicative calculus. Note, however, that a very different conception of universal grammar informs current linguistic theory. Under this conception, inspired largely by Chomsky (e.g., 1966a, 1986), universal grammar represents not the effort to model a material calculus but rather an attempt to account for the phenomena of language acquisition, among other linguistic phenomena.[17] At the core of *this* (relatively narrow) conception of universal grammar is what Chomsky (1986) describes as a "poverty of the stimulus" argument: "The basic problem is that our knowledge is richly articulated and shared with others from the same speech community, whereas the data available are much too impoverished to determine it by any general procedure of induction, generalization, analogy, association, or whatever" (55: cf. Cook 1988: 55ff.; Lightfoot 1988: 303–5; Saleemi 1992: 6–13). Accordingly, Chomsky postulates the existence of a "human biological endowment" (1986: 23)—that is, universal grammar—that permits us to acquire complex and abstract knowledge of language on the basis of very limited experience of language (Cook 1988: 55). As Chomsky puts it, "Surely there is some property of mind P that would enable a person to acquire a language under conditions of pure and uniform experience, and surely P (characterized by U[niversal] G[rammar]) is put to use under the real conditions of language acquisition" (1986: 17). In later refinements of Chomsky's poverty of the stimulus argument, "U[niversal] G[rammar] is [thought of as being] present in the child's mind as a system of principles and parameters. In response to evidence from the environment the child creates a core grammar that assigns values to all the parameters, yielding one of the allowable human languages—French, Arabic, or whatever" (Cook 1988: 56; cf. Lightfoot 1992: 19–20).

V. J. Cook gives a comprehensive account of Chomsky's (and Chomsky-inspired) ideas about universal grammar:

> UG is a theory of knowledge, not behavior; its concern is with the internal structure of the human mind. The nature of this knowledge is inseparable from the problem of how it is acquired; a proposal for language knowledge necessitates an explanation of how it came into being. UG theory holds that the speaker knows a set of principles that apply to all languages, and

parameters that vary within clearly defined limits from one language to another. Acquiring language means learning how these principles apply to a particular language and which value is appropriate for each parameter. Each principle of language that is proposed is a substantive claim about the mind of the speaker and the nature of acquisition. . . . the importance of UG is its attempt to integrate grammar, mind, and acquisition at every moment. (1988: 1–2)

Thus, in contrast to Gardies, a number of researchers have made powerful arguments in support of a higher-order, properly universal grammar—interpreted not as a material calculus but rather as a language-learning apparatus hardwired, so to speak, into human beings as a species.[18]

4.2. I shall not attempt here to adjudicate between Gardies's critique of rational grammars and the conception of universal grammar just outlined. Instead, having acknowledged Chomsky's important modification of older, broader interpretations of universal grammar, I can proceed with the genealogical inquiry that constitutes the main purpose of this introduction. By reviewing three influential proposals for a higher-order grammar construed as a material calculus, I continue to detail relevant language-theoretical contexts—contexts that can help us characterize the links between universal grammar and twentieth-century narrative form. As already indicated, these links are important not just for (literary-)historical reasons but also because of their consequences for ongoing narratological research.

5. Leibniz, Frege, Husserl

In essence, Leibniz's proposal for a "Characteristica Universalis" (Universal Characteristic) can be construed as a scheme for transposing an algorithmic interpretation of language into the material conditions of human communication. It yields the canonic material calculus, so to speak, against which subsequent higher-order grammars measured their failures and successes. Thus, when Frege and Husserl helped make (versions of) the Leibnizian scheme current again around the turn of the century, their efforts unfolded against the backdrop of Leibniz's ideas.[19] As we shall see in section 5.3 below, the Leibnizian inheritance is particularly evident in Husserl's early, prephenomenological writings on the nature of logical analysis.

5.1. Hans Burkhardt (1980) shows how, after 1676, Leibniz increasingly concerned himself with "sprachanalytischen Studien" 'studies in the analysis of language.' As Burkhardt remarks, "[Das] Ziel dieser Untersuchung ist die Konstruktion einer idealen Sprache, von Leibniz *lingua rationalis, universalis* oder *philosophica* genannt" 'The goal of this investigation is the construction of an ideal language, which Leibniz calls rational, universal or philosophical language' (83). Yet, for Leibniz, the ideal language sought for can be constructed in two different ways: "Einerseits kann man a posteriori vorgehen und durch die Analyse von toten oder lebendigen natürlichen Sprachen und deren Vereinfachung zu einer Idealsprache kommen, und anderseits ist eine solche Sprache künstliche herstellbar, wie das Leibniz später Kalkülen durchgeführt hat. In diesem Falle, spricht Leibniz dann von *Characteristica Universalis*" 'On the one hand, one can proceed a posteriori and arrive at an ideal language through the analysis and simplification of natural languages; on the other hand, such a language may be produced artificially and derived through the sorts of calculi Leibniz eventually developed. In the latter case, Leibniz speaks of a Universal Characteristic' (83). However, Burkhardt later identifies the a posteriori mode of analysis in Leibniz as specifically "grammatical" and notes that "Die grammatische Analyse ist für Leibniz . . . ein Ausgangspunkt für den Aufbau einer logischen Syntax und damit eines logischen Kalküls" 'grammatical analysis is for Leibniz . . . a starting point for the construction of a logical syntax and therewith a logical calculus' (138; cf. Heinekamp 1976: 524; and see sec. 1.6ff. below). Higher-order grammar, it seems, is built with the materials of grammar in the narrow sense. Thus, Burkhardt (1987) elsewhere suggests that both a priori and a posteriori modes of analysis—now renamed "analytic-regressive" and "synthetic-progressive" methods of construction—are required for the development of "a *general* or *rational grammar*" one of whose necessary presuppositions is in turn "the simplification of the grammar of a historical language, for which purpose Leibniz selected Latin" (44).

Whatever its original materials and ultimate sources, the Universal Characteristic could in principle yield, according to Leibniz (1973 [1683]), "a kind of alphabet of human thoughts, i.e. a catalogue of summa genera . . . such as *a, b, c, d, e, f,* out of whose combination inferior concepts would be formed" (10).[20] Here, in strictly axiomatic fashion, "All derivative concepts arise from a combination of primitive ones, and those which are composite in a higher degree arise from a combination of composite concepts" (12). At greater length, in a fragment from 1677 anthologized by Louis Couturat (1903), Leibniz asserts that "si l'on pouvoit trouver des caracteres ou signes propres à exprimer toutes nos pensées, aussi nettement et exactement que l'arithmetique exprime les nombres, ou que l'analyse geometrique exprime les lignes, on pourroit faire en toutes les matieres autant qu'elles sont sujettes au raisonnement tout ce qu'on peut faire en Arithmetique et en Geometrie" 'if one could find the proper characters or signs to express all our ideas, as distinctly and exactly as arithmetic expresses numbers or geometrical analysis expresses lines, one could achieve in all matters, insofar as they are subject to rational treatment, all that one can achieve in arithmetic and geometry' (155; cf. Couturat 1901: 283–84; Husserl 1979b [1891]: 390–92; Paul 1978: 356–61).

Thus, implicitly at least, Leibniz suggests that the Universal Characteristic would be distinguished by its fitness both for calculation and for communication. An arithmetic of ideas, a geometry of thoughts, the Characteristic would yield a faultless semiotic technology, as it were—an apparatus built from signs and capable of expressing, with algorithmic or quantitative precision, ideas and relations of a merely qualitative nature. In more modern parlance, a Universal Characteristic would map the digital into the analogic. It is, in short, a highly general art of combinations, or

> the science which treats of the forms of things or of formulae in general (it could also be called generally the science of symbols, or of forms). That is, it is the science of quality in general, or, of the like and the unlike, according as various formulae arise from the combination of *a*, *b*, *c* etc., whether they represent quantities or something else. It is distinguished from algebra, which is concerned with formulae applied to quantity, i.e. with the equal and the unequal. Consequently, algebra is subordinate to the art of combinations, and constantly uses its rules. These rules, however, are much more general and can be applied not only in algebra but also in cryptography, in various kinds of games, in geometry itself, . . . and finally in all matters where similarity is involved. (Leibniz 1973 [1683]: 17)

In this passage, we see how Leibniz "seems to have thought," as Bertrand Russell (1900) would later put it, "that the symbolic method in which formal rules obviate the necessity of thinking, could produce everywhere the same fruitful results as it produced in the sciences of number and quantity" (169). In other words, a truly Universal Characteristic would have under only one of its profiles the features of an algorithm, an algebra, or a calculus; under other profiles it would manifest itself "sous la forme d'une langue ou d'une écriture universelle" 'in the form of a universal language or script' (Couturat 1901: 51), whose range of possible uses is as indefinitely extended as that of any other script.

In theory at least, Leibniz's Universal Characteristic therefore combines operational reliability with universality, to invoke terms borrowed from Gardies in the previous section. It is a calculus that doubles as a language. Some two centuries later, when Frege tried to reinvigorate the Leibnizian ideal under the name of a *Begriffsschrift* or conceptual notation, Frege sought to produce a Characteristic having the same double profile, the same combination of precision and flexibility.

5.2. As Leila Haaparanta (1988) remarks, late nineteenth-century logicians typically adopted one of two different models then available to them. Some, like George Boole, focused on developing what Leibniz would have called a *calculus ratiocinator:* that is, a formal calculus providing rules of inference, the calculus being subject to various interpretations according to the language system adopted (cf. Carnap 1952 [1950]; and secs. **2.6** and **2.7** below) and distinguished chiefly by what Gardies would term its operational reliability. Others, like Giuseppe Peano, attempted to develop what in Leibnizian terms would be called a *lingua characterica,* or "proper language, which speaks about the world" (Haaparanta 1988: 240) with at least some of the flexibility and universality that Gardies ascribes to colloquial languages. In parallel with Leibniz's own Universal Characteristic, however, Frege thought of his *Begriffsschrift* as, simultaneously, both a *calculus ratiocinator* and a *lingua characterica.*[21] As Haaparanta puts it, Frege "thought that his conceptual notation was both an attempt to present the rules of logical inference and an attempt to give a correct conceptual representation of the universe, a representation which contained no ambiguities typical of our natural language" (240).

Specifically, and in contradistinction to the pure calculi (algorithms) constructed by Ernst Schröder and Boole, Frege's notation was supposed to furnish a (material) universal language by satisfying two conditions: (i) it would speak about objects of the world (*Bedeutungen*); and (ii) it would deal with thoughts or intensions (*Inhalte*) as objective or independent of mental acts (Haaparanta 1988: 240ff.; cf. Husserl 1979e [1891]; and secs. **2.4.4.1** and **2.4.4.2** below). Hence "Frege's logic is . . . *inhaltlich* both in the sense that it is related to the real realm of individual objects and in the sense that it is related to the ideal realm of abstract objects" (Haaparanta 1988: 243; cf. Patzig 1969: 12–13). Presumably, by satisfying conditions i and ii, the *Begriffsschrift* would achieve the universality of natural languages but maintain all the operational precision and formal explicitness of a logical calculus.

In fact, from arguments developed in his article "Über die wissenschaftliche Berechtigung einer Begriffsschrift" 'On the Scientific Justification of a Conceptual Notation' (1969d [1882]), we can reconstruct Frege's views concerning the possibility (and desirability) of a material calculus. In this article, Frege attributes to the "Unvollkommenheit der Sprache" 'incompleteness [or imperfection] of language' any number of "Mißverständnisse . . . und zugleich Fehler im eigenen Denken" 'misunderstandings . . . and likewise errors in proper thinking' (91). More specifically, as Frege puts it,

> Die Sprache ist nicht in der Weise durch logische Gesetze beherrscht, daß die Befolgung der Grammatik schon die formale Richtigkeit der Gedankenbewegung verbürgte. Die Formen, in denen das Folgern ausgedrückt wird, sind so vielfältige, so lose und dehnbare, daß sich leicht Voraussetzungen unbemerkt durchschleichen können, die dann bei der Aufzählung der notwendigen Bedingungen für die Gültigkeit des Schlußsatzes übergangen werden. (92–93)

> Language is not so ruled by logical principles that compliance with grammar guarantees, by the same token, the formal correctness of the operations of thought [expressed in well-formed utterances]. The forms in which inferences are expressed are so manifold, so loose and flexible, that presuppositions can easily slip through [the symbolism] unnoticed—presuppositions that we pass over in enumerating the necessary conditions for the validity of the inferences.[22]

Accordingly, we must fashion an artificial language, a conceptual notation, whose grammar *does* in fact ensure formal correctness, over and above providing the conditions for the well-formedness of sentences. Frege suggests that just as "Wir schaffen uns künstliche Hände, Werkzeuge für besondere Zwecke, die so genau arbeiten, wie die Hand es nicht vermöchte, so genügt auch die Wortsprache nicht" 'We build for ourselves artificial hands, work tools for particular purposes, that work in precisely those ways our hands cannot, so too do word languages not suffice [of themselves]' (94).[23] In particular, in connection with his own researches on the foundations of mathematics, Frege discovered that "Wir bedürfen eines Ganzen von Zeichen, aus dem jede Vieldeutigkeit verbannt ist, dessen strenger logischer Form der Inhalt nicht entschlüpfen kann" 'we require a system of signs from which all plurisignificance has been banished, and from whose stricter logical form the content [of a given mathematical idea] cannot escape' (94). Thus, Frege called for an "arithmetischen Formelsprache" 'language of arithmetical formulae' that itself contains expressions for logical connections (e.g., similarity and dissimilarity), instead of forcing us to revert to words in performing various arithmetic operations via the symbolism adopted (96).

However—and this is the crucial point—for Frege the calculi developed by Boole, Graßman, Jevons, and Schröder, for example, are *not* in fact wholly explicit and perspicuous with respect to logical connections or, as Frege also calls them, *Inhalten* (contents, intensions) (96; see the next section and sec. *2.3* below). Frege spells out as follows the minimal conditions for the requisite *Inhaltslogik* or "logic of content," as Husserl (1979e [1891]) would later call it:

> Sie muß für die logischen Beziehungen einfache Ausdrucksweisen haben, die, an Zahl auf das Notwendige beschränkt, leicht und sicher zu beherrschen sind. Diese Formen müssen geeignet sein, sich mit einem Inhalte auf das Innigste zu verbinden. Dabei muß solche Kürze erstrebt werden, daß die zweifache Ausdehnung der Schreibfläche für die Übersichlichkeit der Darstellung gut ausgenutzt. (96–97)

> It must have simple modes of expression for logical relations, modes that, by necessity restricted in number, are thereby easy to master and certain in their use. These forms must be suitably designed, such that they can bind with a given content at the innermost level. By the same token we must search for symbols that can exploit the two-dimensional expanse of the writing surface to yield a total perspicuity of representation [with respect to the logical relations at issue].

Like Leibniz's, then, Frege's goal is an algorithmically simplified language that might nevertheless afford completely perspicuous representations. At issue are representations not only of logico-mathematical concepts but also of all other thought contents that are "sujettes au raisonnement," as Leibniz had put it. After all, Frege's subtitle for the 1879 *Begriffsschrift* was *Eine der arithmetischen nachgebildete Formelsprache des reinen Denkens* (*An Arithmetically Modeled Calculus of Pure Thought*). Such a calculus, arguably, would have to be classed as material, insofar as its operations range over thought contents, that is, relations and properties,[24] as opposed to quantities or magnitudes alone.

5.3. We find what is perhaps a more explicit (re)statement of the ideal of a material calculus, however, in some lesser-known texts of Husserl's, written a few years after Frege's first elaboration of the *Begriffsschrift* but before Husserl began to take his specifically "phenomenological" turn. Of particular interest in this connection is Husserl's (1979d [1891]) review of Ernst Schröder's influential *Vorlesungen über die Algebra der Logik* (*Lectures on the Algebra of Logic*) (1890), together with a draft of that review found in Husserl's *Nachlaß* and later published in *Husserliana* (1979b [1891]). These texts, maybe more clearly than other, better-known Husserlian writings (but see sec. *1.6.2* below), reveal the extent and depth of Husserl's concern with material calculi as well as the strength of Husserl's ties with the whole language-theoretical tradition informing the project of universal grammar.

In the draft of the Schröder review, Husserl states that Leibniz's "größte Entdeckungen beruhen auf der Einführung algorithmischer Methoden in die Analysis" 'greatest discoveries concern the introduction of algorithmic methods into the analysis [of ideas]' (391). Husserl goes on to champion the Leibnizian ideal of a Universal Characteristic in which "gründeten sich auf den charakteristischen Begriffen sogleich mehrfache Operationen der Verbindung und Umsetzung und damit Regeln mechanischer Rechnung" 'manifold operations of connection and conversion, and with them rules for mechanical calculation, are immediately grounded in the symbolized concepts themselves' (391). At the same time, however, Husserl accuses Leibniz of conflating a genuine *Characteristica Universalis* or properly material calculus with the *calculus ratiocinator* or formal algorithm that, as "ein blind rechnendes Verfahren" 'a blindly calculative method' (392), is merely the starting point for a Universal Characteristic in the strict sense.

As Husserl puts it, "Sieht man genauer zu, dann ziegt es sich, daß diejenige Analyse, welche in den mathematischen Disziplinen zu einem calculus ratiocinator führte himmelweit entfernt ist von jener Analysis, die Leibniz bei seiner Charakterbezeichnung der Begriffe im Auge hatte" 'If one examines the matter more closely, it becomes apparent that the sort of analysis that leads to a calculus for reckoning in the mathematical disciplines is heavens apart from the sort of analysis that Leibniz had in mind in connection with his notion of a [Universal] Characteristic' (391). But there are extenuating circumstances. If Leibniz "die Idee einer Universalsprache . . . mit der eines schließenden Kalküls nicht scharf unterscheiden" 'does not sharply differentiate the idea of a universal language . . . from that of a formal calculus for drawing inferences' (392), then the philosopher merely exploits a looseness in the definition of *language* similarly exploited by others:

> Gern sprechen die Mathematiker bei der Umsetzung gegebener arithmetischer Aufgaben in die formalen des Kalküls von einer Übersetzung oder Einkleidung derselben in die "Sprache" des Kalküls, wie schon Newton geradezu von einer traductio ex lingua latina in die lingua algebraica redet, eine Ausdrucksweise, die auch gegenwärtig so verbreitet ist, daß

man ihr kaum entgehen kann. . . . Auf die Spitze getrieben wurde aber die Vermischung von Sprache und Kalkül. (392)

In connection with the conversion of a given arithmetic problem into the formulae of a calculus, mathematicians tend to speak of a translation or a couching of the problem in the "language" of the calculus, just as already Newton speaks of a translation from the Latin language into the algebraic language—a manner of speaking that is presently so fashionable that one can scarcely avoid it. . . . At the extreme, however, this mode of expression leads to a confusion of languages with calculi.

At stake, then, is the very distinction between a language and an algorithm. Or, rather, we are concerned with the distinction between natural language contexts, in which the primary goal is communication, and contexts involving formal languages, where the primary goal is at once effortless and error-free calculation. Husserl sets out his own version of this distinction in the following terms:

Die sprachlichen Zeichen haben die Funktion von sinnlichen, die Gedanken ständig begleitenden Ausdrucksmitteln. Die algorithmischen Zeichen haben die Funktion von sinnlichen, die Gedanken ersetzenden und ersparenden Symbolen, wenigstens vorübergehend, nämlich zum Zweck eines symbolischen Folgerungsprozesses. . . . Ein Algorithmus ist also eine systematische Methode symbolischen Schließens, eine Sprache eine systematische Methode des Ausdrucks von Gedanken und psychischen Phänomenen überhaupt durch Zeichen. Wie es möglich ist, daß ein blinder Mechanismus von sinnlichen Zeichen logisches Denken ersetzen und ersparen kann, das ist die große Frage der Logik der Zeichen, der Semiotik. (394)

The signs of a language function as perceptible means of expression, accompanied always by the ideas [being expressed]. Algorithmic signs function as perceptible symbols that replace and conserve, at least temporarily, the ideas expressed—for the purpose, that is, of drawing inferences through operations on symbols.[25] . . . An algorithm is therefore a systematic method for drawing inferences via symbols, whereas a language is a systematic method for the expression of ideas and psychical phenomena in general through the use of signs. How it is possible that a blind mechanism consisting of perceptible signs can minimize or even replace thinking itself: that is the great question of the logic of signs, of semiotics.

Hence, in the review itself—the critique of Schröder's book being the occasion for Husserl's subsidiary critique of Leibniz—Husserl remarks that "beruht der fundamentale Irrtum, der mit der obigen Charakteristik der neuen Logik begangen wird, auf der Verkennung der wesentlichen Verschiedenheit von Sprache und Algorithmus. Schröder druckt sich beständig so aus, als ob mit der Einführung einer Zeichensprache an Stelle der natürlichen Wortsprache das algebraische Verfahren schon gegeben wäre" 'the fundamental error observed in the previous characterization of the new logic consists in its underestimation of the essential difference between languages and algorithms. Schröder continually speaks as though, with the introduction of a symbolic language in the place of naturally occurring word languages, the algebraic method itself were already given' (1979d [1891]: 21; cf. Husserl 1979b [1891]: 389). For Husserl, Schröder had confused a *calculus ratiocinator* with a truly Universal Characteristic.

As the passage just cited already starts to indicate, we should not overhastily assimilate Husserl's critique of Schröder with Gardies's critique of rational grammars generally. Like Gardies, it is true, Husserl posits an asymmetrical relation between languages proper and algorithms. But Husserl's claim is not that failure to recognize this asymmetry is to suffer (utopian) delusions about the possibility of fashioning a material calculus. Husserl does not suggest that the ideal of a material calculus as such is a figment of the philosophical imagination, the product of an unwarranted superimposition of the functions of languages on the functions of algorithms, and vice versa. Rather, in Husserl's terms a material calculus is a real possibility, hitherto unrealized. Developing such a calculus hinges on our making a twofold distinction between languages and algorithms, on the one hand, and between algorithmic and properly logical analysis, on the other hand. For Husserl, logic is a domain intermediate between the polysemous richness of natural languages and the empty or "blind" formality of algorithmic devices of the sort used in "the mathematical disciplines." To perform a logical analysis in the strict sense is therefore—ideally at least and at this stage of Husserl's thinking—to operate a material calculus.

We can spell out this latter interpretation at greater length. For Husserl, as for Frege, the grammar of natural languages cannot ensure, as the mere unthinking application of an algorithmic device *can* ensure, the formal correctness of the sign combinations being designed and/or interpreted. As Husserl puts it, "Die zugehörige Kunst sprachlicher Bezeichnung ist die Grammatik. Sie lehrt also nicht, wie wir urteilen sollen, sie gibt auch nicht Regeln, wie wir richtige Urteile indirekt durch symbolische Kunstgriffe herleiten können, sondern nur, wie wir

Urteile der Sprache gemäß richtig auszudrücken haben" 'The method or art affiliated with linguistic expression is grammar. Grammar neither teaches how we should draw inferences nor provides rules for the production of correct judgments through symbolic manipulations' (literally, "tricks," "sleights of hand") (1979d [1891]: 21).[26] Thus, in contradistinction to Schröder, Husserl draws a distinction between (i) languages consisting of symbols and (ii) algorithms based on but not exhausted by an initial substitution of symbols for verbal expressions. The grammar of algorithmic formulae is essentially different from the grammar governing the strings of symbols that make up a language.

But further, if for Husserl use of a symbolic language is of itself not a sufficient condition for the construction of an algorithmic device, in turn the construction of an algorithm fails to be a sufficient condition for performing logical analyses in the strict sense—in the sense, that is, of operating a material calculus. In Husserl's formulation:

> Die deduktive Logik geht natürlich nicht auf besondere Begriffe, wie Zahlen, Figuren u. dgl., aber jedenfalls doch auf die logischen Betätigungen, die in allen deduktiven Disziplinen zur Geltung kommen und das Wesen ihrer Methoden ausmachen. Das reine Schließen aber ist nur eine dieser Betätigung. Die deduktiven Wissenschaft schließen nicht allein: Sie operieren auch, sie konstruieren und rechnen. . . . Die Logikkalkül ist also ein Kalkül der reinen Folgerungen, nicht aber ihre Logik. Er ist dies so wenig, als die arithmetica universalis, welche das gesamte Zahlengebiet umfaßt, eine Logik desselben darstellt. Über die deduzierenden Geistesprozesse erfahren wir im einen Falle so wenig als im andern. (6, 8)

> Deductive logic does not of course concern itself with particular concepts, such as numbers, figures, and the like, but rather with the logical operations that achieve validity in all deductive disciplines and indeed constitute the essence of those disciplines' methods. Pure inference, however, is only one such logical operation. Deductive science does not merely infer or conclude; it also operates, construes, calculates. . . . A logical calculus is thus a calculus of strict inferences, but not their logic as such—just as little as universal arithmetic, which encompasses the whole domain of numbers, represents a logic of that domain. We learn as little about the deductive processes of the mind in the one case as we do in the other.

In Husserl's interpretation, then, "Deduktive Wissenschaft" has as its chief concern neither the blindly inferential mechanisms of formal calculi nor that rich particularity of concepts on which, by contrast, precise calculation via natural languages can be expected to founder. Instead, its chief concern is the logical operations that, constituting the "Logik der idealer Inhalte" 'logic of ideal contents' (1979d [1891]: 18ff.), permit us to mediate between languages and algorithms. Logical operations in Husserl's sense are formally rigorous without being blind or empty; their very rigor and ideality ground themselves in the *experience* of judging, construing, inferring, etc.

Admittedly, Husserl's arguments here and in his first book, *Philosophie der Arithmetik,* also published in 1891, were met with Frege's famous accusation of psychologism—Frege's charge that Husserl had conflated the logical with the psychological, producing a host of pernicious results (cf. Mohanty 1982; Picardi 1987). It seems hard to refute (and Husserl himself did not try to refute) Frege's charge in the face of statements such as this: "Wir in den algorithmischen Formeln keineswegs den Kanon der folgernden Erkenntnistätigkeit wiederspeigelt finden" 'In no way do we find mirrored in algorithmic formulas the canon for the *activity* of inferential reasoning itself' (1979d [1891]: 8; my emphasis). My aim is not to plead for the early Husserl's conception of logic, however. Rather, it is merely to situate the Husserlian model in a much larger tradition of thinking about language, grammar, and logic—a tradition stretching back to Leibniz's Universal Characteristic and beyond. As already suggested, Husserl's efforts to ground algorithmic formulae in operations performed on the intensional contents of logical ideas—his attempt to project quantitative methods and distinctions into the domain of properties and relations—may be construed as part of an ongoing effort to model a material calculus.

Against the backdrop of Leibniz's Universal Characteristic, Frege's *Begriffsschrift,* and Husserl's *Inhaltslogik,* we can now pursue the question that prompted comparison of these three schemes in the first place: How do twentieth-century innovations in narrative form pertain to the concept of a material calculus being (re)modeled in contemporaneous language-theoretical discourse? The closing sections of this introduction do not try to frame a definitive response to this question, but they do attempt to indicate how, taken together, subsequent chapters might at least begin to augur an answer.

6. Narrative Grammar as Material Calculus

Although the presuppositions and aims of narrative grammar (and, more specifically, narrative syntax) are discussed in greater detail in the next chapter (see sec. *1.8*ff.), note that from the start narratological models have been interinvolved with the language-theoretical tradition reviewed in previous sections.[27] Indeed, in the very act of christening the then-new science of narratology in his *Grammaire du "Décaméron"* (1969), Tzvetan Todorov remarks that, "tout au long de ce travail, une hypothèse méthodologique va nous guider: celle de l'existence d'une grammaire universelle" 'throughout this work, a methodological hypothesis will guide us: that of the existence of a universal grammar' (14). As Todorov elsewhere (1977 [1971]) puts it, "In the very earliest reflections on language, a hypothesis appears according to which there may be discovered a common structure that transcends the obvious differences among languages. . . . [We can] search for this same universal grammar by studying other symbolic activities besides natural language. . . . A theory of narrative will also contribute, then, to the knowledge of this grammar, insofar as narrative is such a symbolic activity" (108–9). As we have seen, theorists from Aristotle to Chomsky have likewise searched for "a common structure that transcends the obvious differences among languages"; they have developed a host of higher-order grammars that could either "be used for the description of any language whatever in the stead of a respective particular grammar" or else "provide each particular grammar with a basic conceptual apparatus to be used in the construction of this grammar" (Marciszewski 1988: 87; see sec. 3 above). The point is, however, that *both* narratological frameworks like Todorov's *and* the literary narratives under study can be linked to the research tradition that spawned the speculative grammars of the Modistae, the general grammar of Arnauld and Lancelot, and Leibnizian and post-Leibnizian elaborations of the Universal Characteristic.

6.1. In fact, the postulate of universal grammar provides Todorov not merely with an initial, methodological hypothesis but also with a *model* for understanding the situation of narrative discourse relative to grammar and logic:

> A nos yeux, l'univers de la narration obéit également à la grammaire universelle. Mais nous n'aurons pas besoin pour autant de décider si celle-ci reflète ou non la structure de l'univers. On l'a déjà dit: l'objet de ce travail n'est pas les actions, telles qu'elles sont présumées exister dans l'univers, mais telles qu'elles existent dans le discours narratif. La structure de la langue ne sera pas confrontée avec la structure du monde, mais avec celle de la narration qui est un type de discours. (Todorov 1969: 15–16)

> In our eyes, the universe of narration likewise obeys a universal grammar. Yet for all that we shall not need to decide here whether the former [i.e., narration] reflects the structure of the universe itself. To reiterate: the

object of this work is not actions of the sort that are presumed to exist in the universe, but rather actions of the sort that are presumed to exist in the narrative discourse. Thus the structure of language will not be confronted with the structure of the world, but instead with that of the narration, which is but a type of discourse.

Here Todorov situates narrative discourse between the structures internal to a given language *L*, on the one hand, and the rules for framing in *L*, among all other actual or possible languages, propositions about the world (or "universe"), on the other hand. As we might also put it, Todorov modifies Modistic grammars by substituting *discours narratif* for *intellectus* as the link between *vox* and *res*. Narrative discourse now mediates between the structures of language and the structures of the world.

Concomitantly, narrative form assumes a logico-grammatical profile (cf. secs. *1.6.3ff.*), grounded in the contexts of communication but not reducible to them. As we shall explore more particularly in the next chapter (secs. *1.8ff.*), narrative grammars typically situate narrative discourse at a level more general than language but less general than logic;[28] narrative discourse anchors itself in natural language contexts, but it also contains formal features through which, with the help of various narratological tools, we can discern the "common structure" of all such contexts insofar as they pertain to narrative.

To invoke the vocabulary of the Russian Formalists—a vocabulary adopted (and adapted) by Francophone narratologists such as Todorov—we can distinguish between the *fabula* or basic story elements constituting a narrative, on the one hand, and the ways in which those basic elements are disposed (plotted, summarized, focalized, etc.) in the discourse or *sjužet*, on the other hand. The *fabula* concerns what happens; the *sjužet* concerns the presentation of what happens *as* what has happened, as a story. Further, the transmissability of story elements across different formats, languages, and even media is what allows us to produce analogous if not identical paraphrases of the "same" story, whether that story is told in the first person or in the third; whether it is expressed in German, French, English, or Sanskrit; whether it is realized in a written text, in a play, with puppets, or in terms of two-dimensional visual images alone.[29] As classically conceived, narrative grammars aim to furnish what might be termed *structural descriptions* of basic narrative constituents (see Chomsky 1966b [1957]: 13–14; cf. chap. 1, n. 19, and sec. *1.3.3* below). The grammars strive to account for the functioning of formal units with respect to the story and with respect to the discourse; they are also concerned with the effects of different formats, languages, and media on narrative form—that is, with the ways that the different material contexts of stories could affect the design and interpretation of those stories.

Here we start to see the connections between narrative grammar and the higher-order grammars that preceded it. The idea is not that the particular *languages* in which narratives are realized are at once logically transparent and communicatively universal. The idea, rather, is that narrative *discourse*—a supralinguistic construct wider in scope than (the grammar of) any particular language—affords a medium for a material calculus. As Roland Barthes had put it in his powerful "Introduction to the Structural Analysis of Narratives" of 1966,

> It is evident that discourse itself (as a set of sentences) is organized and that, through this organization, it can be seen as the message of another language, one operating at a higher level than the language of the linguists. Discourse has its units, its rules, its "grammar": beyond the sentence, it must naturally form the object of a second linguistics. . . . The general language [*langue*] of narrative is one (and clearly only one) of the idioms apt for consideration by the linguistics of discourse. (Barthes 1977b [1966]: 83–84)[30]

As part of the second linguistics of discourse, narrative grammar can be construed in turn as a second-order grammar. Ideally at least, it roots itself not in a particular language but rather in the forms and functions by virtue of which we recognize sign systems (in general) to be narratively organized. Thus, in the manner of a latter-day material calculus, narrative grammar *exceeds* language without ceasing to be *constrained by* language.

6.2. So far, however, we have not considered how narratological frameworks of the sort just outlined relate to the form of the particular literary narratives that are the focus of this study. The question is whether the medium forces us to rethink the model, to borrow the terms of Shlomith Rimmon-Kenan (1989). As the previous sections indicate, the borders between philosophical, logical, and linguistic inquiry are highly unstable during the period under examination. "Literary discourse" displays a similar volatility, given that it is an always only emergent construct, situated at the crossroads of other discourses and other genres. More specifically, in tandem with contemporaneous language theory, the narratives at issue formally enact the same logico-grammatical enterprise, the same modeling of a material calculus that was discussed in sections 4 and 5 above. These texts work to combine universality and operational reliability in a single symbol system; twentieth-century narrative form starts to orient itself around the twin imperatives of calculation and communication. In this context, therefore, it is not that the model neglects the medium (Rimmon-Kenan 1989) but that the medium anticipates the model, forcing us to reconsider the explanatory power and regulative principles of narratology itself. The narratives under examination are in a sense *theoretically richer* than some of the narratological frameworks that have been used to study them.[31]

Put briefly, through analysis of the grammar of twentieth-century narrative discourse, we are compelled to modify classical conceptions of narrative grammar itself. By carefully observing just *how* the earlier frameworks have to be modified, furthermore, we may be able to glimpse the grail of universal grammarians—or at least its (post)modern image.

7. On the Mutability of Universal Idioms

Tactically speaking, in order to explore links between universal grammar and narrative form, I shall draw on three dimensions of grammatical theory in which, during the present century, the earlier ideas about universal grammar have arguably perpetuated themselves. My claim is that a number of the ideas informing (various incarnations of) universal grammar are now distributed between the three components of grammatical theory that we call *syntax, semantics,* and *pragmatics*—components that first began to be conceptualized, and demarcated, in the years surrounding the publication of the texts under investigation.

Crucially, Charles Morris, synthesizing the ideas of C. S. Peirce, Ludwig Wittgenstein, Rudolf Carnap, and others in arguing for the importance and fruitfulness of a general (properly, universal) semiotics, differentiated as follows between syntax, semantics, and pragmatics in his *Foundations of the Theory of Signs* (1938): syntax studies relations between signs themselves; semantics studies relations between signs and what is signified; and pragmatics studies relations between signs and sign users. In Ducrot and Todorov's (1979 [1972]) restatement of Morris's semiotic system,

> From the ... point of view [of "neopositivist logicians" such as Morris and Carnap] *syntax* determines the rules that make possible the construction of sentences, or formulae, by combining elementary symbols. *Semantics,* in mathematical logic, for its part seeks to provide the means for interpreting these formulae, for setting them into correspondence with something

else; this "something else" may be reality or other formulae (of the same language or of another). Finally, *pragmatics* describes the use that can be made of the formulae by interlocutors seeking to act on each other. (338)

As Stephen Levinson (1983: 1–5) points out, the three dimensions of *semiotic* analysis identified by Morris issued at once into more narrowly *linguistic* theories about syntax, semantics, and pragmatics.[32] Although it will require the rest of this study to explore the linguistic theories at issue, as already indicated (sec. 1 above) my working assumption is that twentieth-century narrative form likewise organizes itself around the syntactic, semantic, and pragmatic concerns being articulated in a wide range of contemporaneous theoretical contexts. Further, although chapters 1–3 associate Joyce's *Ulysses* with syntax, Kafka's *Der Prozeß* with semantics, and Woolf's *Between the Acts* with pragmatics, respectively, the point is not to compartmentalize these texts according to watertight language-theoretical categories. The point, rather, is to highlight (certain) features of the texts that link them with this or that area of linguistic concern. Other permutations of the texts and theories will no doubt suggest themselves.

In any event, the intuition to be tested over the course of this inquiry is that (post)modernist narratives encode into their very design ideas also at work in state-of-the-art theories about the nature and functions of language. The degree to which this intuition is borne out by subsequent chapters will determine just how much (and what kind of) emphasis we should place on the operative conjunction in *Universal Grammar and Narrative Form*.

7.1. At the turn of the century, Louis Couturat (1901) made the following observation about Leibniz's search for a Universal Characteristic: "Comme l'institution de la grammaire rationelle doit nécessairement précéder celle de la langue universelle à laquelle elle est destinée à s'appliquer, Leibniz a besoin d'un idiome auxiliaire qui joue provisoirement le rôle de langue universelle et qui serve d'intermédiaire entre les langues vivantes et la future langue rationnelle" 'Since the institution of rational grammar must necessarily precede that of the universal language to which it is destined to be applied, Leibniz requires an auxiliary idiom that provisionally plays the role of universal language and that serves as an intermediary between living languages and the rational language of the future' (65–66). In the wake of the ancients and the speculative grammarians (and other precedents listed by Aarsleff 1982: 105), Leibniz selected as his "idiome auxiliaire" the Latin language. The hypothesis to be tested over the course of this investigation is whether, around the beginning of this century, we witness a shift in auxiliary idioms—with especially profound consequences for the relation between twentieth-century literary discourse and language theory. Specifically, the question now before us is whether in our century narrative discourse has provisionally and oxymoronically assumed to itself the role of universal idiom, unfolding between the living languages in which narrative takes root and that "future langue rationnelle" into which narrative cannot evolve without thereby ceasing to be.

Part I   Universal Grammar and Narrative Form

1. The Modeling of Syntactic Structures: "Sirens,"
Schönberg, and the Acceptations of Syntax

If we ask why our language allows certain verbal combinations and disallows others, we are to a large extent referred to contingent linguistic habits, to matters of mere fact concerning language, which develop in one way in a speech community and another way in another. In part, however, we encounter . . . *a priori* laws [for] the combination and transformation of meanings, laws which must be more or less revealed in every developed language, both in its grammar of forms and in the related class of grammatical incompatibilities.—Edmund Husserl

1. Logics of Combination

For all the commentary devoted to the musicality of the "Sirens" episode of Joyce's *Ulysses,* it is remarkable that so little attention has been brought to bear on the episode's relation to contemporaneous, early-twentieth-century transformations or rather revolutions in musical form itself. Of particular interest here is the relation of "Sirens" to Arnold Schönberg's radicalization of polyphony—his development of a pure chromaticism, an absolute atonality—through the technique of the twelve-tone row. Yet Schönberg's musical apparatus and the formal innovations of modern music generally can themselves be construed as synecdoches for a more widespread early-twentieth-century concern with forms of construction in general, combinatory apparatus as such. That concern is evident not only in narrative and musical experimentation but also in research on the foundations of mathematics and axiomatic systems; in philosophers' and linguists' work on the syntactic structures of natural as well as artificial languages; in Seurat's, Duchamp's, and others' attempts to develop a pictorial syntax; and so on.[1] Here I can only begin reintegrating "Sirens" into this immense cultural matrix; even some initial arguments in this connection, however, may in the first place help us move "Sirens" interpretation beyond its traditional impasses and current exegetical limits. But beyond this, by reinterpreting Joyce's "Sirens" as an experiment in combinatory apparatus—the modeling of a device for combining and recombining more or less elementary units into (well-formed) structures—I can continue my attempt to redefine the role of narrative itself in shaping the episteme known as *modernism* (sec. *0.1.1*). Arguably, narrative form in Joyce, like musical form in Schönberg, points to the grammatical—more specifically, the syntactic—profile of the modernist episteme.

Note that, in the very broad acceptation recommended early on by Charles Morris (1938), *syntactic analysis* "involves the study of the relations between certain combinations of signs within a language" (13). A similarly broad acceptation of syntax may be found in the work of Rudolf Carnap, for example: "The *syntax* of a language, or of any other calculus, is concerned, in general, with the *structures of possible serial orders* (of a definite kind) *of any elements whatsoever.* . . . Pure [as opposed to descriptive] syntax is thus wholly analytic, and is nothing more than *combinatorial analysis,* or, in other words, the *geometry* of finite, discrete, serial structures" (1937a [1934]: sec. 2, p. 7). Syntax in this usage marks a transdisciplinary field of investigation (as well as a logico-linguistic construct) that first acquired its modern-day scope and contours during the early decades of this century—that is, in the years surrounding the composition of "Sirens" and, for that matter, *Ulysses* as a whole. The period saw logical inquiry assume as its proper domain the analysis, at the most general level possible, of all permissible (i.e., meaningful and also nonabsurd) forms of construction within a given symbolic system. In turn, logicians' attempts to model explicit and consistent (antinomy-free) formal languages shaped linguists' understanding of natural—that is, nonformalized—languages. Hence the importance not only of reexamining "Sirens" in the context of then-burgeoning syntactic theory but also of reexamining syntactic theory via the formal properties of "Sirens." As we shall see, contemporaneous theories of musical structure provide a crucial intermediary link in the conceptual chain binding, in the case of "Sirens," narrative form with universal grammar. Or rather, we can locate the formal properties of Joyce's "Sirens," as narrative construct, at the juncture of early twentieth-century conceptions of musical, logical, and linguistic structure.

1.1. Also falling within the purview of this inquiry, however, are more recent attempts to model a specifically narrative syntax. At issue are the narrative grammars developed by Tzvetan Todorov (1969, 1977 [1971]) and A. J. Greimas (1987 [1969]), among others, during the classical period of (structuralist) narratology—grammars whose starting point was Vladimir Propp's *Morphology of the Folktale* (1968 [1928]). Crucial interconnections between the form of "Sirens" and contemporaneous theories about syntax will compel us to re-evaluate the much more recent postulate of an essentially narrative syntax. Ultimately, the syntactic structures of "Sirens" yield an entire series of questions and difficulties in this connection. At issue is the way in which "Sirens" might pertain to the history of proposals for narrative syntax, when in effect Joyce's text subsumes the operations of narrative itself under the ongoing attempt to model the syntactic structures of symbol systems at large. The difficulty, in other words, is how to characterize the syntax of a narrative whose form and functioning bear demonstrably on syntactic analysis in general, for Joyce's text has consequences both for syntactic theory as it was understood in the earlier part of this century and for later conceptions of syntax developed under the auspices of, for example, phrase-structural and transformational grammars. To put the problem in the most general form possible: In the case of Joyce's "Sirens," how do we go about assorting literature and science? stylistic innovation and language theory? the logic of narrative and the narrative of logic?

2. Vicissitudes of "Sirens" Exegesis

From the beginning, interpretation of "Sirens" has centered largely on how Joyce's text figures, and also whether it or any other purely discursive artifact *can* figure, the relations between music and language. Thus in 1930, basing his remarks on Joyce's schemata for *Ulysses* and on conversations with Joyce himself,[2] Stuart Gilbert very influentially described how "Sirens" "both in structure and in diction goes far beyond all previous experiments in the adaptation of musical technique and timbre to a work of literature" (1958 [1930]: 242; cf. ix). Gilbert's gloss, anticipated by Ernst Robert Curtius's more critical assessment of the episode's construction of "eine Ouvertüre" and its use of the "Wagnersche Leitmotivtechnik" 'Wagnerian technique of leitmotifs' (1954 [1929]: 312ff.), profoundly shaped subsequent interpretations of "Sirens." Critics generally construed the episode as Joyce's more or less (un)successful effort to realize Pater's dictum that all art aspires to the condition of music. The accounts offered by A. Walton Litz (1961: 62–74) and Hugh Kenner (1987b [1980]: 83ff.; cf. Kenner 1987a [1956]: 253–54), for example, perpetuated and refined the musical model, whose most detailed and explicit formulation, perhaps, may be found in a study by Heath Lees (1984).

Recently, however, some dissonant interpretations of "Sirens" have begun to make themselves heard. From a Lacanian and Derridean perspective, Colin MacCabe (1978) subsumes the musical aspects of the text under what might be called a psycho-semiotic interpretation of the episode's linguistic features. Mac-Cabe writes, "As the material of language becomes the concern of the text [in "Sirens"], the reader can no longer pass through signifier to signified, can no longer bathe in the imaginary unity of a full self but must experience him or herself as divided, distanced, as *other*" (79). For Karen Lawrence (1981), "Sirens," together with "Wandering Rocks," marks the first significant departure from the initial style established in the opening chapters of *Ulysses* (cf. Kenner 1987b [1980]: 83; Erzgräber 1985: 298; Zacchi 1986: 190–91; and McHale 1990; but contrast Fludernik 1986). Yet Lawrence argues that the musical analogy alone does not "supply the *raison d'être*" of the episode (1981: 90); rather, "the variations played on the phrases of the overture in the narrative of 'Sirens' illustrate a kind of rhetorical exercise which becomes increasingly obvious in later chapters that do not have music as their 'art.' The text as a verbal composition supersedes the text as an imitation of a musical composition" (91; cf. McGee 1988: 183ff.).

Similarly, Jean-Michel Rabaté (1986) and Daniel Ferrer (1986) take issue with the Joyce-Gilbert *fuga per canonem* theory of "Sirens." Rabaté argues that, instead of "the vocabulary of musicology," the terms and figures of classical rhetoric can be used to characterize the episode (1986: 82–83); Ferrer suggests that we rechristen the episode's technique as "peristaltic" (i.e., digestive) or else—significantly—computational.[3] André Topia (1986), moreover, comments on the episode's transference of the activity of singing to various body parts, arguing that "this simultaneous process of pulverization and reorganization into new units can be paralleled with the relationship between the phonic network, and the syntactic framework of the sentence" (77).[4] Topia's powerful analysis, which is worth quoting at length, and whose concern with "syntactic frameworks" is taken up in what follows, continues thus:

> In a first phase, the syntactic framework (the internal order and hierarchy within the sentence) is systematically broken by Joyce, who substitutes a mere horizontal juxtaposition of isolated units [for] the vertical hierarchic integration which characterizes a syntactic pattern. As a result, the reader is confronted with a succession of punctual, mobile, fluid, interchangeable units which can move in all directions along the chain of the sentence. But in a second phase, Joyce reorganizes his material by coagulating it into new

units, this time according to phonic patterns (variation/permutation/ echo/symmetry) which, as it were, interfere with, subvert, and often replace the syntactic framework of the sentence. (77; cf. Mahaffey 1988a: 187)

As Topia's interpretation in particular suggests, whereas the Joyce-Gilbert paradigm locates the stylistic specificity of "Sirens" in its subordination of linguistic structures and functions to those of music—in an approximation of language to the condition of music—by contrast a critical reorientation has lately called for just the opposite reading. Now the musical techniques and effects structuring "Sirens" are viewed as instrumental to reflection on, and reevaluation of, the structures and functions of language itself. Thus David Hayman (1985), too, retains the musical figure of overture but subsumes it under the specifically rhetorical figure of parataxis (160–61), and Carl Eichelberger (1986) similarly subordinates the musical to the linguistic dimensions of the episode.

2.1. What here appears to be an interpretive chiasmus, however, amounts really to a modulation of positions within a single conceptual framework. Up to now, accounts of "Sirens" have failed to situate the narrative in this larger framework. In consequence, attempts to adjudicate between the respective claims and capacities of music and language in the episode—the way "Sirens" figures the relation of musical to linguistic structure in general—have for the most part oscillated between ascribing now music, now language, dominant status and compositional priority within the episode. Yet, once we begin to take into account how both the notion of music and the notion of language were very much in question at the time Joyce composed "Sirens" (in 1919), and for interrelated reasons,[5] we start to see how the difficulty of determining the relative priority of music and language gives point to a much larger problem in this connection.

The larger problem centers on the discovery and formalization of rules for the (re)arrangement of elements—whatever their material constitution and denotative force—into sequences or strings. In turn, the rules according to which the items ranged in a given repertoire may be linearized and thereby combined—an apparatus for reconciling space and time, as it were—are precisely the object of the syntactic analysis of (both natural and formalized) languages. If therefore the reception history of "Sirens" has so far unfolded as a series of shifts in the relations of dominance between musical and linguistic considerations, we may postulate this hypothesis by way of explanation, a hypothesis to be explored in greater detail in what follows: "Sirens" (self-reflexively) exploits the constructional devices common to both musical and linguistic structures, devices necessarily belonging to the syntactic or combinatory, as opposed to the semantic or referential, dimension of those structures. As Curtius already recognized, it is indeed only by virtue of their syntactic features, the way their basic elements are (re)combined into larger units, that music and language may be said to be analogous in the first place.[6] Further, once researchers began to explore the logical foundations of mathematics, at the end of the nineteenth and the beginning of the twentieth centuries, producing powerful new tools in both logic and mathematics, the notion of a purely logical and *eo ipso* universal grammar regained its old allure, and the remodeling of syntactic theory in particular proceeded, quite explicitly and self-consciously, under the auspices of the search for universal grammar.[7] Both modern music such as Schönberg's and modernist narratives such as "Sirens," arguably, can be viewed as fruits of this same search.

3. "In Music There Is No Form without Logic"[8]

Richard Ellmann (1977) suggests that Gustavo Magrini's *Manuale di musica* (1916)—found among the books Joyce left behind in Trieste when he entrusted to his brother's care the personal library he had assembled there between 1900 and 1920—"was helpful for [the composition of] the 'Sirens' episode" (7–8). Ellmann does not mention in this context, however, another volume that, as Ellmann's own appendix indicates, was also contained in the Trieste library: that is, Ferrucio Busoni's *Entwurf einer neuen Ästhetik der Tonkunst* (*Outline of a New Aesthetics of Musical Art*) (originally published in Italian in 1906).[9] Yet, as Alfred Einstein notes, Busoni's *Outline* represents an important "literary document . . . on the whole school" that, late in the nineteenth and early in the twentieth century, brashly called itself "the New Music"—or, to use Busoni's phrase, the "young classical" movement (Luening 1980: 181). International in scope, this New Music "manifest[ed] itself first of all in pronounced hostility to romanticism and to the hegemony of German music, above all that of Richard Wagner" (Einstein 1954 [1920]: 201–2).

Thus, Busoni (n.d. [1906]) for one argues that, after Wagner, "eine schwelgerische Sinnlichkeit" 'a self-indulgent sensuality' was added to the series of other notions associated with "feeling" in music (e.g., taste, style, and economy); indeed, "[diese] Form der 'Steigerung' im Affekt haben die Komponisten noch heute nicht überwunden" 'even today composers have not yet overcome this form of "intensification" of affect' (29). Busoni also mocks the rarefied connotations of the term *musikalisch* in the German-language tradition—an exalted signification accompanied by a dangerous devaluation of technical mastery in composition and performance (24ff.). At the same time, Busoni takes pains to differentiate between the New Music and the programmatic music associated with composers like Richard Strauss—composers who around the turn of the century attempted to revivify an already moribund Romanticism (Abraham 1979: 694ff.). For Busoni the experience of music "trifft die menschliche Brust mit jener Intensität, die vom 'Begriffe' unabhängig ist" 'strikes the human breast with precisely that intensity which is independent of "the concept."' More generally, "Darstellung und Beschreibung [sind] nicht das Wesen der Tonkunst; somit sprechen wir die Ablehnung der Programmusik aus" 'representation and description do not constitute the essence of musical art; hence we support the rejection of programmatic music altogether' (n.d. [1906]: 8–9).[10] In place of the programmatic ideal, which sacrificed technical ingenuity for sentimentality and affect, Busoni himself developed complex techniques for the analysis and recombination of the traditional seven-note octave into 113 different scales, made up of a layering or terracing (*Abstufung*) of variously flattened and sharpened intervals (41). Indeed, for Busoni, "every composition was merely a transcription or a rearrangement of known sounds" (Luening 1980: 181).

3.1. Even this minimal sketch of the concerns developed in Busoni's *Outline* suffices to show how many of those same issues inform "Sirens" as well. For instance, the episode persistently thematizes how music can promote just that emotional self-indulgence of which Busoni was so critical vis-à-vis Wagner. Despite its being four o'clock, the fatal hour of Molly Bloom's and Blazes Boylan's assignation, Leopold Bloom resists giving himself over to any such self-indulgence—at least prima facie. The outsider, Bloom observes the musical proceedings in the Ormond bar from the distance of the dining room. Removed from the spectacle of Dedalus's performance, Bloom thinks about specific aids and impediments to good singing, rather than admiring the notion of musicality in general (699–700).[11] In addition, like Busoni with his 113 scales, Bloom speculates on the wondrous divisibility and recombinability of intervals into ever new musical relationships (830ff.). As an active interpreter of music, Bloom especially appreciates the "Beauty of music you must hear twice" (1060–62).

Bloom demonstrates awareness, too, of music's (potentially) stupefying or at least anesthetizing effects (as at, e.g., 914).[12] Thus, like Odysseus before him, Bloom takes measures against being utterly overcome by music. He constantly evaluates his own reaction to the siren song of sentimentality—with bald Pat,

Bloom's waiter, having been rendered physically unsusceptible to the charms of music, like the ear-stopped members of Odysseus's crew:

> Braintipped, cheek touched with flame, they listened [as Simon Dedalus sang] feeling that flow endearing flow over skin limbs human heart soul spine. Bloom signed to Pat, bald Pat is a waiter hard of hearing, to set ajar the door of the bar. The door of the bar. So. That will do. Pat, waiter, waited, waiting to hear, for he was hard of hear by the door. (668–72)

Generally, however, the patrons of the Ormond bar are all too ready to subordinate the experience of hearing "The Croppy Boy," say, to the "thrill" of the "Pity they feel"; for most Dubliners the song is merely a pretext for the opportunity "To wipe a tear for martyrs that want to, dying to, die" (1101–2; cf. Gifford and Seidman 1988: 293). In contrast, Bloom, like Busoni, adopts an antiprogrammatic, even Pythagorean view of music. He absolutizes musical structures and deemphasizes the particular phonic substance in which those structures might be realized: "Words? Music? No: it's what's behind" (703; cf. Abraham 1979: 21, 28).[13]

What is more, historical evidence suggests that, at about the time he was writing "Sirens" in Zürich in 1918–19, Joyce did in fact concern himself with modern theories of musical composition. In Zürich, Joyce discussed musical theories and techniques in some detail with the American-born composer and musician Otto Luening (Luening 1980: 197ff.; Martin and Bauerle 1990: 37ff.), at that time a student of Jarnach's and an acquaintance of Busoni's (Luening 1980: 167–85). In casual conversation Joyce ridiculed Wagner; told Luening, "For me there are only two composers. One is Palestrina and the other is Schönberg" (Luening 1980: 194); and was fascinated with Luening's own experiments with "the fanciest kinds of inversions, symmetrical and otherwise, transpositions, and passages in augmentation and diminution, both separately and combined," as well as Luening's use of "the most intricate kinds of canonical passages, in retrograde or in retrograde inversions" (Luening 1980: 196–97). Joyce also "enjoyed giving literary interpretations of the contrapuntal techniques in music. This turned into a kind of intellectual exercise in which he professed to use the devices for his own purposes in his own medium" (197).[14]

3.2. I shall not pursue here, however, the (over)ambitious question with which an authentic source study of "Sirens" might begin: that is, whether Busoni's *Outline*, Luening's ideas about composition, and related developments in modern music provided Joyce with specific themes and concerns reconstituted, in more or less vulgar or at least narrativized form, when Joyce wrote the episode. On the contrary, my claim is that the form of Joyce's narrative itself must be factored into any attempt to reconstitute, to understand, the *Outline*'s themes and concerns at all—along with related themes and concerns. In this connection, I shall bring particular attention to bear on the specifically compositional impetus for Busoni's text. That impetus, arguably, is just the New Music's hallmark or *differentia specifica:* its ever greater radicalization of polyphonic (i.e., fugal) construction; its substitution, to a hitherto unknown extent, of harmonic layering (Busoni's "Abstufung") for any melodic development of the harmonic structures over time; in short, its creation of what Busoni called a "kaleidoskopisches Durcheinanderschütteln."[15] "Sirens" does not merely reflect the radicalized polyphony and superharmonic organization of the New Music. Beyond this, Joyce's text suggests how the organization of modern music can itself be linked to a broader concern with the relation between repertoires of elements, on the one hand, and principles for sequencing those elements into particular patterns, on the other hand. What is at stake here is, in other words, not merely the notion of a global shift to "spatial form," as Joseph Frank (1988 [1945]) would term it, in both music and narrative—a sudden overexaggeration of taxonomies and a concomitant suppression or even (virtual) exclusion of principles of selection and ordering. Instead, we are concerned with a wide-scale attempt to rethink the way taxonomies in general may be linearized, repertoires as such realized.

3.3. Consider Einstein's description of that New Music of which Busoni's *Outline* may be construed as representative:

> [The New Music] sought to expand the traditional range of musical material as such, to invent new types of melody and harmony—or non-harmony—to make renewed use of the whole-tone scale or to divide the scale according to new proportions into third-tones, quarter-tones, and sixth-tones; in other words, to replace the traditional system of harmony, which can be described as a system with an inherent leading-note quality, by a system that allowed the introduction of parallels and combinations. This attempt to give new meaning to melody, harmony, and part-writing was afterwards developed systematically into extremes of freest "linear" treatment, i.e. part-writing which did away with harmonic interplay—extremes which included so-called atonality, polytonality, and every other negation of established norms. (1954 [1920]: 202)

Thus, Busoni himself stresses the generative power of "die Variationenform [die] eine ganze Reihe von Bearbeitungen gibt" 'the forms of variation (that) yield an entire series of elaborations' (n.d. [1906]: 23)—forms whose parallels and combinations afford an apparatus for composition, a machine for the computation of intervals and harmonic relations. That machine's software, however, can no longer be written in a binary code assigning distinct values (0 or 1) to melody versus harmony, linearity versus layering. Instead, Busoni's ideal variational machine would produce a sort of cross-filiation or interbreeding (*Vermischung*) of tones by operating certain transpositions between scales (41ff.). Busoni presents his apparatus as an infinite improvement over the Wagnerian model, specifically. For Wagner's outdated "Kompositionsmachinerie" was crippled from the start by bad programming, its "routines" having all too quickly degenerated into self-cannibalizing loops—"So eng geworden ist unser Tonkreis" 'so restricted has our stock of available tones become' (32–33). In short, for Busoni, the machinery of leitmotifs yielded only an impoverished set of possible variations on a given tone; it produced forms of expression (*Ausdrucksform*) tending always toward repetition and stereotype (33).

Yet the multiscalar apparatus with which Busoni proposes to replace Wagner's outmoded machine for computing tones was itself quickly superseded by another, still more powerful musical technology: Schönberg's twelve-tone row. After reviewing (very briefly) the basic features of Schönberg's system, I can start to indicate how that system pertains to the narrative structures of "Sirens."

3.4. In "Composition with Twelve Tones (I)" (1984a [1941]), Schönberg describes how the twelve-tone technique begins with a "basic set (BS)" that "consists of various intervals" (219). The basic set, however, should not be conflated with a scale, "although it is invented to substitute for some of the unifying and formative advantages of scale and tonality" (219). Specifically, "cadences produced by the distinction between principal and subsidiary harmonies will scarcely be derived from the basic set. But something different and more important is derived from it with a regularity comparable to the regularity and logic of the earlier harmony; the association of tones into harmonies and their successions is regulated . . . by the order of these [basic] tones" (219). The order of the BS—that is, the initial series or "string"[16] of stipulated tones—determines compositional logic by proscribing the repetition of specific tones over too short a stretch of time. Thus, the well-formed atonal musical phrase is marked, essentially, by its resistance to traditional procedures for (para)phrasing series of tones into measures, passages, and so on.

As Schönberg (1984b [1941]) puts it, "The construction of a basic set of twelve tones derives from the intention to postpone the repetition of every tone as long as possible" (246; cf. Abraham 1979: 835). By maximizing the amount of time separating two occurrences of the same tone within the composition, the twelve-tone technique inhibits the effect of regularity, but it promotes this inhibition by means of a highly patterned system for the manipulation and ordering of tones into ostensibly arbitrary sequences. In this connection, Adorno suggests that the twelve-tone technique "can be more correctly compared to the arrangement of colors on a palette than to the actual painting of a picture" (1973 [1948]: 61). Arguably, however, the modern polyphonic composition emerges precisely from the (reconstruction of the) steps taken to arrange tones in a manner that, as effectively as possible, thwarts or at least inhibits the materialization of a given work. Thus, Schönberg's compositions prompt Adorno to conclude that "today the only works which really count are those which are no longer works at all" (30).

But, in "Twelve-Tone Composition" (1984c ·[1923]), Schönberg asserts that "the weightiest assumption behind twelve-tone composition is this thesis: Whatever sounds together (harmonies, chords, the result of part-writing) plays its part in expression and in presentation of the musical idea in just the same way as does all that sounds successively (motive, shape, phrase, sentence, melody, etc.), and it is equally subject to the law of comprehensibility" (207). Thus, in polyphonic as opposed to homophonic music, "motivic shapes, themes, phrases and the like never succeed in stretching beyond a certain length . . . and are never developed, never split off new shapes and are seldom varied: for all (almost all) development takes place through alteration of the mutual relation to each other of the various components of the idea" (208). In Saussurean terms, we might say that the twelve-tone row forces us to reconfigure the syntagmatic (combinatory) dimension of musical composition in relation to its paradigmatic (associative) dimension.[17] More precisely, we must now ascribe a combinatory role to the very layering of tones along the axis of simultaneity itself.[18] Space—here, now—disseminates time.

As Schönberg says,

> *The two-or-more-dimensional space in which musical ideas are presented is a unit.* . . . they reveal their true meaning only through their co-operation, even as no single word alone can express a thought without relation to other words. All that happens at any point of this musical space has more than a local effect. It functions not only in its own plane, but also in all other directions and planes, and is not without influence even at remote points. . . . The elements of a musical idea are partly incorporated in the horizontal plane as successive sounds, and partly in the vertical plane as

simultaneous sounds. The mutual relation of tones regulates the succession of intervals as well as their association into harmonies; the rhythm regulates the succession of tones as well as the succession of harmonies and organizes phrasing. (1984a [1941]: 220)

Here Schönberg himself compares the "cooperation" of sounds in a harmonic network to the cooperation of words via the paradigmatic structures of language. We find in this passage, too, a musicological version of Carnap's effort to detail "the logical structure of the world" by way of a "construction theory [that] considers individual objects as secondary relative to the network of relations in which they stand" (1969 [1928]: sec. 61, p. 99; cf. Schlick 1979 [1925–36]: 373; and see sec. 6.4 below). The Schönberg passage also anticipates Louis Hjelmslev's view that "une structure [linguistique] est par définition un tissu de dépendances ou de fonctions" 'a [linguistic] structure is by definition a tissue of dependences or of functions' (1971c [1943]: 78–79).

I return below to the theories of logic and language affiliated not only with Schönberg's compositional theories but also with the narrative operations of "Sirens." For the moment, however, I want simply to second Adorno's conclusion that, in Schönberg's musical model itself, "the difference between theme and development, the constancy of harmonic flow, and the unbroken melodic line are destroyed" (1973 [1948]: 42). In modern polyphonic composition the organization of sounds in time is, rather, a function of rules for layering tones into more or less complex harmonic strata. Thus, Adorno goes on to remark that, whereas "the true quality of a melody is always to be measured by whether or not it succeeds in transforming the spatial relations of intervals into time," "twelve-tone technique destroys this relationship at its very roots. Time and interval diverge" (74–75).

In sum, once counterpoint is no longer viewed as "a decoration upon the homophonic composition" (Adorno 1973 [1948]: 52), once tones become "at best motivic fragments in the total structuring of the voices" (53), and once we recognize that, "in any music, in which every single tone is transparently determined by the construction of the whole work, . . . [there] is no longer anything which is unthematic . . . [and] the difference between the essential and the coincidental disappears" (57, 59), we must then reorient our strategies for acquiring competence in (designing and interpreting) a kind of music that, to use Schönberg's phrase, "renounces a tonal centre" (1984a [1941]: 217). Since the twelve-tone technique is not merely the haphazard profusion of sounds in a structural vacuum but rather the structuration of harmonic relationships and intervals according to strictly atonal principles, competence in modern music depends on the mastery of rules that assign what we might call a structural description to any given tone in relation to the stock of available (possible, conceivable) tones at any given moment. The same rules would also account for the deviation (or "amusicality," as it were) of certain (relations and sequences of) tones from the kinds of combinations sanctioned by the twelve-tone system.[19]

But furthermore, since deviance from the rules of the twelve-tone system may be defined precisely as conformity to the rules for traditional (or "tonal") methods of composition, competence in modern music presupposes mastery of both sets of rules. By contrast, traditional music suppressed reflection on its rules for construction just to the extent that its forms occluded the atonal, and differently tonal, systems against which such traditional music defined itself. Generally, then, competence in modern music may be identified as the capacity to (re)construct systems of rules according to which permissible combinations of tones are ordered and regulated. A given composition, a specific performance, diachronically unfolds as a unique search for the rules that, from a synchronic standpoint, can be said to determine what constitutes well-formed musical structures in general. The modern musical project, to this extent, is essentially syntactic in nature.[20]

In attempts to substantiate these last, quite broad claims, we must now return to Joyce's "Sirens" and detail affinities between the structure of the episode and Schönberg's conception of musical structure as such. By linking Joyce's narrative techniques to the concepts of polyphonic structure developed by Schönberg, we can in turn start to recontextualize these innovations in both narrative and musical form. Specifically, the narrative and musical experimentation can be resituated in a widespread preoccupation with constructional (a.k.a. axiomatic) systems. These systems form the common root not just of musical and narrative experimentation but also of what at one point came to be called logico-grammatical syntax.

4. "Sirens" and Polyphonic Form: A First Approach

Lees (1984) argues that, in designating the technique of "Sirens" as *fuga per canonem,* Joyce used the term *canonem* in its canonic sense, as it were:

> The musical term *canon* when it was first used in the fifteenth century referred not to the music but to the verbal directions placed before or sometimes within the music. By adhering to these directions, some of

which took the form of perverse puzzles, performers were enabled to realize the "full score" of a piece or the complete course of a melody. . . . It is my contention that Joyce opted for the old title of *fuga per canonem . . .* in order to invoke this medieval practice of providing "cryptic directions" which act as precept or guide to the main unfolding, and I believe that this introduction itself embodies the *canon*. (40–41)

As Richard Hofstadter (1979) notes, by the time J. S. Bach composed his *Musical Offering* (1747) for Frederick the Great, the inclusion of canons at the beginning (and middle) of compositions "was a familiar musical game of the day" (8). The composer's game was to provide "themes and hints" and invite performers to derive the canon for—that is, to (re)construct rules for the performance of— a given piece. Even before Lees, however, commentators such as Curtius (1954 [1929]: 310–12) and Litz (1961: 66ff.) attempted to derive, from the themes and hints set out in the episode's opening lines, the canon of "Sirens" as a whole. Arguably, the half-century-old attempt to reconstruct the technique of "Sirens" has been hindered not by an insufficiently historical understanding of (musical) canons but rather by a failure to take into account the specifically *fugal* structure of Joyce's narrative. More precisely, commentators have failed to situate the structure of "Sirens" in that early-twentieth-century radicalization of polyphonic form already discussed in the context of Schönberg.

   4.1. By presenting a list of its basic narrative constituents in an abbreviated sequence (sixty-three lines) and then expanding that list of constituents into the more extended sequence that makes up the episode proper (1,231 lines), Joyce's text in effect compels us to juxtapose two, differently linearized versions of the episode. Or, rather, even as the episode unfolds in time we are forced to neutralize temporality itself: now by superimposing on the extended sequence of motifs the initial repertoire that provides a sort of legend or key for the narrative as a whole; now by superimposing the episode proper back on the initial repertoire, in order to check that system of coordinates against the (strings of) elements diachronically realized in the text. "Sirens" sanctions and regulates both these (progressive and retrogressive) performative modes, and at the same time—if I may be permitted that locution. In consequence, the episode can be described by means of developmental, "melodic" principles of construction that in effect operate laterally and harmonically, orienting the very evolution of the narrative along an axis of simultaneity. Development, the syntagm—temporality itself—becomes a function of the grouping of indefinitely many (n-tuple) motifs along a vertical, associative axis.[21]

Put otherwise, we read the text as we would listen to a fugue: in the split temporality of a double awareness, the subtle schizophrenia of modern music appreciation, resolving every melodic development back into the stasis of its harmonic situation, the totality of its associative chains, the web of its intermittent paradigms. As my language here implies, my suggestion is that the technique of dual, even self-canceling narrative sequences exploited by "Sirens" reproduces the polyphonic technique of a specifically modern music. Joyce's text disrupts classical narrative form in the same way that Schönberg's twelve-tone technique wreaks change on classical conceptions of music. In modernity at least, music represents, not the continual approximation of particular compositions to an ideal, purely organic compositional form, but rather the creation of unique compositional forms for specific compositions, the constant reformulation of musical grammar. Music ramifies into musics, the accepted logic of melody and harmony into forms that require us to reflect on the conditions for compositional syntax. Similarly, since "Sirens" grounds narrative discourse in a plurality of sequencing techniques, and since furthermore narrative can be *defined* as the representation of events or, in other words, the recounting of sequences of (causally linked) states of affairs (Prince 1973, 1980, 1982), the form of "Sirens" bears accordingly a peculiar relation to standard accounts of narrative form in general. Joyce's narrative form calls into question an entire family of concepts—order, series, duration, development, frequency— by which we tend to explicate the related notions *time, cause, state, event,* and a fortiori *narrative* itself.

I spell out these claims in more detail below (see sec. *8*). The point to stress here is that the two-part structure of "Sirens" compels us to think associatively and in depth as a propadeutic to thinking syntagmatically and in succession. Orienting oneself within the layering of narrative motifs in the first part of the episode becomes a condition of possibility for, or even somehow equivalent to, linearizing those elements into a trajectory, a progression—a narrative—in the second part. Reading itself becomes a back-and-forth, "Fro. To, fro." (47)—or even a "Fro, to: to, fro:" (1113)—process of projecting the initial list of motifs forward into the second part of the episode and of simultaneously projecting the later transpositions and permutations of motifs backward into the opening list. In other words, the narrative always unfolds on two separate planes of successivity. First, we have the structure of the (anticipating) repertoire, which, as we shall see, already situates an apparently static taxonomy within a larger dynamic of permutation and transformation. Second, we have the structure of the (anticipated) realization of the repertoire, a realization that proceeds through transformational operations at work in the episode, and for that matter the novel, as a whole. The narrative discourse thus "progresses" just by always (re)fashioning an emergent network of paradigmatic connections, which link any given segment of the narrative with another—either earlier or later, relatively distant or proximate—narrative segment.

Thus, in "Sirens," as in Schönberg, what figure ostensibly as sequences unfolding along the axis of time produce, in actual fact, structures of coordinate elements along an atemporal axis of association. Such paradigmatic structures evolve, or rather do not evolve, within what we might call a polyphonic temporality of reading; like the processing of Schönberg's compositions, the processing of "Sirens" ideally requires a listener whose interpretive orientation—whose consciousness, whose project, whose very life—develops via a temporality perpendicular or at least transverse to that of the composition.[22] Indeed, for Schönberg my life *must not* evolve in a manner parallel to the development of the composition, lest I fall back into a clandestine and therefore doubly pernicious programmaticism, duped by the premodern promise of a truly organic form, the Romantic fallacy of an aesthesis that is also a mimesis.

Bloom for one listens to Simon Dedalus's performance like a real musical modernist; his idea is that music in general requires not the passive reception of preexistent compositional forms but rather the active structuration of sounds into compositions. That structuration requires, in particular, awareness of the complex temporality by virtue of which one recognizes music *as* music: "Want to listen sharp. Hard. Begin all right: then hear chords a bit off: feel lost a bit. In and out of sacks, over barrels, through wirefences, obstacle race. Time makes the tune" (839–41). But if time makes the tune, that making, divided between the first and the second parts of the episode, is as Bloom says an obstacle race— that is, an *obstacle* race that is also an obstacle *race*. At stake in "Sirens," as in Schönberg's polyphonic compositions, is a mode of linearization that emerges, paradoxically, from a more or less insuperable resistance to all sequence, all linearity. Somehow time and succession emerge, here as in Schönberg, from paradigmatic formations of essentially indeterminate depth.[23]

4.2. So far, as is no doubt all too obvious, my characterization of the polyphonic structure of "Sirens" has succeeded in accounting for (certain aspects of) the episode's form only at a global level. My account of "Sirens" as polyphonic in form merely starts to ask, and in no way resolves, questions about its principles of construction. Despite recourse to the musical analogy, I have not yet begun to describe in any real detail the combinatorial mechanisms of (any one stretch of) the narrative. Nor have I given any account of how, exactly, the techniques of Joyce's narrative might be said to bear on combinatorial mechanisms in general, as opposed to those mechanisms shared by modern music and modernist narratives in particular. Is this lack of detail, explicitness, and explanatory scope in the foregoing analysis to be ascribed to some radical incommensurability between the techniques of narrative as opposed to those of musical construction, as Curtius and later critics postulated? Is it that Joyce's experiment in narrative-qua-music is foredoomed to failure because of the a- or rather antirepresentational nature of music as opposed to narrative?

It seems to me that such claims rest on a mistaken assumption: namely, that since narratives are by definition representational artifacts, and since alternatively music by (modern) definition cannot attempt to represent states of affairs without ipso facto ceasing to be music, therefore any narrative that tries to model itself on musical form will inevitably devolve into a paradoxical and only semirealized possibility, an abortive entity, a grotesque Caliban of cultural production. Any such diagnosis of "Sirens" as a merely monstrous music assumes, in a curious inversion of classical narratological paradigms,[24] that narrative is not only *distinguished* but also *exhausted* by its representational (i.e., referential) functions. Yet, as the previous discussion I hope suffices to show, narratives feature combinatory as well as referential mechanisms; presumably, like the syntax of a language, the syntactic dimension of narrative discourse comprises rules by which the constituent elements of narratives are (re)combined into well-formed sequences and structures. To this extent, a given narrative could very well model its own syntactic structures (at least in part) on the combinatorial mechanisms of music.

Accordingly, the limitations of the polyphonic analogy—its failure to yield an analytic vocabulary rich and nuanced enough to account for the structure of "Sirens"—must be ascribed not to the incommensurability between music and narrative per se but rather to the requirement for a different formal architecture with which to model the structure of "Sirens." From the latter architectonics we may be able to derive applications, ultimately, for both musical and narrative structures. In attempts to begin respecifying the structure of "Sirens" according to an enriched combinatorial logic—whose scope and explanatory power effectively exceed that of the principles regulating either musical or narrative structures taken alone—we require a somewhat wider sample of Joycean discourse. To begin with, we can isolate the various transformations enacted by the discourse on a single lexical item featured in the narrative. The element in question is the term (name) *Bloom,* together with the variants of that term generated by Joyce's wordplay. Ultimately, our concern will be the relation of such wordplay, as well as the rules governing the integration of that verbal play into larger segments of the narrative, to two (overlapping) areas of concern in contemporaneous language theory: (i) techniques for the logical analysis of formal languages and (ii) techniques for the morphological and syntactic analysis of words, phrases, and sentences characteristic of natural languages.

5. The Transformations of *Bloom*

Within the initial repertoire itself, occurrences of the term *Bloom* are themselves embedded, at one level of narrative structure, in a set of permutations or rather transformations. Thus, "A husky fifenote blew." (5) finds, in the next line, its continuance: "Blew. Blue bloom is on the." (6). Likewise, "Jingle. Bloo." (19) immediately precedes "Boomed the crashing chords." (20). Here, in fact, "Boomed" complements "Bloo" both phonetically and orthographically. Two other occurrences are, however, more widely spaced, creating, within the initial taxonomy of elements, that "Fro. To, fro" mode of (non-)progression which the repertoire as a whole induces, given that the list is itself embedded within the entire narrative at another structural level. "I feel so sad. P.S. So lonely blooming." (32) waits some twenty-two lines before finding its complement, in the form of a repetition and transposition, in "Last rose Castile of summer left bloom I feel so sad alone" (54). A final occurrence of *Bloom* stands in isolation—"Bloom. Old Bloom." (49)—although, as already discussed, the ongoing reticulation of the text into a network of verbal associations calls into question the very concept of an isolated narrative element, a single, detachable motif.

In any event, consider the relation between the occurrences (and transformations) of *Bloom* in the opening list and those in the episode proper. Like Schönberg's basic set, the list of narrative elements provided in the opening lines of "Sirens" permits (regulates) the successive combinations of motifs that structure the rest of the episode. Granted, as Litz (1961: 67ff.) has shown, the terms, intervals, and relations encoded in the first part of the episode do not rigidly govern the manner in which the introductory elements are realized in the subsequent portions of the text. To this extent "Sirens" deviates from the quite rigid format required by the twelve-tone technique. Furthermore, in contrast to the basic sets subtending Schönberg's compositions, Joyce's initial list is explicitly included and prominently displayed as a series of quasi-canonic themes and hints in the text itself. Still, the two-part structure of Joyce's text allows us to situate "Sirens" within a combinatorial system as radically structures, as globally operative, as that implemented by Schönberg's twelve-tone row and its fundamental presupposition, the basic set. In effect, the opening list in "Sirens" establishes not the exact sequence but rather the *range* of permissible transformations, the parameters of verbal play, realized in the episode proper; these parameters determine what verbal structures branch or rather, to use Derrida's suggestive term, "fission" (Derrida 1984) from the single lexical element *Bloom,* among many other such elements.

5.1. Arguably, the repertoire performs, and stipulates, three basic kinds of verbal play in connection with *Bloom,* with *Bloom* here serving as a thematic, motivic, phonetic, morphological, orthographic, and characterological root all at once. First, the opening list establishes a pretext for that species of verbal play which links *Bloo-* with *blew* and which therefore sets into play a series of associations spanning breath, the soul (*anima,* πνεῦμα), wind instruments ("husky fifenotes" [5]), singing, and hot air, in the sense of that inflated rhetoric satirized both in the "Aeolus" episode and at the end of "Sirens" itself, where Bloom's fart effectively becomes indistinguishable from Robert Emmet's overheated nationalist rhetoric (1284ff.). In a phrase that recalls and reactivates line 5, for example, the narrator recounts how at one point Simon Dedalus "blew through the flue two husky fifenotes" (218). Further on, the *Bloo-/blew* transformation acquires an additional association with women: "Instruments. A blade of grass, shell of her hands, then blow" (1237). Another element of this transformational series effectively sexualizes the entire set: "See. Play on her. Lip blow. Body of a white woman, a flute alive. Blow gentle. Loud. Three holes, all women" (1088–89).

5.1.1. But, when the narrative records that with a "Light sob of breath Bloom sighed on the silent bluehued flowers" (457–58), the text has already begun to superimpose a second chain of transformations on the *Bloo-/blew* series and its web of attendant associations.[25] What we can call the episode's basic set encodes the schema for this second kind of verbal play as well (e.g., at line 6). In this case, the wordplay consists in punning on *Bloom* and invoking its specifically floral connotations, which are further narrowed by a secondary phonological assimilation of *Bloo-* to *blue* and hence to the blue blooms of, in particular, the rye plant. From the rye bloom derives, as we well know, an anesthetizing agent as powerful as any programmatic music and its self-indulgent appreciation. Thus at line 230 we have "Bloom. Old Bloom. Blue bloom is on the rye" and, at lines 390–91, "Bloom by ryebloom flowered tables." The series of transformations anticipated by the opening list creates an associative network connecting a

Bloom whose punctilious sobriety earns our admiration in the "Oxen of the Sun" episode (cf. 14.275–76) with a species of bloom that intoxicates, once transubstantiated into rotgut.

Yet this associative network linking antithetical (B/b)looms is itself embedded within—or alternatively embeds within itself—another set of associations of flowers with (sexual and other) forms of intoxication. These associations inform the earlier "Lotus Eaters" episode. At the end of that episode, when Bloom takes his bath, Joyce explicitly associates Bloom's penis with a lotus flower (5.572), a species of flora often having (more or less vague) connotations of exoticism, drugged somnambulism, oriental luxuriance, and so on. What is more, we discover in the earlier episode that, for the sake of his erotic correspondence with "Martha," Bloom has adopted the pseudonym Henry Flower (5.63). In "Sirens" itself, even as the text sets into play the series of *Bloom/bloom* transformations preestablished in the introductory list, it inserts that series in the other associative chain linking "Sirens" and "The Lotus Eaters": "Two sheets cream vellum paper one reserve two envelopes when I was in Wisdom Hely's wise Bloom in Daly's Henry Flower bought" (295–96). More generally, in the case of both the *Bloo-/blew* and the *Bloo(m)/(blue) bloom* transformations, the evolution of the narrative finds itself enmeshed in paradigmatic webs that not only extend backward and forward within "Sirens" itself but also encompass other (earlier and later) episodes such as "Aeolus," "The Lotus Eaters," and "Oxen of the Sun."[26]

5.1.2. The two series of transformations characterized thus far—*Bloo-/blew* and *Bloo(m)/(blue) bloom*—can be grouped with another class of transformations also introduced by the basic set. The mechanisms of this third transformation are more difficult to specify than the other two, but the difficulty involved here will provide a convenient transition to the next stage of the analysis. That stage centers on how the logics of combination exploited by both modern music and modernist narrative can themselves be recontextualized in a larger network of discourses. At issue are philosophico-linguistic discourses concerned with the syntactic analysis of both formalized and natural languages.

Meanwhile, we can approach *Bloom's* third transformation through the concept of the name, or rather through the various syntactic functions on which we tend to confer nominal, pseudonominal, or pronominal status, as the case may be. In this connection, note that the initial list in effect makes *Bloom* and its assorted transformations merely one set of lexical elements among many others. The first part of the episode does not rank the various elements according to any known actantial paradigm, any familiar characterological model; it refuses to set literary characters above their environments or even above the objects found within their environments. The introductory list thereby opens up space for a series of grammatical or, more precisely, morphological operations on the word *Bloom* construed as a (proper) name. More specifically, the narrative conflates the nominal functions of *Bloom*, its capacity to designate an individual, with the pronominal (anaphoric) functions that might otherwise be ascribed to a term like *Bloom*—were it to lose its status as a proper name. Thus, *Bloom* operates throughout as an indeterminate part of speech, an ambiguous *modus significandi.* In effect, *Bloom* functions now as a nominal and therefore categorematic term, now as a pronominal and therefore syncategorematic term.[27]

This dual functioning of *Bloom* can be glimpsed in a series of constructions in which the name acquires, over the course of the narrative, morphological signatures that are specific to the grammar of personal and relative pronouns alone. More to the point, English, being an analytic (uninflected) as opposed to a synthetic (inflected) language, does not ordinarily assign case markings to nouns, except in the genitive case (e.g., *Lena's, artist's*). Thus, neither *Lena* nor *artist,* for example, requires modification according to whether the term functions syntactically as a subject ("Lena loves the artist") or as an object ("The artist loves Lena") within a given sentence. By contrast, both personal pronouns (*he, his, him*) and relative pronouns (*who, whose, whom*) take case markings according to their various possible syntactic functions. "Sirens," however, elides the difference between English nouns and pronouns by assigning case markings to (variants of) the proper noun *Bloom.* We find evidence of the nominative case in "Bloowho went by Moulang's pipes" (86), of the genitive case (of the relative pronoun as opposed to the noun) in "Bloowhose dark ey read Aaron Figatner's name" (149), and of the dative case in "Winsomely she on Bloohimwhom smiled. Bloo smi qui go. Ternoon" (309–10).[28] Note furthermore that, in the midst of this series of transformations, *Bloom* reappears in its orthodox nominal form as a one-word line at 102. Here the form of the narrative skews the ongoing pronominalization of *Bloom* through a sudden reassertion of the term's capacity to name—its ability to operate independently of other terms or, as we might also put it, to function categorematically and not merely syncategorematically.

Thus, the third transformation of *Bloom* centers on the morpho-syntactic profile of English, denaturalizing the principles according to which grammatically acceptable phrases and sentences of the language incorporate that class of terms we call (proper) nouns, and foregrounding as well the principles that regulate the grammar of nouns and pronouns, respectively. The narrative thus brings our attention to bear on the combinatorial logic(s) pertaining to words, phrases, and sentences, depending on the level of grammatical description chosen. In attempts to specify this third transformation of *Bloom*, however, we have gotten ourselves entangled in concepts and distinctions—morphological signatures versus syntactic functions, modes of syntactic integration, levels of grammatical description, etc.—that first began to assume their modern-day form only in early-twentieth-century discourses centered on language, in a theoretical as opposed to a narrative setting. Yet if we discover that we are bound to mention these concepts and distinctions in discussing the form and functioning of "Sirens" as a narrative construct, this suggests in turn that Joyce's text bears importantly on both the theory and the (literary) practice of language. It is not that we must apply linguistic or logical theory in order to "get" what is going on in "Sirens" but that the narrative is instrumental in showing us just where and how applications of the theory first become thinkable.

5.2. In what follows, I first examine "Sirens" vis-à-vis contemporaneous discourse on the structures and principles of formal languages (sec. 6). From the start, efforts to model the syntax of natural languages gained impetus from philosophers' and logicians' attempts to model the syntax of formal languages. Devised for more convenient analysis of arguments according to the rules for valid inference (cf. sec. 0.5.2), the history of twentieth-century theories about formal and natural languages suggests that, in modern as well as ancient times (sec. 0.2), grammar has always been (more or less) philosophical grammar. Next, in section 7, I attempt to situate Joyce's narrative in the context of discourse on the syntax of natural languages, keeping in mind that the two fields of logico-syntactic and more narrowly syntactic inquiry are historically and conceptually intertwined in quite complicated ways. Thence, in section 8, I move on to consider the form of "Sirens" in the context of efforts to model a specifically *narrative* syntax.

Thus, I seek to determine how "Sirens" pertains to the notion of syntax taken in what prima facie appears to be a series of progressively more specialized acceptations: from syntax in its logical acceptation, to syntax in its linguistic acceptation, to syntax in its narratological acceptations. (As we shall see, however, narrative syntax in fact operates at a level of specificity intermediate between that of logical and that of linguistic syntax.) It is not only that, in interpreting the formal mechanisms of Joyce's narrative, we must begin to model its structure using all three acceptations of syntax pertinent here. What is more, the narrative form of "Sirens" helps define the grounds on which these acceptations of *syntax* can be assorted—conceptualized—in the first place.

6. "Sirens" and the Logical Acceptations of Syntax

At issue, first, is the relation between "Sirens" and contemporaneous efforts to fashion a formal language according to the principles of a wholly logical syntax. In this connection, my task is to determine whether the structure of "Sirens" can be construed as, or at least as being more or less analogous to, a quasi-formal calculus. A more specific version of the previous question is, How does the two-part format of the episode pertain to the axiomatic or constructional systems on which the structures of first formal and then natural languages have been modeled?

6.1. Classical accounts of formal languages traditionally posit two criteria for a language in the most basic sense: (i) the stipulation of a set of primitive terms and (ii) the sequencing of those terms into "strings"—into formulae or sentences—according to so-called formation and transformation rules. More precisely, as Alfred Tarski says in "The Semantic Conception of Truth and the Foundations of Semantics" (1944):

> To specify the structure of a language, we must characterize unambiguously the class of those words which are to be considered *meaningful.* In particular, we must indicate all words which we decide to use without defining them, and which are called "*undefined* (or *primitive) terms*"; and we must give the so-called rules of *definition* for introducing new or *defined* terms. Furthermore, we must set up criteria for distinguishing within the class of expressions those which we call "*sentences.*" Finally, we must formulate the conditions under which a sentence of the language can be *asserted.* In particular, we must indicate all *axioms* (or *primitive sentences*), i.e., those sentences which we decide to assert without proof; and we must give the so-called *rules of inference* (or *rules of proof*) by means of which we can deduce the new asserted sentences from other sentences which have been previously asserted. Axioms, as well as sentences deduced from them by means of rules of inference, are referred to as "*theorems*" or "*provable sentences.*" (52; cf. Carnap 1971 [1938]: 159; Körner 1960: 74ff.; Nagel and Newman 1958: 45–56)

Accordingly, what was characterized before as the basic set of "Sirens," by analogy with the twelve-tone row, can now be recharacterized by way of a logical analogy. The episode's first sixty-three lines can be construed as a list of the primitive, undefined sentences or axioms of the narrative discourse; they form "those sentences [that the discourse] . . . assert[s] without proof" or rather stipulates to be meaningful in the context of the narrative system. Lines such as "Chips, picking chips off rocky thumbnail, chips" (3) or "Rrrpr. Kraa. Kraandl" (60), although not strictly speaking sentences (in the English language) at all, nonetheless operate as axioms of the narrative, permitting what Tarski calls the deduction[29] of "the new asserted sentences" comprising the episode proper. On this model, interpreting the episode requires that we "deduce" "Into their bar strolled Mr Dedalus. Chips, picking chips off one of his rocky thumbnails. Chips" (192–93), and "Prrprr. . . . Fff! Oo. Rrpr. . . . Tram kran kran kran. Good oppor. Coming Krandlkrankan. . . . Kraaaaaa. . . . Pprrpffrrppfff" (1286–92), "from [the] other sentences which have been previously asserted" in the first part of the episode. Those primitive "sentences" contain too the primitive, undefined terms, "the class of those words which are to be considered *meaningful*" in the context of the narrative discourse.

6.2. Up to now, however, I have suppressed certain more or less obvious incongruities (or at least complications) in the logical analogy in order to outline the comparison in a first, rough form. Of crucial importance to any comparison of Joyce's text with an axiomatized symbol system are what Tarski specifies as the requirement for an *unambiguous* characterization of the primitive terms, on the one hand, and what he calls the requirement for a statement of the language's rules of definition and inference, on the other hand. I discuss the latter requirement first, gradually working back around (in secs. 6.5 and 6.6) to the requirement for unambiguous primitive terms.

Notice that, whereas Tarski carefully discriminates between rules of definition and rules of inference with respect to an axiomatized language, the Danish logician Jørgen Jørgensen, writing a few years earlier but within the same philosophical tradition, tends to group both sets of rules under a single domain that he terms "syntax": "Within each language the symbols pertaining to [that language] are manipulated according to certain rules which are the criteria of 'correct language.' Such rules are called 'syntactical rules,' and the systematic statement of the rules governing a certain language is called the syntax of the language in question" (1939: 219).[30] Similarly, Charles Morris (1938) groups both rules of definition and rules of inference under the heading *syntax*. Thus, in that subset of semiotic inquiry which abstracts away from semantic and pragmatic considerations and studies only the syntactic dimension of signs and sign combinations, "language (i.e., L_{syn}) becomes any set of things related in accordance with two classes of rules: *formation rules*, which determine permissible independent combinations of members of the set (such combinations being called sentences), and *transformation rules*, which determine the sentences which can be obtained from other sentences. These may be brought together under the term '*syntactical rule*'" (14). We might wonder, however, how both the rules according to which we introduce new terms and the rules according to which we deduce theorems (i.e., provable sentences) belong to the "syntax" of a language. More to the point, it remains unclear how the combinatorial mechanisms at work in Joyce's text pertain to a logical syntax prescribing both how we define and how we infer within the framework of a (formalized) language.

Provisionally, at least, we can say that Joyce's text encodes into its very form issues faced by logicians in their efforts to map syntactic categories and relations from grammatical into logical models (and vice versa). Here we have to recall that Tarski's distinction between the rules of definition and the rules of inference—rules that Jørgensen brings under the single heading *syntax*—can be traced back ultimately to Husserl's powerful and influential distinction between *Unsinn* (nonsense or ill-formedness) and *Widersinn* (absurdity or contradictoriness) in the fourth of his *Logical Investigations*, which is concerned with "Der Unterschied der selbständigen und unselbständigen Bedeutungen und die Idee der reinen Grammatik" 'the distinction between independent and dependent meanings and the idea of pure grammar.'[31] In this *Investigation*, Husserl seeks to establish a fundamental distinction between grammar, or syntax in the narrow sense, and logic, which Husserl and those influenced by him thought of as syntax in a broader sense. As Husserl puts it,

> [Es gibt] Gesetze, welche in der Sphäre der Bedeutungskomplexionen walten und die Funktion haben, in ihr Sinn von Unsinn zu trennen, sind noch nicht die im prägnanten Sinn sogennanten logischen Gesetze; sie geben der reinen Logik die möglichen Bedeutungsformen, d.h. die apriorischen Formen komplexer, einheitlich sinnvoller Bedeutungen, deren "formale" Wahrheit bzw. "Gegenständlichkeit" dann die im prägnanten Sinne "logischen Gesetze" regeln. Während jene ersteren Gesetze dem Unsinn, wehren diese letzteren dem formalen oder analytischen Widersinn, der formalen Absurdität. (1984 [1913]: 301–2; cf. Husserl 1969 [1929]: 50ff., and 294ff.)

> [There are] laws that, prevailing over the sphere of meaning-complexes, have the function of separating sense from nonsense. Such laws are, how-

ever, not so-called logical laws, in the most pregnant sense of that term; rather, they yield merely the pure logic of possible forms of meaning— i.e., the forms to which significantly complex unities of meaning can be known a priori to adhere. In turn, the "formal" truth or "objectivity" of the complex meanings is regulated by "logical laws" in the salient sense. Whereas the former principles guard against nonsense, the latter guard against formal or analytic countersense, or formal absurdity proper.

On the one hand, nonsense (*Unsinn*) marks the abrogation of grammar; it comes from ignoring formation rules, the rules for forming strings, sentences, or formulae, depending on how we choose to characterize the basic units of the symbol system at issue. In sequencing terms into strings, the aim is to avoid the nonsensicality that derives from ill-formedness (as in, e.g., "view the Seems now hazy expansive yet" or "avez maintenant d'abord vous avec les autres" or, to use Carnap's 1975 [1931] example, "Caesar ist und"). On the other hand, absurdity (*Widersinn*—literally, "countersense") marks the abrogation of logic; it comes from ignoring transformation rules, that is, rules for transforming one (class of) sentence into another (class). When deriving corollaries and inferences from the undefined axiomatic sentences, the prime directive, now, is to avoid contradiction in concatenating two or more primitive sentences (as in, e.g., "A round thing is a round thing, and it is also a square thing" or "An old person is a young person; therefore, she is not only old but also young").

But in the same *Investigation* Husserl *also* attempts to map the distinction between *Unsinn* and *Widersinn*—and a fortiori the distinction between grammatical and logical principles—into a second-order logico-grammatical framework that he terms "reinlogische Grammatik" 'purely logical grammar' and that he explicitly associates with "die alte Idee einer allgemeinen, und spezieller, die einer apriorischen Grammatik" 'the old idea of a general grammar and, more particularly, the idea of an a priori grammar' (1984 [1913]: 302).[32] Thus transplanted, the grammar-logic distinction yields both a "rein logisch-grammatische Formenlehre" 'pure logico-grammatical morphology' (336ff.)— that is, a "theory of the pure forms of judgments . . . implanted as a germ in the old analytics [such as Aristotle's] but not yet developed" (1969 [1929]: 50)—and also a "consequence-logic" (1969 [1929]: 53ff.). By proscribing contradictory combinations of the more elemental forms of judgment—"S is p" ("the dog is rabid") being more elemental than "Sp is not-q" ("the rabid dog is not curable")—the latter logic provides "Einsicht in die apriorische Konstitution des Bedeutungsgebietes nach Seiten all derjenigen Formen, die in den Grundformen ihren apriorischen Ursprung haben" 'insight into the a priori constitution of areas of meaning according to all those forms that originate a priori in the basic forms [from which the more complex forms can be derived through various combinatorial operations]' (1984 [1913]: 340).[33] The grammaticization of logic, so to speak, allows us to specify the most elemental forms in which judgments must be cast in order for them *to be* judgments at all. Meanwhile, the logicization of grammar permits us to speak of deductive operations that, performed on the elementary judgments, guarantee noncontradictory second-order judgments (i.e., inferences).

The following paradox emerges. Husserl eventually resubsumes under a logico-grammatical framework the very distinction between nonsense and absurdity that was supposed to demarcate grammatical from logical analysis in the first place. As a result, syntax in Husserl's scheme acquires a peculiarly indefinite profile. Syntax must now account both for the combinations of terms permitted by the grammar of a given language and for all logically permissible combinations of terms—combinations that, built up according to a priori principles, pertain by definition to all modes of expression that can be formulated (in principle) in any language whatsoever.

Analogously, if "the function of grammar is to define those laws in virtue of which an expression avoids . . . nonsense, whereas the function of logic is to define those laws in virtue of which expressions which . . . are already free of nonsense also avoid absurdity" (Gardies 1985 [1975]: 18), we can offer a Husserlian diagnosis of Jørgensen's suggestion that "syntax" is what accounts for *all* allowable manipulations of symbols within a given language. Jørgensen's usage indicates that the term *syntax* itself has migrated from a narrowly grammatical acceptation to a broader acceptation spanning both grammar and logic. As Morris (1938) puts it, "Logical syntax deliberately neglects . . . the semantical and pragmatical dimensions of semiosis to concentrate upon the *logico-grammatical* structure of language" (14; my emphasis).

6.3. "Sirens," arguably, also unfolds within a framework of logico-grammatical rules; it too overdetermines the very notion of syntax through forms of construction that project grammar into logic, logic into grammar.[34] The narrative requires that, in interpreting Joyce's text, we distinguish between the formation rules chiefly operative in the first part of the episode and the transformation rules whose main function is to regulate the (re)combinatory operations that build up the rest of the episode—from what Husserl might call the *Grundformen* provided in the first sixty-three lines. Insofar as the introductory section of the episode brings our attention to bear on what counts as sensical and nonsensical within the (English) language and, indeed, begins to defamiliarize the principles of sense for that language, the first class of rules may be termed *grammatical rules*. The second class of rules, by contrast, may be termed *logical*, insofar as these rules determine which linearizations, what recombinations, of the introductory elements are to be viewed as absurd or "countersensical" over the course of the narrative. (Here again, Joyce's text presses against the very bounds of what we habitually deem sense vs. nonsense, contradiction vs. consistency.)

At the same time, however, the two-part format of the episode also invites applications of the axiomatic analogy that I invoked earlier, in connection with Tarski's definition of formal languages. The narrative makes recounting itself a quasi-deductive operation; consequently, Joyce's (narrative) grammar is effectively resubsumed, at a higher or at least a different level of description, under the domain of logic. "Sirens" as a whole, we might say, evolves along a strictly Husserlian trajectory. The syntax of the narrative situates itself within a larger, "rein logisch-grammatische Grammatik," itself quite difficult to situate, however, vis-à-vis the respective claims of grammar and logic.

A more detailed analysis of the way Joyce's narrative generates syntactic structures at the intersection of logic and grammar requires a more developed and systematic presentation of the logico-grammatical framework that Husserl merely outlines, in rudimentary fashion, in his fourth *Logical Investigation*. The more developed account may be found, specifically, in Rudolf Carnap's descriptions of "logical syntax," as set out in a series of widely influential publications (cf., e.g., Carnap 1969 [1928], 1975 [1931], 1937a [1934], 1937b, 1979 [1935], 1971 [1938], and 1963). My chief concern will be the status of Joyce's narrative discourse in "Sirens" relative to Carnap's project of logical syntax as well as ways in which Carnap's account short-circuits grammatical and logical considerations in the study of language.[35] As we shall see, once Joyce's narrative techniques are situated within the logico-grammatical system built up by Carnap on Husserlian foundations, "Sirens" begins to suggest how narrative syntax generally may be specified as a set of principles belonging to a domain of inquiry—for short, call it "universal grammar"—whose field of application occupies the uncertain border between logic and linguistics.

6.4. It was in *The Logical Structure of the World* (1969 [1928]) that Carnap began to pursue, in the name of "constructional systems," what Ludwig Wittgenstein had recommended earlier under cover of a strictly logical syntax. In Wittgenstein's *Tractatus Logico-Philosophicus* (1986 [1922]) we read:

In the language of everyday life it very often happens that the same word signifies in two different ways—and therefore belongs to two different symbols—or that two words, which signify in different ways, are apparently applied in the same way in [a given] proposition. . . . In order to avoid these errors, we must employ a symbolism [*Zeichensprache*] which excludes them, insofar as they do not apply the same sign in different symbols, nor apply signs in the same way that signify in different ways. A symbolism, therefore, which conforms to *logical* grammar—to logical syntax. (3.323, 3.325, p. 55; cf. Wittgenstein 1973 [1929]: 31)

Of crucial importance in this connection is Wittgenstein's idea of "truth-operations," or operations "which must happen to a proposition in order to make another out of it" (1986 [1922]: 5.23, p. 115). Having included denial, logical addition, logical multiplication, etc. under the heading *operations* (5.2341, p. 115), Wittgenstein proceeds to define *truth-functions* as the "result" of such operations: "All truth-functions are results of the successive application of a finite number of truth-operations to elementary propositions" (5.32, pp. 119–20; cf. 5.3, p. 119). In short, "by presenting a proposition as the result of an operation which produces it from other propositions (the bases of the operation) . . . [the] operation is the expression of a relation between the structures of its result and its bases. . . . [Thus] truth-functions of elementary propositions are results of operations which have the elementary propositions as bases" (5.21, 5.22, 5.234, p. 115).

For Carnap, likewise, axiomatic or constructional systems necessitate the "stepwise" formation and transformation of structured sequences (results) of elements (bases). As Carnap puts it, "to reduce *a* to *b, c* or to *construct a* out of *b, c* means to produce a general rule that indicates for each individual case how a statement about *a* must be transformed to yield a statement about *b, c*. This rule of translation we call a *construction rule* or constructional definition. . . . By *constructional system* we mean a step-by-step ordering of objects in such a way that the objects of each level are constructed from those of lower levels" (1969 [1928]: sec. 2, p. 6). A constructional rule thus affords those "Bestimmungen über Ableitbarkeit" 'determinations with respect to derivability' which a few years later Carnap would make the sine qua non of all meaningful (i.e., non-metaphysical) expressions (1975 [1931]: 152–53). On this view, an expression becomes meaningful just to the extent that we can, at least in principle, furnish rules for deriving it from the observational sentences or "Protokollsätzen" 'protocol sentences' in which Carnap at one point tried to ground all non-metaphysical modes of utterance.[36]

More generally, and to invoke terminology similar to that used by Schönberg when he describes his own system for constructing musical compositions, in order "to lay down the basis of a constructional system, we need not only the basic elements, but also certain initial ordering concepts [*Ordnungssetzungen*], since otherwise it is not possible to produce any constructions starting from the basic elements" (Carnap 1969 [1928]: sec. 75, p. 122). The requisite "initial ordering concepts," in turn, are what Carnap would eventually identify with syntax and syntactic rules. At stake are "rules for step-by-step operations through which ["a given subject"] *A* can arrive at the construction of certain schemata ('inventory lists') which correspond to the individual objects that are to be constructed" by *A* over time (sec. 99, p. 157; cf. sec. 26, pp. 47ff.). A sentence too—and this is precisely the point—can be represented by virtue of certain schemata, which in turn represent how the sentence may be generated, or "constructed," out of an inventory of more basic elements (terms) through a step-by-step, sequential ordering of the elements via the recursive application of certain syntactic rules. Such, essentially, is the legacy of Chomsky, who had himself inherited, through Goodman and Quine in particular, the constructional program of Carnap and a fortiori the earlier axiomatic tradition informing Carnap's own constructionalism.[37] For Chomsky, too, the syntactic "derivation [of any sentence from a string of "phones" or rather "formatives" (Chomsky 1965: 16)] is roughly analogous to a proof, with *Sentence* playing the role of the single axiom, and the conversions [i.e., the grammatical transformations or 'applications of rewrite rules' (Chomsky 1975 [1955]: 73)] corresponding roughly to rules of inference" (Chomsky 1975 [1955]: 67).

Once again, however, we are getting ahead of ourselves. Focusing for the moment on Carnap's idea of constructional systems and the logico-syntactic principles governing such systems, and using a descriptive vocabulary pertinent both to Schönberg's compositions and to Joyce's "Sirens," we can say that Carnap's constructional theory encompasses two dimensions of analysis. On the one hand, constructional systems include a spatial or taxonomic dimension, entailing the enumeration of basic elements along with an adequate (or, as Tarski put it, "unambiguous") nomenclature for the primitive elements so itemized. On the other hand, constructional systems also include a temporal or selective dimension, prescribing the possible combinations, according to a particular rule, of the elements itemized in the initial repertoire. Within the selective dimension itself, furthermore, we must pose a distinction between rules of formation and rules of transformation vis-à-vis the elements of the symbol system. Thus, in *The Logical Syntax of Language* (1937a [1934]), and following Husserl's lead, Carnap identifies the formation rules with "grammar" as such, or syntax in the narrower sense (sec. 2, p. 4; cf. Carnap 1979 [1935]: 46). Alternatively, Carnap identifies rules of transformation with the various logical rules of inference (1937a [1934]: sec. 10, pp. 27ff.), using the term *syntax* in the widened, logico-grammatical acceptation similarly adopted by Jørgensen and Morris, for example. In Carnap's scheme as well, the scope of syntax includes both the (grammatical) rules of definition and the (logical) rules of inference: "The difference between syntactical rules in the narrower sense and the logical rules of deduction is only the difference between *formation rules* and *transformation rules*, both of which are completely formulatable in syntactical terms" (sec. 1, p. 2).[38]

But again, once the term *logical syntax* is admitted into our theoretical vocabulary, our grammar of inquiry—the grammar of grammar, as it were—has registered a profound change. On the basis of syntactic categories, not only do we now attempt to account for the limits of sense, given "the possible forms of meaning" specific to a certain (natural) language; we attempt to account, furthermore, for the limits of valid deduction, the horizon of permissible inference, given certain a priori formal requirements not specific to any particular language. These latter formal requirements prescribe what might be characterized as conditions of possibility for all languages whatsoever, insofar as they can be used to state, judge, and infer. To this extent, the logical analysis of natural languages underwrites a (meta)language in which can be formulated the grammar of an artificial language wholly isomorphic with the dictates of logic itself. But, in turn, the very notion of grammar must undergo logico-axiomatic reconstruction before it allows us to conceive as a "language" the calculus whose formation and transformation rules the metalanguage specifies.[39] Elaborating the grammar of a logical calculus, in other words, results in an ongoing logicization of grammar itself, a wholesale "Kalkulisierung der Grammatik" (Hermanns 1977).

Put still otherwise, language provides a paradigm for (and medium of) logical inquiry only insofar as it is a calculus whose various operations are borne out by logico-syntactic investigation; but to what extent languages can be viewed as calculi results from a prior (logical) determination of what the logical syntax regulating calculi is and does. As Carnap (1937a [1934]) puts it, "In the widest sense, logical syntax is the same thing as the construction and manipulation of a calculus; and it is only because languages are the most important

examples of calculi that, as a rule, only languages are syntactically investigated"
(sec. 2, p. 5).[40] Visions of bootstraps—and vicious circles—begin dancing in
one's head. At the very least, we can conclude with Chomsky (1955) that logico-
grammatical acceptations of syntax may have the effect of encouraging us "to
make a blind leap from mathematical systems to ordinary linguistic behavior"
(39). After all, "artificial languages [unlike physics experiments] are neither
special cases nor idealized versions of natural languages" (contrast Roberts
1993: 116–17); consequently we "cannot measure the deviations in the behavior
of actual languages from that of the artificial systems that we invent" (Chomsky
1955: 43). The problem is thus one of *locating* syntax once we say that its scope
is to be fixed not by logical, or by grammatical, but by logico-grammatical
coordinates.

Theorists of logico-grammatical syntax were not unaware of this problem.
Hence, following Carnap's suggestion that the syntax of a given language can
"without the emergence of any contradictions . . . be formulated within this
language itself" (1937a [1934]: sec. 18, p. 53), Leonard Bloomfield writes that "a
formal dialect, such as a system of symbolic logic, may very well be used to state
the rules which govern its use. This means simply that the formal dialect
suffices for statements about word-order, selection, and substitution. It neither,
on the one hand, removes the system from its linguistic status, nor, on the other
hand, gives it the standing of an independent 'language'" (Bloomfield 1971
[1939]: 263). Debatably, however, both Carnap's argument for the language-
internal formulation of syntactic rules and the last sentence of the Bloomfield
passage just quoted encounter difficulties once we make the transition from
what Carnap calls "special" (i.e., logical *or* grammatical) syntax to what he calls
"general" (i.e., logico-grammatical) syntax—"that is to say, . . . syntax which
relates not to any particular individual language but either to all languages or to
all languages of a certain kind" (1937a [1934]: pt. IVA, p. 153). Just how to
characterize the difference between general and special syntax—just what constitutes generality and specificity in this connection—remains very much in
question.

6.5. My claim is that "Sirens" encodes the very same problem—the problem
of determining how syntactic structures are to be distributed between logic and
grammar—into its narrative form. Joyce's narrative, as we might also put it,
unfolds as an ongoing situation of syntactic structures amid both grammatical and logical constraints; "Sirens" plots the logical adventures of grammar
against the grammatical adventures of logic. More precisely, the narrative forces
us to negotiate between two different modes of linearization, two sorts of

syntactic structure, specific to two different types of system. Both systems, each a kind of structural complement of the other, encompass both formation and transformation rules, rules of definition,and rules of inference. What differentiates the two systems, and the syntactic structures specific to them, is the *scope* of the rules of concatenation, and the scope of the rules accounting for the syntactic structures of "Sirens" may be defined against, or rather as a quotient of, the scope of the other two classes of rules (the other two systems) in question. As a logico-grammatical object, located at the border between logic and language, Joyce's narrative syntax may be characterized via principles whose field of application is the union of two sets: (i) the set of logical rules accounting for axiomatized languages' syntax and (ii) the set of grammatical rules accounting for unaxiomatized (natural) languages' syntax.

In the first place, we have logico-syntactic rules whose scope is virtually infinite or, as it were, translinguistic. *These* rules strive to account, through the combinatory mechanisms of a given language, for the operations of language in general. At issue is the reconstruction of a calculus at the heart of the empirical word, the λόγος at the core of all mundane discourse. Here, precisely, is where the axiomatic analogy invoked earlier gains its greatest force. In this context, we would argue that "Sirens" too linearizes its own most basic elements into "sentences," and then its sentences into suprasentential (i.e., "inferential") structures, according to syntactic principles that all possible languages whatsoever, and hence no language in particular, must necessarily and by definition embody.

Yet Joyce's text imposes a restriction of scope on the logico-syntactic rules governing constructional systems, axiomatized languages.[41] Specifically, insofar as the syntactic structures of the episode are realized in a particular language—namely, (a certain complex variant of) English—the narrative necessarily deviates from the pure λόγος of calculation. Perforce it falls back on the material structures of an empirically given, merely more or less logical language. Put otherwise, insofar as "Sirens" resubsumes its two-part, quasi-deductive format under the syntax of a natural language, it fails to meet Tarski's second requirement for an axiomatized language. The "primitive terms" of Joyce's narrative discourse are not subject, and cannot be subject, to an unambiguous characterization from the outset. Rather, already formed from the lexicon of an empirical language—formed, indeed, from that sublexicon which in its totality provides the complete concordance to *Ulysses* and to the Joycean corpus as a whole—the episode's introductory list is rooted in polysemy, not monosemy; plural, not singular meanings.

How, for example, could we circumscribe de jure the possible lexical functions of just the first word of the introduction, *Bronze?* We must gradually delimit the scope of the term's significance, in intuitive and piecemeal fashion, over the course of reading "Sirens." Or, rather, reading the episode requires retroactive definition of the term via the range of uses—spanning descriptions of the color of Lydia Douce's hair (64), the "gildedlettered" bar mirror (119–20), the coins given by the customers to the barmaids at different points in the episode, and so on—built up over the course of "Sirens." The episode's primitive terms are in this sense anything but primitive; they are not stipulated beforehand but decoded ex post facto. This ongoing and retrospective disambiguation of terms—this ad hoc coping with an inherently polysemous lexicon by means of constantly "harking back in a retrospective sort of arrangement" (798) to the terms' prior contexts of use—is just what the axiomatization of sign systems proposed by Tarski was designed to circumvent.

6.6. We can describe the nonaxiomatized and nonaxiomatizable mechanisms of the episode in another way—a way that anticipates issues connected with syntax in its narratological acceptation (see sec. *8* below). In classical narratological frameworks, narratives encompass a set of inputs, which comprise what has been variously termed the *fabula,* story, or narrated. Treatment of these inputs according to operations for disposing of the order, duration, and frequency of the brute narrative data yields in turn a specific output: the *sjužet* or discourse of the narrative in question (Genette 1980 [1972]; Chatman 1978; Prince 1982). In reading the opening lines of "Sirens," however, we are forced to review what we might call the raw narrative data without benefit of any device, any program, for operating on those inputs in a way that would yield the output "Sirens." Or, to speak somewhat more carefully, the opening lines so accelerate and compress the sequence input → operation → output that Joyce's narrative form prevents us from deriving, in any explicit and uniformly reproducible way, the rules by which the text transforms the givens of the story into the sequences constituting the discourse as a whole.[42] Whereas axiomatized systems require absolute explicitness when it comes to such (trans)formational rules, by contrast Joyce's text promotes an irreducibly ad hoc interpretation of the mechanisms generating its sequences.

Significantly, shortly after Joyce's "Sirens" indicated some of the possibilities and limits of (quasi-)deductive apparatus in natural-language environments, Kurt Gödel (1931) pointed out the limits of formalized systems in general. Gödel's incompleteness theorem showed that "the axiomatic method has certain inherent limitations, which rule out the possibility that even the ordinary arithmetic of the integers can ever be fully axiomatized"—or rather that it is impossible to *demonstrate* certain crucial propositions in arithmetic (Nagel and Newman 1958: 6ff.; cf. Plotnitsky 1994: 196ff.). In the broad view, and to use terms suggested by Gödel's own theorem, we might draw an analogy between Joyce and Gödel by suggesting that both construe the idea "true in a system" as a broader notion than "provable in a system" (Nagel and Newman 1958: 10). In Gödel, this insight produced the proposition "that there is an endless number of true arithmetical statements which cannot be formally deduced from any given set of axioms by a closed set of rules of inference. It follows that an axiomatic approach to number theory, for example, cannot exhaust the domain of arithmetical truth" (Nagel and Newman 1958: 98–99; cf. Hofstadter 1979: passim). In Joyce, the same insight yields a *form* of narrative discourse that highlights the inexhaustibility of grammar by logic, syntax by deduction. The axioms of the episode yield combinations and inferences of which, however, we cannot give a formal proof.

Ultimately, we shall discover that neither linguistic nor logical formalization per se captures the syntactic operations of Joyce's narrative. Rather, "Sirens" is so designed as to produce verbal structures according to formal principles, or principles of formalization, at work along jointly logical and linguistic lines. Therefore, it may be in Joyce, not Carnap, that we find the most compelling presentation of "logical syntax" extant. In the Joycean presentation, the yoking together of logic and syntax produces its most powerfully (and productively) oxymoronic effect—an effect born of the interanimation of logical by grammatical principles, a priori by a posteriori concerns. As we might also put it, as narrative discourse, "Sirens" occupies a position intermediate between the "natural" and "artificial" modes of signification distinguished by A. J. Greimas in *Structural Semantics* (1983 [1966]): "In the case of artificial signifying ensembles, the discrete elements would be established a priori, while the natural signifying ensembles would disengage their discrete constitutive units only a posteriori" (10).

6.7. Before attempting to come to grips with the syntactic structures of "Sirens" insofar as they are subject to linguistic as well as logical description, I should like to make a brief digression on another issue related to Joyce's construction of a quasi-axiomatic system in "Sirens." At issue, specifically, is Derrida's use of the metaphor of the computer in his writings on Joyce. The metaphor of the computer—and the idea (and ideal) of computation—appears in both of Derrida's two major essays on Joyce, producing a set of positive, substantive claims about Joyce's texts. Derrida uses computational metaphors in association with both the Joycean corpus itself and Joyce interpretation at large. In "Two Words for Joyce" (1984), for example, Derrida describes *Finnegans Wake* as a sort of massive lexical mainframe, capable of calculating, at incredible speeds, the etymological and semantic relations between verbal roots, even as they multiply into the polysemous vocabularies of forty different tongues.[43] Alternatively, in "Ulysses Gramophone" (1988c), Derrida uses the metaphor of the computer in describing the Joyce Industry itself. Extrapolating from critics' ongoing efforts to recapture allusions and reconstitute meanings in the Joycean corpus, Derrida postulates what would be the ideal device for future Joyce Studies: a computer that replicates Joyce's own mind (cf. 36, 47–50, 57–58). Throughout the suggestion is that no feat of programming, however ingenious, could produce a computational machine, an artificial intelligence, adequate to the production and reception of Joyce's texts.

Yet Derrida nowhere provides any *general* explanation as to why the figure of the computer should acquire special pertinence vis-à-vis the formal and/or thematic mechanisms of Joyce's texts. (Nor for that matter does Derrida's analysis acknowledge the vast amounts of evidence in support of the view that there can in fact be more and less successful approximations of quite astounding computational routines.) Why, one may find oneself asking after reading Joyce and then Derrida on Joyce, should computational metaphors prove so compelling when it comes to discussing the form of Joyce's text? To put the same question another way, What work does the figure of the computer do, precisely, in Derrida's own critical deductions? To the extent that the axiomatic analogy holds for "Sirens," we have perhaps discovered the unstated motivations for Derrida's use of the computational metaphors. Work on axiomatic systems— and on the foundations of mathematics more generally—of course issued directly into the computer technologies developed slightly later in the twentieth century (Boyer 1968: 670ff.). Thus, among other Joycean texts, and along with other artifacts like Schönberg's compositions, "Sirens" helped write the (master) program by means of which we process the very notion *computer.* Fuller substantiation of this claim, however, would require more detailed study of the links between Joyce's (and Schönberg's) logics of combination and the technologies of computation that such cultural artifacts helped underwrite.

7. "Sirens" and the Linguistic Acceptations of Syntax

Theories about the syntax of natural language have evolved in the wake of theories about logical syntax. At least since the seminal researches of Bloomfield, syntax has been defined against morphology in a way that recalls how, in formalized languages, rules of inference are defined against rules of definition, transformation against formation rules. For Bloomfield (1933, 1936, 1971 [1939]), the grammar of a language consists of rules for the integration of phonemes and morphemes into individual words (phonology and morphology, respectively) as well as rules for the way words are to be integrated into phrases and sentences (the task of syntax).[44] Take Bloomfield's (1971 [1939]) characterization of phonemes:

> The ordering and formalizing effect of language appears, first of all, in the fact that its meaningful forms are all composed of a small number of meaningless elements. . . . The forms of every language are made up out of a small number . . . of typical unit sounds which have no meaning but, in certain fixed arrangements, make up the meaningful forms that are uttered. These signals are the *phonemes* of the language. . . . once the phonemes are established, any form of the language is completely and rigidly definable (apart from its meaning) as a linear or quasi-linear sequence of phonemes. (239, 242)

The influence of Tarski's and Carnap's conceptions of formalized languages is unmistakable. Phonemes, here, are virtual stand-ins for primitive, undefined terms at the basis of axiomatic systems. Further, in characteristically behaviorist parlance, Bloomfield argues that the way we arrange sets of words according to principles of parallelism reveals "habits" that can be renamed *morphological constructions*. The same habitual arrangement of sets of phrases can be labeled *syntactic constructions* (1971 [1939]: 243). In general, "In presenting the description of a [given] language, . . . we begin with the constituents and describe the constructions in which they appear" (243). Bloomfield's (behaviorist) methodology everywhere betrays his allegiance to constructionalism, as does the publication of his "Linguistic Aspects of Science" (1971 [1939]) in the *International Encyclopedia of Unified Science*—one of whose editors (and contributors) was none other than Rudolf Carnap.

Note that, around the same time as Bloomfield, although on avowedly Saussurean foundations (Garvin 1954: 90–91), Hjelmslev was constructing a model for linguistic analysis whose (quasi-)axiomatic profile is even more pronounced than that of Bloomfield's model. Part of the logical empiricist enterprise spawned by the Vienna School (Pavel 1989: 55; Hjelmslev 1971b [1948]: 40) and perpetuated by Carnap and Bloomfield, Hjelmslev's glossematics "aims to produce . . . an immanent algebra of language . . . and we use *glossemes* to mean the minimal forms which the theory leads us to establish as bases of explana-tion, the irreducible invariants" (1969 [1943]: 80; note that, in 1926, Bloomfield had already used *glosseme* to signify "whatever has meaning" in a language). Hjelmslev's basic assumption is "that any process can be analyzed into a limited number of elements recurring in various combinations. Then, on the basis of this analysis, it should be possible to order these elements into classes according to their possibilities of combination. And it should be further possible to set up a general or exhaustive calculus of the possible combinations" (9). Thus, the Hjelmslevian "procedure [for syntactic analysis] is purely formal in this sense that it considers the units of a language as consisting of a number of [un-defined] figurae for which certain rules of transformation hold. These rules are set up without consideration of the substance in which the figurae and units are manifested" (96). The last sentence in particular reveals the indebtedness of glossematics to "la théorie logistique du langage" 'the logistic theory of lan-guage' that Hjelmslev traces back to Carnap (Hjelmslev 1971b [1948]: 40). On this model, syntax acquires a translinguistic (i.e., logico-grammatical) applica-bility: "Precisely because the theory is so constructed that linguistic form is viewed without regard for 'the substance' (purport), it will be possible to apply our apparatus to any structure whose form is analogous to that of a 'natural' language" (Hjelmslev 1969 [1943]: 102).

We find ourselves back on familiar (Carnapian) territory here, insofar as Hjelmslev seeks to determine the syntactic structures of language in general—what Hjelmslev himself calls a "general calculus"—but in a manner that still reflects the facts of natural language(s). Bracketing the substance of any partic-ular language, glossematics apparently produces an "apparatus" adequate to all languages. In his telling exposition of Hjelmslev's *Prolegomena,* Thomas Pavel (1989) shows how, "in defining the different notions of his theory, Hjelm-slev constantly emphasizes its formal character in accordance with logico-empiricism. But as his work progresses, not only the *theory* is formal, but also its *object* exhibits a formality of its own which seems to compete with that of the deductive calculus" (58). Accordingly, "natural languages, far from being sim-ply the *target* of a logical description, form *part of the family* of logical struc-tures" (59). Put otherwise, given Hjelmslev's assumptions and methods, it be-comes difficult to determine the scope of syntactic as over against logico-syntactic rules, natural as opposed to formal languages.

Certainly, Hjelmslev did not have the last word in syntactic theory; his *Prolegomena* date back more than a half century and thus precede the Chom-skyean revolution, that is, the advent of transformational generative grammars.

But, arguably, the constructionalist program subtending both Hjelmslev's and Bloomfield's models has outlived the models themselves (Hermanns 1977), and, in any event, that program helps frame issues also set into play by Joyce's "Sirens." Joyce's text encodes the distinction between natural and formal languages as a distinction between the linguistic materials and the formal operations of the narrative discourse. (As we shall see in sec. 7.4, these components of Joyce's discourse stand in a relation of analogy, not identity, to what Chomsky describes as the deep and the surface structures of [natural] languages.) More precisely, the form of Joyce's narrative consists (at least in part) of a kind of ordered unraveling, a rigorous disintegration, of various levels of structure with respect to the language in which the episode happens de facto to be cast.

7.1. At various points in the episode, Joyce's discourse resolves word and phrase constructions—morphological and syntactic structures—back into the more elementary units from which those structures derive. Manipulating structures both at the level of the word and at the level of the phrase, "Sirens" thereby figures as a logico-grammatical object par excellence. Joyce's text is caught between the specificity of the language in which the narrative unfolds and the linguistically non- or aspecific operations that *constitute* the narrative—operations that maintain a necessary and de jure applicability to language in itself and as such.

7.1.1. Over the course of "Sirens," we witness a variety of inverted word and phrase constructions, as it were. (One is tempted to speak here of word and phrase *deconstructions*, were that term not already reserved for different, more notorious uses.) For example, note how the text begins to reduce words to their morphemic (and phonemic) constituents in the transition from

> —I saved the situation, Ben, I think.
> —You did, averred Ben Dollard. I remember those tight
> trousers too. That was a brilliant idea, Bob. (480–82)

to the form that these same utterances assume in the provenance of Bloom's interior monologues: "Father Cowley blushed to his brilliant purply lobes. He saved the situa. Tight trou. Brilliant ide" (483–84). Bloom's truncated speech reports perhaps suggest an attempt to economize on mental effort;[45] perhaps, too, they register a kind of static that, entering through the open channel of Bloom's memory, scrambles the intermittent signal of thought. Beyond this, however, we can point to the specifically grammatical effects of the verbal truncations and distortions themselves. Thus, consider this passage, in which we witness not only a disintegration of words into the morphemes that constitute them but also an agrammatical, or at least differently grammatical, recombination of the elementary constituents as such:

> It was the only language Mr Dedalus said to Ben. He heard them as a boy in Ringabella, Crosshaven, Ringabella, singing their barcaroles. Queenstown harbour full of Italian ships. Walking, you know, Ben, in the moonlight with those earthquake hats. Blending their voices. God, such music, Ben. Heard as a boy. Cross Ringabella haven mooncarole. (849–53)[46]

As before, the speech reports (in this case, the reports are indirect instead of direct) undergo a secondary filtration, as it were, through the grammar and lexicon regulating the provenance of pure thought. To speak with Dorrit Cohn, "Every quoted interior monologue, no matter how disjointed its syntax, *attributes linguistic activity to fictional minds*" (1978: 86; my emphasis). The episode's disintegration and repartitioning of verbal matter reflects, we are to assume, the mechanisms of an aspecific language of thought, which, however, operates *through* the richness and ambiguity of the original linguistic material. Necessarily, Joyce's breakdown and recomposition of verbal structures (phonemes and morphemes)—a procedure that at the limit furnishes the logic of puns—roots itself in the phonic substance of a given material language.

7.1.2. Joyce, then, does not renounce the body of the word for the ideal of calculability; characteristically, he redistributes morphemic constituents across both actual and virtual networks of sound and sense. These networks converge on the figure of the (Joycean) pun. The text itself reflects on the formation of puns via the transpositions of morphemes, as in "He heard Joe Maas sing that one night. Ah, what M'Guckin! Yes. In his way. Choirboy style. Maas was the boy. Massboy" (610–12). Or take the even more self-reflexive pun on a phrase originally included in Martha's letter to Bloom ("I do wish I could punish you for that" [5.244]): "How will you pun? You punish me?" (890–91). A line like "Croak of vast manless moonless womoonless marsh" (1012), further, displays the logic of puns even more accentuated in Joyce's *Finnegans Wake* (1939). We witness here a realignment of morphemes according to the grammar of an otherwise virtual language—a language in which it is possible to ascribe to women lunar qualities in nonfigurative fashion and which is momentarily exposed by the pun before falling back into its virtuality with the reassertion of standard morphological norms. By the time of *Finnegans Wake,* however, we are forced to read in the absence of such norms, engaged instead in the infinite task of cataloging and cross-referencing an entire universe of polysemic puns.

7.1.3. Note that "Sirens" also recombines morphemes to produce specifically onomatopoetic effects, as in "Her wavyavyeavyheavyeavyevyevyhair un comb:'d" (808–9) or "snakes *hiss*. There's music everywhere. Ruttledge's door: *ee creaking*. No, that's noise" (964–65; my emphases; cf. 936, 984, 1125; the tapping of the blind stripling's cane as it punctuates approximately the last third of the episode; and of course Bloom's fart in the closing lines). If puns represent the partial virtualization of grammar under pressure of alternative morphological norms, onomatopoeia marks the momentary eclipse of syntactic by morphological features of verbal structure. For onomatopoetic word constructions cannot be integrated into phrase constructions according to syntactic principles. Here we can adapt the terminology of Husserl's third and fourth *Logical Investigations*. Onomatopoeia marks the breaking free of otherwise nonindependent meanings (*Momente*)—that is, morphemes whose significance derives from their situation in word constructions—toward that independence of meaning which Husserl associates with the "the piece" (*das Stück*). In effect, the onomatopoetic word construed as piece constitutes the limit of language itself. Wholly enmeshed in its phonic substance, its morphemic materials, onomatopoeia produces meanings that cannot be integrated into the generative structures of the syntagm itself (see, however, Saussure 1959 [1916]: 60); it represents a kind of linguistic irrationality, an irrationality of language. Joyce's narrative form continually traffics in unreasonable language.

7.2. Besides reshuffling the basic constituents of word constructions, Joyce's narrative discourse performs a variety of operations at the level of syntactic structures proper. In passages previously cited we have already begun to see modes of decomposition and displacement at the syntactic as well as the morphological level of the discourse. For example, the truncated "Hell did I put?" evokes (or presupposes) "Where the hell did I put them?" just as "Heard them as a boy" marks a truncated version of "He heard them as a boy in Ringabella." In fact, throughout the episode we witness a number of different forms of syntactic disintegration and/or displacement. We have, for example, constructions that, placed in series, represent an ongoing disruption of syntactic norms for English. The series tend in two different directions—now toward greater, now toward lesser complexity of structure—but ultimately with the same disintegrative effect on the syntax itself.

7.2.1. On the one hand, we have series building toward greater syntactic complexity, but in a manner that contravenes the syntactic rules that permit such complex expressions to retain grammatical structure. Of this type is the series linking the well-formed strings "—Exquisite contrast, miss Kennedy said"

(68) and "Ladylike in exquisite contrast" (106) with the ill-formed, quasi-recursive string "inexquisite contrast, contrast inexquisite nonexquisite" (464–65), toward which the prior two occurrences of the phrase build. (Although the first instance of the phrase "exquisite contrast" occurs *before* Bloom enters the Ormond bar, the discourse nonetheless requires that we once again imagine the series of transformations performed on that phrase as iterative, recombinatory operations associated with Bloom's cognitive grammar, so to speak.) A similarly progressive, or perhaps hyperstructured, series involves the names *Lydia Douce* and *Mina Kennedy*, together with the increasingly more complex or even chaotic associations of bronze and gold linked in pseudometallurgical fashion with each woman (cf. 64–74, 174–76, 717–20).

7.2.2. On the other hand, we also witness regressive, or hypostructured, series working in the other direction, in parallel to the modes of morphemic disintegration commented on earlier. In this case, elements structured into phrases and sentences are deintegrated or "deconstructed" through the play of Joyce's discourse. Thus, we have both localized regressive series, as in

> Dollard and Cowley still urged the listening singer out with it.
> —With it, Simon.
> —It, Simon. (653–55)[47]

and also more globalized series, as in the chain of transformations linking

> —Come on to blazes, said Blazes Boylan, going.
>   Lenehan gulped to go.
> —Got the horn or what? he said. Wait. I'm coming. (430–32)

with the closing sentences of this passage:

> By Bachelor's walk jogjaunty jingled Blazes Boylan, bachelor, in sun in heat, mare's glossy rump atrot, with the flick of whip, on bounding tyres: sprawled, warmseated, Boylan impatience, ardentbold. Horn. Have you the? Horn. Have you the? Haw haw horn. (524–27)

Other passages combine local with global modes of syntactic disintegration, as in this description of Bloom eating:

> Pat served, uncovered dishes. Leopold cut liverslices. As said before he ate with relish the inner organs, nutty gizzards, fried cods' roes while Richie Goulding, Collis, Ward ate steak and kidney, steak then kidney, bite by bite of pie he ate Bloom ate they ate. (519–22)

This passage at once decomposes over the course of its own elaboration, points ahead to a further, even more radical disintegration—"Bloom ate liv as said before" (569)—and reactivates as a prior syntactic norm, as it were, an earlier passage that opens the "Calypso" episode:

> Mr Leopold Bloom ate with relish the inner organs of beasts and fowls. He liked thick giblet soup, nutty gizzards, a stuffed roast heart, liverslices fried with crustcrumbs, fried hencods' roes. Most of all he liked grilled mutton kidneys which gave to his palate a fine tang of faintly scented urine. (4.1–5)

7.3. At the same time, we have atypical (ill-formed) strings interspersed throughout the text, promoting a somewhat more piecemeal disintegration of syntactic structure; such (non-)strings represent, perhaps, the syntactic equivalent of the pun. Again, two further subdivisions of syntactic play may be isolated in this connection. On the one hand, the discourse sometimes scrambles word order; on the other hand, it introduces punctuation (colons, full stops, question marks) at unusual junctures within sentences and specifically within the sentences "uttered" by Bloom in the context of his various interior monologues.

7.3.1. First, then, we find many instances (and modes) of syntactic scrambling in "Sirens." In some cases, the scrambled word order involves merely a displaced preposition or adverb or the coy omission of a noun, and the resulting sentence retains a minimal but recognizable syntactic structure. Such is the case with "Shrill, with deep laughter, after, gold after bronze, they [i.e., Lydia and Mina] urged each each to peal after peal, ringing in changes, bronzegold, goldbronze, shrilldeep, to laughter after laughter. And then laughed more" (174–76), and also with "Bald Pat in the doorway met tealess gold returning" (453). Similarly, we find instances of anacoluthon—that is, the illicit transition from one syntactic construction to another over the course of a single sentence—that nonetheless preserve a more or less intelligible and recoverable syntactic profile. Such is the case with "The voice of dark age, of unlove, earth's fatigue made grave approach and painful, come from afar, from hoary mountains, called on good men and true" (1007–8), and also with "Quitting all languor Lionel cried in grief, in cry of passion dominant to love to return with deepening yet with rising chords of harmony" (736–37).

But in a passage like "A liquid of womb of woman eyeball gazed under a fence of lashes, calmly, hearing" (1104–5), we enter a domain of syntactic disorganization marked by mixed metaphor and synaesthetic adverbial modifications, together with the omission of a definite or indefinite article (or possessive pronoun) before "eyeball" and a resulting transfer of adjectival functions to the noun *woman*. Here, more *interpretation*—a more concerted application of our knowledge of the grammar of the language in which the episode happens to be cast—is required before we can confer at least some syntactic structure on the sentence at issue, make some sense of the effects of the anacoluthon. But then what are we to make of sentences such as "With patience Lenehan waited for Boylan with impatience" (289)? In this case, the anacoluthon yields two (incompatible) interpretations. Because the adverbial phrase *with impatience* ambiguously modifies two subjects, Lenehan and Boylan, it produces two, contradictory readings depending on which subject we stipulate as modified by the phrase in question—given that Lenehan has already been characterized as waiting "with patience." No amount of interpretation restores genuine syntactic structure in this case, but only (at best) a structural description that accounts for how the sentence in fact deviates from syntactic norms through anacoluthon. As we might also put it, the discourse momentarily (and nonsensically) activates a kind of virtual syntax, in which contradictory modifiers and incompatible predicates bind one and the same subject, even when that predication is performed in the same tense (i.e., not "*S* was *p* but is now not-*p*" but rather "*S* is *p* and *S* is not-*p*"). It proves difficult, however, to imagine (let alone formalize) the operations of what might be termed a *dialectical syntax* encompassing antithetical predicates that modify one and the same subject at one and the same time.

7.3.2. Another species of syntactic play unfolds, once again, according to the dictates of what I have termed Bloom's rational or cognitive grammar—or, rather, what Joyce's narrative encourages us to hypostatize as the grammar of thought, of mental representation, as such. We can approach the syntactic features at issue through the text's nonstandard punctuation, specifically. Throughout, atypical punctuation produces a fragmentation of syntactic structures, such that the discourse effectively empties the language of principles that might integrate words into phrases, phrases into sentences. Note, for example, the nonstandard use of colons in this passage: "Miss Douce, miss Lydia, did not believe: miss Kennedy, Mina, did not believe: George Lidwell, no: miss Dou did not: the first, the first: gent with the tank: believe, no, no: did not, miss Kenn: Lidlydiawell: the tank" (818–20). Here the narrative unfolds as a segmentation of phrase structures that cannot be ranked according to modes of subordination, superordination, or (non-)dependency. It would be difficult if not impossible to diagram, by way of a tree-like or any other representation of phrase structure, the phrases here conjoined by colons. The phrases aspire to a kind of pure parataxis (cf. Hayman 1985); their juxtaposition thwarts any ranking or derivation according to the ordered application of rewrite rules. Joyce's narrative form works in the absence of—indeed, disallows—any syntactic structure that might gather up these framentary phrases (what Benveniste 1971 [1966] terms "phrasemes") into the unity and coherence of a syntagm.

The foregoing remarks apply, furthermore, to the complex combination of nonstandard punctuation (here, full stops and question marks), morphological partitioning, and syntactic decomposition at work in another passage, which again centers on Bloom's writing (and his thinking about writing) to Martha:

> On. Know what I mean. No, change that ee. Accep my poor litt pres enclos. Ask her now answ. Hold on. Five Dig. Two about here. Penny the gulls. Elijah is com. Seven Davy Byrne's. Is eight about. Say half a crown. My poor little pres: p.o. two and six. Write me a long. Do you despise? Jingle, have you the? So excited. Why do you call me naught? You naughty too? O, Mairy lost the string of her. Bye for today. Yes, yes, will tell you. Want to. To keep it up. Call me that other. Other world she wrote. My patience are exhaust. To keep it up. You must believe. Believe. The tank. It. Is. True. (865–73)

It is no accident, arguably, that the most severe and prolonged deformations, or rather eradications, of syntactic structure are precisely the signature of Bloom's interior monologues. Throughout, syntactic decomposition marks that sudden access of anguish to which Bloom repeatedly falls victim over the course of the episode—it being the hour in which Blazes Boylan and Molly are to fulfill their adulterous scheme.[48] The discourse, as we might also put it, consists in a sort of global reprocessing of prior verbal material, previously structured utterance, through grammatical operations performed by a fictional mind.[49] Thus, when Bloom imagines Molly and Blazes together—and, in the long passage cited above, some of the disjointed phrases suggest the lovers' tryst ("Jingle, have you the [horn]?"; "To keep it up"; etc.)—we again witness anomalous punctuation, as well as scrambled word order and a pun (on "rose"): "At each slow satiny heaving bosom's wave (her heaving embon) red rose rose slowly sank red rose. Heartbeats: her breath: breath that is life" (1106–7; cf. 523–27, quoted above). Even more strikingly, nonstandard punctuation disrupts Bloom's (unsuccessful because overly painful) attempt to conceptualize and give utterance to the moment Blazes actually arrives at Molly's door: "Jing. Stop. Knock. Last look at mirror always before she answers the door. The hall. There? How do you? I do well. There? What? Or? Phial of cachous, kissing comfits, in her satchel. Yes? Hands felt for the opulent" (689–92). Eventually, the effort to conceive and verbally represent the lovers' tryst becomes intolerable; Bloom's monologues are then left with the merest remnants of syntactic structure, phrases paratactically frozen in an agony of inner speech. Hence Bloom's impoverished, hypostructured imagination of the words exchanged by Blazes and Molly, words that Bloom's memory superimposes on the words he himself once exchanged with Molly on the occasion of their first meeting: "Will? You? I. Want. You. To" (1096).

In short, through a series of operations on the de facto structures of the English language, Joyce's discourse sets into play principles that apply de jure to all possible morphological and syntactic structures—principles grounded in what we infer to be the operations of Bloom's mind. As we might also put it, "Sirens" articulates the grammar of the expressible with the grammar of the expressed.

7.4. A question that suggests itself is whether this distinction between syntax de jure and syntax de facto—this distinction between the *discourse* of "Sirens" and the *language* that it draws on—can be likened to Chomsky's opposition between the deep and the surface structures of language. As it turns out, the analogy between Joyce's narrative and Chomsky's treatment of syntactic structures is only partial at best. By charting the limits of the linguistic analogy in this connection, however, we start to see in greater detail how the syntactic structures of "Sirens" function as truly logico-grammatical objects. As we shall see, narrative form in "Sirens" helps rethink models for (narrative) grammar and syntax, instead of merely being subject to description by way of such models.

7.4.1. Note that Chomsky's opposition between deep and surface structure represents a reaction both to structuralist models like Saussure's and to logico-syntactic models for formal languages. As Chomsky puts it, "One might briefly characterize the syntactic theories that have arisen in modern structural (taxonomic) linguistics [of, say, the Saussurean stripe] as based on the assumption that deep and surface structures [of sentences] are actually the same" (1965: 16). Meanwhile, "The grammars of the 'artificial languages' of logic or theory of programming are, apparently without exception, simple phrase structure grammars in most significant respects" (Chomsky 1965: 136) and are thus devoid of transformational operations in the specifically grammatical sense that Chomsky goes on to spell out. "The central idea of transformational grammar," he says, "is that [deep structure and surface structure] are, in general, distinct and that the surface structure is determined by repeated application of certain formal operations called 'grammatical transformations' to objects of a more elementary sort" (1965: 16–17). At greater length:

> We can distinguish the "deep structure" of a sentence from its "surface structure." The former is the underlying abstract structure that determines its semantic interpretation; the latter, the superficial organization of units which determines the phonetic interpretation and which relates to the physical form of the actual utterance, to its perceived or intended form. . . . *The underlying organization of a sentence relevant to semantic interpretation is not necessarily revealed by the actual arrangement and phrasing of its given components.* (Chomsky 1966a: 33; my emphasis; cf. Chomsky 1965: 16)

The point is that sentences with different surface structures may nonetheless exhibit the same deep structure, and therefore be subject to the same semantic interpretation, regardless of overt differences of organization and phrasing. Hence, by assuming that deep and surface structures differ, we can greatly reduce the number of explanatory principles needed to account for the linguistic phenomena (i.e., sentence constructions). In short, postulating the existence of a deep structure greatly simplifies (explanatory models for) the grammar— more specifically, the syntax—of a language. Thus runs the argument.[50]

In order to illustrate the previous claim, we can adapt and expand an example provided by Geoffrey Horrocks (1987: 43–44). Take the sentence

(S) What did Georgina put into her briefcase?

The deep structure of (S) can be represented (nondiagrammatically) as

(DS) Georgina put what into her briefcase

while the surface structure of (S) can be represented as

(SS) What did Georgina put into her briefcase.

As Horrocks comments, the difference between the deep and the surface structure of a sentence like (S) manifests itself in the fact that the object (i.e., *what*) appears in two different positions in each case. Keep in mind, too, Horrocks's observation that we can "set up a transformational rule to express the nature of the relationship between deep structures such as [DS] and surface structures such as [SS]" (44; cf. Matthews 1981: 283–91).

Now consider the following two contexts. In the first context, an incredulous coworker, amazed that Georgina had the gall to take a stack of hundred-dollar bills sitting right under the nose of her tyrannical boss and put it into her (Georgina's) briefcase, asks, "Georgina put *what* into her briefcase?" In the second context, a slightly annoyed coworker who has been competing with Georgina for a promotion, discovers that he is missing a few important documents and, under the assumption that Georgina may have taken those documents either accidentally or (what he deems more likely) on purpose, asks another coworker, "What did Georgina put into *her* briefcase?" Although here the surface structure of the two sentences differs; and although intonational features connected with the *utterance* of the two sentences (in tandem with elements of background knowledge) license vastly different sorts of inference about the meaning of each sentence, nevertheless, syntactically speaking, we can assume that the two sentences have an identical deep structure. (Put otherwise, in the first instance, the surface structure and the deep structure coincide, whereas they do not in the second instance.) More precisely, making this assumption greatly reduces the number of sentence constructions that we have to account for on the basis of the syntax of the language; it thereby obviates the risk of adhocity, that is, the tendency to multiply syntactic rules and other grammatical principles indefinitely, in attempts to account for the syntactic organization of every one of the (in principle infinite) sentences generated by the grammar of a language. Instead of framing a new *syntactic* rule for every new sentence, we postulate a finite number of deep-structural components, together with a finite number of *transformational* rules for mapping those components (and their combinations) into the surface structures of the language.

7.4.2. Early on Chomsky (1975 [1955]) described such transformational rules as follows:

> Just as on lower levels we can represent a sentence as a sequence of pho-nemes, morphemes, words, syntactic categories, and (in various ways) phrases, so we can, on the transformational level, represent each sentence as a sequence of operations by which it is derived from the kernel [phrase]. Each such sequence of operations [may be] interpreted as a string in a concatenation algebra and [as] originating ultimately from a fixed sequence of kernel elements. . . . The complexity of the grammatical statement is substantially reduced, since sentences with complex phrases and involved structure can be constructed transformationally out of already formed simpler sentences. (73)[51]

Note that, in Chomsky's *grammatical* scheme, the operative concept of transformation bears a meaning (or function) distinct from the one it bears in

Carnap's *logical* model and in other axiomatic/constructional systems, whose rudiments may be found in Husserl's distinction between *Unsinn* and *Widersinn* (see sec. *6.1* above). In Carnap and Tarski, for example, transformation rules are simply rules of deduction that presuppose prior, more elementary rules of definition. Such secondary or transformation rules permit more complex propositional structures to be built up, in wholly calculable fashion, from strings already stipulated to be well formed in the framework of the deductive system itself. In Chomsky, by contrast, transformation rules serve precisely to define where natural languages deviate from formal languages. More accurately, according to limits that can be determined only a posteriori and with respect to particular instances of linguistic structure, the transformational mechanisms of a grammar determine ways in which (i) the syntax governing formal languages, and used to represent the underlying logical organization of components, functions, and relations called *deep structure,* can be articulated with (ii) the syntactic and other grammatical components, functions, and relations pertaining to the surface structures of a given (natural) language.

Hence, grammatical as opposed to deductive transformations account for how the abstract deep structures generated by the "rules of the base," as Chomsky puts it, can be mapped into the concrete lexical and phonetic features that characterize the surface structures specific to particular languages:

> The branching rules of the base (that is, its categorial component) define grammatical functions and grammatical relations and determine an abstract underlying order . . . ; the lexicon characterizes the individual properties of particular lexical items that are inserted in specified positions in base Phrase-markers. Thus when we define "deep structures" as "structures generated by the base component," we are, in effect, assuming that the semantic interpretation of a sentence depends only on its lexical items and the grammatical functions and relations represented in the underlying structures in which they appear. (1965: 136)

7.4.3. As already indicated, "Sirens" rearranges or rather disintegrates both morphological and syntactic structures in a sustained bid to highlight, through the mechanisms of the narrative discourse itself, the "underlying structures" of the linguistic materials on which the discourse operates. But what, exactly, are these abstract underlying structures that relate, through transformational rules of some description, to the narrative surface and its organization into morphemes and phrasemes? Presumably, the abstract underlying organization of the discourse constitutes the deep structure of the narrative—the deep structure whose relation to the (language-specific) surface structures it is precisely the task of a narrative grammar (including a narrative syntax) to ascertain. (This, as we shall see, is the position of, e.g., Greimas 1987 [1969].)

The problem here, arguably, is that of determining just where an analysis of "Sirens" based on the foregoing assumptions may be situated, in conceptual space, relative to the operations of Joyce's narrative itself. From the start, the formal mechanisms of Joyce's text supervene on the mechanisms that, in a transformational *theory* of the narrative discourse, might be used to account for the form and functioning of "Sirens." In effect, "Sirens" realizes the grammatical apparatus that Chomsky by contrast locates not in the *performance* of actual utterances within a given (stretch of) discourse but rather in the domain of linguistic theory proper and correlatively in the set of cognitive capacities and behavioral dispositions that linguistic theory seeks to reconstruct under the heading *competence* (Chomsky 1975 [1955]: 35ff.; Chomsky 1966b [1957]: 15, 92; Chomsky 1965: 14ff.; Lyons 1970: 90–121).

To the extent that it reprocesses prior verbal material through a secondary grammatical machinery anchored in the mind of Bloom, Joyce's text unfolds as an ongoing correlation of actual utterances (the surface structure of the narrative) with a more abstract sequence of elementary operations (the deep structure of the narrative), and vice versa. The text, we might say, *encodes degrees of depth of structure within the narrative discourse itself.* By the same token, we witness more or less profound complications of the notion *transformational rule,* as applied to the richly differentiated verbal structures fashioned by Joyce. Strict adherence to a transformational model—strict discrimination between the narrative's surface structures and its deep structure, on one hand, and between performance and competence, on the other—would seem to involve us in a vicious regress of some sort. We would require a deeper level of deep structure mapped by way of transformational rules into a surface structure that nonetheless constitutes (in some sense) the deep structure of the narrative. At stake are verbal structures now both superficial and deep, both material and idealized, both sui generis and widely if not universally applicable as an abstract underlying order, asymmetrical with any de facto manifestation in the language of a narrative.

7.4.4. One might make the case that this (indefinite) multiplication of levels of structure in narrative discourse has steadily increased in scope and frequency ever since the radicalization, during the nineteenth century, of narrative techniques for representing consciousness—techniques including not just interior monologue and modes of speech representation (cf. Cohn 1978; Fludernik 1993a; and chap. 4 below) but also the use of multiple, internal, and hypothetical (Herman 1994c) modes of focalization and the representation of ratiocinative thinking in detective fiction (broadly defined). Such innovations promote what we might call a stratification, in narrative discourse, of levels of expressibility as well as an emphasis on the constraints determining what can or cannot be expressed. Or rather, with the advent of such techniques, narrative form itself becomes increasingly subservient to this ranking and differentiation of the structures of the expressible. Narrative discourse unfolds as the construction of its own abstract underlying order, the ongoing projection of the manifest discourse into an a priori domain of what can, might, should, could, or would be said, barring certain conditions whose a posteriori realization accounts for what *is* in fact said over the course of the narrative. The ranking and differentiation of degrees of depth in (narrative) structure become at once formal device, external constraint, and privileged theme.

Although the previous claims are of course subject to empirical (dis)confirmation, another, somewhat weaker claim is perhaps already warranted by the foregoing discussion: namely, that Joyce's text exploits formal features that compel us to rethink techniques for the analysis and reconstitution of the verbal structures out of which they are made. These formal features pertain to a whole family of formal mechanisms that help illuminate the combinatorial mechanisms studied under the heading *syntactic theory.* The formal features in question are not merely *instances* of language use susceptible of language-theoretical analysis. Rather, as description of the syntactic structures of "Sirens" in particular reveals, the narrative discourse itself unfolds *as* a logico-grammatical apparatus, not just a discursive artifact to which such an apparatus may be applied, after the fact, as a descriptive and/or explanatory framework. Thus, "Sirens" and narratives with formal affinities to Joyce's text must be classified as logico-grammatical devices both historically and conceptually interlinked with axiomatic systems and transformational generative grammars.

In examining the third acceptation of syntax pertinent here, I shall survey, very briefly, some (classical) narratological models for understanding *narrative* syntax. By and large, these models construe narrative discourse as language use to which various sorts of (logico-)grammatical devices can be applied, in order to reveal, clarify, and more or less explicitly formalize the syntactic structures of a given narrative. The question that I pose here, however, is one already broached in a variety of forms: Where exactly, relative to "Sirens," are we to *situate* models for understanding narrative syntax, given that Joyce's narrating itself participates in the modeling of syntactic structures?

8. "Sirens" and the Question of Narrative Syntax

As previously indicated (sec. *0.6*), Todorov for one associates the search for a grammar of narrative with the (prior) search for universal grammar. Articulating the research program "d'une science qui n'existe pas encore, . . . la *narratologie*, la science du récit" 'of a science that does not yet exist, . . . *narratology*, the science of narrative' (1969: 10), Todorov cautions that "we must not forget that we are adopting the perspective of a logical and universal grammar, not that of a particular language" (1977 [1971]: 225; cf. Todorov 1969: 14–15). Conversely, the much-delayed realization of universal grammar requires that we study "other symbolic activities besides natural language"—one of the "few extended explorations of the grammar of symbolic activities" being "Freud's study of oneiric language" (Todorov 1977 [1971]: 109). Linguists in particular "have failed to consider [narrative] when they inquire into the nature of a universal grammar" (109). (Todorov is at this time manifestly unaware of, say, William Labov and Joshua Waletzky 1967.) A few years earlier, in his contribution to *Communications* 8, perhaps the single most influential publication in the history of narrative theory, Roland Barthes had expressed a similar, although more optimistic, view, commenting, "The new linguistics of discourse has still to be developed, but at least it is being postulated, and by the linguists themselves" (1977b [1966]: 83; cf. sec. *0.6.1*).

Together, Todorov's and Barthes's remarks suggest crucial interconnections between, on the one hand, the surge of interest in *narrative discourse* (and *narrative grammars*) beginning in the mid-1960s and, on the other hand, the development of techniques for *discourse analysis* beginning with the work of Zellig Harris (1952).[52] Both projects aspire to universality by studying units of language larger than the sentence (Hendricks 1967; cf. Herman 1994b), although in one case the object of study is that subset of discourse that has the additional property of being narratively organized. Be that as it may, both the discourse-analytic and narratological theories reject Bloomfield's "structuralist" model, which makes the sentence the upper limit of linguistic structure: "In any one utterance a form which, in this utterance, is not a constituent of any larger form is a *sentence*" (1971 [1939]: 245; cf. Bloomfield 1926: definition 27, p. 158; Benveniste (1971 [1966]: 108–9). Further, if we say with Barthes (1977b [1966]) that "the most reasonable thing is to posit a homological relation between sentence and discourse insofar as it is likely that a similar formal organization orders all semiotic systems" (83), then we can expect (narrative) discourse to have a syntax that is but the syntax of the sentence writ large (cf. van Dijk 1972).

Simply assuming an isomorphic relation between sentences and discourses, however, does not tell us exactly how to go about formulating a narrative syntax. At issue, still, are the minimal constituents of narrative structures and the rules for concatenating those elements into stories of varying complexity and interest. As Claude Bremond recounts (1973: 11–47), in their efforts to develop a theory of narrative syntax, the early narratologists turned to Vladimir Propp's *Morphology of the Folktale* (1968 [1928]). In particular, they focused on Propp's idea of "function" and its relevance for a grammar of narrative based on (certain permissible combinations of) *actions*. In the *Morphology* itself, Propp says that "definition of a function will most often be given in the form of a noun expressing an action (interdiction, interrogation, flight, etc.). Secondly, an action cannot be defined apart from its place in the course of the narration. The meaning which a given function has in the course of the action must be considered. . . . *Function is understood as an act of a character, defined from the point of view of its significance for the course of the action*" (21). Interdefining function and plot, Propp therefore locates the minimal units of story in what Marie-Laure Ryan (1991: 125ff.) has termed "plot-functional elements" of narrative discourse. In the Proppian scheme, narrative syntax can be formulated on the basis of constituent actions together with the rules that determine which combinations of the actions are legal, that is, constitutive of (well-formed) plots. Accordingly, Pavel (1985a) offers this diagnosis of Propp's (still rudimentary) syntax of plot-functional motifs: "Propp's analyses approach the object from a syntactic perspective; each folk narrative belonging to the corpus is shown to manifest the same abstract structure, independently of the particular motifs involved in the story. The similarity to linguistic analysis is striking; indeed, syntax discovers combinatory patterns of abstract categories . . . independently of the lexical units which may form the actual sentence" (87).

Thus, although he traces his own narrative grammar back to the great speculative grammars of the medieval Modistae, transposing onto narrative structures the Modists' distribution of grammatical categories into *modis significandi* (see secs. *0.3.1* and *0.3.2* above), Todorov's more immediate precedent is the actantial model set out in Greimas's 1966 study *Sémantique structurale* (Todorov 1969: 17, n. 8), which bears throughout the imprint of Propp's *Morphology* and its emphasis on actions as plot-functional constituents of narrative discourse.[53] The actantial model transmitted by Greimas from Propp to Todorov offers a set of formation and transformation rules for concatenating primitive deeds, atomic actions, into stories. The model is to this extent avowedly and irremediably anthropocentric. In his analysis of the grammar of Boccaccio's *Decameron,* for example, Todorov describes in actantial terms the deep structure, or base, of narrative discourse generally: "L'unité syntaxique de base sera appelée *proposition.* Elle correspond à une action 'indécomposable'" 'The syntactic unit of the base will be called *proposition.* It corresponds to an "non-decomposable" action' (19). In turn, addressing the question of formation rules first, Todorov writes, "La grammaire de la narration possède trois catégories primaires qui sont: le nom propre, l'adjectif, et le verbe" 'The grammar of narrative has three primary categories, which are: the proper name, the adjective, and the verb' (27). Whereas, "syntaxiquement, le nom propre correspond à l'agent" 'syntactically, the proper name corresponds to the agent' (28), the adjective corresponds to predicates ascribable to the agent at a given time. Meanwhile, the verb corresponds to the actions performed by agents (or *on* agents to the extent that they have become patients), such that different classes of predicates will be ascribed to the agent before and after the action in question (30ff.). Thus, Todorov tries to model the combinatory logic of Boccaccio's discourse on the basis of syntactic features pertaining to the sentence, using the anthropocentric concepts *action* and *actant* as mediating links between sentence and discourse levels of grammatical structure.

The same procedure subtends Todorov's treatment of transformation rules for the syntactic structures of narrative. He describes three such rules: "l'enchaînement, l'enchâssement et l'alternance" 'conjunction, embedding and alternation' (1969: 69ff.).[54] These rules generate complex, molecular actions from atomic actions, those indissoluble unities (what Hjelmslev would call "solidarities") of agent, predicate, and act which are accounted for through the formation rules. The transformation rules, by contrast, regulate the supra-propositional units that Todorov calls narrative "sequences" (1969: 53ff.; cf. Todorov 1977 [1971]: 116ff.; Barthes 1977b [1966]: 101–4; and Bremond 1973: 139ff.). (Indeed, Todorov 1977 [1971]: 219 will go on to distinguish a total of four levels of grammatical description in the context of narrative discourse: "predicate [or motive, or function], proposition, sequence, text.") Hence, we can say that "les propriétés syntaxiques des relations [i.e., 'les relations possibles entre propositions' (Todorov 1969: 55)] déterminent la structure de la séquence" 'the syntactic proprieties governing relations [i.e., "the possible relations between propositions"] determine the structure of the sequence' (Todorov 1969: 60). An ill-formed narrative sequence would be one in which a nongrammatical series of propositions, derived in turn from the successive application of incompatible predicates to an agent or to several agents, produces a discourse that cannot be analyzed into a chain of (causally linked) atomic actions. Such a sequence would contain a series (or rather an amalgam) of propositions having the structure of, say, "With patience Lenehan waited for Boylan with impatience" (289).

8.1. As the previous example from Joyce suggests, there are grounds for questioning the applicability of Todorov's grammatical apparatus for analysis of a narrative like "Sirens." Two (interlinked) difficulties suggest themselves in this connection: first, the explicit anthropocentrism of Todorov's model; second, the model's apportionment of narrative discourse into atomic and molecular actions, together with the formation and transformation rules pertaining to each level of actantial complexity.

8.1.1. As indicated earlier in the discussion of the transformations of *Bloom* (sec. 5), Joyce's text makes character and a fortiori agency an effect of grammar rather than predicating narrative grammar on agency (or action), as does the Proppian research tradition. In a manner that inverts Todorov's founding reduction of names to agents and thence to actants, "Sirens" typically reduces actants to names, which disintegrate in turn into bits of verbal material transposed and recombined through grammatical operations rooted in Bloom's mind, as in this passage: "First Lid, De, Cow, Ker, Doll, a fifth: Lidwell, Si Dedalus, Bob Cowley, Kernan and big Ben Dollard" (1271–72). If anything, Bloom is what we might call a *grammatical actant;* he may be an agent, but he is an agent of (or for) the grammar. Joyce's text thus subordinates the actions being described under grammatical acts, which furnish the basis for making descriptions as such. Arguably, Todorov's model lacks the conceptual resources to account for the peculiar species of agency (if we can really call it that) at work in the episode. To put the same point another way: the minimal units of "Sirens" cannot be readily discovered using the actantial search parameters.

8.1.2. At the same time, the structures of "Sirens" force us to reconsider the scope and applicability of Todorov's rules for concatenations of minimal units. These are the rules by means of which Todorov seeks to map what might be termed the deep structure of agency into the surface structure of narrative propositions and the larger sequences to which the propositions contribute. Here we discover a strange conjunction of anthropocentric and logico-syntactic ideas. Note that, even more explicitly than Todorov, Greimas (1987 [1969]) attempts to relate the deep and surface structures of narrative syntax by using a logico-grammatical apparatus to characterize the anthropomorphic domain of actants and actions. For Greimas, the enterprise of narrative grammar depends on our distinguishing between "an apparent level of narration, at which the diverse manifestations of narrative are subject to the specific requirements of the linguistic substances through which it is expressed, and an immanent level, which is a kind of common structural trunk where narrativity is located and organized at the stage preceding its manifestation" (64). Mediating between the immanent and the apparent levels of narration, presumably, is what Gerald Prince describes as the "expression component" required by narrative grammars. The latter component is "equivalent to a given medium of representation—say, written English—or, rather, to its grammar and it will allow us to rewrite in that medium the information provided by the other components" (1980: 61; cf. Prince 1973: 34–35; Prince 1982: 100–101, 170; Prince 1987: 62). ("Sirens," however, highlights conceptual difficulties bound up with formulating expression rules in this sense. See secs. 6.2–6.5 above.)

In any event, in a manner that recalls the formal mechanisms of Joyce's text, Greimas inverts the scheme set up by Todorov, locating the deep structure or "common structural trunk" of narrative not in the transcendental domain of agency but in the sphere of logico-grammatical operations encompassed by narrative syntax:

> Starting with the elementary operations of the deep grammar (which follow the process of the actualization of signification) and continuing with the combinations of the syntagmatic series of the surface grammar (which are nothing more than anthropomorphic representations of these operations) the contents, through the effect of the performances, become invested within the narrative utterance. These are organized in linear sequences of canonical utterances that are connected, like the links of a single chain, by a series of logical implications. (Greimas 1987 [1969]: 82–83)

If Todorov roots in the structures of action the syntactic proprieties of sequences, Greimas grounds actantial repertoires in a network of "logical implications." Yet, insofar as Joyce's text troubles the border between "deep grammar" and "surface grammar," forcing us constantly to negotiate between logical relations and their material manifestation in the structures of language, "Sirens" constitutes an anomaly, and perhaps more than just an anomaly, with respect to Greimas's division between deep and surface grammar. (For analogous remarks in connection with Chomsky's model, see secs. 7.4.1ff. above.) Joyce creates a surface grammar that is, on Greimas's own terms, already deep. Greimas makes the point that, "because of their *anthropomorphic nature*, the constitutive elements of [the narrative's] surface grammar can be distinguished from the *logical nature* of the categories of the deep grammar"; "conversion (the movement from one grammatical level to another) can thus be defined as being the equivalence between operation and doing"—between "*syntactic* operation and syntactic *doing*" (1987 [1969]: 70). "Sirens," however, contains syntactic structures that are preconverted, so to speak. Here syntax *is* action, action syntax. Given that the text features both the verbal material of prior utterances and the reprocessing of those utterances through (Bloom's) deep-grammatical operations, neither Greimas's nor Todorov's actantial model is rich enough, it seems, to capture the syntax of Joyce's narrative discourse. The formation and transformation rules subtending "Sirens" must be anchored in some other domain, situated at some other level of (logico-)grammatical description.

8.2. Subsequent narratological models have by and large deanthropomorphized narrative syntax. (The actantial model lives on in refined form in Coste 1989: 134ff., having been importantly modified, also, by Pavel 1973, 1976, and 1985b on the basis of ideas and methods taken from transformational generative grammar.) The anthropocentric investment of later narratological schemes decreases in exact proportion as they register the shift from a primarily anthropological paradigm supplemented with certain techniques of formalization borrowed from linguistics, to a primarily linguistic paradigm marked by a more or less residual complement of anthropological considerations. In the later models, as in the earlier ones, narrative syntax encompasses both formation and transformation rules; its domains are both strings of elements (subjects, predicates, states, events, etc.) so concatenated as to produce structures recognizably and indeed intuitively narrative in nature and the longer stretches of discourse into which such "minimal stories" (Prince 1973: 16ff.) may be inserted by means of conjunction, alternation, and/or embedding (see Prince 1973, 1980, 1982). But given that (some of) the later models proceed from the principles of transformational generative grammar, and given, too, that the status of "Sirens" as logico-grammatical object may complicate use of the generative paradigm in this instance; further consideration of Joyce's text and of other texts with structural affinities with "Sirens" would perhaps require extensive remodeling of the notion *narrative syntax*. That task, however, must be reserved for another place.

8.3. Of primary importance here are the multiple profiles assumed by "Sirens" itself under different conditions of observation. Viewed from one perspective, "Sirens" presents a logico-syntactic profile, its forms and techniques continuous with Carnap's attempt to reconstruct, through the logical analysis of particular languages, the basic features of language in general. Viewed from another perspective, the episode presents a profile whose contours can best be outlined via syntax in its linguistic acceptation. Under this profile, the episode appears as sets of syntagms that gather, knot, and unravel over time; the emphasis is now on aspects of discourse that cannot be assimilated to a wholly logical language, to some perfect calculus at the heart of a fallen speech. But the episode presents yet another profile. From this third perspective, the structures of "Sirens"—ambiguous between logic and language, interstitial, of indefinite makeup and extent—are regulated by a narrative syntax that is both diffuse and dense, both generalized and limited. It is logic's double, rooted not only in the plenitude and ambiguity of the living word but also in the transmissability of stories across different cultures, languages, and epochs. Only a fuller treatment of the interrelations among logic, language, and narrative, however, can illuminate the combinatory mechanisms of Joycean narrative and of narratives generally. Conversely, in the ongoing effort to model syntactic structures in all their richness and differentiation, musical structures may provide additional, if heterodox, routes of access to an enriched (dare I say universal?) syntax.

2. Semantic Dimensions: Objects and Models in Kafka's *Der Prozeß*

Ich selbst werde meiner Subjektnatur, meiner Ichheit, bewußt in Setzung von Sinn, als ein Sinn Setzender. . . . Alles Sinnfindenund Sinnerfüllen ist unabgeschlossen. Jeder erreichte Sinn weist über sich hinaus.—Ernst Mally

I become conscious of my subject-nature, my I-ness, in the positing of meaning, as a sense-positing being. . . . The discovery and fulfillment of every meaning is inconclusive. For each attained meaning points beyond itself.

1. The Problem of Meaning in Narrative

A number of calls for a semantics of story have been issued from a wide variety of sources and with decidedly mixed results.[1] At least since Vladimir Propp (1968 [1928]) tried to isolate a set of "functions" whose (re)combinations would exhaust the semantic resources of a particular corpus of stories (i.e., Russian folktales), researchers have attempted to explain how narratives in general *mean*. Thus, Claude Lévi-Strauss (1963 [1958]), searching for not just a syntax but also a semantics of mythic discourse, analyzed the Oedipus myth into a set of minimal constituents grouped paradigmatically according to their semantic functions, irrespective of their situation on the syntagmatic chain subtending Sophoclean discourse. Lévi-Strauss's results, to be sure, were far from being uniformly reproducible; his analysis did not yield discovery procedures (Doležel 1972: 55) for identifying and classifying universal semantic constituents but rather interpretations as ad hoc as they were ingenious. By investing narrative form with sociocultural significance, however, Lévi-Strauss anticipated later efforts to characterize what might be termed the *semantic saturation* of narrative sequences. Hence, A. J. Greimas and François Rastier (1987 [1968]; cf. Prince 1987: 85–86) sought to refine Lévi-Strauss's approach by developing a structural or rather generative semantics of narrative. They based their model on an emergent structure of logico-semantic relations linking propositions, their contraries, and their contradictions—a dynamic, evolving network of conceptual relations that, despite surface variations, purportedly underlie all those sequences of propositions that we call stories.

More recently, researchers such as Lubomír Doležel (1976a, 1976b, 1979, 1983, 1984, 1989), Uri Margolin (1984, 1991), Thomas Pavel (1986), Ruth Ronen (1994), and Marie-Laure Ryan (1991, 1992) have discussed narrative applications for that class of semantic theory which is premised on the concept of possible worlds. To what extent these and other, prior accounts of narrative meaning achieve descriptive and explanatory adequacy is a matter subject to dispute; as I proceed, I shall evaluate possible worlds semantics in particular as a resource for characterizing the mechanisms by which narratives mean (secs. 6 and 7).[2] By analogy with the previous chapter, however, my working hypothesis is not merely that stories of all sorts are subject to various kinds of semantic analysis. Beyond this, my guiding assumption is that semantic analysis of twentieth-century literary narratives can help us retell the story of semantics itself. More precisely, my assumption is that, through their very forms and techniques, the narratives at issue affiliate themselves with ideas about meaning being developed contemporaneously in language-theoretical settings. I test the possibilities and limits of this hypothesis by examining Franz Kafka's *Der Prozeß* (*The Trial*), a novel first published posthumously in 1925 but written some ten years earlier.

1.1. One might argue that the basic *aims* of semantic theory have not changed all that much since the very inception of grammatical inquiry (sec. **0**.2). In R. H. Robins's (1989) concise formulation, "What one is really trying to do in semantics, or in making statements about meaning, is to explicate, to make explicit the ways in which words, and sentences of various grammatical constructions, are used and understood by native or fluent speakers of a language" (22). Yet the *methods* of semantic research changed dramatically around the time Kafka composed his novel. As we have seen, the period during which Kafka lived (1883–1924) was also the period of the rebirth of universal grammar; that period spawned, along with the (logico-)syntactic theories discussed in chapter 1, a host of strategies for correlating the grammatical forms of a language and the meanings that those forms encode. Thus, in a recent textbook on linguistic semantics, William Frawley (1992: 17–60) surveys a gamut of semantic models, ranging from theories of meaning as logical form, to theories of meaning as conceptual structure, to theories of meaning as context and use, to theories of meaning as reference, to theories of meaning as culture. It would be beyond the scope of the present chapter to examine how Kafka's novel bears on all these models—although the models themselves can be traced back to developments in language theory in the years surrounding the composition and publication of *Der Prozeß*. Mine is a more modest goal: namely, to study how interpretation of Kafka's narrative compels us to recontextualize, and hence rethink, theories about meaning and reference.[3]

1.2. The first phase of this investigation will focus on what can be called object-theoretical aspects of Kafka's text. Arguably, *Der Prozeß* encodes in its narrative form a concern with the nature of objectivity and hence participates in an entire network of late nineteenth-, early twentieth-century discourses oriented around the problem of objects. Furthermore, the foundations of modern-day semantic theory were constructed in parallel with those of object theory and in response to many of the same issues—notably the ontologico-referential status of the meanings bound up with the design and interpretation of linguistic expressions. Thus, this chapter explores the role of object theory in the evolution of semantic theories about meaning and reference, but the chapter also uses Kafka's forms and techniques to conduct that exploration.

Classical object theory belongs to a research tradition stemming from Franz Brentano's reconstruction of the medieval doctrine of intentionality in his extraordinarily influential *Psychology from an Empirical Standpoint* (1973 [1874]).[4] The concepts and methods set out in Brentano's "descriptive psychology" perpetuated themselves in the work of philosophers such as Kasimierz Twardowski, Anton Marty (who happened to be Kafka's instructor at the Charles University in Prague), Alexius Meinong, Ernst Mally, and Edmund Husserl, to name only some of the more important representatives of object-theoretical discourse (see sec. 4 below). Globally speaking, object theory is a theory about what sorts of objects we must include in any inventory of the real (and irreal), how these objects bear on one another, and the logico-semantic resources by means of which, conceptually and communicatively, we manipulate the different sorts of objects included in our ontological inventories.

My claim is that we find similar concerns built into the structure of Kafkan objects. Specifically, in representing Josef K.'s modes of sense assignment, the circumstances under which he must perpetually posit meanings (epigram), Kafka's text helps us reframe ideas about objects variously characterized as intentional, immanent, logical, irreal, ideal, synsemantic, or fictive, depending on the nomenclature adopted. (For a partial history of the relevant terminology, see Morscher 1972; and Wolf 1972; cf. secs. 4ff. below.) More specifically

still, Kafka's objects point up limitations of two broad trends in contemporaneous object theory. A nominalist trend ascribed fictitious or at best heuristic
status to the objects of verbs such as *consider* in statements like "Consider that
gold mountain" or "Consider an object such that it is impossible for that object
to exist." Conversely, a realist trend inventoried such objects as components of
the real. The divergence of these two trends in object theory prefigured the
subsequent polarization of extensional (set-theoretic) and intensional (model-
theoretic) approaches to meaning (sec. 3).

By contrast—and this constitutes the second phase of the investigation—
Kafkan objects resist description in either nominalist or realist terms. Rather,
Der Prozeß embeds objects in what I shall go on to characterize as model worlds
(secs. 6 and 7). Kafka's narrative thus performs a crucial metasemantic role. By
generating multiple model worlds, competing frames of reference, the novel
also generates what can be termed *species of radical semantic indeterminacy.*
Such indeterminacy derives not from the multiplicity of available frames but
rather from an uncoupling of frames of reference from the contexts that make
them model worlds as opposed to merely possible worlds in the first place.
Study of Kafka's narrative form therefore yields the following inference: Understanding the mechanisms of meaning ultimately requires that semantic models
be supplemented with contextual considerations usually grouped under the
heading *pragmatics*—considerations that will be the chief concern of chapter 3.

1.3. Note that mine is the *kind* of interpretive strategy pursued by commentators ever since Kafka's friend and literary executor, Max Brod, claimed that
Kafka himself had no capacity for abstract thought or theoretical argumentation. Brod's view was that "Kafka did not love theories. He spoke in images
because he thought in images" (quoted in Heidsieck 1989: 489). The sheer
volume of Kafka commentary amassed over the past three-quarters of a century
(cf. Corngold 1973) suggests something about the quality of Brod's assessment.
Further, the research itself has revealed sociological, religious, philosophical,
and more broadly theoretical implications of Kafkan discourse (cf. Adorno
1986b [1967]; Bense 1952; Kurz 1987, 1989; Miles 1983; Oblau 1979; and Robertson 1985, among many others). Indeed, Susanne Kessler (1983) has persuasively
argued that Kafka's very "theoretischen Verschlossenheit" 'theoretical reserve'
(7) figures as the expression of a larger tradition of *Sprachskepsis* and *Sprachkritik* that became widespread in German-language philosophical and literary
writing around the time of the *Jahrhundertwende:* for example, in the language
critiques put forth by Fritz Mauthner and Ludwig Wittgenstein (cf. Janik and
Toulmin 1973: 120ff.).

Roughly coeval with the fin de siècle interest in *Sprachkritik,* the object theories surveyed below (sec. *4*) also help illuminate the theoretical ramifications of Kafka's narrative form. More than this, however, just as Joyce's "Sirens" participates in the modeling of syntactic structures, Kafka's *Der Prozeß* helps us reconceptualize the object-theoretical discourse in which it is embedded. Whereas object theorists tried to paraphrase talk about meaning into the language of objects or else to paraphrase talk about objects into discourse on meaning, Kafka's novel speaks both idioms at once. The result is a peculiar nonsense, which helps illuminate the scope and nature of sense.

2. Strategies of Immanence

From the outset, Kafka represents Josef K.'s experiences, and the inferences that he draws from those experiences, in paradoxical fashion. The internally focalized narrative (Genette 1980 [1972]: 189–211), which forces us to share K.'s severely limited point of view, confers on K.'s experiences and inferences a kind of pure immediacy, an absolute incorrigibility; but at the same time the text assigns to what K. undergoes, or rather to what he concludes about what he undergoes, a kind of radical uncertainty, an ongoing fall into deception and delusion. During his exegesis of the parable about the man waiting before the law, the Priest asserts that "Richtiges Auffassen einer Sache und Mißverstehen der gleichen Sache schließen einander nicht vollständig aus" 'The correct interpretation of a thing and misunderstanding of the same thing do not completely exclude one another' (Kafka 1986 [1925]: 185).[5] Similarly, and equally paradoxically, we can doubt neither that K. experiences what he does nor that what K. construes about those experiences enjoys at best a drastically mediated relation to the world that we in turn strive to understand, at another inferential level, on the basis of information supplied over the course of the narrative as a whole. By virtue of its participation in object-theoretical discourses at large, and more specifically in discourse centered on intentional objects, Kafka's text resolves even as it elaborates this paradox, which indissolubly joins interpretation with (some degree of) misinterpretation: that is one of the claims to be argued over the course of this chapter.

During K.'s arrest at the opening of the novel, when K. asks one of his warders who he is, with the warder ostensibly ignoring him, we read that it is "als müsse man seine Erscheinung hinnehmen" 'as though one simply had to put up with his appearance' (Kafka 1986 [1925]: 7). Like the reader facing Kafka's narrative for the first time, K. must accept as a sort of premise or given—

as a datum in the strict sense—the more or less inexplicable appearance of the warder in his bedroom. A moment later, K. looks on as the same warder

> turned to the door [of K.'s bedroom] and opened it slightly so as to say to someone who was evidently [*offenbar*] standing just behind it: "He wants Anna to bring him his breakfast." A small laugh from the next room followed; one couldn't be sure from the sound whether or not more than one person had participated in the laugh. Although the strange man could not have learned anything from the response that he did not already know, still he now said to K. with the tone of one who is making an announcement: "It is impossible." (Kafka 1986 [1925]: 7)

Here, in relating only the sort and the amount of information immediately available from within K.'s own perspective, that is, in being rigorously internally focalized, the text denaturalizes the process of inference itself, indexing each inferential step with some degree of uncertainty ("evidently," "one couldn't be sure whether or not," "although . . . still").[6] With classically phenomenalist (Hirst 1967) insistence, the text subordinates the process of inference, which necessitates that we accept as data things only indirectly (mediately) known, to the data experienced directly and immediately *as* phenomena and therefore known in the strict sense—even if our knowing now consists only in knowing that we do not know.

In fact, as the narrative proceeds, K. realizes more and more that the sorts of inferences that he habitually draws are just that—inferential habits, customary assumptions, even outright prejudices. These belief structures base themselves on data whose principles of organization escape even K.'s own much-vaunted *Organisationstalent* as the Bank's Chief Clerk—as K. himself must eventually acknowledge. In consequence, K. finds himself relinquishing, more and more, *all* belief structures whatsoever (see sec. *6.1.1ff.* below). K. therein increasingly models his behavior on that of the Court Usher, for example, who at any given moment acts "als sei die Ansicht K.s genau so richtig wie seine eigene" 'as if K.'s view [on the matter at hand] were just as correct as his own' (Kafka 1986 [1925]: 56). Taking refuge from such wholly relativized systems of belief, K. savors the brute phenomenality of sensory experiences, whose larger consequences and interrelations K. no longer presumes to infer. K. thereby subordinates analysis of his surroundings to the search for unmistakable evidence that at least some phenomenon or another is, somehow, in the process of occurring somewhere.

Consider the scene involving K., the manufacturer, and K.'s archenemy, the Assistant Manager of the Bank. At this point in the novel, K. is so distracted by his case that he is unable even to concentrate on, let alone understand, the complex series of transactions proposed by the manufacturer in K.'s office. After managing to mutter, "It is difficult," K.

> looked up, but only very feebly, as the door of the Manager's office opened and there—not entirely clearly, somewhat as if behind a screen of gauze— the Assistant Manager appeared. K. did not reflect any further [*dachte nicht weiter darüber nach*] on all this, but merely pursued its immediate effect [*Wirkung*], which was very gratifying to him. For immediately the manufacturer jumped up from this chair and hurried over to the manager—though K. would have had him do so ten times more quickly, since he feared that the Assistant Manager might once more disappear. (Kafka 1986 [1925]: 112)

In this passage, K. welcomes the immediate and indisputable fact of the Assistant Manager's intervention, powerless, however, to infer either the reasons for or the ultimate consequences of that intervention. Like some vague aura through which K.'s world is hazily refracted, these reasons and consequences surround with a nebulous significance the immediate, isolated datum of the Assistant Manager's otherwise gratifying apparition. In effect, K. now values the certainty afforded by the isolated sense datum more than he esteems his own position at the Bank. K. actually fears the disappearance of a man whose sole purpose and raison d'être, it seems, is to ensure K.'s own more or less rapid downfall within the hierarchy of the Bank. Such highly phenomenalistic habits of mind account, perhaps, for the narrator's remark early on in the novel that "it was not usual for [Josef K.] to learn from experience" (Kafka 1956 [1925]: 4).

Yet if we find it paradoxical that K. attempts to derive absolute certainty from the bracketing of all but the most immediate, phenomenal evidence—the indistinct apparition of, say, a human shape glimpsed through a half-open door—we should recall that this enterprise is by no means unprecedented in the discursive environment of *Der Prozeß*. For example, the neopositivist Ernst Mach (1902 [1886]) had influentially attempted to derive all knowledge from a matrix of potentially verifiable sensations (*Empfindungen*). Mach construed such (purely phenomenal) "elements" as a species of ultimate, originary data at once psychical and physical in their constitution and configuration (235–36; cf. Alexander 1967: 116–17). More pertinent to my own investigation is Brentano's descriptive psychology. Brentano's (1973 [1874]) concern was to redescribe phenomenality by way of what the philosopher variously termed "intentional," "immanent," or "inexistent" objects. For Brentano, the realm of the phenomenal must be broken down, at least heuristically, into mental acts and the intentional objects toward which those acts are directed. As opposed to Mach, however, Brentano does not (or does not at first) situate the objects constitutive of mental acts in the field of empirically verifiable and spatiotemporally organized experience. Rather, in Brentano's scheme, as formulated initially, such generalized or intentional objectivity stands in a certain relation to experienceable objects in the narrow sense.

I attempt to characterize this relation, and *its* relation to Kafkan objects, in greater detail in sections *4* and *5* below. Before studying Brentano's and others' theories about intentional acts and objects, however, I shall conduct a preliminary investigation of what semantic theorists started to call *intensions* (and intensional properties) during the same era. Arguably, by starting to situate intentions in the context of intensions, we shall be better equipped to explore, in later sections, key (meta)semantic aspects of Kafka's narrative form.

3. Intensions and Extensions

The concept of intensions can be traced back to Gottlob Frege's groundbreaking analyses of meaning and reference (1969b [1891], 1969c [1892], 1969e [1892]), together with Bertrand Russell's (1905) post-Fregean analysis of naming and denotation. Distinguishing between intensional and extensional aspects of meaning, the Fregean-Russellian tradition has produced a division of labor in semantic research, as described by Katz (1972: 234–43), Danto (1981: 71–72), and Doležel (1983: 121–22), among others. On the one hand, researchers typically construe the *extensions* of terms and propositions (set theoretically) as sets of entities and states of affairs denoted by the terms and propositions in question. Such sets are "picked out" by words and sentences, and the conjunctions, disjunctions, and intersections of the sets produce relations of entailment, exclusion, presupposition, etc. between the terms and propositions themselves. (For a more complete list of these logico-semantic relations, see, e.g., Eco 1984: 48–49.) Extensionally speaking, therefore, our chief concern in semantic inquiry is the logic of referring expressions—what those expressions pick out in the world and, concomitantly, what logical inferences the expressions themselves presuppose, entail, and/or disallow.

On the other hand, researchers commonly construe the *intensions* of terms and propositions as properties, or "contents," attaching to those terms and propositions in a given context of use (cf. Hintikka and Hintikka 1989: 73ff.; Palmer 1981: 190–201; Eco 1976: 62ff.). Intensionally speaking, our chief concern is the variable semantic profile assumed by expressions whose meaningfulness is anchored in contexts that might feature propositional attitudes (attitudes of believing, knowing, hoping, etc.), modalized statements (attributions of necessity or impossibility to states of affairs), or other elements yielding what Willard V. O. Quine (1980) called "referential opacity." Intensions account for why "a name may occur referentially in a statement S and yet not occur referentially in a longer statement which is formed by embedding S in the context 'is unaware that . . .' or 'believes that . . .' " (Quine 1980: 142). Thus, the extension or, as Frege called it, the *reference* (*Bedeutung*) of the term *Mars* in the statement

(S) Mars is the fourth planet from the sun

and in the statement

(S') Bob believes that Mars is the second planet from the sun

is identical, but the intension or *meaning* (*Sinn*) of the term differs in each case (Frege 1970 [1892]: 58; see sec. 6.3 below). Mars *is* the fourth planet from the sun; but, still, (S') is not necessarily a false statement, Bob having perhaps momentarily confused Mars with Venus. Even though both (S) and (S') may be true, however, the position of Mars relative to the sun has not changed (or has not changed *that* much) in the time it took Bob to utter (S'). Rather, the meaning of the term *for Bob* is what varies. Since therefore the referents of expressions remain constant while their meanings may vary, we must acknowledge that extensions and intensions are distinct properties of utterances. Otherwise, we shall involve ourselves in logico-epistemological paradoxes of the most pernicious sort.

3.1. Further elaboration may help. Whereas the extensional definition of a term consists in listing the members of the class designated by the term, "alternatively, and perhaps more commonly, we can define a class on the basis of some property (or set of properties) which [the members of that class] have in common. . . . This would be an intensional definition: the intension of a term is the set of essential properties which determines the applicability of the term" (Lyons 1977: 1:158–59).[7] If I say *cat*, extensionally speaking I denote, refer to, anything whose anatomical structures and behavioral patterns conform to those of the creatures we call cats. Depending on context, however, the intension of *cat* can range from "nonhuman" to "alternately affectionate and aloof" to "mouse killer" etc. The term's intension, that is, consists of the meaning(s) imputed to *cat* across widely variable situations of use. Thus, in saying *cat*, intensionally speaking I may connote any number of things.[8]

We therefore conclude that two classes—say, the class of brown tabbies, C_{bt} and the class of creatures with brown-hued feline fur, C_{ff}—may share the same members "and yet be different classes by virtue of their intensional definition" (Lyons 1977: 1:159). Although the membership criteria for C_{bt} overlap with those for C_{ff}, C_{bt} and C_{ff} are not symmetrical; they center around different *sorts* of properties attaching to the set of referents (objects) constituting the extension of both classes. C_{bt} is a class whose membership criteria are of special pertinence to veterinarians, cat breeders, cat owners, and the like; by contrast, the membership criteria for C_{ff} are important primarily to those who have allergic reactions to cats—or perhaps to those who simply favor hairless over furry floors.

3.2. The distinction between intensions and extensions has further consequences for semantic theory—consequences that Kafka's novel helps us sort through. When characterizing the intensions of terms and propositions, researchers often define these (variable) contents as functions from possible to actual worlds. More precisely, intensions are construed as functions from truth conditions obtaining in one or more possible worlds to the truth conditions obtaining in a reference world, that is, the world that counts as actual relative to any number of possible worlds over which the intensional functions might range (Partee 1989: 97, 108; cf. Frawley 1992: 384–436; Herman 1994a; Ryan 1991; and sec. 6 below). In a possible world W', *Mars* means "the second planet from the sun"; in that possible world, Bob's statement that "Mars is the second planet from the sun" would amount to a proposition having a positive truth value. In the reference world W subtending the vast majority of propositions that we hold to be true about the solar system, however, Bob's statement amounts to a proposition with a negative truth value. Or, as we might also put it, in W *Mars* more commonly means "the fourth planet from the sun."

As a result, using now a set-theoretic framework for the analysis of extensions, now a model-theoretic or possible worlds apparatus for the analysis of intensions, researchers institute a more or less rigid distinction between issues of ontology (reference) and issues of epistemology (meaning) in the characterization of meaning (Champigny 1972: 22, n. 6; Partee 1989: 116ff.; Ronen 1994: 19ff.). The extensionalist approach puts a premium on what linguistic expressions denote, as opposed to what we think we know while we are denoting things with the expressions, during particular acts of meaning production and interpretation (cf. Katz 1972: 234). Indeed, for Quine (1960), who argues that "the underlying methodology of the idioms of propositional attitudes contrasts strikingly with the spirit of objective science at its most representative" (218), the intensional properties putatively bound up with propositional attitudes (e.g., "Bob believes that Mars is the second planet from the sun") are superfluous entities, subject to removal by Ockham's razor: "All [propositional attitudes] can be thought of as involving something like quotation of one's own imagined verbal response to an imagined situation" (219).

Conversely, the intensionalist approach puts a premium on *how* we mean when we mean—on the epistemic properties of linguistic expressions used to connote particular meanings in particular contexts (cf. Eco 1976: 62). Insofar as intensional or model-theoretic semantics postulates that "the mode of fixing the reference [of sentences] is relevant to our epistemic attitude toward the sentences expressed" (Kripke 1980: 20–21)—insofar as "the sense of an expression is supposed to determine its reference" (Green 1989: 42)—we find a different research program for semantic theory than the one prescribed by the more parsimonious extensionalists. For example, researchers now try to map epistemic modality, or "the content of an expression that reflects the speaker's attitude or state of knowledge about a proposition," into grammatical mood, or "the inflectional expression of a subset of modal denotations" (Frawley 1992: 386; Palmer 1990; cf. Herman 1994a; and secs. 6.3ff. below). More generally, the intensionalist approach leads to the conclusion that "language treats possibility and truth as a conceptual/semantic system: not as a system that relates language to the world, but as one that connects language to its users" (Frawley 1992: 408).

As I discuss in the next section, the extensionalist and intensionalist outlooks, respectively, were anticipated by nominalist and realist object theories in circulation around the turn of the century. In effect, the nominalists (Brentano, Oskar Kraus) and realists (Husserl, Meinong) helped set the parameters for later semantic research—for subsequent models for meaning and reference. Eventually, by starting to reattach Kafka's *Der Prozeß* to surrounding object theories— more precisely, by examining how the structure of Kafkan objects exceeds the explanatory resources of both the nominalist and the realist approaches (secs. 5ff.)—we can at the same time recontextualize the object-theoretical schemes and their bearing on more recent semantic inquiry.

4. Intentional Objects: Inexistence or in Existence?

A. R. Lacey (1986) remarks that "intentionality, though historically different from intensionality, is often confused or equated with it" (111). On Lacey's account, "Intentional situations may be thought of as those where a relation appears to exist but does not really, as 'want' in 'I want a unicorn' seems to relate me to a unicorn" (111; cf. Brentano 1973 [1874]: 271ff.; and sec. 4.3 below). Thus, we might assume that intentional contexts are a subset of intensional contexts, intentions a subset of intensions. If I intend a unicorn, I may enjoy an irreal relation with a horse that has a horn on its head; but the intensional properties bound up with statements about unicorns are just a specific variety of the properties (e.g., propositional attitudes such as belief, conjecture, etc.) attaching to statements about automobiles, squirrels, and articles of furniture. However, the definition of *intentional situations* as those involving a merely specious relation is itself based on the view of intentions found in Brentano's later, nominalistic object theory; as we shall see, for realist object theorists like Husserl and especially Meinong, any such definition begs the question. For the realists, the speciousness of our relations even to intentional objects like unicorns and round squares does not go without saying. Where intensions end and intentions (in Lacey's sense) begin: that is the core of the dispute between object-theoretical realists and nominalists.[9] In effect, Kafka's *Der Prozeß* unfolds as an attempt to adjudicate this dispute, circumvent this dilemma.

4.1. I have gotten ahead of myself, however; it is time to characterize object theory itself in somewhat greater detail. We can begin with Brentano's remark, in book 2 of *Psychology from an Empirical Standpoint,* that "nothing distinguishes mental phenomena from physical phenomena more than the fact that something is immanent as an object in them. For this reason it is easy to understand that the fundamental differences in the way something exists in them as an object constitute the principal class differences among mental phenomena" (1973 [1874]: chap. 6, sec. 2, p. 197). For Brentano, these class differences span, in order of increasing complexity, presentations or presentational acts (*Vorstellungen*); judgments (*Urteilen*), which presuppose presentations; and (aesthetic as well as ethical) feelings and interests (*Gemütsbewegung, Interesse*), which in turn presuppose both presentations and judgments.

Note that Brentano's classification of the modes of immanence of intentional objects, a latter-day incarnation of the Porphyrian tree (cf. Eco 1984: 46–86; Smith 1987: 207–9), finds an important analogue in Kafka's own stratified and hierarchicalized characterization of the Court.[10] Based as it is on relations of presupposition and implication (i.e., levels of inclusiveness), with each higher level permitting certain combinations of elements found at the previous level(s), the typology of intentional acts, like the Court system, features functional strata ranked according to scope and complexity. In the Kafkan scenario, these levels progress like arithmetically scaled orders of magnitude; to each level corresponds an unopened and unopenable door of the Law, as described in the

Priest's parable (Kafka 1956 [1925]: 213ff.). At the lowest level we find portrait painters, students, ushers, and would-be Court-typists such as Fräulein Bürstner (25); at the next stratum, we discover warders, inspectors, and whippers; still higher are the bands of ineffectual pettifogging lawyers; thence we move on to well-connected attorneys such as Huld; Chief Clerks of the Court (104–5), jurisprudential analogues for Josef K., himself formerly Chief Clerk at the Bank; and aged Examining Magistrates with their inscrutable advisers (see sec. 6 below). Finally, at the highest, all-inclusive level, we have Judges whose fearsome, properly sublime power, like the awesome size of the Cathedral, strikes one "as bordering on the limit of what human beings could bear" (208–9; cf. 190ff.). Thus, Titorelli the painter remarks to K., "The ranks of officials in this judiciary system mounted endlessly, so that not even the initiated could survey the hierarchy as a whole" (119).

This joint bureaucratization of mind and world in Kafka and Brentano has implications that cannot be fully considered here (cf. Horkheimer 1974 [1967], 1972 [1968] on the "instrumentalization of reason"; but contrast Menger 1985: 333ff.).[11] Its pertinence to our investigation as a whole is made explicit in a remark of Brentano's from 1895, as quoted by Oskar Kraus in his introduction to the 1924 edition of the *Psychology:* "The task of [descriptive psychology] is to exhibit all of the basic mental phenomena. All other mental phenomena are derived from the combination of these ultimate psychological elements, just as all words are built up out of letters. Completion of this task could provide the basis for a *characteristica universalis* such as Leibniz, and Descartes before him, envisaged" (369; cf. sec. *0.5.1*). For the moment, however, we need to focus more particularly on the status of that "something" which—combined and recombined in Brentano's progressively more complicated levels of presentation, judgment, and feeling—inheres in, is immanent to, all levels of mental phenomena, all types of conscious functioning. At issue, in short, are the modalities of immanence attributed to intentional objects and how those ontological modalities bear in turn on the structure of Kafkan objects.

4.2. Dissatisfied with Descartes's and Kant's wholly negative definition of *mental phenomena* as what lacks extension in space (cf. Brentano 1973 [1874]: bk. 1, chap. 4, sec. 1, p. 65), Brentano finds in intentionality the positive feature of—indeed the criterion for—mental phenomena in general. As already indicated, this criterion is just the structural directedness of all mental phenomena toward an object. Hence, mental phenomena can be described exhaustively by means of their intentional properties, together with their nonlocalizability in space. But furthermore, as the phenomena of feeling and interest demonstrate, the objects toward which mental acts are (constitutively) directed need not themselves be objects in the customary sense. We do not grasp intentional objects, in every case at least, by virtue of some spatially proximate or temporally current relation to, some co-presence with, an object subsisting outside us. We may grievingly intend someone long after that person has died. Indeed, we may intend characteristics of certain subatomic particles, for example, to which we have not had, and in principle cannot ever have, direct or immediate access, but at best only the highly mediated access afforded by complex observational instruments.[12] Put otherwise, if "one thing certainly has to be admitted; [namely, that] the object to which a feeling refers is not always an external object" (bk. 2, chap. 1, sec. 5, p. 90), more generally we can say that

> every mental phenomenon is characterized by what the Scholastics of the Middle Ages called the intentional (or mental) inexistence of an object, and what we might call, though not wholly unambiguously, reference to a content, direction toward an object (which is not to be understood here as meaning a thing), or immanent objectivity. . . . This intentional inexistence is characteristic exclusively of mental phenomena. No physical phenomenon exhibits anything like it. We can, therefore, define mental phenomena by saying that they are those phenomena which contain an object intentionally within themselves. (Bk. 2, chap. 1, sec. 5, pp. 88–89)

If only in the terms and categories it somewhat haphazardly invokes[13]—content (*Inhalt*), inexistent or immanent object (*Gegenstand, Objekt*), and existent or transcendent thing (*Ding, Wesen, Reales*)—this passage defines the scope of subsequent object-theoretical inquiry. In assigning immanent objectivity or intentional inexistence to the objects we intend, as opposed to the things in which our intentions and their objects are (sometimes) grounded, Brentano brings into focus a set of issues both epistemological and ontological in nature. At stake here are, among other things, the status of universals and the role of existential quantifiers (*some, all, none*) in the logical analysis of statements about nonexistent and/or impossible entities or states of affairs (Russell 1905) as well as the problem of relating meaning contents (intensions) to the denotata of acts of meaning (extensions).

It would require a more specialized study than this one to explore all the ramifications of Brentano's account of intentionality. (For a more complete list of the relevant issues, see Smith 1987: 205–6.) But one can pose the central question suggested by Brentano's analysis of immanent objectivity. The question is this: Do we or do we not ascribe, and if so to what degree (and in what mode), fictivity and/or irreality to what Brentano calls immanent objects? In this connection, we can identify on the one hand a nominalist line of object-theoretical inquiry, in which immanent objectivity finds its place in the domain of the heuristic, fictive, or irreal, depending on the specific character of the nominalistic scheme adopted. On the other hand, in what can be identified as a realist line of object-theoretical discourse, we discover (at the limit) the tendency to abolish the domain of the fictive itself, to characterize every possible mode of directedness toward an object as an instance or aspect of the real.[14] Whereas nominalistic object theory reduces intensions to extensions, anchoring immanent in nonimmanent objects, the realist version reduces extensions to intensions or, rather, posits just as many extensions as there are intensions. Object-theoretical nominalism subordinates epistemologico-semantic concerns to the demand for a noncluttered ontology; object-theoretical realism sacrifices a parsimonious ontology for a richer, more flexible account of both knowledge and meaning.

4.3. The later Brentano himself can be adduced as perhaps the most prominent example of the nominalistic approach to immanent objects (but see also Vaihinger 1913).[15] Immanent objectivity, for *this* Brentano, now names a more or less innocuous species of fiction, a helpful but in principle disposable heuristic device. In Roderick Chisholm's (1967) formulation: "In [Brentano's] later writings, he said that 'unicorn' in the sentence 'John is thinking about a unicorn' has no referential function; a contemplated unicorn is not a type of unicorn. 'Unicorn,' in such sentences, is used syncategorematically to contribute to the description of the person who is said to have a unicorn as the object of his thought" (202).

Put otherwise, if I say that I grievingly intend a dead person as an object, or if I say that my intention of a quark includes immanently as objects any number of mathematically determinable features of that particle, then I am speaking loosely and by virtue of what the later Brentano, following Aristotle, would call an improper (*uneigentlich*) notion of being. According to this improper notion, even an object such that it could not possibly exist does at least in a certain sense exist—that is, in the sense that I speak about *it* as nonexistent.[16] As Brentano remarks in the ninth appendix to the 1911 edition of the *Psychology*, "In many cases the fiction that we can have something other than a real thing as an object—that non-beings, for example, may be objects just as well as beings—proves to be innocuous in logical operations; and in fact these operations can even be facilitated by this fiction because it simplifies our form of expression and even our thought processes themselves" (295; cf. Brentano 1966: 340–46).

Thus, the function of irreal, idealized geometric figures, for example, is merely that of "serving as a guideline for the association of thought-determinations" (Brentano 1981a [1929]: 67; cf. Husserl 1979f [1894]: 327). But, although "fictive" statements about "nonthings" such as isosceles triangles or $\sqrt{-1}$ enable us to express ourselves more efficiently than we could without them, still we should not forget that such statements can in principle be paraphrased back into "a more strict and proper mode of expression" (Brentano 1981b [1907–17]: 24).[17] It is too bad that "the fact that such fictions are useful in logic has led many to believe that logic has non-things as well as things as its object and, accordingly, that the concept of its object is more general than the concept of a thing" (Brentano 1973 [1874]: app. 9, p. 300). But, in principle at least, this situation is not irremediable.

In brief,

> In many cases, the things to which we refer [in mental references] do not exist. But we are accustomed to saying that they then have being as objects. This is a loose [*uneigentlicher*] use of the verb "to be," which we permit with impunity for the sake of convenience, just as we allow ourselves to speak of the sun "rising" and "setting." . . . Because reference to things is a distinctive characteristic of someone who is mentally active, we have been led to talk about objects having being or subsisting in the mentally active subject. (Brentano 1973 [1874]: app. 9, p. 291)

Thus, in discussing "Mental Reference as Distinguished from Relation in the Strict Sense" (271ff.), Brentano follows Aristotle in distributing minimal (two-termed) relations between a fundament and a terminus but remarks that, whereas in relations in general both fundament and terminus are real (*Reales*), in the relation we designate as mental reference or presentation only the terminus is real. It is just that our habitual modes of discourse sometimes make us think otherwise.

As this last claim suggests, the later, nominalistic Brentano seeks to expose types of looseness in talk about existence—for example, the colloquial application of existential quantifiers to various classes of nouns—by postulating a grammar of well-formed existence claims, a class of properly phrased locutions concerning "the real" (cf., in this respect, Carnap 1975 [1931], 1937a [1934]; Descombes 1986 [1983]: 118–37). Thus, in the appendix "On Objects of Thought" added to the 1924 (posthumous) edition of the *Psychology*, Brentano asserts that "anyone who is thinking must have a thing [*Reales*] as his object and have this as his object in one and the same sense of the word" (321–22). Conversely, as

Brentano puts it in the appendix "On Ens Rationis," "We must . . . acknowledge [with Aristotle] that what has being in potentiality and its actuality are not real things. *But it does not follow from all this that anything other than a thing is ever the object of our thought*" (346). More strongly still, Brentano writes in a letter to Anton Marty dated 7 January 1903, "Es ist, scheint mir, *unmöglich, daß einem Nichtrealen anders als in Dependenz von einem Realen Tatsächlichkeit zukomme*" 'It is impossible, it seems to me, that a nonreal [entity] can have any actuality other than in its dependence on a real one' (Brentano 1966: 106). Here, Brentano subordinates immanent objects to their dependency relations vis-à-vis nonimmanent objects; put otherwise, he seeks to paraphrase, to translate, intension-laden varieties of talk into talk that centers on extensions. Ontological parsimony necessitates that we fictionalize or at least virtualize both the objects of thought and the semantic contents of expressions. Hence, the later Brentano's nominalistic object theory works toward at least some version of the extensionality thesis, as succinctly described by Lacey (1986):

> Extensions are simpler than intensions, and in one loose but intelligible sense they are more objective: they concern the world rather than how we look at it. So logicians prefer extensions, and would like to dispense with intensions, by translating statements containing intensional notions into statements free from them. The view that this can be done is called the *extensionality thesis* . . . and defended by . . . those who prefer a sparse and austere universe. It is attacked by those who accept the richness and complexity of the universe at its face value. (111; cf. Church 1950)[18]

4.4. Among those who "accept the richness and complexity of the universe at its face value" are those who embrace what can be called the realist version of object theory. Object-theoretical realism confers on intentional objects not fictive or heuristic status but a mode of existence that cannot be explained away as loose talk—as logical shorthand or investigative slang. To the contrary, the realist approach issues in a glut of entities, an ontological plenum. In extremis— as we shall see, Meinong defines this extreme—anything conceivable, anything possible to intend, enjoys at least some mode of existence or subsistence and a fortiori the status of an object. Accordingly, objects are not extensional anchors that halt the play of irreal ideas but rather the medium of ideation itself, instantaneously self-actualizing contents of thought. In turn, the notion of a bad, erroneous, partial, or outmoded representation of an object becomes difficult, if not impossible, to capture in Meinongian terms (see Ryle 1972; Herman 1993d: 67–68; and sec. 4.4.2 below).

4.4.1. A notable proponent of the realist version of object theory is Edmund Husserl.[19] Arguably, Husserl's object-theoretical realism stems from his attempt (1979e [1891]) to develop a logic based on the contents of judgments (*Inhaltslogik*), as opposed to a set-theoretic logic based on the extension or referential scope of judgments (*Umfangslogik*) (see sec. *0.5.3* above). (This early *Inhaltslogik* would be renamed *phenomenology* later on.) From the start Husserl attempts to refute "eine häufige Behauptung, daß nur die 'Interpretation' aller Urteile als Klassenurteile zu einem schließenden Kalkül führen könne" 'a common proposition [among contemporary logicians], namely, that only the "interpretation" of all judgments as judgments about classes [of entities] could lead to a complete calculus' (44; cf. Mally 1912: 77ff.). Husserl follows Ernst Schröder's differentiation of "den 'faktischen Inhalt' eines Begriffs (das ist nichts anderes als der Inhalt in dem gewöhnlichen Sinne der Logik) von dem 'idealen.' Dieser umfaßt die Gesamtheit gültiger Merkmale, welche einem Begriffsgegenstande als solchen zukommen" 'the "factual content" of a concept (which is nothing other than its content in the customary logical sense) from the "ideal" content. This last comprises the totality of valid signs marking the object of a concept as such' (47). But whereas Schröder held a strictly intensional logic to be impossible (47), by contrast Husserl suggests that a logic of ideal contents yields results that are just as significant, if not more significant, than the results yielded by an extensional or set-theoretic logic (47–48).

This is because—and here we uncover the roots of Husserl's object-theoretical realism—Husserl had reacted to Frege's charges of psychologism (see Mohanty 1982: 18–42) by redescribing what Schröder called the *factual* content of ideas as their *psychological* content. Husserl then set this psychological content over against the ideal *meanings* subtending our ideas (cf. Welton 1989; Morscher 1972: 69–72). Thus, one must differentiate between the having of the idea of the number 4 at a certain moment or set of moments and the various arithmetic operations that one can perform, at any given moment, with the content of the idea "4" itself (cf. Mally 1912: 80). Hence, too, Husserl (1979f [1894]) talks about "die Unterscheidung des idealen von dem psychologischen Gehalt der Vorstellungsakte. Der erstere weist ja hin auf gewisse Identifizierungszusammenhänge, in denen wir die Identität der Intention erfassen (eventuell mit Evidenz erfassen), während die einzelnen Vorstellungen doch nicht irgendein psychologisch-identisches Bestandstück gemein hätten" 'the distinction of the ideal from the psychological content of acts of presentation. The first points back to certain identifying connections, in which we grasp the identity of the intentions (eventually in their pure evidence), whereas the particular presentations [linked together by these identifying connections] need not necessarily have any psychologically identical component in common' (sec. 4, pp. 311–12). Ultimately, in the fifth *Logical Investigation*, Husserl would go on to locate these "gewisse Identifizierungszusammenhänge" in what he termed the *semantic essence* of intentional acts: "To the extent that we deal with acts, functioning in expressions in sense-giving fashion, or capable of so functioning . . . we shall speak more specifically of the semantic essence of the act. The ideational abstraction of this essence yields a 'meaning' in our ideal sense" (Husserl 1970 [1913]: sec. 21, p. 590; cf. Sözer 1989).

Indeed, the role of (semantic) essences in the constitution of objects is what leads the realist Husserl, in his second *Logical Investigation*, to include meanings in the domain of objectivity itself, one of whose proper subsets is now the domain of *ideal* objectivity corresponding to intentions and, for that matter, intensions:

> It is naturally not our intention to put the *being of what is ideal* on a level with the *being-thought-of which characterizes the fictitious or the nonsensical*. The latter does not exist at all, and nothing can be properly predicated of it. . . . Ideal objects, on the other hand, exist genuinely. . . . we . . . have insight into certain categorial truths that relate to such ideal objects. If these truths hold, everything presupposed by their holding must have being. If I see the truth that 4 is an even number, that the predicate of my assertion actually pertains to the ideal object 4, then this object cannot be a mere fiction, a mere façon de parler, a mere nothing in reality. (1970 [1913]: sec. 8, pp. 352–53)

Yet, in the fifth *Investigation*, Husserl accords even "the being-thought-of which characterizes the fictitious" a mode of actuality—irrespective of the possibility or impossibility of fictitious objects and situations. The result is a peculiar actuality, a "mode of mindedness," by means of which Husserl reconceptualizes ideal, fictitious, and nonsensical objects as articulations of the order of the real:

> I have an idea of the god Jupiter; this means that I have a certain presentative experience, the presentation-of-the-god-Jupiter is realized in my consciousness. This intentional experience may be dismembered as one chooses in the descriptive analysis, but the god Jupiter naturally will not be found in it. The "immanent," "mental object" is not therefore part of the descriptive or real make-up . . . of the experience, it is in truth not really immanent or mental. But it also does not exist extramentally, it does not

exist at all. This does not prevent our-idea-of-the-god-Jupiter from being actual, a particular sort of experience or particular mode of minded-ness. . . . If, however, the intended object exists, nothing becomes phenom-enologically different. It makes no essential difference to an object pre-sented and given to consciousness whether it exists, or is fictitious, or is perhaps completely absurd. (Husserl 1970 [1913]: sec. 11, pp. 558–59)

4.4.2. Note that the last sentence of this passage invokes precisely those three ontological modalities—existence (*Sein*), subsistence (*Bestehung*), and extraex-istence (*Außersein*)—through which Meinong seeks to confer on every possible (and impossible) content of consciousness at least some measure of objectivity. In his 1904 essay "Über Gegenstandstheorie" 'On the Theory of Objects' (1971 [1904]), Meinong recapitulates what his student Ernst Mally famously formu-lated as "das Prinzip der Unabhängigkeit des Soseins vom Sein" 'the principle of the independence of being-so from being' (sec. 3, p. 490) and then remarks that

der Geltungsbereich dieses Prinzips erhellt am besten im Hinblick auf den Umstand, daß diesem Prinzipe nicht nur Gegenstände unterstehen, die eben faktisch nicht existieren, sondern auch solche, die nicht existieren können, weil sie unmöglich sind. Nicht nur der vielberufene goldene Berg ist von Gold, sondern auch das runde Viereck ist so gewiß rund als es viereckig ist. . . . Wer paradoxe Ausdrucksweise liebt, könnte also ganz wohl sagen: es gibt Gegenstände, von denen gilt, daß es dergleichen Ge-genstände nicht gibt. (491)

the scope of the validity of this principle becomes most evident in view of the circumstance that not only objects that in fact do not exist, but also such objects as could not possibly exist, are subject to the principle. Not only is the all-too-familiar golden mountain really made of gold, but also the round square is certainly just as round as it is four cornered. . . . Whoever loves paradoxical modes of expression could thus in all propriety say: there are objects of which it holds that these same objects do not exist.

The principle of independence suggests how object-theoretical realism repre-sents, in contradistinction to nominalist object theory, discourse that puts a premium on intentions and/or intensions. The principle highlights the con-tents of terms like *round square*—and also the contents of propositions or, as Meinong calls them, "objectives" (*Objektiven*) (1971 [1904]: sec. 4, pp. 492ff.) like "there are objects of which it holds that these same objects do not exist"—as opposed to the truth conditions by means of which the extensions of such expressions might be defined. Hence this remark of Meinong's: "Sein ist eben nicht die Voraussetzung, unter der das Erkennen gleichsam erst einen Angriffspunkt fände, sondern es ist selbst schon ein solcher Angriffspunkt. Ein eben so guter ist dann aber auch Nichtsein" 'Being is decidedly not the presupposition that must be adopted if knowing is to find, as it were, its point of attack, but rather is itself just such a point of attack. But in consequence one serving just as well would be that of nonbeing' (1971 [1904]: sec. 4, p. 494). As a "partisan of ontological tolerance" (Pavel 1986: 28), Meinong clearly resists the extensionality thesis. Meinong's, rather, is what might be called an intensionality thesis: that is, that to every intension corresponds an extension, no matter what empirical or even logical laws would have to be abrogated thereby. There are as many things in the universe as we can frame thoughts and/or utterances about—although some of those things do not exist in the narrow sense but rather subsist or extraexist.

In direct contrast to the later Brentano's efforts to dissipate immanent objects, then, for Meinong we can in principle never leave the domain of objectivity. As a result, thought itself merely ascends and descends along the static hierarchy of existent, subsistent, and extra-existent objects and their more or less complex determinations. The negation of an object or a state of affairs becomes the affirmation of that object or state of affairs at the next level of objectivity: the not-being of a red object, for example, becomes a higher-order object, specifiable as the being of the not-being of the red object. (For a fuller account of the so-called superiora and inferiora, see Meinong 1978 [1899]: 144ff.) But—as Kafka's representation of the Court suggests—never to be able to escape and never to be able to enter a given domain are in a sense two manifestations of one and the same problem. To die before the stupefying sameness of the Law, which narrowly prescribes the same "exact regulations for the interior dispositions of [all its] offices" (Kafka 1956 [1925]: 164), is no less fatal than deciding, as K. at first quite injudiciously decides, to impute an essential impropriety, a constitutive looseness, to the claims of the Court. Surely, in order to negotiate the intricate ontologies of the Law, we need a different theory of objects—a different kind of model for understanding what, and how, things mean.

5. The Structure of Kafkan Objects

Note that Arnold Heidsieck (1984, 1986, 1989) has already uncovered important links between Kafka's corpus and (some varieties of) the object theory inspired by Brentano's *Psychology*. Heidsieck points to the influence that Brentanian doctrine had "on Kafka during his formative years as a writer," arguing that object theory "left many traces in [Kafka's] mature fiction" (1986: 11; cf. Heidsieck 1989: 489). In 1902, at the Charles University in Prague, Kafka had attended Marty's lecture course on "Fundamentals of Descriptive Psychology," together with a course on "Philosophical Ethics" given by Meinong's student Christian von Ehrenfels. Further, Kafka had ties with Hugo Bergmann (cf. Hayman 1982: 22), another student of Marty's; Bergmann himself developed object-theoretical arguments in his study of the evidence yielded by introspection or "inner perception" (see Bergmann 1908, esp. secs. 5, 6, 10, 18; cf. Brentano 1930). There is also evidence that "from 1902 to 1905 . . . [Kafka attended some of] the bi-weekly gatherings of philosophy faculty and students who read papers and conducted discussions on Brentanian philosophy at the Café Louvre" in Prague (Heidsieck 1986: 12; cf. Waggenbach 1958: 174; Neesen 1972). On the basis of such evidence, Heidsieck argues mainly that Kafka's work was *influenced by* the object-theoretical discourse to which the writer was exposed at various points in his life.

Debatably, however, *Der Prozeß* also *participates in* contemporaneous discourse on objects. True, Brentano's *Psychology*, and particularly the philosopher's discussion of intentional objects, set the immediate precedent for those features of Kafka's narrative which tend to denaturalize, to place in question, the very idea of an object. Yet, after an initial survey of the structure of objects in *Der Prozeß*, we shall discover that Kafka's denaturalizations differ significantly from those of Brentano and, for that matter, those of the object-theoretical realists who argued against Brentano. Indeed, Kafka focuses not on objects but on objects-in-models, that is, entities, events, and states of affairs whose meaning depends on the provisional, emergent frames of reference in which they are situated. Although situating objects in frames of reference does not *exhaust* the meanings of those objects, such situatedness is a necessary condition for their having meaning.[20] Thus, Kafka's text suggests that the ultimate constituents of meaning, the atoms of sense, are not objects; the minimal units of significance, rather, are objects-in-frames-of-reference—or, more precisely, entities, events, and situations as interpreted from within what will be characterized below as model worlds (secs. 6 and 7).[21]

5.1. During K.'s first encounter with a representative of the Court at the beginning of the novel, one of K.'s warders wears "a closely fitting black suit furnished with all sorts of pleats, pockets, buckles, and buttons, as well as a belt, like a tourist's outfit, [which] in consequence looked eminently practical, though one could not quite tell what actual purpose it served" (Kafka 1956 [1925]: 1). The incommensurability between the form and the purpose of the warder's uniform reveals, in turn, what might be called the objective (i.e., *gegenständlich*) structure of its constituent entities, whose possible uses, possible meanings, cannot be exhausted by any one institution, any given set of official functions. In the frame of reference in which K. gives it a significance, or at least tries to give it a significance, the warder's uniform connotes something like eminent practicality; but, as the text emphasizes, the uniform means more than that. In principle it could always be situated in some other possible frame of reference; it could serve purposes of which K. does not happen to be cognizant.[22]

Analogously, when K. faces the Inspector in Fräulein Bürstner's room, the Inspector is "with both hands rearranging the few things [*Gegenstände*] that lay on the night table, a candle and a matchbox, a book and a pincushion, as if they were [*als seien es*] objects [*Gegenstände*] which he required for his interrogation" (Kafka 1956 [1925]: 10). One might point to the metafictional profile of these Kafkan objects, insofar as they can be construed as props in a game of make-believe embedded within another such game, that is, Kafka's fiction itself (cf. Walton 1990: 11–69). Beyond this, however, notice Kafka's use of an *as if* construction in this context. To anticipate my later discussion of the modal operators encoded in the grammar of Kafka's discourse (see sec. *6.3.3* below): the *as if* construction, together with the subjunctive grammatical mood (*seien*), confers doubtfulness, uncertainty, on the narrator's characterization of the Inspector and his props. Such grammatical features suggest a lack of commitment to the truth of the description at issue. More precisely, the narrative hedges on whether the objects are in fact items required by the Inspector during the interrogation; indeed, the text even hedges on whether the items *appear to the Inspector himself* as requisite objects or devices in this connection.

The doubtfulness encoded into Kafka's description derives, in turn, from a particular kind of object-theoretical argument: namely, the argument that not even an institution as powerful and as all encompassing as the Court can circumscribe every possible function, every conceivable meaning, of a candle, a matchbox, a book, or a pincushion. Rather, the text suggests that the Inspector's props should be construed as what Itamar Even-Zohar (1980) terms "realemes," "i.e., [as part of] *an aggregate of items governed by system relations*, which constitutes the way a culture can convey information about reality." Like the Inspector's props, realemes are "members of a structured system, which is the source of their existence and the principle governing their appearance in utterances [or propositions], i.e., a constraint on their insertability" (65–67). In Kafka, objects do not simply reduce to the functions and meanings that they accrue in different frames of reference; there is, furthermore, a constraint on the insertability of such realemes across alternative frames (cf. secs. 5.3ff.).

The polysemousness of the pleats, pockets, buckles, and buttons on the warder's uniform; the mock functionality of the objects that the Inspector manipulates and whose counterparts appear later on when K., now hopelessly distracted by his case, sits in his office at the Bank and "instead of working . . . twisted in his chair, idly rearranged the things [einige Gegenstände] lying on his writing-table, and then, without being aware of it, let his outstretched arm rest on the table"; even, perhaps, the haphazard construction of Titorelli's patchwork blanket (Kafka 1956 [1925]: 113, 144), fabricated from the most heterogeneous materials: these are the traits of the entities populating the world(s) of the novel, the items listed in Kafka's catalog of the real. What the text persistently emphasizes is that these items might possibly figure as different sorts of objects, realemes of a different order, if inserted into other systems of relations, subsumed under other institutions and norms. The point is that it is impossible in principle to know, exactly and exhaustively, just what these objects mean—to grasp all and only the meanings attaching to this or that entity in Kafka's universe.

5.2. Yet that is not all there is to Kafkan objects. Another noteworthy feature of the narrative is a sporadic overaccumulation of things, an occasional hyperdensity of objects, that contrasts markedly with K's usual environs, in which emptiness, insufficiency, even desolation predominates.[23] For example, when the warders commandeer and possibly rearrange Frau Grubach's living room at the opening of the novel, the text reads: "villeicht war in diesem mit Möbeln, Decken, Porzellan und Photographieren überfüllten Zimmer heute ein wenig mehr Raum als sonst, man erkannte das nicht gleich" 'in this room, which was overcrowded with furniture, rugs, china and photographs, there was perhaps a little more space today than usual, [although] one did not perceive that immediately' (Kafka 1986 [1925]: 8). Such clutter may have Meinongian implications; in effect, it offsets the object-theoretical parsimoniousness that we discovered in the later Brentano. Then, too, even though Kafka began composing Der Prozeß in 1914, aspects of the novel could perhaps be interpreted as anticipatory illuminations of "die neue Sachlichkeit" 'the new objectivity' documented by John Willett in The New Sobriety (1978). A constructivist, antiexpressionist aesthetic movement grounded in "the sober, functional, technologically conscious, socially-orientated mid-European culture" of the 1920s (Willett 1978:

98), the new objectivity developed as part of an emergent "concern with the object, the 'Veshch' or 'Gegenstand,' and . . . objective art. . . . By definition subjectivity, the personal viewpoint, was [in this objectivist aesthetic] very largely ruled out," leaving little "room . . . for the human being as a theme for art" (105).[24] Frau Grubach's overcrowded living room likewise delimits the space, the very possibility, of "the personal viewpoint." Here, as in the new objectivity, any such viewpoint would seem to be merely a function of the position or disposition of the objects being viewed.

More than this, however, the structure of the room is such that, in conducting an inventory of its constituent entities ("Möbeln, Decken, Porzellan und Photographieren"), Josef K. fails to configure those objects into, to recognize them as part of, a larger (meaningful) situation. K. grasps the constituents but not the *Gestalt* of Frau Grubach's room; he sees the world atomically, not molecularly. Similarly, when Fräulein Montag moves her things into Fräulein Bürstner's room, "She seemed to be always forgetting some article of underwear or a scrap of drapery or a book that necessitated a special journey to carry it into the new apartment" (Kafka 1956 [1925]: 75). Fräulein Montag's objects, although many, again cannot be configured into a whole. To invoke the language of Husserl's third *Logical Investigation,* her and Frau Grubach's belongings constitute unstructured aggregates, mere collocations, as opposed to founded wholes. Here, it seems, the meaning of a room is less than the meaning of the sum of its constituent objects. Meaning is additive and incremental, not cumulative. In this sense, what I have called the internal focalization of the narrative (sec. 2), which is told from Josef K.'s partial and limited perspective, can be viewed not only as a stylistic choice but also as the formal corollary of an ontological axiom—or, rather, as the corollary of an assumption that statements about objects of all sorts are subject to radical indeterminacies of meaning.

5.3. I shall return to this latter assumption and its formal corollaries below (cf. secs. *5.4* and *6.3ff.*). But, first, recall Kafka's description of Fräulein Montag in particular. Hers is an attempt to transport objects across frames of reference; but, significantly, she never quite finishes. Like the ostensibly innocuous detail of Fräulein Bürstner's slip—an item left hanging carelessly on a window latch during K.'s interrogation by the Inspector (Kafka 1956 [1925]: 10) and the focus of K.'s obsessive interest as time goes on (27, 132)—the objective traces of Fräulein Montag's move constitute fragments of a real that exists, of a resistant reality. These are the fugitive elements of an environment not wholly amenable to interpretation; in the face of such surroundings, K. finds himself fetishizing this or that world fragment as significant. Objects, for K., mark a sudden cathexis of meaning, a powerful affect of intension, whereby the odd scrap and article becomes all that really matters. Yet in other frames of reference, as K. painfully discovers, those fragments of the world which he judges to be important are deemed trivial, and vice versa.

We may therefore be able to establish parallels between Kafka's objects and Michael Thompson's (1979) ingenious "rubbish theory." Drawing on René Thom's catastrophe theory, Thompson develops an explanatory model for sudden "transfers" of once transient objects across the threshold of value (via rubbish) into durability. Where such transfers happen mark sites of confrontation between worldviews (87ff.); the transfers correspond to different conceptions of rubbish, of where to draw the line between meaningful versus meaningless objects. In this connection, note that the scene in which K. witnesses the warders being whipped for insubordination occurs in a closet or junk room (*Rumpelkammer*) at the Bank. The *Rumpelkammer* is, in more ways than one, a site of confrontation, marked by the clash of competing worldviews. The text reads: "It was, as [K.] had correctly assumed, a lumber-room. Bundles of useless old papers and empty earthenware ink bottles lay in a tumbled heap behind the threshold" (Kafka 1956 [1925]: 83). Thus, although the scene suggests contact or at least contiguity between the Court and the Bank, it is significant that the Court can conduct its business only in the rubbish room of the Bank. The props of the Law constitute the rubbish of the Bank; and the converse proposition also holds, as is suggested by K.'s ever more serious dereliction of duties at the Bank as the novel proceeds. Likewise, in proportion as he increases his communication (*Verkehr:* literally, "intercourse") with the Court, Titorelli loses his "verve" as an artist, his "künstlerische Schwung" (Kafka 1986 [1925]: 130).

Kafka also uses the washerwoman's living room to stage the conflict between alternative, properly antagonistic, frames of reference—this time, the conflict between frames corresponding to the public and the private domains. Not only is the relation of the washerwoman's room to the Examining Magistrate's offices exactly symmetrical with the relation of Frau Grubach's object-ridden room to the place of K.'s arrest; what is more, although the living room contains only a washtub when the Court is in session, when the Court is not in session and no competing and more powerful worldview relegates the contents of the room to the category of rubbish, the washerwoman's is "ein völlig eingerichtetes Wohnzimmer" 'a fully furnished living room' (Kafka 1986 [1925]: 46). In this room, as in the rubbish room at the Bank, competing frames of reference impute different meanings, strictly irreconcilable functions to the objects at hand (cf. Thompson 1979: 90). More precisely, what count as extraneous and useless objects in one setting are, from another perspective, woven into the very fabric of life.

5.4. As might be expected, therefore, the structure of Kafkan objects displays itself especially prominently in those sections of the narrative where K. finds himself traveling *between* the frames of reference bound up with various institutions—notably, the Bank and the Court. At such moments K. traverses an indeterminate space; the functions and meanings of objects are manifestly underdetermined by the worldviews impinging on those objects from every direction, but now only in a highly mediated fashion, as if from a great distance. In one such intermediary space, in which K. makes his way toward the interrogation to be conducted by the Examining Magistrate (cf. secs. 6.3ff.), he sees

> Near him a barefooted man [who] was sitting on a crate reading a newspaper. Two boys see-sawed on a handcart. A sickly young girl stood at a pump in a dressing-jacket and gazed at K. as the water poured into her can. In one corner of the courtyard a line had been stretched between two windows, where washing was already being hung up to dry. A man stood below and superintended the work with a couple of shouts. (Kafka 1956 [1925]: 35; translation modified)

This remarkable passage situates a manifold of objects against a backdrop of utter desolation. But, furthermore, the passage registers an ongoing transposition of objects across alternative frames of reference, different systems of use. Here, a crate functions as a chair; a handcart serves as a seesaw; a dressing jacket finds use as work clothes. Kafka thus denaturalizes objects by broadening; even distending, the cultural repertoires by virtue of which they function as realemes (Even-Zohar 1980: 66). It is as if, no longer anchored in official frames of reference, objects have begun to migrate across functional categories, mobile and nomadic fragments of a slowly disintegrating world.

Even more remarkable, perhaps, is another, later scene that also occurs in the space separating Court and Bank. In the passage at issue, the text represents constraints on realeme insertability—in other words, the impossibility of exhaustively characterizing the potential meanings of a thing—by figuring gaps in the very structure of the real. Acting on the advice of the manufacturer, K. leaves his office at the Bank in attempts to secure Titorelli, the official portrait painter for the Court, as an ally. Along the way K. discovers that Titorelli lives in a poor neighborhood with darkened houses, the streets filled with sludge oozing about slowly on the top of the melting snow. In the tenement where the painter lived only one wing of the great double door stood open, but beneath the other wing the wall had been breached: and out of the resulting cavity [*Lücke*] issued, just as K. approached, a yellow, steaming fluid, from which in turn some rats fled into the nearby canal.[25] At the foot of the stairs a small child lay prone on the ground and cried. But one could barely hear its cries on account of the deafening noise that came from the tinsmith's shop across the way. The door of this workshop was open, and three apprentices stood in a semi-circle around some piece of work [*Werkstück*] on which they beat with their hammers. . . . K. cast upon all this only a fleeting glance. (Kafka 1956 [1925]: 141; translation modified)

Deep in the ghettos of Prague, where an abandoned child, one object among many, is dwarfed by an entire panorama of filth and disrepair, we find a lattice-work of breaches, openings, voids. These spaces—the open door of the noisy workshop and the semicircle formed by the apprentices; the dirty tenement's partially blocked entrance; and the repulsive, micturating breach in the wall—are essentially prohibitive, like the paradoxically impenetrable entrances to the Law. Such voids mark the limits of the intelligible; more precisely, they signal the essential incompleteness[26] of frames of reference. The text suggests the impossibility of listing all the intensional properties that might accrue to a thing, given the (in principle infinite) number of perspectives that we might adopt on it, the indefinitely many frames that might embed it. Kafka's gaps thus represent not the absence of meaning but rather the oversaturation of the world by possibilities for meaning.

5.5. In order to start substantiating these last remarks, I must reformulate the argument subtending my analysis of Kafkan objects—an argument presented in somewhat piecemeal fashion over the course of previous sections. At issue are the semantic properties of Kafka's objects and the relation of those semantic properties to classical object theory, on the one hand, and to current models for understanding meaning and reference, on the other hand. As we have seen, Kafka's text figures at once the incompleteness, the innumerability, and, to adapt an idea of Quine's (1960: 26–79; cf. sec. **0.3.2** above), the only indeterminate translatability of the frames of reference embedding objects. Where frames collide, we find either oversupply or vacuum, either gluts of objectivity or voids in the space of the real, either junk or dearth. These ontological pressure points, as it were, reveal the contours of Kafka's (narrative) semantics. Specifically, while making the meanings of objects model dependent, the text also suggests that there are indefinitely many different sorts of model dependency—as many sorts, in fact, as there are models. For Kafka, objects are only in part what we choose to make of them; beyond this, objects are what others have chosen and might yet choose to make of them. The result is not only that, as the Priest puts it, "The correct interpretation of a thing and misunderstanding of the same thing do not completely exclude one another" (Kafka 1986 [1925]: 185). Moreover, *Der Prozeß* figures forth a semantics that, although it gives scope to both intensions and extensions, supports neither the extensionality thesis (sec. *4.3*) nor the intensionality thesis (sec. *4.4.2*)—at least in their classical forms.

Given that objects are multiply and simultaneously insertible, as realemes, within multiple frames of reference, we are barred from Meinong's plenum of intensional contents. Such contents, rather, are predicated on particular frames; they have the character that they do because of the specific frames in which they are situated, not because every possible thought content actualizes itself in a single, although incalculably large, domain of existent, subsistent, and extra-existent entities, states, and events. And there can be no synoptic survey of all possible frames. The very same considerations, however, work against object-theoretical parsimony as well: in shifting from talk about objects to objects-in-frames-of-reference, we relax the later Brentano's requirements for an uncluttered universe, an ontology restricted to nonimmanent objects. Such requirements work against the model dependency of meaning; in effect, they disallow multiple modes of realeme insertability. In Kafkan terms, the object-theoretical nominalist is doomed to a fate like K.'s, overextending the scope of the fictive, the irreal, in attempts to reduce the complexity of what is. By contrast, the object-theoretical realist is apt to get lost in the corridors of the Court, much like the pettifogging lawyers and their obsequious clients; these characters come to ascribe *too much* meaning to statutes, institutions, and related abstract objects. Kafka's suggestion is not that we try to linearize the labyrinth of the Law, nor that we submit wholly to its logic, but that we recontextualize the Court itself as one institution among many, one frame of reference among multiple available and interacting frames.

5.6. As we shall now go on to explore, however, making the difficult and sometimes disorienting transition from objects to objects-in-models is not enough to guarantee a successful semantics; that transition is only a first step toward a viable theory of what and how things mean. Caught in a multiplicity of models, and unable to rank them according to importance or priority, Josef K. dies like a dog ("Wie ein Hund!") (Kafka 1986 [1925]: 194) at the hands of his Court-appointed executioners. K.'s experiences teach us that, in order to distinguish situations true in some possible world(s) from situations presumed to be true in the world(s) we call our own, we cannot remain equally committed to any and all available frames of reference. Rather, we must commit ourselves to a particular model world anchored in a particular set of contextual coordinates. Thus, we have to modify as follows the formulation included in section *5.0:* the minimal units of sense are not objects-in-frames-of-reference but rather objects-in-frames-of-reference-in-contexts. Put otherwise, meaning is a function of model worlds vis-à-vis other, demonstrably only possible worlds.

Note that, in discussing the interdependencies of meaning and model worlds in *Der Prozeß,* we shall shift from an object-theoretical to a predominantly model-theoretic (or "possible worlds") vocabulary. As already suggested (secs. *3* and *4*), however, model theory and object theory are at once historically and conceptually interlinked. The next two sections do not ground themselves explicitly in the object-theoretical arguments previously discussed; implicitly, however, the following sections sketch a continuum leading from object theory to model theory—from intentional objects to intensional contents (cf., e.g., sec. *6.3.1*). Further, by focusing more particularly on the grammatical features of Kafka's discourse than I have up to now, I can more fully integrate into my genealogy of universal grammar and narrative form ideas of a jointly object-theoretical and model-theoretic provenance.

6. Meaning, Model-Theoretic Semantics, and Model Worlds

As already indicated in section *2.1,* in model-theoretic schemes the meaning or intension of a term or proposition—as opposed to the reference, denotation, or extension of that term or proposition—can be described as a function, in the strict sense.[27] Specifically, meaning is a function from some possible world to the truth conditions defining the world stipulated to be actual for the purposes of a given (semantic) analysis. That stipulated frame of reference has been characterized both as an "indexical" (Lewis 1973; cf. Frawley 1992: 387–88) and as a "reference world," that is, as a world "for which [a given expression, proposition, or] text claims facts" (Ryan 1991: vii; cf. Herman 1994a: n. 6). Here the stipulated frames will be called *model worlds.* This term derives, in part, from the account of model sets given by Jaakko Hintikka (1969) and is meant to carry somewhat less actualist connotations than *reference world.* Or, rather, the term is meant to suggest how, model theoretically speaking, frames of reference function as (emergent) models, constructs, systems of postulates, on the basis of which we set about fixing the sense—and reference—of linguistic expressions. I return to this last point in section 7.

A model world, then, is a world assumed or stipulated to be a frame of reference vis-à-vis other possible worlds—worlds that, relative to the stipulated model world, remain possible in the strict sense. To cite Green's (1989) formulation, which is based in turn on Montague's (1974) formal semantics: in model theory "the sense of an expression is supposed to determine its reference, and the goal of the intensional logic that makes explicit the mechanism by which this can happen is to determine the possible sorts of functions from possible *indices* (coordinations of worlds, times, speakers, etc.) to their *extensions* or *denotations* (the entities or sets of entities denoted by an expression at an index" (42). Thus, if terms and propositions can mean different things to different people at different times or different things to the same person at different times, model theoretically we can account for this as follows: whenever they are used, and in whatever context, the terms and propositions pick out (denote) entities and states of affairs that obtain, that is, have positive truth-value, in some possible world. The congruence or fit, as it were, of any number of possible worlds with an adopted frame of reference, a (model) world deemed actual, can be more or less exact, more or less convenient, and more or less elegant.

6.1. On a first approach (see sec. 7.2 below), we can formalize the model-theoretic conception of meaning thus:

$$F_{int}(x'_{W_p}) = x_{W_a}.$$

Or, to invoke terms that require fuller characterization in what follows, a meaning (or intensional function) F_{int}, operating on an argument x', which designates a object, situation, or event obtaining in some possible world W_p, defines the truth-value of propositions about x' in terms of the truth conditions holding for propositions about the object, situation, or event x in world W_a. W_a is thus the frame of reference stipulated as the actual or, better, the model world required for F_{int} to assign any meaning to x' at all. The point is that, once we adopt W_a as our model world or frame of reference, what we *mean* by statements about x is a function that projects the (indeterminately large) domain of truth-values for statements about x' in W_1, W_2, W_3, . . . , W_n into the more narrowly delimited range of truth values for statements about x in W_a.

For example, substitute for the variable x' the argument *red*. Assume that across possible worlds W_1, W_2, and W_3, respectively, the applications of the term *red* vary quite widely. Suppose that *red* covers everything from a certain temperature (in world W_1), to a certain location (in world W_2), to light waves with a certain frequency, amplitude, etc. (in world W_3). Assume now that the truth conditions defining our stipulated frame of reference or model world are such that the truth-values of the propositions "Red is a temperature corresponding to sixty-five degrees on the fahrenheit scale" and "Red is a town in northernmost Lithuania" are 0 (or false) in each case. We conclude that the meanings of the term *red* (x') in worlds W_1 and W_2, respectively, cannot be transferred to, superimposed on, the meaning of *red* (x) in our stipulated frame of reference or model world W_a, which happens to correspond (at least in this respect) to possible world W_3. *Red* in world W_a (or W_3) simply does not mean what it does in worlds W_1 and W_2.

6.1.1. More generally, we can say that intensions are determined by—their truth-values must be defined on the basis of—the model world to which they are a function from some possible world or another. Conversely, however, it is only by means of a (very large) set of intensional functions that one would be able to characterize something like a model world, a frame of reference, in the first place. If it were possible for our beliefs to be shattered instantaneously and in toto, perhaps we should bear the full brunt of the otherwise not noticeably vicious circle linking meanings with model worlds, for we should then have to pull ourselves up by our ontologico-epistemological bootstraps, attempting to reconstruct a frame of reference out of meanings that, however, presuppose such a frame from the start.

In fact, appeal to the foregoing dilemma might support the argument that, at least to some extent, changes of taste and opinion, and revisions of (scientific and other) theories, occur not all at once and apocalyptically but rather gradually and in a manner that perpetuates certain aspects of the abandoned frame of reference in the one newly adopted. (For arguments to the contrary, however, see Kuhn 1989, among others.) To be sure, within a structure of beliefs, the meaning of a term or proposition will denote an entity or state of affairs true only in some possible world W', rather than a model world W_a, as soon as the term (e.g., *phlogiston, ether*) or proposition (e.g., "The moon is unreachable by humans") starts to conflict too obviously with that vastly large set of other terms and propositions whose truth-values collectively define W_a. But this vastly large set can itself be disactualized[28]—projected *as a whole* into the domain of possibility—only were a complete and completely other world already in place to fill the vacuum of belief left in the wake of the departing world.

We shall find ourselves increasingly occupied with the question of vanishing worlds, and vacuums of belief, when we return to the model worlds connected with Kafka's text. Meanwhile, however, we should remember that struggles for the status of actuality more often take place at the peripheries than at the center of belief structures.[29] Or, at least, such struggles often confine themselves to the margins until such time as (if ever) the set of peripheral beliefs forced by new discoveries or better interpretations into the domain of the merely possible reaches a point at which it is larger than the set of (unthreatened) nonperipheral beliefs. For it is only on the perhaps dubious basis of these latter beliefs—themselves describable as dispositions, prejudices, assumptions, or even superstitions (Bartsch 1987: 25ff.; Quine 1960: 125ff.)—that we can presume to doubt the beliefs that may under certain circumstances appear relatively peripheral by contrast.

6.1.2. In what follows, I reassess what I have thus far divided up too simplistically into peripheral and nonperipheral beliefs. (Since, for my purposes, I need not consider the different semantic properties attaching to different species of propositional attitudes, let the term *belief* here be coextensive with the more general terms *meaning* and *intension*. Compare, however, Herman 1994a.) The first part of the discussion that follows centers on an example that approaches the limit case of indeterminacy with respect to so-called peripheral beliefs. This sort of semantic indeterminacy displays as its hallmark a special form of triviality. Here, the meaning of a term or proposition can be indeterminate—that is, its truth-values can vary—across a wide range of possible worlds that nonetheless remain (mutatis mutandis) identical except with respect to the single intensional variable at issue. According to traditional ontological taxonomies, this first form of semantic indeterminacy would be equivalent to the category *accident* (with respect to a particular frame of reference, a particular model world). By contrast, culled from *Der Prozeß*, the second class of examples represents a form of semantic indeterminacy that bears on what traditional schemes for ontology construed as *essences* (again, with respect to a particular model world).

More precisely, Kafka's text suggests that if an intension or meaning m is nonperipheral in some frame of reference, and if furthermore m varies across possible worlds $W_1, \ldots, W_n$, then an entire chain of associated intensions—an intensional chain that is at the limit infinite—will as a result also acquire different truth-values across $W_1, \ldots, W_n$. Hence, in traveling from world to world, as it were, we should have to change frames of reference, adopt different model worlds, in each case. To this extent, indeterminacy with respect to m yields not just an indefinitely extended range of possible worlds, parasitical on some primary ontological instance, some frame of reference associated with a more or less perdurable model world, but rather an indeterminate number of model worlds—an indefinite multiplication of frames of reference as such. Yet we should concede beforehand that no example imaginable will reflect either the limit case of pure accidentality (of purely isolated intensional variables) or the limit case of pure essence (of a totally concatenated, worldwide variability of meaning). An example of the former sort of indeterminacy would be too trivial for us to notice even in principle. An example of the latter sort of indeterminacy would be too stupendous for us to process; that is, since every intension would be premised on its variability in relation to every other one, it would be impossible to establish even a provisional model world vis-à-vis the now totally indeterminate configuration of meanings. We would instead become, perhaps to an even greater extent than Kafka's Josef K., between-worlds creatures, faced with series of intensional magnitudes that could not be organized into a structure, a world, at all. (Here, however, we should not forget that Deleuze and Guattari 1986 [1975] call such series "assemblages" and valorize them in the name of the non- or rather anti-model worlds structured according to a strictly schizophrenic logic.)

6.2. Taking the two classes of indeterminacy in order, suppose, first, that we have a set of propositions describing states of affairs that obtain in possible worlds $W_1, \ldots, W_n$. Suppose too that these states of affairs have characteristics that are different but not obviously or rather interestingly inconsistent across the various possible worlds in which they obtain. The problem is then how to assess the truth conditions for propositions about an indefinitely large domain of different but not obviously incompatible possible states of affairs and so determine which states of affairs can be designated as actual with respect to a certain frame of reference.

Specifically, consider a state of affairs that varies as follows across an indeterminately large set of alternative possible worlds. Given that $n = 1,000,000$, and given a set of possible worlds $W_1, \ldots, W_x$, we define the relation between worlds such that if in W_1 Mr. Jones has n hairs on his head, in W_2 Mr. Jones has $n + 1$ hairs on his head, in W_3 Mr. Jones has $n + 2$ hairs on his head, and so on. Generally, in W_x Mr. Jones has $n + (x - 1)$ hairs on his head. In this case, further, given a proposition like

(P) Mr. Jones's head has more hair on it than Mr. Smith's,

where Mr. Smith has 1,000,002 hairs on his head, (P) is false except where $W_x >$ W_3. Although the proposition in question is strictly speaking false in W_2, however, it is by no means obviously or rather interestingly false, other things being equal. Provided that we make the simplifying assumption that $W_1, \ldots, W_x$ are identical except for the one variable feature n, it would be virtually impossible to disconfirm that (P) does in fact have a positive truth-value in W_2. Nor would (P) be obviously true across any number of possible worlds, where $W_x > W_4$, until we reached perhaps W_{1001}, assuming that it takes maybe a thousand hairs to constitute one barely visible tuft.

We could therefore argue that—in effect, and presupposing the usual *pragmatic* constraints (see sec. 7 below)—the truth-values for (P) are indeterminate where $W_x < W_{1001}$. Assuming that we remain constituted (perceptually, e.g.) *as* human beings across $W_4, \ldots, W_n$, only where $W_x > W_{1001}$ does (P) become interesting enough for (P) to be given a meaning or determinate truth-value—relative to all but a very small and (in the technical sense) marked subset of frames of reference.[30] In the frames of reference in which we are by and large constrained to function—the worlds in which we must gather meanings that count—we are after all subject to quite distinct perceptual, temporal, and other limitations. More loosely, we do not have time to go around counting people's hairs unless perhaps we are brilliant microscopists gone haywire.

6.3. For illustrations of a more interesting because more radical kind of semantic indeterminacy, we can return to an analysis of narrative form in Kafka's *Der Prozeß*. What sets the Kafkan examples apart from the previous sort of indeterminacy can be described as follows. The novel represents objects, events, and states of affairs that, although perhaps not strictly (or logically) incompatible with one another, are nevertheless obviously and interestingly different across the various possible worlds that fall within the scope of the narrative discourse. We are therefore concerned, in Kafka, with species of nonperipheral semantic indeterminacy. In this connection, I should like to focus attention on the scene in which K. undergoes his first and, as it turns out, last interrogation by the Examining Magistrate. As this scene shows, even when a set of propositions *can* be termed interesting in relation to a particular frame of reference—even when one's very fate hinges on the truth-value assigned to this or that statement about the world—the propositions in question may resist ready assessment of their truth-values across any number of possible worlds. To put the same point another way, Kafka's text works against any rigid demarcation of possible from model worlds, in a way that helps us reflect on the conditions and limits of semantic theory itself.

6.3.1. In the scene at issue, the Examining Magistrate and some courtroom auditors, the latter divided (ostensibly) into Right and Left "parties" (*Partein*), respond ambiguously to the plaintiff, Josef K. In turn, facing unknown charges amid highly complex legal codes and jurisprudential procedures, K. speaks out against the vagaries of the court system that he has all too quickly learned to despise (Kafka 1986 [1925]: 37–45; Kafka 1956 [1925]: 37–48). Throughout the scene, the text persistently poses, but never completely resolves, this question: What, precisely, is the *meaning* of the Magistrate's and the auditors' response to K.'s often quite heated diatribe? Arguably, the response to K., as represented in the world(s) of the novel, has no readily determinable significance. As we shall see, the (nontrivial) semantic indeterminacy produced in this connection can be redescribed as an unchecked proliferation of model worlds. The text generates multiply emergent frames of reference with covariant sets of truth conditions;[31] and into this matrix of truth conditions we, along with K., are compelled to project the intensional variables—the objects, situations and events—whose meaning we never fully comprehend but that we cannot stop trying to interpret, on pain of an ignominious death.

Thus, when K. snatches from the Magistrate's hand what seems to him to be an important notebook, the text reads: "It could only be a sign of deep humiliation, *or must at least be interpreted as such,* that the Examining Magistrate now took up the notebook where it had fallen on the table, tried to put it to rights again, and made as if to read in it once more" (Kafka 1956 [1925]: 41–42; translation modified, my emphasis). Here, Kafka's account of the Magistrate's actions unfolds by reducing the explanatory scope of that very account. K.'s interpretation of the event is in part an interpretation of the constraints placed on interpretations in general; K.'s assessment follows not with the inevitability of truth but only insofar as certain conclusions can be drawn from a set of stipulated or—hence Kafka's "must" (*mußte*)—nonperipheral meanings. So, when K. struggles to discern whether the Magistrate is making signs to the audience in order to orchestrate their response to his testimony, we find the following construction: "[K.] glaubte er zu bermerken" 'K. believed that he observed' (Kafka 1986 [1925]: 42) the Magistrate to be making such signs. The text hedges on the degree to which any given observation, let alone any inference based on that observation (see sec. *3.1* above), is corrigible. By the same token, the narrative evolves by reminding us of its own limitations; the discourse (*sjužet*) signals that it is merely making a *bid* to capture and (re)present the objects, events, and situations constituting the story (*fabula*).[32]

In thus working to erode the border between model worlds and possible worlds, the text resorts to a variety of grammatical devices functioning as evidentials (Chafe and Nichols 1986); or, rather, the novel incorporates modal operators with jointly epistemic and alethic functions.[33] Collectively, these operators help virtualize states of affairs on whose actuality, however, K., for better or worse reasons, has come to presume. Kafka's narrative form, as we might also put it, scrambles the instructions for assigning modal status to a given object, event, or situation found in the narrative itself. I now go on to examine several such scrambling devices and in particular the way they root themselves in the grammatical structures of the narrative discourse. At issue are modal operators encoded through a variety of grammatical features, including the verb *to seem* (*scheinen*); *as if* constructions, in tandem with subjunctive verbal moods; rhetorical questions; and the disjunctive particle *or*. These are not the only formal features helping disactualize Josef K.'s model world(s), but a more comprehensive study will have to be reserved for another place.

6.3.2. Toward the end of K.'s impassioned speech and just after K. bangs his fist on the table for emphasis, we read:

> Immediately there was silence, so completely did K. already dominate the meeting. No one shouted in confusion as at the beginning, nor did anyone clap with approval any longer; rather, people seemed [*schien*] already convinced or about to be convinced [by K.'s speech]. (Kafka 1956 [1925]: 45; translation modified)

This passage yields at least a minimal characterization of the narrated events. To paraphrase: in its impassive behavior the audience fails either to protest or to support K.'s self-defense. Note, however, Kafka's use of the verb *seemed* in this context. *Seemed* here functions both alethically (as a modal operator encoding possibility vs. actuality) and epistemically (as a modal operator encoding doubt vs. certainty). The scope of this dual operator covers not the what (the lack of both protest and support) but rather the why, the meaning, of the narrated events (whether the audience's impassiveness means that they have been or are about to be convinced, or not). Thus, *seemed* makes explicit that K.'s is in fact a model world: things at most *seem to K.* to mean in such and such a way; and the primacy of K.'s quite tentative model world over other (available, possible) interpretive systems, far from being guaranteed de jure, has a merely de facto primacy over other such model worlds, a primacy that begins to be impugned, as we shall see, over the course of its very construction in the text.

6.3.3. Now contrast the form of the narrative when, a little later on in the scene, the old men in the courtroom begin pressing up against K. and clutching at him in response to the disturbance caused by the washerwoman's shriek. Here the text omits *seemed* as a marker of evidentiality, a modal operator; but other grammatical features of the passage yield analogous effects:

> K. no longer gave any thought to [the man fondling the washerwoman in
> the courtroom]: to him it was as though [*ihm war, als werde*] his freedom
> were being restricted, as though he were in all gravity being arrested, and
> he sprang down, heedlessly, from the podium. (Kafka 1986 [1925]: 44)

This passage firmly anchors the ostensible arrest in K.'s model world: the *as though* construction supports (at most) the inference that it is "to him"—that is, within K.'s markedly limited frame of reference—that what the old men do has the appearance of an arrest. Furthermore, the use of a subjunctive verbal mood (*werde*) grammatically encodes "a judgment of relative factuality" (Frawley 1992: 387) into the narrative discourse; by means of the subjunctive mood, the discourse signals a lack of commitment to the truth of the proposition concerning the restriction of K.'s freedom. To put it the other way around, the discourse (indirectly) asserts the nonactuality of K.'s arrest by the old men.

To this extent, the scope of the semantic indeterminacy set into play by the passage covers not just the why, the meaning of the narrated events, but also the what, the very nature of those events. Before, the problem presented by the silent audience was not that we could not discern what the audience was doing but rather that we (and K.) could find no compelling reason for placing this or that interpretation, as opposed to any number of other interpretations, on what the audience was doing. By contrast, the problem presented by the old men is that we cannot discern just what it is that they are doing, let alone place more or less cogent interpretations on why they would be doing that. In consequence, over the course of the description the model world that K. inhabits, or at least tries to inhabit, becomes as it were flattened out, modally dedifferentiated, ranged alongside other possible model worlds. Such multiple model worlds can no longer be separated from other possible (nonmodel) worlds subtending the description—that is, worlds with no stipulated actuality vis-à-vis still other possible states of affairs. In all these possible systems or worlds, the inscrutable events of the narrated might, in strictly indeterminate fashion, figure equally importantly but with wholly different kinds of importance. Thus, Kafka's narrative unravels into discourse about sets of unbounded possibilities at the level of the story.

6.3.4. Indeed, when the text poses a series of rhetorical questions concerning the nature and significance of the story elements, the model world subtending the narrative discourse becomes virtualized, assimilated to other possible frames of reference, before K.'s (and the reader's) very eyes. Notice that the passage embedding the questions can be construed as an instance of what

Dorrit Cohn (1978: 11–12, 21–57) would call "psycho-narration"; that is, the passage presents a character's state(s) of mind through the mediation of a narrator's discourse, situating us at once inside and outside K.'s model world and thus further decentering the modal structure of an already decentered narrative universe (Ryan 1991: 109–23; Derrida 1978b [1966]):

> Had [K.] judged the people [in the courtroom] correctly? Had he credited his speech with too much of an effect on them? Had they been putting up some pretense as long as he was speaking and then, when he came to the end of his argumentation, had they had their fill of that pretense? (Kafka 1986 [1925]: 44–45)

It is by no means accidental that Kafka's text broaches questions about the power or efficacy of *language*—its ability to describe, interpret, conclude, convince, or intimidate—with respect to K.'s audience. Just as the questions themselves bear on the power of illocutionary acts both to represent and to create states of affairs in any number of possible worlds, any number of hypothetical scenarios, the narrative discourse embedding *these very illocutionary acts* affixes a question mark to each element of the story that we no longer know to have been told at all. We therefore witness a post hoc interrogation and virtualization of the story by the discourse. Such is the (metasemantic) trajectory from which Kafka's narrative never fails to deviate, in all its self-corrosive exactitude.

6.3.5. Use of the disjunctive particle *or* in the following passage introduces (or at least formally marks) what is perhaps an even more compelling instance of nonperipheral semantic indeterminacy in Kafka's text.[34] Immediately after K. accuses the Magistrate of making secret signs to the audience of the proceedings, the text reads:

> Whether out of embarrassment or impatience, the Magistrate fidgeted in his chair. The man behind him, with whom [the Magistrate] had been talking, leaned over to him again, either to encourage him in general or to give him some special word of advice. (Kafka 1956 [1925]: 44; translation modified)

Disjunction, arguably, is the rhetorical figure (or logical symbol) that typifies Kafka's self-virtualizing narrative discourse. Split between the two segments of each disjunction, K. has no basis for choosing among alternative possibilities. According to the very logic (and ontology) of the narrative discourse, he cannot differentiate between what could be either real embarrassment or else stern impatience, either innocuous encouragement or else vicious insinuation.

More precisely, since he is unable even to stipulate a model world for himself, K. loses the ability to partition his surroundings into the actual and the virtual; he cannot distinguish between propositions true of some possible world and propositions true of the world he postulates as his own. The narrative discourse thus acquires unusual semantic properties; in particular, meanings can no longer be construed as intensional functions from objects, events, and situations obtaining in possible worlds to the truth conditions of the (model) world assumed to be actual. Instead, meanings index undecidably virtual and/or actual story elements to their equally indeterminate counterparts across an indefinite range of possible worlds. Across W_1, W_2, . . . , W_n, the meanings of objects, states, and events differ so crucially that K. *must* decide between them or else die. But, insofar as each such world devolves into a matrix of possibilities, a welter of the (in)actual, there can be no model world to support judgments of the sort K. nevertheless finds himself constantly compelled to make.

To be sure, K. can hypothesize alternative sets of truth conditions and so glimpse the structure of innumerably many model worlds. Possibly, the Magistrate is really embarrassed, and thus the set of possibilities x follows in turn; but possibly, too, the Magistrate is furiously impatient, and thus the set of possibilities x' follows. Possibly, the Magistrate's adviser has it out for K., and thus the set of possibilities y follows in turn; but possibly, too, the Magistrate's adviser is discussing some matter completely unrelated to K.'s case, and thus the set of possibilities y' follows. Ad infinitum. Yet K. cannot find a reason, or stipulate a criterion, for choosing any of these belief systems, any of these model worlds, over any of the others. Hence, K.'s entire experience ironically confirms Rudolf Carnap's (1952 [1950]) thesis that relations between possible language systems cannot be specified in cognitive, but only in noncognitive, terms. Like meaning's virtual double, its troubled and flickering ghost, K. inhabits the irrational space between always only possible worlds.

7. Model Worlds and Metasemantics

As we have seen, Josef K. finds himself paralyzed between indefinitely many meanings and the contours of his world blurred by intersecting frames of reference; K. haunts, like some doubly irreal figment, some hyperfictional fiction, an indeterminate position in the text's (onto)logical space. K.'s trial highlights, in turn, problems bound up with framing and delimiting possible worlds by model worlds; at issue is the ranking of worlds (and world fragments) according to modal status. As we might also put it, *Der Prozeß* compels us to reflect on the minimal conditions for model worlds, which are themselves a necessary condition for meaning. The narrative suggests that a world becomes a model world by virtue of the way it is anchored in a particular context (cf. secs. 5.2, 5.4.2, and 5.5 below). By the same token, the text indicates that models for meaning and reference must be articulated with pragmatic models (cf. Green 1989: 47–61)—that is, models for understanding how features of context license inferences about meaning—on pain of nonperipheral semantic indeterminacy of the sort that K. for one finds fatal.

7.1. An analogy drawn from predicate logic—itself a technique for logical analysis developed late in the nineteenth and early in the twentieth centuries, in conjunction with research on the foundations of mathematics—may help illuminate these metasemantic aspects of Kafka's text. In particular, consider the distinction often posed between first- and second-order predicate logics (or calculi), second-order calculi having been developed in attempts to capture the complexities of natural, as opposed to strictly formalized, languages. In a richer, more complex second-order predicate logic, in contrast to simpler first-order calculi, the scope of quantifers (*all, some, none*) ranges over, or "binds," variables standing not just for objects but also for relations and properties. (See, e.g., Allwood, Andersson, and Dahl 1977 [1971]: 148ff.; Blumberg 1967: 27–33.) Arguably, the narrative discourse of *Der Prozeß* enacts what might be termed a *third-order calculus*—with respect to modal as opposed to strictly truth-functional features of the discourse, however. In Kafka's text, modal operators bind not just individual objects—and not just relations (e.g., events) and states of affairs—that are possible relative to a given model world; what is more, the modal operators range over the very model worlds embedding judgments about the relative factuality, about the actuality or inactuality, of objects, events, states, etc.

The modal structure of the discourse thereby takes on a recursive profile; Kafka frames descriptions that can be paraphrased along the following lines: "It is possible that there might be a model world W_m in which the Examining Magistrate's fidgeting in his chair out of irritation and impatience is a state of affairs that obtains in W_p, which is in turn a world merely possible relative to W_m." The result is what might be termed a *model-theoretic regress*. Kafka's text widens indefinitely the scope of operators of possibility and doubt; each story element thereby attaches itself to multiple frames of reference, all of which, however, are coded as potential candidates for the status of model world vis-à-vis the other available candidates. In this way, an overabundance of possible worlds produces a peculiar worldlessness, for, as Josef K. comes to discover, a world unpartitioned (or unpartitionable) into the virtual and the actual is really no world at all.

7.2. In turn, K.'s worldlessness can be construed as a metasemantic argument built into the structure of Kafka's text. The argument is this: Only by anchoring themselves at essential points to particular contexts can model worlds furnish us with instructions for partitioning modality; that is, model worlds stipulate what is actual just by encoding certain spatiotemporal and more broadly contextual coordinates as primitive, or nonnegotiable, in contradistinction to other possible coordinates.[35] The coordinates at issue help determine the truth conditions by virtue of which the relative factuality of statements might be assessed—again, with respect to a given model world. By generating multiple model worlds with covariant sets of contextual coordinates and at the same time denying us sufficient textual information to rank any one of those sets as primary (or primitive) relative to other more or less similar sets, Kafka's narrative suggests that the model dependency of meaning (cf. sec. 5.5) cannot be characterized without recourse to pragmatic as well as semantic considerations.

7.2.1. Although I cannot embark here on a full-blown analysis of the semantico-pragmatic profile of model worlds, by reviewing the various stages of the discussion thus far I may be able to indicate areas where future research on the modal structure of narrative universes would do well to focus. Recall that, initially (sec. 6.1), I tried to formalize the model-theoretic conception of meaning using the following string of symbols:

$$F_{int}\left(x'_{W_p}\right) = x_{W_a}.$$

The incorporation of model worlds into the analysis requires that I modify the previous formula, however. Insofar as we interpret meaning as a function from propositions true of some possible world to the truth conditions of the world that *counts as,* or is *stipulated to be,* the actual world, we obtain a formula like

$$F_{int}\left(x'_{W_p}\right) = x_{W_m},$$

or, perhaps better,

$$W_m[F_{int}(x'_{W_p}) = x_{W_a}].$$

This latter formula stresses that the (model) world *presumed* to be actual is what grounds judgments of relative factuality. Model worlds can thus be construed as emergent, global frames of reference supporting any number of local, and hence sequential, assessments of the actual and the virtual—assessments that enter into every story we might conceivably tell about the world(s) we call our own.

As K.'s experiences powerfully illustrate, however, when we begin to question our presumptions about actuality in the very process of describing or recounting what we construe to be (or to have been) actual, varieties of nonperipheral semantic indeterminacy result. Such indeterminacy derives from a judgment that the model world subtending a given proposition, description, or story is itself merely one possible world among others. That judgment can be expressed in the following form:

$$W_{m/p}[F_{int}(x'_{W_p}) = x_{W_a}].$$

Semantic indeterminacy of the Kafkan stripe, in other words, roots itself in undecidably actual and/or possible worlds; and such undecidability stems, in turn, from the higher-order modal operators binding K.'s (and the narrator's) judgments of relative factuality.

7.2.2. It follows that, if there is to be a world at all, the scope of alethic, epistemic, and other operators—for example, operators of possibility and doubt—must somehow be delimited. Only then can the scope of possibility, for example, be reduced to the point where not every possible world figures, at all times, as a model world in its own right or every model world as a merely possible world. What we require are grammatical (and conceptual) resources for ranking possible worlds as better and worse candidates for model worlds in a given case. Such resources might help us avoid the radical disactualizations in which Kafka's narrative form continually involves us.

As the previous analysis suggests, however, the needed resources cannot be derived from just the semantic properties of the text. Arguably, the resources at issue are to be found in other—that is, pragmatic—features of the grammar regulating narrative discourse. Here we can build on a characterization offered by Green (1989) in her account of meaning and reference in language use generally. Green remarks that "the mechanism by which referring expressions enable an interpreter to infer an intended referent is not strictly semantic or truth-conditional, but involves cooperative exploitation of supposed mutual knowledge" (47; cf. Schiffrin 1990). Green's point can be recast as follows via the semantics of *Der Prozeß:* The knowledge and manipulation of the contexts of (narrative) discourse by discourse participants is what delimits the scope of possibility enough for meaning to happen, for reference to occur. Or, schematically (where C stands for "context"):

$$C\{W_m[F_{int}(x'_{w_p}) = x_{w_a}]\}.$$

Insofar as the form of *Der Prozeß* works to block inferences about contexts—to suppress or occlude contextual information that might help both K. and the reader resolve indefinitely many possible worlds into a stipulated model world—Kafka's text unfolds as a kind of antimodel of meaning. The novel allegorizes just the conditions under which meaning is impossible and so creates new possibilities for understanding what meaning is and how it works.

It would perhaps require another, separate book-length study to test and refine the previous remarks about meaning, contexts, and model worlds—in Kafka's narrative and in other narratives formally affiliated with *Der Prozeß*. The foregoing comments are as yet more speculative than substantive. At this point, however, I must shift my focus, going on to explore other links between universal grammar and twentieth-century literary narratives. Having pointed to the necessity of anchoring of model worlds in contexts, I conduct, in the next chapter, a more detailed investigation of the nature of context itself and of some of the ways in which narrative discourse encodes information about context. Thus, in turning from objects and models in Kafka's *Der Prozeß* to representations of discourse itself in Virginia Woolf's *Between the Acts,* my investigation of universal grammar and narrative form will reorient itself around specifically *pragmatic* issues and concerns—issues and concerns manifest, once again, in both language-theoretical and literary settings.

3. Toward a Metapragmatics of Represented Discourse: Prague School Functionalism and Woolf's *Between the Acts*

They were talking—not shaping pellets of information or handing ideas from one to another, but rolling words, like sweets on their tongue.—Virginia Woolf

1. Contexts of Discourse Representation

This chapter attempts to link two kinds of theories that have unfortunately evolved more or less in parallel, despite appearances of mutual borrowing and cross-fertilization. One kind of theory, a part of narratology, studies represented discourse in narratives—that is, narrative discourse that represents the discourse of one or more characters.[1] (In order to simplify the presentation, this chapter sometimes subsumes under *theory of narrative* terms and concepts in actual fact elaborated under the rather different auspices of *stylistics*, as in Ullmann 1964.) The other kind of theory, linguistic pragmatics, is of a much more general character. In its modern-day form at least, linguistic pragmatics studies how speech contexts paired with speech tokens produce, in nonrandom and hence predictable ways, the meanings that speakers and hearers jointly confer on the utterances that they exchange. More simply, pragmatics "is the study of the use of context to make inferences about meaning" (Fasold 1990: 118; cf. Leech 1983; Levinson 1983; Green 1989; Herman 1994b; and sec. 4 below). Thus, the communicative skills studied in pragmatics constitute a crucial part of grammatical competence; without them we could not mediate between the formal *design* of locutions and the contexts on the strength of which those linguistic forms license particular *interpretations*. Although linguistic pragmatics as it is currently conceived emerged only after the seminal researches of language theorists like J. L. Austin (1963 [1940], 1962), Yehoshua Bar-Hillel (1954), and H. P. Grice (1989), one of my chief concerns is to explore how ideas pertaining to the genealogy of pragmatics are rich in applications for, and indeed conceptually affiliated with, the innovative discourse representations found in (post)modernist literary narratives.

In particular, I use Virginia Woolf's 1941 novel *Between the Acts* to reconceptualize the narratological and pragmatic theories already mentioned. By analogy with chapters 1 and 2, the overarching claim is that Woolf's narrative sets into play—helps us powerfully and productively frame—issues and concerns found in adjacent theoretical settings. As we saw earlier, the study of the structures of Joyce's "Sirens" helps illuminate, and is illuminated by, logicians' and linguists' efforts to model syntactic structures as such. Meanwhile, the semantic dimensions of Kafka's *Der Prozeß* help reframe classical concepts of meaning and reference. By contrast, the present chapter explores how, in *Between the Acts,* Woolf's multiple and highly various representations of discourse bear on issues pertaining to the problem of context—as that problem manifests itself both in narrative theory and in more broadly pragmatic theories.

1.1. Recently, a number of commentators have provided useful descriptions of the way narratives not only contain but also represent discourse.[2] These researchers have in addition furnished suggestive and fruitful accounts of the various (stylistic, thematic, and more broadly epistemological) indices and effects of each strategy for representing discourse in narrative contexts. Nevertheless, extant accounts of represented discourse require fuller grounding in the pragmatic models that first began to be developed, by researchers in semiotics, linguistics, and the philosophy of language, around the same time that Woolf composed her novel in 1939. Indeed, the lack of any sustained historical interinvolvement of pragmatic models with the study of narrative[3] may account for why the problem of free indirect discourse, for example, has for so long resisted precise description, let alone resolution, in the framework of narrative theory as classically formulated. In turn, the historical separation of pragmatics from narrative theory may be attributed to the grounding of (Francophone) narratology in Saussurean or at least Saussure-inspired linguistic and semiological models. Such structuralist models typically *background* contextual concerns in the analysis of languages and, more generally, sign systems (see sec. *4.1* below; cf. Herman 1992b). Hence the importance of meshing pragmatic with narratological terms and categories, in a manner that the original situation of narrative theory—its position relative to other theoretical discourses—perhaps did not permit.

1.2. More specifically, my suggestion is that we can work toward a pragmatics of represented discourse by drawing on the functional linguistics fashioned by the Prague School. The bulk of the Prague School's work issues from the years between the wars—although Roman Jakobson's influential essay "Linguistics and Poetics" was published in 1960 and a younger member (or at least immediate descendant) of the Prague School, Lubomír Doležel, has more recently addressed the issue of represented discourse specifically in his *Narrative Modes in Czech Literature* (1973). It is not just that Prague School functionalism helps illuminate the form and functioning of represented discourse in Woolf's text, however; what is more, Woolf's representations of discourse can throw new light on the scope and limits of functionalist models such as the one jointly shaped by Jan Mukařovský and Jakobson—models with demonstrable importance for the evolution and refinement of pragmatic theories. Indeed, examination of Woolf's techniques for representing discourse requires that we re-examine, at the same time, the grounds on which linguistic pragmatics might be articulated with narratological theories and acceptations in the first place. Sketching the pragmatics of represented discourse in Woolf may therefore yield the rudiments of a richer, more powerful account of the relations between context, language, and narrative generally.

Limitations of space dictate that, in setting out the argument, I begin not with an extended synopsis of theories of represented discourse in narrative but rather with a diagnosis of those theories based on standard accounts already available in a number of sources and widely discussed in the literature. The diagnosis presented here will suggest how, in general, the standard accounts are marred by an impoverished account of the role of context in both the design and the interpretation of represented discourse in narrative. The same under-theorization of context has resulted in an overrestricted inventory of (possible) types of represented discourse as well as a failure to grasp the irreducibly polyfunctional status of the discourse types included in standard inventories. My working hypothesis: that the ways in which narratives represent discourse correspond to *modes of encryption of contexts-of-use into narrative form itself.* Or, as we might also put it, the capacity of narratives not just to embody but also to represent diverse types of illocutionary performances makes of narrative discourse itself a series of more or less complexly embedded speech acts (cf. Ryan 1991: 61ff.). Arguably, only a general theory of contexts—and *eo ipso* a narrative pragmatics (cf. Prince 1983a)—will permit us to develop special theories under whose scope an analysis of represented discourse properly falls.

Toward this end, I factor into the debate on represented discourse Jakobson's and Mukařovský's polyfunctionalist pragmatics, their persistent thematization of contexts-of-use as functionally overdetermined, along both modal and temporal dimensions. Equipped with the Prague School's pragmatics—or, more precisely, with their "metapragmatics"—I attempt to model an enriched typology of represented discourse through important illustrative instances from Woolf's *Between the Acts*. Somewhat more elliptically, our task is to trace the often surprising route leading from Prague to Bloomsbury, taking care to note what stops and detours we have to make along the way.

2. Some Ambiguities of Context

In synopsizing standard accounts of represented discourse, we can streamline the discussion by focusing on just one subdomain of the research: that is, that subdomain concerned with free indirect discourse (FID) specifically. Although researchers posit both transformational (Bally 1912; Lips 1926) and nontransformational (Vološinov 1973 [1929]; Banfield 1982) relationships between direct discourse (DD), indirect discourse (ID), and FID—that is, although FID acquires in the different accounts more or less derivative or autonomous status relative to the two discourse types described as DD and ID—discussions of FID expose the fundamental assumptions, the theoretical postulates, grounding the accepted typologies. Specifically, accounts of FID typically reveal the failure of narrative theory to include (sufficiently developed) postulates about the role of context in narratives' representations of discourse, let alone in our efforts to process the types of discourse represented. The lack of such general postulates helps explain Norman Page's (1973) remark that "a substantial task of analysis and definition remains to be undertaken in the field of categories of speech-presentation" and his further comment that "there would seem to be a number of constructions, by no means rare in works of literature, for which a precise and generally-accepted terminology is lacking" (38).

2.1. From the start, stylisticians and narratologists have agreed that we can isolate certain linguistic features proper to FID, plotting those features against the distinctive features proper, in turn, to DD and ID. The real dispute about FID centers on the precise extent to which that discourse type is subject to grammatical (e.g., syntactic and lexical) description and also on the scope and nature of the discursive residuum left over after the resources of grammar have been exhausted in this connection.

Charles Bally (1912, 1914), for example, seems to hedge on how far FID can be specified through properly grammatical means. Although Bally begins by resorting to syntactic criteria for the identification of ID—"le style indirect comprend ... l'ensemble des formes de syntaxe servant à reproduire les paroles ou les pensées d'un tiers" 'the indirect style comprehends the ensemble of syntactic forms serving to reproduce the words or the thoughts of a third party' (1912: 549)—he goes on to introduce a sort of uncertainty principle into the grammar of represented discourse as a whole. Bally suggests that, the more carefully and exhaustively we approximate the grammatical features of each type of represented discourse, the less certainly we can locate FID at any definite remove from (or in any definite position relative to) either ID or DD: "Voyons comment il [i.e., le style indirect libre] s'éloigne insensiblement des formes classiques de l'indirect, et comment il se rapproche toujours plus du style direct pur" 'let us see how it [FID] distances itself imperceptibly from the classical forms of the indirect, and how it draws ever nearer to the direct style in its pure form' (552). Bally's point is that we witness no difference in kind but rather merely a difference in degree between "le caractère subjectif de l'énoncé" 'the subjective character of the enunciated' marking FID and the non- or rather less subjective character of other types of represented enunciations (553). Ultimately, although we can, through certain transpositions of verb tenses (e.g., "la transposition du futur en conditionnel" 'the transposition of the future into the conditional' [597]), go some distance toward identifying and typologizing the possible syntactic forms assumed by FID, such syntactic criteria nevertheless cannot capture "la valeur subjective ajoutée à l'idée verbale" 'the subjective value added to the verbal idea' (597) that also defines FID. Indeed, that subjective value appears peculiarly resistant to grammatical description in any strict sense.

We can use a brief example to confirm Bally's intuition that syntax alone cannot specify what sets FID apart from DD and ID. Note that, whereas the shift from the future to the conditional is a necessary condition for FID as opposed to DD, by itself that shift is not sufficient to distinguish FID from ID. Thus, in progressing from

(S) Unflinching, Lucia said: "By God, I will be ready for anything"

to

(S′) Unflinching, Lucia said that she would be ready for anything

and then

(S′′) Lucia stood there unflinching. By God, she would be ready for anything

we cannot simply point to the shift from the future to the conditional in trying to explain why (S′) is an instance of ID whereas (S′′) is an instance of FID. As Ullmann (1964) puts it, unlike ID, but like DD, FID gives "the utterance a subjective colouring; [we find in FID] colloquial, vulgar and slang terms which are expressive of the speaker's character and attitude" (97). But then the problem is how FID entails an ongoing supplementation of "l'idée verbale" with "la valeur subjective"—how it amounts to a "subjective colouring" of the reported utterance, despite the apparent absence of grammatical indices that would provide necessary and sufficient conditions for a given occurrence of FID.

In fact, commentary on FID consists of a series of more or less ingenious attempts to project the subjective residuum of FID toward the limit of grammatical description as such. At this limit, on this border, lie disparate concerns all too readily lumped together under the heading *context* or *contextual considerations*. Beginning with Bally himself (1914: 410–12) and then throughout the literature on FID, we find persistent use of the notion of context as a sort of primitive term in arguments about the impossibility of specifying FID grammatically. Yet we also find different usages of the term *context* in researchers' bid to indicate the minimal conditions—to explain the stylistic perceptibility—of FID relative to DD, ID, or, for that matter, the "nonrepresented" discourse embedding the subsidiary discourse representations. As Ducrot and Todorov (1979 [1972]) point out, context is sometimes used to designate "the set of circumstances surrounding the occurrence of an act of enunciation (whether written or oral)" and sometimes used to talk about "the strictly linguistic surroundings of an element (a word or phonic unit) within an utterance, that is, the series of elements that precede and follow it in the utterance" (333). Ducrot and Todorov propose to eliminate the ambiguity at issue merely by encouraging the adoption of a conventional rule to define context in a relatively narrow way. By contrast, my argument is that, in discussions of represented discourse, narrower usages of context are regularly and confusingly interchanged with wider usages, precisely because narrative theory has for the most part evolved in the absence of any general theory of context, any pragmatics.

2.2. In her important study of techniques for representing consciousness in fiction, Dorrit Cohn (1978) renames and reconceptualizes *style indirect libre* as "narrated monologue"—that is, as "a transformation of figural thought-language into the narrative language of third-person fiction" (100; cf. 99–140)[4]—and goes on to remark,

> The problem of delimiting the narrated monologue from narration generally is . . . complex, since purely linguistic criteria no longer provide reliable guidelines. Cloaked in the grammar of narration, a sentence rendering a character's opinion can look every bit like a sentence relating a

fictional fact. In purely grammatical terms "He was late" . . . could be a
narrator's fact, rather than a character's thought. Within a broader context
it might become possible to attribute it to a figural mind: for instance, if
the next sentence belied the idea that "he was late"; or if the statement were
embedded in a recognizable thought sequence. (106)[5]

Here the notion of context functions intratextually or, as we might also put it,
intersententially. In this case, we might say that narrated monologue resists (or
transcends) purely grammatical description because detection of the formal
device is context dependent in the following sense: only an intratextual pattern
(context) of thought representations permits us to identify, via recurrent or
habitual modes of consciousness, where species of thought (and utterance)
mark a narrator's "*identification*—but not his *identity*—with the character's
mentality" (112).

Extrapolating from contexts of fictional consciousness to contexts of represented discourse, we might offer the following account. It is possible to detect
FID *as* FID just by contextualizing bits of represented discourse in a set of
(analogous) discourse representations constituted over the course of a narrative. Only thus do we arrive at the inference that a given stretch of text belongs
to the class of utterances subtending the discourse habits of a given character,
together with that class subtending the narrator's discourse. Instances of FID,
moreover, may be more or less widely spaced in the contextual—the intersentential—chain. Hence, Brian McHale (1978), following Roy Pascal (1977: 26–27),
suggests that besides "cues in the immediate context" (267)—for example, verbs
of speech or thought that occur immediately before or after an instance of
FID—"General context . . . has a considerable effect on the perceptibility of
FID," particularly in cases where "the point of view is always that of a character,
never that of an omniscient narrator." In the latter instance, "general context"
for McHale includes "any expression which directs the reader's attention to a
particular character [and which thus serves] as a 'bridge' between narration
and FID" (268).

Yet recent work in discourse analysis and in text grammar warrants at least
some caution in connection with this (intratextual or intersentential) usage of
context in the literature on FID. With this intratextual usage commentators on
FID assimilate the problem of context to the broader problem of how to establish and recognize cohesiveness among the various local utterances contained
in longer stretches of talk—that is, how to capture (and manipulate) the critical
property of coherence that makes for a discourse or a text in the first place (cf.

Halliday and Hasan 1976; Brown and Yule 1983; Schiffrin 1987, 1990; Herman 1994b). But, although we are making a true statement when we say that FID can be recognized and interpreted because of its status as part of a larger discourse, that statement is only trivially true. The more interesting question, presumably, concerns the exact nature of those "discourse markers" (Schiffrin 1987: 31ff.) that bracket the units of talk constituting instances of FID within a larger discourse. Thus, to invoke the (overly general) notion of context in attempts to account for this particular mode of patterning in discourse is, in effect, to substitute the *explanans* for the *explanandum*.

What is more, text grammarians like Teun A. van Dijk have argued that intersentential relations can in principle be brought within the bounds of grammatical competence. Early on van Dijk (1972) hypothesized that, by means of text grammar, relations between sentences can be mapped onto "textual surface structures" through syntactic principles like those governing definitivization (article selection) from sentence to sentence, such that "the 'contextual' conditions for definitivization, normally left over to performance, are thus explicitly brought within the scope of the [text] grammar" (8; cf. 42ff.). Van Dijk hypothesized, too, that intersentential relations can be described via semantic principles, such as the ones allowing us to establish topic-comment relations between different sentences more or less proximate to one another in the textual chain: "The identification of a topic (and thus of a comment) in a sentence is regulated by rules analogous to those determining definite descriptions, pronominalization and presupposition . . . , which are all functions of certain identity-, equivalence- and other semantic relations with previous sentences" (9; cf. 73ff., 109ff.). Subsequently, van Dijk (1977: 93ff.) came to emphasize the importance of world knowledge, or knowledge frames, in allowing us to recognize and exploit multisentential units *as* coherent discourses. Whatever we think about the text-grammatical enterprise in its classical and postclassical formulations (contrast Herman 1994b), however, the point is that to talk about intersentential contexts (as an index of FID) is to beg questions that have been asked with considerable sophistication by text grammarians, among others.

2.3. Meanwhile, context in an alternative usage informs V. N. Vološinov's (1973 [1929]) and Mikhail Bakhtin's (1984 [1929]) bid to define the structure and functions of FID—or, as Vološinov calls it, "quasi-direct discourse" (137ff.).[6] In contrast to Cohn's, McHale's, and other commentators' intersentential usage of context, the notion of context in Vološinov-Bakhtin functions in a manner we can term *intertextual*. In fact, in the framework of stylistics generally, this intertextual usage of context provides Bakhtin (1984 [1929]) with something as basic as his founding distinction between (monologically oriented) linguistics and (dialogically oriented) "metalinguistics":

> Stylistics must be based not only, and even *not as much,* on linguistics as on metalinguistics, which studies the word not in a system of language and not in a "text" excised from dialogic interaction, but precisely within the sphere of dialogic interaction itself, that is, in that sphere where discourse lives an authentic life. . . . [The word] never gravitates toward a single consciousness or a single voice. The life of the word is contained in its transfer from one mouth to another, from one context to another context, from one social collective to another, from one generation to another generation. In this process the word does not forget its own path and cannot completely free itself from the power of these concrete contexts into which it has entered. (202)

Context taken in this metalinguistic or intertextual sense presumably allows us to specify, as a kind of reflexive instance of the inherently dialogical, "vari-directional" nature of discourse in general, those "double-voiced" discourse phenomena that Bakhtin-Vološinov associates with certain forms of represented discourse in particular. At issue are all those forms of "discourse with an orientation toward someone else's discourse (double-voiced discourse)" (Bakhtin 1984 [1929]: 199).

On the one hand, "Direct, unmediated discourse directed exclusively toward its referential object, as an expression of the speaker's ultimate semantic authority," and "objectified discourse (discourse of a represented person)" (199) are context-backgrounding discourse types, insofar as they suppress or occlude, to the highest degree possible, the dialogic situation of a given utterance. (As we shall see in a moment, however, on Bakhtin-Vološinov's own terms there can be no such thing as a backgrounding of dialogic contexts, strictly speaking.) On the other hand, properly double-voiced phenomena—later assimilated to the "dual-voice" hypothesis made current by Paul Hernadi (1972) and especially Pascal (1977)—are context-foregrounding features of discourse. Thus, for Bakhtin-Vološinov, genuinely double-voiced discourse, which we can classify here under the more familiar heading *FID*, inscribes within narrative form itself the dialogic situation of words, phrases, and (in principle) all other possible units of narrative and more broadly verbal structure.[7] In processing FID, we must come to grips with the embedding of two or more—irreconcilable or, as Bakhtin puts it, "internally undecided" (1984 [1929]: 198)—contexts on the single plane of the discourse currently being processed. Through FID, as we might also put it, (narrative) discourse at once thematizes and enacts, both mentions and uses, its own irreducibly dialogic status. Thus, Vološinov comments that, in double-voiced discourse, the represented discourse

> becomes more forceful and more active than the authorial context framing it. . . . The authorial context loses the greater objectivity it normally commands in comparison with reported speech. It begins to perceive itself . . . as subjective. . . . The narrator's speech is just as individualized, colorful, and nonauthoritative as is the speech of the characters. The narrator's position is fluid, and in the majority of cases he uses the language of the personages depicted in the work. He cannot bring to bear against their subjective position a more authoritative and objective world. (Vološinov 1973 [1929]: 121)

As should already be apparent, however, on Bakhtin-Vološinov's own terms context conceived as a (global) intertext cannot serve as an index or a marker of FID. Instead, and conversely, FID must be construed as one particularly explicit marker—among other less explicit indices—of the contextual (over)determination of all discourse, all meaning. It follows that, rather than being isolable according to its (extragrammatical) *differentia specifica,* FID loses all specificity in the face of severe restrictions of the explanatory scope of grammar itself.

We can detail as follows the problem just indicated. For Bakhtin-Vološinov, FID exposes in particularly explicit fashion the "metalinguistic" or intertextual mechanisms by which contexts of speech are perpetually embedded one within another under pressure of particular utterances made by particular speakers in particular circumstances. Still, insofar as every utterance is inherently dialogic—insofar as every speech act is postulated to be operative in indefinitely many contexts at one and the same time and hence at some level subject to ongoing metalinguistic description—we have yet to explain what sets FID apart from what Bakhtin-Vološinov must admit to be any number of other context-foregrounding features present in all types of discourse, including putatively monologic, single-voiced discourse. If we say that to speak is to traverse (or invoke) innumerably many other contexts of speech bearing in principle on our own current speech act, then we must infer that grammar as ordinarily conceived falls far short of accounting for language use in general, let alone FID in particular. The context-activating and -foregrounding features of discourse now include just those sorts of features projecting text T into texts $T_1, T_2, \ldots,$ T_n: for example, (more or less recondite) allusions or "hidden polemics," as

Bakhtin puts it; variations in dialect; species of shoptalk; slang; terms of address; modes of emphasis; techniques of paraphrase; reiterated verbal tags; diminutives; in fact anything that smacks of some supra- or transtextual pattern of acceptation, some larger ethos of utterance. At issue are features that point to the discursive genotype underwriting a current or phenotypic discourse—to use the language of Julia Kristeva. On Bakhtin's-Vološinov's metalinguistic interpretation, FID functions as a metonymy for this whole family of context-foregrounding features. But then we are left with the question with which we began: How do we go about characterizing FID in contradistinction to other forms of (represented and nonrepresented) discourse? How do we capture the intuition that FID marks a discourse phenomenon that, to a larger degree than other discourse phenomena, requires for its disambiguation, its interpretation, attention to the different values that an utterance may in principle acquire across different contexts?

In neither its intratextual nor its intertextual sense, it seems, does the notion of context help us pinpoint—account for—the context-foregrounding mechanisms corresponding to that peculiar "valeur subjective" that we generally recognize as subtending all and only instances of FID. Yet by relegating to the domain of context those features of FID which resist description according to syntactic, lexical, or other grammatical rules, existing accounts of FID suggest that the notion of context must itself be spelled out in this connection, lest we merely beg the question about the *differentia specifica* (and narrative functions) of FID. Hence the crucial importance of the Prague School's contributions to a general theory of contexts-of-use. As we shall see, in parallel with the analytic techniques of the Prague School, Woolf's narrative techniques in *Between the Acts* highlight the pragmatic mechanisms (properly, functions) according to which sentences get paired with contexts to produce particular utterances having particular meanings. Like the Prague School's analysis of functional contexts, Woolf's discourse representations traffic in what can be called *metapragmatic* issues and concerns.[8] Accordingly, in Woolf's novel we face a narrative artifact that is not merely *susceptible* of a specific type of grammatical (in this case, pragmatic) description and analysis. Beyond this, Woolf's narrative can help us rethink the role of context in the design and interpretation of language and so help *generate* linguistic models for understanding illocutionary acts. Through a first approximation of the discourse representations embedded in Woolf's text, we can start to characterize the metapragmatic motifs also at work in Mukařovský's and Jakobson's functionalist models.

3. Discourse Representations in *Between the Acts*: A First Approach

Note that the chief protagonist of Woolf's novel is not a character or, more precisely, not any one particular character or group of characters. Rather, it is the discourse, the talking, the (acts of) speech operative *between* characters, that figures most prominently in the narrative. What the narrator characterizes as "voices" (151; cf. 156ff.)[9] ultimately assume the most prominent role in Woolf's text. The narrative thus foregrounds the logic of conversation, the principles of turn-taking and exchange, governing the play of its various voices. Admittedly, this predominance of the voice does sometimes take on Dionysian overtones: "It didn't matter what the words were; or who sang what. Round and round they whirled, intoxicated by the music" (94). Before we overhastily construe Woolf's text as celebrating a wholly unconstrained, random play of voices, however, we had better start characterizing in somewhat more detailed terms the various discourse representations included in the novel.

3.1. In its classical formulation, narratology offers at least the rudiments of a descriptive vocabulary in this connection. If, at the level of the *fabula,* the events of Woolf's novel unfold between the acts of Miss La Trobe's pageant, at the level of the *sjužet* we must ceaselessly negotiate between the various acts of speech, the different modes of enunciation, embedded in the discourse of the narrative. Thus, the novel begins with the representation of an enunciative act; the syntax of the opening sentence subordinates the topic of utterance (the *énoncé*) under the act (and the context) of the uttering (the *énonciation*): "It was a summer's night and they were talking, in the big room with the windows open to the garden, about the cesspool" (3). Syntactically at least, in this sentence what "they" are talking about is less prominent than the nature and context of their illocutionary act itself. Likewise, the novel ends with a sentence whose syntactic structure, although more elementary than that of the first sentence, also foregrounds the process over the product of speaking, the act over the topic of utterance: "They [i.e., Giles and Isa] spoke" (219).[10]

The text's emphasis on speaking over what has been spoken shapes the narrative discourse in a number of different ways and with a number of different effects. For example, we find persistent stress on the material substance, as opposed to the lexical functions or referential force, of words. Thus, after the performance of her pageant, Miss La Trobe sits in a bar and contemplates her next dramatic endeavor: "She raised her glass to her lips. And drank. And listened. Words of one syllable sank down into the mud. She drowsed; she nodded. The mud became fertile. Words rose above the intolerably laden dumb oxen plodding through the mud. Words without meaning—wonderful words" (212). Similarly, the text represents as follows the minister's plea for contributions from the audience toward "the illumination of our dear old church" (193): " 'each of us who has enjoyed this pageant has still the opp. . . .' The word was cut in two. A zoom severed it. Twelve aeroplanes in perfect formation like a flight of wild duck came overhead" (193; cf. also 21–22, 71, 208, and the epigraph for this chapter).

Indeed, in direct proportion as it grounds words in their material, phonic substance, their modes of realization as sounds, the narrative widens the scope of the notion *utterance* itself so that it comes to include a range of sounds—even visual inputs—not typically associated with speech. For instance, the narrator at one point attributes speech to a butterfly: "the tortoiseshell butterfly beat on the lower pane of the window; beat, beat, beat; repeating that if no human being ever came, never, never, never, the books would be mouldy, the fire out and tortoiseshell butterfly dead on the pane" (17). At another point, a room sings: "Empty, empty, empty; silent, silent, silent. The room was a shell, singing of what was before time was" (36). Later, a view and then a herd of cattle reiterate the propositional content curiously ascribed to a gramophone that "gently stated certain facts" (133) through a tune played during an intermission in the pageant: "The view repeated in its own way what the tune was saying. . . . the view was saying how after toil men rest from their labours; how coolness comes; reason prevails. . . . The cows, making a step forward, then standing still, were saying the same thing to perfection" (134). Still later, a tree synesthetically becomes "a rhapsody, a quivering cacophony, a whizz and vibrant rapture" (209).

At the same time, the narrative extends the scope of *utterance* in the opposite direction so that the idea comes to include, too, the gaps and interstices of speech. Utterance comprises conversational pauses, silence—in short, non-utterance itself (cf. Weber 1986). Consider the many conversations in which silence figures importantly, as detailed in passages that include: "In all this sound of welcome, there was an element of silence, supplied by Isabella, observing the unknown young man [i.e., William Dodge]" (38); " 'what are your rings for, and your nails, and that adorable straw hat?' said Isabella, addressing Mrs. Manresa silently and thereby making silence add its unmistakeable contribution to talk" (39); "[Isa] half turned in her seat. 'No, not for us, who've the future,' *she seemed to say*" (82; my emphasis); and "[Bart] knocked the ash off his cheroot and rose. 'So we must,' said Lucy; *as if* he had said aloud, 'It's time to go' " (118; my emphasis; cf. sec. *9.1* below). Consider, too, the all-important asides that, in Miss La Trobe's pageant, represent silences that speak not on the plane of dramatic discourse itself but on the plane of our interpretation of that discourse (128–30).

3.2. In addition, the text suggests how words, viewed as bits of phonic substance, first take on meaning in the course of particular enunciative acts matched to particular contexts of production and reception. Hence Woolf's representation of a host of dialects, idioms, and registers of speech. In this connection, consider the utterances of the Olivers' nurses, at once related and recounted through the more elevated parlance of the narrator's illocutionary acts: "How cook had told 'im off about the asparagus; how when she rang I said: how it was a sweet costume with blouse to match;' and that was leading to something about a feller as they walked up and down the terrace" (10); the discourse explicitly marked as cliché and adopted by Isa as a way of ameliorating painful introspection about her marriage with Giles: "'The father of my children,' she added, slipping into the cliché conveniently provided by fiction" (14; 48); the frequent shifts in dialect indexed to differences in class, education, and experience: "[the cat's] drawing-room name Sung-Yen had undergone a kitchen change into Sunny" (32; cf. 34 for a stereoscopic representation of Mrs. Sands's and Lucy Swithin's thoughts, two parallel interior monologues differentiated by dialect and placed in series in the narrative); and that poetic register regularly adopted by Isa (cf., e.g., 15, 18, 83, 104, 118, 180) and then generalized with the coloration of the narrative discourse by the language of Miss La Trobe's pageant. The pageant for its part represents a speech register by turns elevated and archaic, but in any case explicitly marked throughout via the use of italicized type (76ff.).

3.3. Of greater significance, perhaps, is the highly reflexive discourse representation set into play when the minister, the Reverend G. W. Streatfield, attempts to sum up the "message" of Miss La Trobe's pageant as a whole. Here, rather than encouraging us to focus on the illocutionary force of Streatfield's statements, the discourse highlights instead Streatfield's ongoing attempt to construct, on the basis of discrete words arranged serially in time, a syntagm intelligible to its recipients or interpreters:

His first words (the breeze had risen; the leaves were rustling) were lost. Then he was heard saying: "What." To that word he added another "Message"; and at last a whole sentence emerged; not comprehensible; say rather audible. "What message," it seemed he was asking, "was our pageant meant to convey?" (191)

In this passage, the discourse not only draws our attention to the minister's fitful elaboration of an ultimately dubious syntagm but also indicates the extent to which contextual considerations must in general be brought to bear on utterances before their significance can be decided. Put otherwise, we face in the minister's (non)utterance a peculiarly reflexive embedding of enunciative acts—one is tempted to speak of a kind of discursive *mise en abyme*—that might be termed the hallmark of represented discourse in *Between the Acts*. On the one hand, the minister produces an utterance whose "message" cannot be fully determined, given its contexts of reception; what he says is not "comprehensible" in the strict sense but rather only barely "audible" over rising breezes and rustling leaves. On the other hand, however, the context does allow the audience at least to surmise that the topic of the utterance concerns (or seems to concern) strategies that the audience itself should use in order to determine the message of the pageant. More precisely, the minister offers rules for how the audience should go about mapping into current-day contexts of reception the (large) set of scripted sentences corresponding to Miss La Trobe's drama. An utterance whose interpretation cannot finally be fixed bears, therefore, on the fixing of an interpretation for sentences such that they may be construed as meaningful utterances, as messages in contexts, in the first place.

Indeed, locutions whose design encodes the underdetermination of the sentences' meaning by their contexts of reception—contexts that do, however, figure as *necessary* conditions for the interpretation of these and all other locutions—virtually saturate the discursive environment of Miss La Trobe's pageant. (For a discussion of analogously designed sentences in Woolf's *Orlando*, see Herman 1991c: 78–79.) To cite just a few examples (in all of which the ellipses and emphases are part of Woolf's text itself): "A long line of villagers in shirts made of sacking began passing in and out in single file behind her between the trees. They were singing, but not a word reached the audience" (77–78); "They were singing; but only a word or two was audible '. . . *wore ruts in the grass . . . built the house in the lane. . . .*' The wind blew away the connecting words of their chant" (80); "*The Queen of this great land . . .* those were the first words that could be heard above the roar of laughter and applause" (83–84); "She bawled. They bawled. All together they bawled, and so loud that it was difficult to make out what they were saying" (90); "She spoke too low at first; all they heard was . . . *reason holds sway*" (123); "The wind blew the words away" (125); "the stage was empty; the emotion must be continued; the only thing to continue the emotion was the song; and the words were inaudible" (139); "The words died away. Only a few great names—Babylon,

Nineveh, Clytemnestra, Agamemnon, Troy—floated across the open space. The wind rose, and in the rustle of the leaves even the great words became inaudible; and the audience sat staring at the villagers, whose mouths opened, but no sound came out" (140); and "The voices of the pilgrims singing, as they wound in and out between the trees, could be heard; but the words were inaudible" (163–64).

We can recharacterize as follows the discursive structure that underlies the sorts of utterances just quoted. The utterances are *themselves* so designed as to point up a kind of asymmetry between the formal design of sentences and the conditions under which those same sentence designs are interpreted as utterances. In other words, the quoted passages suggest how the grammar of an utterance always underdetermines the range of meanings that may accrue to that utterance in all its contexts of use. Grammar underdetermines meaning to the extent that no de facto context of use is definitive; rather, a given context bears in principle on indefinitely many other contexts; in the totality of those contexts one and the same utterance might conceivably assume very different discourse functions, very different meanings. Conversely, however, meanings can accrue to sentences only if and when the sentences are realized *as* utterances matched to specific contexts—realized, that is, at particular times and places and under particular conditions of use. Yet—and this is the crucial point—the rules corresponding to the pragmatic component of grammars seek to account for just this asymmetrical relation between sentences (well-formed strings) and utterances (sentences in contexts). Woolf's discourse representations therefore ground themselves in the same concerns that spawned the pragmatic frameworks developed in language theory over the course of this century. Below (secs. 7ff.) I turn to a more considered analysis of the (meta)pragmatic dimensions of narrative form in *Between the Acts*. First, however, we need a brief synopsis of pragmatic theory itself, and more particularly of those elements of Prague School functionalism pertaining to pragmatics—elements whose narrative corollaries may be found in the discourse representations featured in Woolf's novel.

4. The Pragmatic Matrix

Of primary importance in linguistic pragmatics are the scope and nature of what Gerald Gazdar (1979) has characterized as functions mapping utterances into the contexts that license inferences about the utterances' meaning(s). As such, pragmatics attempts not only to establish that, but also to specify how, a context paired with a sentence produces a (meaningful) utterance to begin with. Most broadly, therefore, we can say that pragmatics attempts to derive a function f_p that can map the domain E (the set of all possible utterances) into the range M (the set of contexts for utterances) (Gazdar 1979: 4ff.). This pragmatic function, in turn, takes on a more or less properly mathematical character—that is, f_p has to a greater or lesser degree the structure of the relation holding between mutually dependent variables—according to how we characterize M itself. As we shall see, Prague School functionalism assigns to M what can be described as an ontologically stratified structure, encompassing both de facto and de jure contexts—that is, classes of context distributed between the actual and the possible, the real and the virtual (see, in particular, sec. 6 below). Predictably, this stratification of contexts yields, in Jakobson and Mukařovský, a particularly rich version of Gazdar's f_p. Furthermore, we find similarly stratified speech contexts in *Between the Acts,* such that the most abiding subject of Woolf's discourse is in effect the modes of indexing speech to speakers—the (pragmatic) mechanisms by which speakers and hearers anchor utterances in infinitely variable communicative contexts.

Both Gazdar (1979: x, 2–4, and 89ff., esp. 161–68) and Stephen Levinson (1983: 33–35) point out that the contexts in which language is used supply language users with information that cannot be derived from just the syntactic and/or the semantic features of a language. Whereas syntax and semantics may be necessary conditions for the design and interpretation of meaningful utterances, these grammatical components do not suffice to explain how utterances—that is, locutions embedded in a particular place, time, and sociocultural environment—produce the inferences that constitute what we call their meaning (Levinson 1983: 18–19; Fasold 1990: 118ff.). Sentence meaning, that is to say, seems to be a function not only of the syntactic rules for incorporating phrasemes into well-formed increments of speech, and not only of the truth conditions pertaining to that speech segment, but also of the context in which the utterance in fact gets said—of the materialization of an otherwise merely idealized configuration of lexical units and logical properties.

The irreducibility of context makes itself felt in a particularly obvious way when an utterance contains a deictic term like *I, now,* or *this;* after all, *I am stupid* cannot be given a meaning until we determine the speech context in which the *I* anchors itself (Green 1989: 17–21; cf. Herman 1994e). Beyond this, however, the underdetermination of utterance meaning by syntax and semantics is what gives language its inherent flexibility as a vehicle for communication (sec. *0.4*). Thus, the truth conditions for the well-formed string (S)

It's raining are such that the sentence is true if it is raining and false if it is not. Yet the sentence can *mean* everything from (M_1) "Water is falling from the skies" to (M_2) "Maybe the crops will do better now" to (M_3) "I don't want to play tennis just yet." Without positing an interdependence of context and meaning, it would be impossible to account for the indirect speech acts (Searle 1991 [1975]) performed by way of (S) to produce meanings M_2 and M_3. More generally, unless the grammatical form and the logical properties of speech tokens underdetermined their meanings, we would not be able to do everything that we can in fact do with words.

It is important to remember, however, that pragmatic argumentation of the sort just outlined emerged only gradually over the course of this century, under the impress of intellectual trends as diverse as American pragmatism, Prague School functionalism, and the Ordinary Language Philosophy inspired by the later Wittgenstein. By sketching (part of) the prehistory of pragmatics, we start to see in turn how the Prague School's polyfunctionalist model and Woolf's experimental discourse representations pertain to a single matrix of concepts spanning both universal grammar and narrative form. Put otherwise, we start to see that the recognition of the importance of context has its own context.

4.1. Note that, when Charles Morris (1938) isolated syntax, semantics, and pragmatics as three interactive dimensions of semiosis, he thought that he was contributing to an international project envisaged by the founding members of the Vienna Circle—the project, namely, of the unification of the sciences. But, ironically, a half century after Morris specified these three dimensions of semiosis in what no doubt seemed to him a highly general and thus noncontroversial manner, consensus about what falls within the scope of each semiotic dimension remains split roughly along the lines of researchers' nationalities. Herman Parret (1983) has shown how, in general, scholars working in the Anglo-Saxon or Peircean ("analytic") semiotic tradition find themselves pitted against researchers in the ("structural") Continental tradition, which began with Ferdinand de Saussure, extends through Louis Hjelmslev, and perpetuates itself in post-Hjelmslevians like A. J. Greimas (23–88).[11] Specifically, the dispute between the analytic and the structuralist factions centers on the element of dynamism that Peircean semiotics, in contrast to the Saussurean/Hjelmslevian tradition, builds into the very nature of semiosis (cf. Eco 1987). Historically speaking, Morris's dream of a general semiotic,[12] which would provide a metalanguage into which the various subsidiary scientific languages might be translated, never got past the first, rather mundane stage of translating Saussure into Peirce, and vice versa.

As Parret puts it, "The dynamism of the sign relation in Peirce is in fact due to the functioning of the third term, the interpreter, which is simultaneously a sign itself and an essential ingredient of any sign relation" (1983: 29). Thus, whereas Peirce's analytic semiotics evolves "a *logic of action*" (30), the dyadic concept of the sign operative in structural semiotics produces chiefly "a *relational* logistics" (30), providing "no perspective either on the dynamism and the creativity of the sign and the meaning process or on the *interpretation* regularities and rules of *inference*" (31) at work in that process. We are left with a dispute about whether semiotics should be viewed primarily as a formal or as a functional grammar (36; cf. Dik 1978)—with the analytic semioticians setting up semiosis on a functional basis, the structural semioticians by contrast urging for signs' closed, immanent systematicity. Over the course of this long dispute, as should by now be apparent, the question of pragmatics has occupied an especially prominent position. Indeed, the delayed and largely piecemeal introduction of the analytic model into a structuralist tradition (Pavel 1989) perhaps accounts for the very different conceptions of pragmatics held even today by Anglo-American and European language theorists (cf. Levinson 1983: 2; Verschueren 1985).

In *Semiotics and Pragmatics*, Parret himself seeks to "homologate" the analytic and structuralist perspectives; he attempts to bridge the form-function dichotomy via a sufficiently broad notion of semiosis as a process comprising both communicative and logical dimensions (1983: 40; cf. 89–128). Arguably, however, even while what Parret characterizes as the analytic-structuralist dispute was beginning to take shape, the Prague School had begun to point beyond the very terms in which that debate was being cast. Stratifying context itself into de jure and de facto classes of context, the polyfunctionalism of Mukařovský and Jakobson features a quite sophisticated apparatus for linking, rather than dichotomizing, forms and functions, grammar (and logic) and meaning.

4.2. In discussing Mukařovský's and Jakobson's metapragmatic stratification of context into the actual and the virtual, our aim is not to multiply (meta)levels and generate neologisms gratuitously. Our aim, rather, is to use the Prague School's concept of functional contexts as a way of contextualizing the idea that contexts help determine meaning. As the polyfunctionalist model teaches us, to say that meaning is pragmatically determined is to say that the resolution of meaning into contexts—more precisely, the resolution of utterances into sentences paired with contexts—is a forever incomplete operation. A context is by definition always only more or less, never absolutely, specifiable (cf. Derrida 1982c [1971], 1988b); furthermore, there are indefinitely many (possible) contexts. For Mukařovský and Jakobson, this interminable divisibility and multipliability of contexts can be halted only temporarily and provisionally,[13] and again only within a particular sociocultural context, by assigning *dominance* (cf. Jakobson 1971b [1935]) to one function of an utterance vis-à-vis its other functions, its other meanings (see sec. 6). Thus, we can say that the Prague School, admittedly *avant la lettre*, built its pragmatics on the basis of a metapragmatics, or at least on the basis of the idea that, in principle if not in fact, any given portion of the context of an utterance always bears on another portion of that context or on some other context, any context C_n on context C_{n+1} or on context $C_o, C_p, \ldots, C_z$.

5. Stratifications of Context; Metapragmatic Rules

I can better describe the metapragmatic profile of the Prague School's polyfunctionalism by situating it against the backdrop of Mary-Louise Pratt's *Toward a Speech Act Theory of Literary Discourse* (1977). The account of Prague School structuralism found in this important book has been influential in scholarly discussion at large; unfortunately, because the account is misleading or at least incomplete, Pratt's study has assisted in the trend that assimilates the Prague School either to Russian Formalism or alternatively to the Francophone structuralists working in the 1960s and the 1970s. We should recall at the outset, however, that Pratt's study appeared *just before* Peter Steiner and John Burbank (among others) undertook their translations of the work of the Prague School into English.[14] Thus, the bulk of the Prague School materials to which we now have access were unavailable to Pratt herself when she wrote her book nearly twenty years ago.

Be that as it may, arguing that "a socially-based, use-oriented linguistics is a prerequisite toward sealing the breach between formal and sociological approaches to literature" (1977: xix), Pratt attributes this breach to what she calls "the Poetic Language Fallacy" (6ff.), a fallacy of which both the Russian Formalists and the Prague School structuralists were guilty, according to the author (xii). As Pratt convincingly points out, the quasi-linguistic categories of "poetic" versus "practical" language represent not empirically falsifiable divisions of language use but rather a more or less ingenious way of articulating a foregone conclusion. Postulating "a separate grammar of poetry which is related analogically to the grammar of language" (11) at large, the Poetic Language Fallacy commits us to the view that "intrinsic textual properties constitute 'literariness'" (26). Yet "the weakness of the 'poetic language' argument immediately surfaces as soon as 'ordinary language' is treated not as a vacuous dummy category but as a real body of data" (25). As Pratt aptly demonstrates, those data bear out the conclusion not that literary discourse is a separate *kind* of language but rather that literature marks a particular *use* of a single stock of linguistic resources—resources that happen to be exploited somewhat differently in discourse that (because of genre expectations and other factors) we are not inclined to label *literary.*

Admittedly, the Poetic Language Fallacy does in fact operate, at least to some degree,[15] in a text like Èjchenbaum's "Theory of the 'Formal Method'" (1971 [1926]). Here Èjchenbaum's claims that "the basis of our position was and is that the object of literary science, as such, must be the study of those specifics which distinguish it from any other material" (831); he also points to "the contrast between poetic and practical language that served as the basic principle of the Formalists' work on key problems of poetics" (832). But what must be stressed is that, even *if* we grant Pratt's assertion that "the Formalists were only interested in the structural properties of literary utterances" (1977: 6),[16] and even *if,* furthermore, we grant that the Formalists in this respect took their cue from Saussurean structural linguistics, which on Pratt's view "does not claim to describe real utterances of any kind but rather the abstract set of rules which underlies real utterances" (7), still we need not accede to the claim that Prague School structuralism merely continues, in a different time and place, the work of the Formalists. Nor must we grant Pratt's contention that "Prague School structural linguistics, though it made a point of calling itself 'functional,' was, like Saussure, almost uniquely concerned with the function of elements within the linguistic system rather than with the functions the language serves within the speech community" (7). Peter Steiner (1982), for his part, has stressed the historical implausibility of viewing the relation between Russian Formalism and Prague Structuralism as "a mere transfer of ideas" (175; cf. Steiner 1984: 268–70). Instead, Steiner argues that an indigenous Czech tradition of aesthetic inquiry made the Prague School particularly receptive to only certain of the Formalists' concerns (1982: 184ff.; cf. Jakobson 1971a [1936]: 547–48).

But how, specifically, does Prague School functionalism differ from its avowedly Formalist antecedents? For one thing, to say that Mukařovský's functionalism is situated (primarily) on "the linguistic system" rather than "the speech community" (Pratt 1977: 7) is to gloss over important historical differences between the formalist and the structuralist movements. Debatably, by misreading Mukařovský in this fashion Pratt fails to recognize the ways in which Mukařovský's claims about social collectivities actually anticipate Pratt's own ideas about speech communities. More generally, a detailed examination of some key texts by Mukařovský and Jakobson shows that it is wrong to characterize the functional contexts of the Prague School as merely the notion of literariness in disguise. Matters are much more complicated than that. Far from rigidly demarcating functional contexts according to different genres of discourse (the poetic vs. the practical, say), the Prague Structuralists assigned indefinitely multipliable contexts for any and all utterances—including the utterances constituting pragmatic inquiry itself—through what may be termed two metapragmatic rules. As I now go on to spell out, these rules can be construed as (i) a rule for the dialectical interplay of functional contexts one within another at any given time and (ii) a rule for the relativization, via the social collectivities in which particular functions arise, of functional contexts over time. Although in this connection Mukařovský's and Jakobson's arguments are of a generally semiotic as opposed to a narrowly linguistic provenance, I shall attempt to draw out the language-theoretical applications of their ideas, particularly since I am working my way back around (in secs. 7ff.) to a discussion of analogous metapragmatic mechanisms in Woolf's *Between the Acts.*

5.1. Granted, Mukařovský does in some instances seem to vacillate between, on the one hand, positing merely a difference in degree between poetic and other utterances and, on the other hand, making poetic utterances a class of language use different in kind from other sorts of utterances. Thus, in the first section of his essay "On Poetic Language," "Poetic Language as a Functional Language and as a Material," Mukařovský at one point asserts

> that no single property characterizes poetic language permanently and generally. Poetic language is permanently characterized only by its function; however, function is only a *mode of utilizing* the properties of a given phenomenon. Poetic language belongs among the numerous other functional languages. (1977 [1940]: 3–4)

Immediately after this passage, however, Mukařovský makes the following claim:

> The aesthetic "orientation toward the expression itself," which is, of course, valid not only for linguistic expression and not only for verbal art but for all arts and for any realm of the aesthetic, is a phenomenon *essentially* different from a logical orientation toward expression whose task is to make expression more precise, as has been especially emphasized

by the so-called Logical Positivist movement ("Viennese Circle") and in particular by Rudolf Carnap. (4)

Arguably, any approach to language use that calls itself functionalist cannot legitimately label as "essential" the difference between one "mode of utilizing" language and another. Nor is it permissible for a functionalist approach to brand "the Logical Positivist notion of language [as] *completely* different from the notion of language as a means of communication in everyday life" (5; my emphasis). Here Mukařovský's self-contradictory propositions—the proposition that we must ground meaning in modes of language use and the proposition that philosophical and communicative uses of language are absolutely distinct—seem to bear out the criticism that "[Mukařovský] end[s] up maintaining a difference in kind and denying it at the same time" (Pratt 1977: 26), for, once we grant a difference in kind between the use to which language is put in logico-syntactical analysis and the use to which it is put in communicative situations at large, it is but a short step to the dreaded Poetic Language Fallacy.

Yet there is in turn a difference in kind between identifying inconsistencies in Mukařovský's functionalist argument and resolving the functionalist position itself back into the view to which Prague School (poly)functionalism is manifestly opposed: the view, namely, that utterances are bestowed with intrinsic properties, of a given sort, even apart from the contexts—and in particular the speech communities or, in Mukařovský's parlance, "collectivities"—in which the utterances are designed and interpreted. Consider what Holenstein (1979a: 10–11) and Steiner (1982: 198–99) have characterized as the monofunctionalist tendencies evident in the Russian Formalist Lev Jakubinskij's 1916 essay "On the Sounds of Poetic Language." Jakubinskij's is a restricted functionalism that, as Holenstein argues, ultimately reduplicates the ordinary language–poetic language distinction ("den Unterschied zwischen gewohnlicher und poetischer Sprache in finaler Perspektive" [11]). For Jakubinskij, the test for "practical" as opposed to "poetic" language is this: are the means of expression wholly subordinated to the communicative function (= practical language), or, conversely, are the means of expression accorded independent value, as defined against the communicative function (= poetic language)? In *this* species of functionalism, in its clear-cut opposition between the communicative function of language and its non- or extracommunicative (poetic) function, we do in fact find that covert search for literariness with which Pratt stigmatizes functionalism generally.

Even in the Prague School's own 1929 "Theses"[17] we find evidence to support the charge that what should be a commitment to functional gradualism—a mere difference in degree between different uses of language—all too often manifests itself as a commitment to generic differences of kind, as either-or distinctions between kinds of utterance. Thus, in the thesis "On the Functions of Language," the members of the Prague School assert that "*In its social role* one must distinguish *speech according to its relation to extralinguistic reality.* It has either *a communicative function,* that is, it is directed toward the object of expression, or *a poetic function,* that is, it is directed toward the expression itself" (Steiner 1982: 12). Accordingly, continues the thesis, "It is advisable to study those forms of speech in which one function *totally predominates* and those in which manifold functions interpenetrate" (12; my emphasis). In the first part of the quoted passage, the members of the Prague School seem to be hedging their bets against precisely that manifold interpenetration of functions which the second part of the passage makes room for—an interpenetration that points beyond what can only be a spurious distinction between poetic and ordinary language.

Other, more developed accounts of functional contexts by the Prague School, however, do not prove so susceptible to charges of the Poetic Language Fallacy. Of particular importance here are Mukařovský's extended analysis, in a number of different texts, of the role of the aesthetic function vis-à-vis the other functions and also the well-known six-function schema set out, long after the heyday of the Prague School, in Jakobson's "Closing Statement: Linguistics and Poetics" (1960). It is not just that these polyfunctionalist accounts make it impossible to distinguish between literary and nonliterary discourse in any absolute or generic sense. More than this, through the two metapragmatic rules mentioned previously—one concerning the dialectical interplay of functions at any given time, the other concerning the relativity of those functions over time—Jakobson and Mukařovský indefinitely multiply the contexts in which a given utterance is in principle operative at a given time t_n as well as the contexts within which an utterance will potentially be operative, or has possibly been operative, at time t_{n+1} or t_{n-1}.

5.2. In "Linguistics and Poetics" (1960), Jakobson states at the outset that

> language must be investigated in all the variety of its functions. Before discussing the poetic function we must define its place among the other functions of language. An outline of these functions demands a concise survey of the constitutive factors in any speech event, in any act of verbal communication. (353)

At about the same time that J. L. Austin (1962) was conducting his own post-Wittgensteinian researches into how to do things with words, Jakobson built on the theory of communicative functions already in place in Karl Bühler's *Sprachtheorie* (1934). That theory, whose structuralist extensions have been carefully documented by Holenstein (1979a), marks an attempt "die Funktionen den konstitutiven Komponenten des Sprechereignisses zuzuordnen und in ihnen zu verankern" 'to coordinate the functions of the constitutive components of speech events and to anchor those functions in such speech occurrences' (Holenstein 1979a: 13).[18] Yet Jakobson also stresses the polyfunctionality of any given utterance: its constitutive dependence on a field of interpenetrating functions; its status as an illocutionary act whose effects, far from being restricted to any one communicative function (the referential, say), distribute themselves, in fundamentally indefinite magnitudes, *among* the other communicative functions in which the speech act is (simultaneously) either in fact or in principle engaged. As Jakobson puts it,

> Although we distinguish six basic aspects of language, we could, however, hardly find verbal messages that would fulfill only one function. The diversity lies not in a monopoly of some one of these several functions but in a different hierarchical order of functions. The verbal structure of a message depends primarily on the predominant function. But even though a set [*Einstellung*] toward the referent, an orientation toward the *context*—briefly the so-called *referential,* "denotative," "cognitive" function—is the leading task of numerous messages, the accessory participation of the other functions in such messages must be taken into account. (1960: 353)

Insofar as Jakobson emphasizes "the [potential] accessory participation of the other functions" in each particular manifestation of linguistic function, his model avoids driving a wedge of generic, absolute difference between literary and nonliterary discourse and thereby falling victim to the Poetic Language Fallacy.

At one point Pratt comments that, with respect to the poetic function specifically, Jakobson "does not provide any criteria for determining when [the] presence [of the poetic function] has reached the point of dominance" (1977: 33). Arguably, however, the very existence of such criteria would entail not a mobile interpenetration of the functional contexts in which any given utterance participates—not a continuously shifting configuration of functions comprising, at all times, a host of accessory functions *in potentia*—but rather a static structure of functional relations to which one and the same set of criteria could be applied, over and over again, in order to determine the dominance of this or that particular function. In effect, to demand set criteria for functional dominance is to place form over function, text over context. Or at the very least it is to choose a monofunctionalist over a polyfunctionalist model.

5.3. We can further illuminate Jakobson's emphasis on the accessory participation of functions by examining Mukařovský's analyses of the aesthetic function and of functional contexts in general. Mukařovský's arguments quite explicitly couple the first metapragmatic principle, involving the simultaneous interplay of various functions, with the second such principle, involving the attachment of particular functional configurations to particular social collectivities. Indeed, as Mukařovský's stratifications of contexts suggest, the two metapragmatic rules taken together bear a striking analogy to that difference and that deferral which Derrida assigns to the structure of signification in general: "*Différance* as temporization, *différance* as spacing" (1982a [1968]: 9).

In assembling Mukařovský's polyfunctionalist statements, we find, first, those propositions which bear on the interpenetration, the accessory participation, of functions. In his essay "The Place of the Aesthetic Function among the Other Functions" (1978d [1942]), for instance, Mukařovský proposes to "revise" the (monofunctionalist [37]) emphasis hitherto at work in "functional architecture and functional linguistics" (34–35), remarking,

> We are not concerned with the aesthetic as a static property of things, but with the aesthetic as an energetic component of human activity. For this reason we are not interested in the relation of the aesthetic to other metaphysical principles, such as the true and the good, but in its relation to other motives and goals of human activity and creation. (32–33)

In consequence, as Mukařovský observes in the same essay, "there is not an insurmountable difference between practically and aesthetically oriented activities" (34); in consequence, too,

> not even the most ordinary colloquial speech is, in principle, devoid of the aesthetic function. And so it is with all other human activities. . . . In brief, we shall find no sphere in which the aesthetic function is essentially absent; potentially it is always present; it can arise at any time. It has no limitation, therefore, and we cannot say that some domains of human activity are in principle devoid of it, while it belongs to others in principle. (35)

As Mukařovský puts it, "there are cultural forms [like "folklore culture"] . . . in which functions—among them, of course, the aesthetic—are almost indistinguishable from one another, in which they appear with every act as a compact bundle" (36). And if "any function, not just the one which the acting subject ascribes to his [or her] act or creation, can always be evoked" (36–37), then Mukařovský is quite justified in drawing a broader "conclusion pertaining to functions in general": the conclusion, namely, that "can be formulated as the basic polyfunctionality of human activity and the basic omnipresence of functions" (37).

Propositions of this class—propositions about the polyfunctionality not just of linguistic utterances but of all human activity and about the impossibility, therefore, of indexing a single function to a given activity or utterance—can be found throughout Mukařovský's corpus. Thus, in the essay "On the Problem of Functions in Architecture," Mukařovský asserts that "every act in which an object is used can simultaneously pursue more than one purpose" (1978c [1937–38]: 237) and also that "there are potentially present in every act and its result functions other than those which the act obviously fulfills" (239). More poetically, if we can risk that term here, Mukařovský, describing the aesthetic function as "always potentially present, waiting for the least opportunity for revival" (244), goes on to suggest that "the aesthetic function clings closely to and follows the other functions just as space fills up with air everywhere that an object has withdrawn, or just as darkness penetrates a fold of space from which light has retreated" (244). Similarly, in his "Poetic Reference," Mukařovský reiterates that "the boundary separating the aesthetic function from practical functions is not always apparent, and, in particular, it does not coincide with the dividing line between art and other human activities. Even in a fully autonomous artistic expression, practical functions . . . are not entirely suppressed" (1976 [1936]: 158).

Further, in his book-length study *Aesthetic Function, Norm and Value as Social Facts* (1970 [1936]), Mukařovský links (i) the set of propositions in which he stresses the accessory participation of functions with (ii) the set of propositions in which he distributes functions across different temporal (and/or sociocultural) contexts. Restating that "there is no definite borderline between the aesthetic and the extra-aesthetic" (1) and that "the aesthetic sphere develops as a whole and is, in addition, constantly related to those aspects of reality which, at a given point in time, do not exhibit the aesthetic function at all" (19), Mukařovský clarifies his position thus: "There are no objects or actions which, by virtue of their essence or organization would, regardless of time, place or the person evaluating them, possess an aesthetic function and others which, again by their very nature, would be necessarily immune to the aesthetic function" (1–2).

Thus, we find, in the second place, various propositions enjoining us to relativize the fit between functions and things. Such relativization proceeds by way of the temporal or, more broadly, sociocultural contexts in which the fit between functions and things is to be determined. As Mukařovský (1970 [1936]) puts it,

> The aesthetic function manifests itself only under certain conditions, i.e. in a certain social context. A phenomenon which, in one time period, country, etc., was the privileged bearer of the aesthetic function may be incapable of bearing this function in a different time, country, etc. . . . As soon as we change our perspective in time, space, or even from one social grouping to another (e.g. from one [social] stratum to another, one generation to another, etc.) we find a change in the distribution of the aesthetic function and of its boundaries. (3, 5)

Hence, if "the aesthetic function is, in itself, neither a real property of an object nor . . . explicitly connected to some of its properties," and if the "aesthetic function of an object is likewise not totally under the control of an individual," then we must conclude that "stabilizing the aesthetic function is a matter for the collective and is a component in the relationship between the human collective and the world" and, furthermore, that "any given distribution of the aesthetic function in the material world is tied to a particular social entity" (18). In "The Problem of Functions in Architecture," Mukařovský explicitly connects the dialectical interplay of functions with the temporal and social contexts in which the configuration or "structural bond" of functions is most fundamentally located. As Mukařovský puts it, "Because of the dominance of the structural bond among functions over individual functions it is sometimes possible to identify one and the same function in two different historical or social contexts only with great difficulty" (1978c [1937–38]: 238). Inescapably, we must deal with a "set of functions [both] lodged in the awareness of the collective and bound by internal interrelations into a structure" (237). Hence, if within a certain structure of functions "an object can change its conventional function in the course of time," this temporal variability of functions in turn derives, "on the one hand, [from] the collective that associates certain functions with a particular object and, on the other hand, [from] the individual who uses the object for his personal aims and largely determines this usage" (237). Indeed, the dialectical antinomy, as it were, between individual and collectivity, with the individual introducing "a constantly renewed structure of accidentality into the functional process and thus [setting] [a given] structure of functions into motion" (237), ensures that the manner in which a social collectivity embodies a functional configuration can be determined only on a temporary basis. What *you* call a poetic utterance, for instance, *I* do not; yet in a moment, under the right kind of (peer) pressure, I may have to grant your point and thereby extend, once again, the protean domain of the aesthetic function.

6. General and Special Theories of Context

On the basis of the preceding discussion of Jakobson and Mukařovský, we can reformulate as follows metapragmatic rule i:

> At any given time, it is impossible to rule out *in principle* the accessory participation of one or more communicative (or more broadly behavioral) function in another such function;

and metapragmatic rule ii:

> The function assigned to a fragment of linguistic or other behavior occurring at time t_n cannot *in principle* be determined by the application of any one set of functional criteria embedded in a social collectivity at time t_{n+1} (the future) or time t_{n-1} (the past) or indeed, factoring in the additional constraint of rule i, at time t_n (the present) itself.

Note the emphasis on the phrase *in principle* in both formulations. Without some such restriction of their scope—a restriction that Mukařovský for one explicitly recommends—the metapragmatic principles would cease to be metapragmatic and would instead become pragmatic. Or, rather, they would become antipragmatic because they would in effect rule out the very possibility of establishing *any* rule-governed connections between forms and functions, sentences and meanings. In this scenario, speech acts, for example, could not be linked in more than a random way to the contexts in which they occur. There would be no principled way of distinguishing (quickly and efficiently) between the string *I'm going to kill you* uttered as a joke and the same string spoken in earnest. The concept of killing out of self-defense would have to be extended to unmanageable proportions in order to cover the violent reactions of those persons to whom such undecidably ambiguous threats and/or jokes had been addressed.

But the point is that Prague School functionalism *does* restrict the scope of its metapragmatic rules; an emphasis on the potential revisability of pragmatic rules does not diminish the necessity and regularity of those rules' de facto application. Rather, nonrandom connections between forms and functions—texts and contexts, sentences and meanings—result from the (always provisional, always temporary) application of the operator "dominance" to a given structure of functional interrelations (cf. Jakobson 1971 [1935]).[19] Dominance marks the threshold at which functional contexts produce in fact, and because of inescapable local constraints, local structures of meaning (cf. Plotnitsky 1987). De facto the linguistic string *I'm going to kill you* derives, from the particular context in which it is designed and interpreted, a rule-governed (pre)dominance of one communicative function over other possible functions. To be sure, further information or a change of context might in principle cause a shift of dominants, that is, the attribution of a different (primary) communicative function to the string. But, without suppressing the *possibility* of other contexts and hence other meanings, the metapragmatic stratification of contexts ensures that a particular functional context actually (nonrandomly) yields a dominant meaning when brought to bear on a particular fragment of linguistic or other behavior.

6.1. Having outlined the general theory of context subtending Prague School functionalism—namely, the stratification of contexts into de jure and de facto classes of contextual constraint and the two metapragmatic rules bound up with this stratification—I can now work toward a special theory of context vis-à-vis strategies for discourse representation in Woolf. (By implication, at least, the special theory will have a bearing on the representation of discourse in narratives generally.) It is not just that Woolf's discourse representations highlight the mechanisms by which linguistic forms get paired with contexts to produce meaningful utterances. Beyond this, and in parallel with Jakobson's and Mukařovský's polyfunctionalism, Woolf's text encodes a stratificational model for understanding context itself. The illocutionary acts represented in the novel can be situated along an array stretching from types that background the bearing of other possible contexts on the current context(s) of utterance, to types that foreground just this indefinite multipliability of contexts, eliding the difference between actual and possible, de facto and de jure contexts of utterance. I shall attempt to substantiate the previous claims through examination of both the themes (sec. 7) and the forms (secs. 8ff.) of Woolf's novel.

7. Thematizing (Indefinitely Multipliable) Contexts

Thematically speaking, Woolf's narrative encodes a polyfunctionalist stratification of contexts in the contrast between the aging Bart Oliver and his sister,

Lucy Swithin. This contrast is set out in the early sections of the novel, before the text's later generalization and pluralization of "voices" begins to place in brackets the very idea of a character or (discrete) identity.

7.1. When we first meet Lucy

> she had stretched for her favourite reading—an Outline of History—and spent the hours between three and five thinking of rhododendron forests in Piccadilly; when the entire continent, not then, she understood, divided by a channel, was all one; populated, she understood, by elephant-bodied, seal-necked, heaving, surging, slowly writhing, and, she supposed, barking monsters; the iguanodon, the mammoth, and the mastodon; from whom presumably, she thought, jerking the window open, we descend. (8)

More generally, Lucy is "given to increasing the bounds of the moment by flights into past or future; or sidelong down corridors and alleys" (9). She thereby exploits the same temporal and modal displacements at the basis of Mukařovský's and Jakobson's polyfunctionalist scheme—a scheme according to which the meaning of a sentence, say, varies as a function of the illimitable variety of circumstances in which that sentence might be (or have been) uttered.

Lucy must sometimes forcibly remind herself that her own actions unfold in "actual time" as opposed to "mind time" (9). By and large, however, Lucy lives according to mind time; she occupies the place of the (historical) imagination, of memory, and of the book. Her chief concern is in effect the relativity of utterances' meaning across different contexts. The result is that the determination of the truth or falsity of a given proposition about some state of affairs—for example, the position of the sea relative to one's present position on land (29)—is of secondary importance when set over against the fact that the state of affairs in question might have been (and once was) otherwise: " 'Once there was no sea,' said Mrs. Swithin. 'No sea at all between us and the continent. I was reading that in a book this morning. There were rhododendrons in the Strand; and mammoths in Piccadilly' " (29–30). Later, too, Lucy reflects on the migratory patterns of the swallows in the barn's rafters, remembering once again the way things were "Before there was a channel, when the earth, upon which the Windsor chair was planted, was a riot of rhododendrons, and humming birds quivered at the mouths of scarlet trumpets, as she had read that morning in her Outline of History" (108). Yet Lucy fulfills the obligations of memory and the imperatives of the imagination just by neglecting present interpretive responsibilities. She remembers and imagines at the cost of being deemed irrelevant and even trivial with respect to her assessment of current states of affairs. Hence the condescending thoughts and smiles all too often bestowed on Lucy: "Well, if the thought [that 'the agony of the particular sheep, cow, or human being is necessary'] gave her comfort, William and Isa smiled across her, let her think it" (175; cf. 27).

As we might also put it, Lucy's is the peculiar powerlessness that derives from subsuming contextual determinants operative de facto at time t under any number of other possible contexts operative merely de jure at times $t_1, t_2, \ldots, t_n$. It is not whether or how a thing is so but rather under what conditions the thing might have been or may yet be so that most occupies Lucy's imagination.

7.2. Conversely, Bart tends to subsume contexts possibly operative at some time or another under the particular contexts in which he finds himself compelled to act at the moment. Bart is thus the ultimate pragmatist, in more than one sense of that term. Not only does he propose to use umbrellas instead of prayer to circumvent rain (23); furthermore, he faults his sister precisely for her lack of fixity relative to the present moment, the current context: "She would have been, he thought, a very clever woman, had she fixed her gaze. But this led to that; that to the other. What went in at this ear, went out at that" (24; cf. 204–5). It falls to Bart, therefore, to consult the encyclopedia in order to isolate the exact origin and significance of the expression "Touch wood"—to grasp a literal meaning at the heart of the figurative, the idiomatic (28). Yet if, in general, "What [Lucy] saw [Bart] didn't; what he saw she didn't—and so on, *ad infinitum*" (26), nonetheless, once his sister replaces speculation and superstition with (dis)confirmable observations—about past states of affairs, say, or procedures for determining whether fish is fresh (29)—Bart readily concurs: "A fact that was." In short, Bart's chief concern is to avoid error in the determination of particular facts, not to assess the limits of the domain of the factual by imagining alternative contexts in which a different version of the facts might have gained, or might yet gain, currency. Thus, asked how far away the sea is, Bart responds "as if he had whipped a tape measure from his pocket and measured it exactly" (29). Bart's situation is in a sense best defined by the legacy of strictly delimited choices that he has passed down to Giles, his son: "Given his choice, [Giles] would have chosen to farm. But he was not given his choice. So one thing led to another; and the conglomeration of things pressed you flat; held you fast, like a fish in water" (47). Like Giles's, Bart's interpretive orientation may be measured against what Isa describes as a sort of paradigm case of non- or antifactuality, a situation intolerable to Giles's fixation on actual as opposed to mind time and later reproduced in the events surrounding the performance of Miss La Trobe's pageant: "Books open; no conclusion come to; and he [i.e., Giles] sitting in the audience" (59).

8. The Contexts in the Form

Yet Woolf's text encodes different modalities of context not only through its themes but also through its forms. Put simply, the narrative discourse of *Between the Acts*—more particularly, its use of represented discourse—is so designed that we can adopt neither the assumptions of Lucy nor those of Bart (or Giles) in interpreting the text. Generating an entire matrix of discourse representations, the narrative compels us to adjudicate between classes of contextual constraint of the de facto and de jure types. The text unfolds as a metapragmatic search for the very conditions of functional dominance, the scope and limits of meaning-in-context.

Schematically, assume that the narrative discourse D posits an utterance U issued by character x in a speech situation involving an interlocutor y. Character x might be represented as having issued U_a, at some indefinite time prior to present time t, through some speech act(s) narrativized through D but allowing for a range of factors $f_1, f_2, \ldots, f_n$ that might have produced certain infelicities in the narrative transcription of U_a into D via the illocutionary acts represented in the text. In that case, U_a is subject to a quite different order of contextual constraints than, say, what D merely posits as U_b said by x to y three minutes prior to t. The point is that Bart would reduce represented discourse of the first, complex type to represented discourse of the second, less complex type, forcibly assimilating utterances having the structure of U_a to those having the same structure as U_b. Lucy, by contrast, would perform just the opposite reduction, counterfactualizing U_b into U_a, as it were. Yet interpreting Woolf's text requires that, ideally at least, we avoid both sorts of reduction; instead, the highly variegated profile of the voices encoded in the text forces us to acknowledge a whole gamut of speech situations with their attendant contextual constraints.

Hence, interpretation of the narrative form, whose description demands an enriched typology of illocutionary acts, requires that we accommodate an entire spectrum of discourse representations. At the outer limits of that spectrum are classes of utterance whose paradigm cases are U_a and U_b; between those limits are intermediate classes, their boundaries marked by a metapragmatic polarity par excellence. One boundary is defined by (i) the de jure infinite multipliability of contexts for utterances and/or behaviors across particular collectivities at different times and among different collectivities (or possibly the same collectivity) at the same time. The other boundary is defined by (ii) the de facto selection of a functional dominant, and the suppression of indefinitely many other (communicative) functions, according to constraints at work in all language use, all (linguistic and other) behavior.

9. An Enriched Typology of Discourse Representations

By working toward a finer-grained taxonomy of the novel's discourse representations, then, one can prepare the way for further analysis of the metapragmatic profile of Woolf's novel. Arguably, the ways in which the narrative represents discourse exceed the scope of the standard typologies. Thus, the discourse types customarily designated DD, ID, and FID must be supplemented by some hybridized (and, over longer stretches of the text, concatenated and embedded) discourse types if we are to capture the discursive acts so richly dramatized in *Between the Acts*.[20] Attention to just those discourse types on which standard narratological paradigms would otherwise confer anomalous or at least derivative status—together with a pragmatically enriched narratological vocabulary— can help us outline a metapragmatics of represented discourse.

As suggested in section *8,* the types of discourse represented in *Between the Acts* can be ordered along a continuum; the increments of the continuum mark degrees to which the various species of illocutionary acts highlight contextual determinants of their production and reception. The lower end of the continuum might be defined as a kind of zero-degree discourse. Engaged in zero-degree discourse, speakers take no consideration whatsoever of the possible meanings that could in principle accrue to a given utterance through a change of contexts. In this instance, the discourse does not in any way allude to other possible contexts but rather brackets them under pressure of the particular contexts bearing on it. The upper end of the continuum, by contrast, may be defined as discourse that highlights the contextual considerations bracketed by discourse of the zero degree. In this instance, the functioning of an utterance in some current discourse induces (metapragmatic) reflection on how we should set about situating that very utterance in the current discourse. Or, to put it otherwise, the utterance is so designed that, in processing it, we are compelled to ask how it relates both to other contexts, past and present, in which the utterance might in principle be operative and to other ways in which the utterance could de jure function vis-à-vis the present context itself. By now it should be apparent that no (represented) utterance could strictly speaking be categorized either as zero-degree or as absolutely context-foregrounding discourse. But, still, we can specify differences between utterances located at different points on the continuum. For example, what was schematized in section 7 as U_a versus U_b can be situated somewhere at the upper (context-foregrounding) end versus the lower (context-backgrounding) end of the continuum, respectively. The task at hand, therefore, is to fashion an enriched typology of represented discourse on the basis of differences that can be mapped more or less directly into increments segmenting the continuum just described.

Before examining how Woolf's discourse representations can be ranked incrementally along the continuum just described, we should take note of an important precedent for an analysis of the sort proposed.[21] At the same time I can discuss the basis of the symbolism used below for the sake of descriptive convenience. The ensuing inventory of discourse types will be modeled, at least in broad outline, on Lubomír Doležel's (1973) account of DN (narrator's discourse) as a theoretical or idealized base with respect to which different distributions of distinctive features may be used to define different forms of represented discourse. But since in the proposed analysis the category of represented discourse would include both what Doležel calls DC (character's discourse) and what he terms RD (represented discourse) in a narrower sense, and since even within what Doležel names RD the present analysis identifies a wider variety of subtypes than the two Doležel designates "compact" and "diffused" (50ff.), as a result the analysis proposed attempts to account for proportionately more complex distributions and permutations of distinctive features, relative to the idealized discourse base here designated simply D (for "discourse").

In fact, D represents the zero-degree discourse described a moment ago: that is, a limiting case in which changes of context can have no conceivable bearing on utterance meaning. Thus, D amounts to the theoretical postulate of a maximally descriptive (purely diegetic) discourse. For a point of reference, we can compare the Scholastics' postulate of "adequation" at the base of their theory of truth as *adaequatio rei et intellectus*. (The latter formulation is Saint Thomas Aquinas's, as cited by Frederick Copleston 1962 [1950]: 185–86.) However, in the case of D, what is postulated is not an adequation of discourse relative to what the discourse strives to represent or approximate but rather an adequation of a particular discourse design relative to a particular discourse interpretation. Adequation of the sort just described could not in fact be realized in any empirical utterance, just to the extent that language qua language is subject to interpretation in contexts that cannot be foreseen or second-guessed at the moment a given unit of discourse is designed. Yet D can nonetheless serve a useful heuristic function, viewed as a theoretical base that forms too the (lower) endpoint of the continuum of discourse types. Furthermore, in the inventory that follows, the "lowest" discourse type actually identified is D_n—roughly analogous to Doležel's DN ("narrator's discourse") but here distinguished from D specifically by the sorts of context-foregrounding features that make the narrator's discourse relatively more opaque, more subject to (re)interpretation, than D would be (by definition).

Equipped with the postulates just set out, and working within the framework of a special theory of context, I can now go on to sketch a partial inventory of the discourse types found in *Between the Acts*. The analysis will include, first, a simple list of the types of discourse representation, which will then be indexed to illustrative passages taken from Woolf's novel (sec. *9.1*). These constituent types are in turn subject to various forms of concatenation and embedding over the course of the narrative; therefore, I next examine a few longer stretches of the text in order to indicate the richness and complexity issuing from combinations of the constituent types cataloged (sec. *9.2*). Finally, in section *10*, my task is to indicate how the proposed typology, even in the merely rudimentary form that it attains here, can be plotted against the metapragmatic continuum stretching from utterances having roughly the structure of U_b to those having roughly the structure of U_a.

9.1. The following is a synoptic listing of the discourse types that will be inventoried via Woolf's text.[22] The catalog offered immediately afterward will detail some of the relations and contrasts between the various types listed; but an initial overview of constituent types, arranged as it were into families of discourse representations, may assist readers in drawing their own conclusions about intercategory relations.

I. Synopsis of Discourse Types

D_n = discourse of the narrator
AD = attributive discourse

DD = direct discourse
ID = indirect discourse
FID = free indirect discourse

IM = interior monologue
PDD/TIM = pseudo−direct discourse/transmissible interior monologue

indefDD(1) = restricted indefinite direct discourse (representation of
  utterances issuing from unknown member of a restricted set of speakers)

indefDD(2) = unrestricted indefinite direct discourse (representation of utterances issuing from unknown member of an unrestricted set of speakers)

indefID(1) = restricted indefinite indirect discourse (reported utterances issuing from unknown member of a restricted set of speakers)

indefID(2) = unrestricted indefinite indirect discourse (reported utterances issuing from unknown member of an unrestricted set of speakers)

II. Catalog of Discourse Types

D_n (= discourse of the narrator): "The audience was assembling. The music was summoning them. Down the paths, across the lawns they were streaming again" (118); "Isa, whose eyes had been wandering, shook her head" (175); "She [Miss La Trobe] thrust her suit case in at the scullery window and walked on, till at the corner she saw the red curtain at the bar window" (211).

AD (= attributive discourse, as described by Prince 1978): in the examples of DD that follow, "said Mrs. Swithin, at a venture," "Mrs. Swithin mused," and "she exclaimed" are instances of AD. Further, note this passage, which may be construed as an extended instance of "discours attributif," disattached, however, from any specific utterances at the moment of the attribution itself: "She [Lucy] spoke simply. She spoke with an effort. She spoke as if she must overcome her tiredness out of charity towards a stranger, a guest" (70).

DD (= direct discourse): " 'How those birds sing!' said Mrs. Swithin, at a venture" (9); " 'That's Mrs. Neale!' she exclaimed. 'A perfect marvel of a woman, aren't you, Mrs. Neale!' " (107); " 'The Victorians,' Mrs. Swithin mused. 'I don't believe,' she said with her odd little smile, 'that there ever were such people. Only you and me and William dressed differently' " (174–75).

ID (= indirect discourse): "Bart put his finger inside his mouth and projected the upper row outside his lip. They were false. *Yet,* he said, *the Olivers hadn't married cousins*" (30);[23] "Mrs. Parker was deploring to Isa in a low voice the village idiot. . . . 'But surely,' said Mrs. Parker, *and told Giles how creepy the idiot*—'We have one in our village'—*had made her feel.* 'Surely, Mr. Oliver, we're more civilized' " (110–11).

FID (= indirect discourse): "Then they went in to lunch, and Mrs. Manresa bubbled up, enjoying her own capacity to surmount, without turning a hair, this minor social crisis—this laying of two more places. *For had she not complete faith in flesh and blood? and aren't we all flesh and blood? and how silly to make bones of trifles when we're all flesh and blood under the skin—men and women too!* But she preferred men—obviously" (40); "*This afternoon?* Mrs. Manresa was aghast. *Was it the pageant? She had never dreamt it was this afternoon. They would never have thrust themselves in—had they known it was this afternoon"* (45–46); "[Mrs. Manresa] drew [Giles] down the Barn, in and out, from one to another. *She knew 'em all. Every one was a thorough good sort. No, she wouldn't allow it, not for a moment—Pinsent's bad leg.* 'No, no. We're not going to take that for an excuse, Pinsent.' *If he couldn't bowl, he could bat.* Giles agreed" (107–8).

IM (= interior monologue): "Mrs. Manresa laughed. She remembered. An anecdote was on the tip of her tongue, about a public lavatory built to celebrate the same occasion, and how the Mayor . . . *Could she tell it? No.* The old lady, gazing at the swallows, looked too refined. *'Refeened'*—Mrs. Manresa qualified the word to her own advantage, thus confirming her approval of the wild child she was, whose nature was somehow just human nature" (102);[24] "[Bart] could not find his son. He had lost him in the crowd. So old Bartholomew left the Barn, and went to his own room . . . standing in front of the book case. *Books: the treasured life-blood of immortal spirits. Poets; the legislators of mankind. Doubtless it was so. But Giles was unhappy"* (115); " 'Tut-tut-tut,' Mrs. Lynn Jones expostulated. 'There were grand men among them . . .' *Why she did not know, yet somehow she felt that a sneer had been aimed at her father; therefore at herself"* (164).

PDD (= pseudo–direct discourse, not to be confused with Vološinov's "quasi–direct discourse" [i.e., FID], and alternatively specifiable as *TIM* [= transmissible interior monologue]. Here typical markers [tag clauses, punctuation] of DD are retained, but surrounding discourse allows us to identify the verbal material in question as the unspoken utterances proper to IM. Yet those "unspoken" utterances function in the text as if they were in fact spoken):

> Giles then did what to Isa was his little trick; shut his lips; frowned; and took up the pose of one who bears the burden of the world's woe, making money for her to spend.
>
> "No," said Isa, as plainly as words could say it. "I don't admire you," and looked, not at his face, but at his feet. "Silly little boy, with blood on his boots." (111)

Compare, too, "At that she smiled a ravishing girl's smile, as if the wind had warmed the wintry blue in her eyes to amber. . . . 'I took you,' she apologized, 'away from your friends, William, because I felt wound tight here. . . .' She touched her bony forehead upon which a blue vein wriggled like a blue worm" (72–73); and, even more strikingly,

He [Giles] said (without words), "I'm damnably unhappy."

"So am I," Dodge echoed.

"And I too," Isa thought. (176)[25]

indefDD (= indefinite direct discourse, which retains quotation marks and other features specific to DD but which represents discourse attributable not to an individual character but rather to a collective or, to use the language of the text itself, a group of voices.) Compare this passage: "Over the tops of the bushes came stray voices, voices without bodies, symbolical voices they seemed to her [Miss La Trobe], half hearing, seeing nothing, but still, over the bushes, feeling invisible threads connecting the bodiless voices" (151). IndefDD may be subdivided according to the scope of the indefiniteness involved: that is, whether a given utterance is (1) indefinitely or undecidably attributable to some definite pair or group of characters or (2) undecidably attributable to any number of unspecified characters:

1. In the dialogue represented on pp. 158–60, the text attributes the utterances contained in this dialogue to two (minor) characters, "old Mrs. Lynn Jones (of the Mount)" and "Etty Springett, with whom, since both were widows now, she shared a house" (158). But tag clauses are omitted, and ellipses mark the space where those tag clauses together with attributive discourse would otherwise be inserted in order to help us decide who is saying what. (Note, too, the sporadic insertion of a term of address without a definite addressee—" 'D'you remember?' "—throughout this dialogue.)

2. In the following passage (which in its entirety spans pp. 120–22), note the use of an initial and appropriately vague tag clause, which acts as a kind of illocutionary quantifier whose scope is effectively infinite. This passage uses the term of address (minus a definite addressee) and the elliptical suppression of attributive discourse that we find in type 1 but distributes the utterances between a unrestricted set of unnamed speakers:

"They're not ready. . . . I hear 'em laughing" (they were saying). ". . . Dressing up. That's the great thing, dressing up. And it's pleasant now, the sun's not so hot. . . . That's one good the war brought us—longer days. . . . Where did we leave off? D'you remember? The Elizabethans. . . . Perhaps she'll reach the present, if she skips. . . . D'you think people change?" (120–21)

indefID (= indefinite indirect discourse, which like ID is marked by an absence of quotation marks but which like indefDD involves utterances undecidably attributable to two or more characters. Also as with indefDD we find two subtypes of indefID, differentiated according to the scope of the indefiniteness involved):

1. In the following passage we are, on the basis of previous discourse, able to infer who is present and therefore who falls under the scope of "they" and "we" (i.e., that subset of "the audience" composed of Bartholomew, Lucy, Isa, Giles, Mrs. Manresa, and William Dodge) mentioned at different points in the passage (note by the way that the passage itself thematizes indefiniteness of place or location): "There was nothing for the audience to do. Mrs. Manresa suppressed a yawn. They were silent. They stared at the view, as if something might happen in one of those fields to relieve them of the intolerable burden of sitting silent, doing nothing, in company. *Their minds and bodies were too close, yet not close enough. We aren't free, each one of them felt separately, to feel or think separately, nor yet to fall asleep. We're too close; but not close enough.* So they fidgeted" (65).

2. By contrast, in this next passage the scope of "they" is such that it covers the whole audience, indiscriminately: " 'The Victorian Age,' Mrs. Elmhurst read out. *Presumably there was time then for a stroll round the gardens, even for a look over the house. Yet somehow they felt—how could one put it—a little not quite here or there. As if the play had jerked the ball out of the cup; as if what I call myself was still floating unattached, and didn't settle. Not quite themselves, they felt*" (149).[26]

9.2. As a first, relatively uncomplicated example of how the discourse types can be concatenated, consider one of the passages that furnished an instance of FID above. (Slash marks between symbols at the head of individual sentences and clauses indicate ambiguity or undecidability between two or more discourse types, or at least between available descriptions of those types.) The passage may be represented thus:

> ^{Dn}Then they went in to lunch, and Mrs. Manresa bubbled up, enjoying her own capacity to surmount, without turning a hair, this minor social crisis—this laying of two more places. ^{FID}For had she not complete faith in flesh and blood? and aren't we all flesh and blood? and how silly to make bones of trifles when we're all flesh and blood under the skin—men and women too! $^{Dn/FID}$But she preferred men—obviously. (40)

The second sample combination, of considerably more complexity, may be represented schematically as DD + AD + D + IM + IM/PDD (or TIM) + D_n:

> ^{DD}"Swallows," ^{AD}said Lucy, holding her cup, looking at the birds. ^{Dn}Excited by the company they were flitting from rafter to rafter. ^{IM}Across Africa, across France they had come to nest here. Year after year they came. Before there was a channel, when the earth, upon which the Windsor chair was

planted, was a riot of rhododendrons, and humming birds quivered at the mouths of scarlet trumpets, $^{IM/PDD}$as she had read that morning in her Outline of History, they had come . . . ^{Dn}Here Bart rose from his chair. (108)

Finally, consider this narratologically remarkable passage, in which we discover a complex fusion of both undecidable and embedded discourse types (embedded types are indicated with brackets):

^{Dn}Feet crunched the gravel. Voices chattered. The inner voice, the other voice was saying: $^{indefID(2)}$How can we deny that this brave music, wafted from the bushes, is expressive of some inner harmony? $^{indefDD(2)}$"When we wake" ($^{Dn/AD}$some were thinking) "the day breaks us with its hard mallet blows." $^{indefDD(2)}$"The office" ($^{Dn/AD}$some were thinking) "compels disparity. $^{indefDD(2)}$Scattered, shattered hither thither summoned by the bell. $^{indefDD(2)[indefDD(1)]}$'Ping-ping-ping' $^{indefDD(2)}$that's the phone. $^{indefDD(2)[I_{df}DD(1)]}$'Forward!' 'Serving!'—$^{indefDD(2)}$that's the shop." $^{IndefID(2)/Dn}$So we answer to the infernal, agelong and eternal order issued from on high. $^{indefID(2)/Dn}$And obey. $^{indefDD(2)}$"Working, serving, pushing, striving, earning wages—to be spent—here? Oh dear no. Now? No, by and by. When ears are deaf and the heart is dry." (119)

The last passage in particular suggests how the analysis of represented discourse generally must, for the sake of both descriptive and explanatory adequacy, be grounded in turn in a special theory of context—for reasons that I can try to address in the next, concluding section of the chapter.

10. On the Continuum

As the foregoing examination of Woolf's discourse representations suggests, we can usefully rearrange the order of the types listed in the initial synopsis by ranking each constituent discourse type according to its relative opacity vis-à-vis the theoretical postulate of a wholly transparent D. More precisely, whereas D corresponds to an (impossible) adequation of discourse to context— an intelligibility of utterance irrespective of the particular context in which the utterance happens to be issued—we can create, at least in principle, an inventory of discourse representations such that each successive type inventoried deviates more and more radically from this postulated base of the idealized type D. A scaled inventory of this kind might look something like figure 1.

Figure 1. The metapragmatic continuum

←(context backgrounding) .... (context foregrounding)→

D D$_n$ DD ID IM FID indefDD(1) indefID(1) indefDD(2) indefID(2) PDD/TIM {embedded types}
|
AD

Thus, DD, for example, figures a speech situation comprising at least three instances: the instance of the speaker and his or her speech; the instance of the interlocutor to whom the speech is addressed; and the instance of the narrative discourse itself, that global discursive situation subsuming (representing) the interlocutors' respective situations. Then, farther up the continuum of scaled deviations from D, we have indefDD(1) and then indefID(2). Here the various instances comprised by the speech situation cannot be so readily enumerated, let alone specified. In the case of indefDD(1) or indefID(1), we have one well-defined instance—that of the narrative discourse—and any number of less well-defined instances, corresponding to a set of recognizable interlocutors any one of whom may be responsible for the instance of speaker and/or hearer realized through a given utterance. In the case of indefDD(2) or indefID(2), however, the *number* as well as the *specification* of possible instances has been rendered indeterminate. We do not know exactly who the interlocutors are or exactly how many of them might be speaking/listening at a given moment.

Next consider PDD/TIM. In the case of pseudo–direct discourse or transmissible interior monologue, it is possible to specify neither the number, nor the nature (identity), nor even the conditions of possibility of the instances comprised by the speech situation at issue. The scope of the very notion of (interpersonal) "speech" has been widened such that it now includes nonverbal as well as verbal behavior, a flashing thought as well as a quip. In principle, at least, a speech situation of the type PDD/TIM might encompass the total number of human beings even barely sentient at the moment of "utterance." Thus, we approach a speech situation—just as impossible as D but for precisely the opposite reasons—whose design foregrounds the de jure infinite multipliability of contexts-of-use.

Furthermore, combinations of differently ranked constituent types produce more or less complexly fused and/or embedded discourse types. Thus, whereas the first sample combination listed in section 9.2 permits on the whole ready differentiation of constituent types, the situation of the sentence "But she preferred men—obviously" relative to the other speech representations produces an utterance ambiguous between FID and D$_n$. In the second passage, likewise, the situation of "as she had read that morning in her Outline of History" relative to "Here Bart rose from his chair" confers on the first sentence an ambiguous status. The narrative leaves it undecided whether there is a causal relation between Bart's getting up and Lucy's starting to rattle on (in her mind?) about rhododendrons and the like. If we posit a causal relation, then we have PDD/TIM; if we posit a noncausal relation, then we have IM.

Finally, the embedding of discourse types in the third passage cited produces discursive opacities within other opacities. We face here a Chinese-box structure of doubly indefinite contexts (instances) coextensive with the global speech situation represented. For example, and as the symbolism indicates, the single phrase "Ping-ping-ping" involves an embedding of indefDD(1) *within* indefDD(2). Although it is difficult to imagine what a discursive structure farther up the continuum from D might look like, it is important to keep in mind here that in principle there is no restriction on the possible depth of such illocutionary embedding. Any restriction of embedding would stem, rather, from a breakdown of our processing mechanisms past a certain threshold of embedding or else, to put the same thing another way, from an oversaturation of the narrative discourse with concatenated and embedded types, such that the text at issue becomes boring, confusing, or unreadable—depending on whom one asks.

The larger point to be stressed here is this: we can begin to model a special theory of context, and thus (part of) a narrative pragmatics, only by articulating together two sorts of schemes: schemes for understanding (concatenated and embedded) types of discourse representations and schemes for understanding the contextual profile of the speech situations subtending each such discourse type. Prague School functional linguistics may be an as yet insufficiently exploited theoretical resource for schemes of the second, more general sort. In tandem with the study of narratives like *Between the Acts,* we may be able to develop a polyfunctionalist model for discourse representation in narrative contexts. To put the same point another way, with the help of Mukařovský's and Jakobson's metapragmatics, we may be able to make some headway in identifying and interpreting an entire family of formal features in narrative. At issue in this connection is that family of features that—like the pragmatic component of grammars—compels us to rethink the nature of utterances-in-contexts, as over against the principles for combining linguistic items into larger units, or the logic according to which expressions mean and refer.

Part II   Applications and Extensions

4. Postmodernism as Secondary Grammar

[Discourse] is a space of exteriority in which a network of distinct sites is deployed.
—Michel Foucault

To the Babylonians the stars were "the writing of the sky."—Ernst Robert Curtius

1. Via Satellite

I should like to begin as synoptically as possible, measuring the postmodern all at once and as if from some immense orbital apogee, launched, adrift, but actively scanning—via satellite. I shall thus adopt a position like that of Joseph McElroy's orbiting cyborg—human brain transmogrified into Interplanetary Monitoring Platform (IMP Plus)—processing a series of signals that have been transmitted to us in complex code (McElroy 1987). The signals, scripting our movements and orientation, direct our sensory apparatus toward a quite large, as yet ill-defined informational site. A synoptic perspective should help us register the terrains, contours, and appurtenances of the topic (or topos) it is our purpose to monitor. The area of concern—no *topos ouranios*, surely—is the place of the postmodern. Information about postmodern topology is always on the way but always coded, it seems, in terms of both time and space, as irreducible posteriority and yet also (topographical) difference. *Its* space and time, we can infer by extension, will bear a peculiar relation to space and time as such.

But let us speak less elliptically. Our data processors have had some difficulty deciphering the postmodern code, particularly its spatial component. Some technical repairs or at least supplementations are in order. Specifically, in attempts to decode the notoriously nebulous signals of postmodernism, we must resort to a device that allows us to plot, not only the emergence and half-life of postmodern phenomena on the axis of time, but also, along a spatial axis, the field and configuration of those postmodern events. Optimally, the supplemental technology that we seek will allow us to plot the postmodern—to *plot* the postmodern: both to locate and to narrativize it. Yet we seek to plot postmodernism not as some always forthcoming (hence "unpresentable") cultural and aesthetic event. Rather, we can characterize the postmodern as an ongoing effort to reorient the very concepts of place and position, of plotting itself.

Ernst Robert Curtius (1953 [1948]) once charted a number of textual intersections or citational networks as places defining the very scope of Western literature.[1] By contrast, the discourses of postmodernism reconceive places in general as the intersection or networking of textually organized structures. In particular, what has come to be designated as postmodern "theory" both enacts and thematizes an always unfinished citation or sampling of its own (and other) discourses.[2] The discourses of theory will thus be construed here as one of a series of emergent technologies—broadly telecommunicational in nature—for rethinking the notion of place (origin, locus, situation, trajectory, telos) as such. Accordingly, we must reconnoiter for a data-processing device, a programming system, that might help us decode the principles and effects of such postmodern technologies of place. My argument is that postmodern discourse technologies can be processed by means of another, very old, ostensibly earthbound, but nonetheless highly functional technical system for analyzing the formation, coordination, and transformation of positions. I have in mind a particular subsystem of the technical systems developed through the ideal of grammar and refined during the long practice of grammatical analysis. The technical subsystem (deciphering device) in question: that which has been elaborated by way of the syntactic analysis of language(s).[3] To complete one full orbital revolution around the topos at hand, postmodernism can be synopsized, provisionally decoded, as the making-syntactic of the world itself.

2. Scanning: Temporal Code

First things, first, however. Let us rebegin by noting the overpowering strength of the temporally coded signals having issued up to now from postmodernism, as (ambiguously) both concept and occurrence. Answering the question, What is postmodernism? has been a task reserved, often enough, for appendices (as in Lyotard 1984 [1979]); it has come afterward, as an afterthought to the thinking of what it means to be absolutely or always after, belated, behind the times. Yet, having thus been left unanswered, the question, What is postmodernism? then hallucinogenically doubles as the answer it awaits. Putting off the definition of a postmodernism that one has already presupposed in the articulation of one's (postmodernist) discourse, it seems, is the content or definition of *postmodernism* itself. Thus for Jean-François Lyotard, to whom my phrasing thus far has of course been indebted, postmodernism is just this oddly deferred begging of the question. The circularity at stake in defining (and experiencing) postmodernism is for Lyotard the cultural and aesthetic counterpart to Kant's notion of reflective judgment, on whose terms we must "respond to a case without criteria." This unprepared but at the same time tardy response becomes "itself a case in its turn, an event to which an answer, a mode of linking, will eventually have to be found" (Lyotard 1988b: 27). Postmodernist discourse amounts, then, to a set of second-order reflective judgments about the results of other reflective judgments; it is a series of phrases by which we more or less belatedly and incompletely link onto a particular interrogative phrase—"What is postmodernism?"—that we are always and in general underprepared to hear.

Hence, as Rainer Nägele describes it, the postmodernist *phrase* is also—indeed, essentially—a *phase*, a matter of timing, such that, if "the notion of Modernism as a specific historical-cultural term rather than a relative concept has shifted the quality of temporality to the position of content itself," "Postmodernism intensifies that displacement and subverts even more the substantial identity of cultural demarcations," defining a "boundary which always comes 'after,' [an] indefinite postponement and displacement" (1980: 5–6). By yielding to the very strong temptation to define the postmodern as pure happening, as absolute diachronicity, we might find ourselves in phase with what Lyotard says about postmodernism as an instance or inflection of the sublime (1984 [1979]: app.). Conversely, if the postmodernist project is to present the unpresentable, how can postmodernism itself be defined except as a perpetually unfolding event, whose character we can never define without having missed, lost, second-guessed, prejudged, or generally misconstrued that event? Postmodernism, to this extent, also names a mechanism for the production and broadcasting of information (books, articles, lectures). Such information consists in reporting—through the more or less redundant or noisy channels of title, theme, style, and (proper) name—on the mechanism by which the information itself is licensed and emitted. This informational circuit and its assorted channels merit close inspection as much as professional cynicism. A phenomenon that is always just a little ahead of the efforts expended in attempts to define it, postmodernism might just figure the condition and limit of interpretive labor as such. On its own terms, postmodernism will never be exhausted by any particular, time-bound attempt to say precisely why it is that some artifact or another, this discursive frequency as opposed to that one, may be classed or regulated, here and now, as postmodern. Postmodernism outguesses, among other agencies, the FCC.

3. Scanning (Continued): Spatial Code

Although the foregoing remarks themselves emerge, opportunistically enough, from the very frequency of postmodernism's self-renewing, self-generative definitions, I shall nonetheless here try to avoid, as best I am able, recourse to some primordial belatedness in attempting to characterize the phenomenon of post-modernism.[4] Do not get me wrong; I am not after pre-postmodern origins or searching for lost presences amid a merely specious, fleeting present. It is not even that I wish to juxtapose theories of the postmodern with a specific form of experience, a particular set of conditions, whose very pain and necessitousness compel us to engage in concrete, strategic, and perhaps for that reason anti-postmodernist thinking. My aim, instead, is to pit postmodernism against itself, to find within discourse construed as postmodern a different strategy for thinking the question, What is postmodernism?

True, the case can be made (and has forcibly been made) for the view that postmodernism does not allow for the political organization of events into a collective history but rather absolutizes, under cover of the postmodern sublime, events as such—the being-innovative of innovation proper.[5] Yet the discourses of postmodernism do not speak only of a total diachronicity that rules out anything resembling purposive, concerted action; beyond its emphasis on inexhaustible happening, we find in postmodernist discourse a quite generalized and pervasive emphasis on synchronicity—on strategies for situating items and events in relational networks. To this extent, postmodernism marks not the wholesale failure of strategic thinking but rather the proliferation of strategies for forming strategies. Description of such second-order strategizing demands, in addition to the syntactic technology outlined in what follows, semantic and pragmatic devices as well (as outlined in Morris 1938; cf. Herman 1993d; Plett 1975: 52–119). To bring all these devices to bear on the powerful matrix of postmodern signals, however, would overload the quite minimal database that I have managed to assemble in this place. For the same reason, I cannot discuss here, except in preliminary terms, the relation between post-modernism and technology in general. Instead, my analysis will center itself chiefly on the possibility—the interest or fruitfulness—of characterizing post-modern discourses as a subset of one particular set of technologies. That set of technologies, designed to optimize the transmission of data, the relay of information, I have termed *telecommunicational* (in the broadest sense).

A number of commentators, building on the grammatological model set out by Jacques Derrida in *Of Grammatology* (1974 [1967]), have already characterized postmodernist or, more specifically, poststructuralist notions of *écriture* and (arche-)writing as essentially technical, technological, even teletheoretical concepts at root. As such research suggests, we must construe the Derridean concept of writing in the broadest possible—indeed, in a properly transcendental—sense. "Writing," for Derrida does not restrict itself to the various empirical phenomena associated with making and reading inscriptions on the walls of caves, clay tablets, paper, or what have you. In its Derridean acceptation, writing bears instead on the conditions of possibility for communication in general—not only in the postmanuscript era of print but also, at least by extension, in the postprint era of electronic media.[6]

Even in its very earliest formulation in *Edmund Husserl's "Origin of Geometry": An Introduction* (1988a [1962]), Derrida's conception of (the transcendental function of) writing highlighted how the iterability and transmissability of written information is what constitutes a tradition. Tradition, in turn, "is only mediacy itself and openness to telecommunication in general" (50). Furthermore, according to Derrida's early exegesis of Husserl's late writings, concepts, knowledge, experience itself, all are possible only as particular reactivations of a given (supraempirical and omnitemporal) tradition of concepts and judgments (12–13 and passim).[7] Such reactivations must always be placed in writing, documented. Later, Derrida would designate the indefinite transmissability or "openness to telecommunication in general" represented by writing as *différance*, to list just one of its many specifications. The structure of documentation on this model determines the conditions of possibility for things, experiences, and something like a (geometrically describable) earth to begin with. Conversely, no temporal or earthly experience determines, of itself, the telecommunicational mechanisms (the *Überlieferung*) by which the experience of mundanity can be handed down *as* such an experience, one element in the continuously reactivated and thereby modified tradition of knowing things about the world.

This inversion of the relative priority of writing with respect to experience has by now become a deconstructive commonplace. Nevertheless, we can emphasize how, spanning the Derridean corpus, poststructuralism's ongoing and persistent thematization of the text, and of the world as interpretable according to textual principles and structures, imputes in effect a special grammatical profile to the world-constituting and telecommunicational technics of writing.[8] Universalizing the very notion of grammar, stretching the skein or network of linguistic structure, the rules and principles of language use, across the entire surface of the earth, arche-writing or *écriture* is itself another origin of geometry, another institution of precisely definable relations and positions. Only the lines that it inscribes on the pages and planes of the world—sketching in the figure of all that can be known—are lines of communication, linkage, traditionality as such.[9]

4. Writing the Program: Some Technicalities

Accordingly, my purpose here is not simply to posit an analogy between postmodernist theories of writing and contemporaneous revolutions in communications technologies; moreover, I seek to reestablish communications between postmodernism and the tradition of (universal) grammar.[10] Grammatically speaking, I shall try to download the data on postmodern communications through syntactic programming in particular. The matrix of signals, however, is still too large, still too powerful; let us close off part of the information circuit in order to maximize redundancy and minimize the noise. The assumption guiding my analysis is that postmodernism can be plotted as a set of techniques, a set of discourse technologies, that extend and generalize (at an inter- vs. intratextual level) the techniques described via the syntactic analysis of sentences. In order to bring the analysis within shorter compass, I shall focus more particularly on the (metasyntactic) role of citation—as theme, function, and device— in the discourses that have come to be labeled *theoretical* in a specifically postmodern sense.

Analyzed in these discourses under the name *intertextuality*, citation can be construed as what we might call a higher-order syntax, which in its radicalized form affixes to every discursive fragment at least some coefficient of citedness or quotation. *Citation* points to a quotational syntax that exhausts all possible relations between texts and/or bits of text.[11] Thus, Heinrich Plett (1985), for example, grounds the possibility of an "Intertextualitätspoetik" in what he terms a "secondary grammar" ("Sekundärgrammatik") (87), based in turn on a series of syntactic or, more precisely, metasyntactic rules. These rules—addition, subtraction, substitution, permutation, and repetition—link cited texts and text fragments with the texts and text fragments that cite them (82; cf. Plett 1975: 226–50). We can extrapolate. In an intratextual or primary grammar, the analysis of syntactic structures has traditionally sought to provide a device that captures (and formally models) an ideal speaker-hearer's intuitions about grammatically acceptable versus grammatically unacceptable linguistic strings, that is, sequences of lexical items (cf. Chomsky 1965: 8–15). Thus, primary syntax "is concerned with the principles according to which words can be combined to form larger meaningful units, and by which such larger units can be combined to form sentences" (Horrocks 1987: 24; cf. Ducrot and Todorov 1979 [1972]: 209ff.; Sells 1985; and secs. *1.7ff.* above). Primary syntax, in essence, aims for an explicitly formalized representation of a speaker-hearer's intuitions about acceptable ways to sequence different classes of linguistic units (e.g., definite noun phrases, indefinite noun phrases, verb phrases, etc.) into syntagms; and syntagms, in turn, are just the larger linguistic units into which the smaller units can be placed as constituents or by which the smaller units are governed via sets of dependency rules (Matthews 1981: 71–95). At the limit, the syntagms form sequences of sentences (or propositions) grouped, by way of relations of "information coherence" (Givón 1984: 240ff.), into a discourse or into a text (Petöfi 1990; cf. Broch 1977 [1946]: 248ff.; van Dijk 1972; Ducrot and Todorov 1979 [1972]: 281ff.; Hendricks 1967). At stake in an intertextual or secondary grammar, however, are (among other things) the metasyntactic relations between different classes of text fragments and texts. A secondary grammar would model intuitions about how to decompose, permute, reassemble, and more generally manipulate text-sized structures—not necessarily along lines prescribed by relations of information coherence (e.g., foreground-background relations, topic-comment structures, etc.), but rather according to the looser, more relaxed communicative constraints imposed by the quotational operations that we group together under the heading *citation* (see sec. *7* below).

Secondary grammar thus specifies, in two senses of the term, a global or globalized version of the syntactic rules operative in primary grammars. On the one hand, a grammar of intertexts would ideally characterize second-order or text-level transformations of the rules applying to linguistic structures at the level of individual sentences or propositions (Pfister 1985: 25ff.). Using the rules of secondary grammar, we project into *textual* structures the linguistic and logical properties pertaining to *sentences* and *propositions.* At issue here are considerations that can be called *technical* in a particular sense of that term, a sense whose analysis must be reserved for another place. On the other hand, however, a globalized or secondary syntax of intertexts yields, too, a syntax of the globe, broaching issues that can be termed *technical* in a different sense, a sense that will be my main concern in what follows. As already indicated, much of what is called *postmodern* and/or *poststructuralist theory* locates the conditions of possibility of experience itself in textual principles, structures, and functions. To this extent, a metasyntax of textual relations amounts, really, to a theory about the organization and structure of the world as such. Postmodernism, whose various manifestations can be identified with more or less explicitly formulated secondary grammars—or so I shall go on to argue—therefore constitutes not just a cultural semiotics but also a transcultural syntax, a metaphysical topology.[12]

In contrast to the notion of spatial form, which Joseph Frank (1988 [1945]), for example, associated with specifically modernist texts, and which obeys principles of juxtaposition and montage as opposed to sequencing in the representation of events, the postmodernist construction of citational networks introduces what might be termed *hyperspatial* or *telecommunicational form*—the more or less instantaneous and multiply directed relay of information through that worldwide space of discourse which Foucault defines as a network of sites (epigram). Hyperspatial form is the broadly discursive counterpart to a global economy, and we should preserve the many senses of *economy* (fiscal, informational, and anthropological) operative here. Indeed, to enter the citational economy that Sergej Karcevskij (1982 [1929]) specified as homonymic and that entails (at least) one signal on which a given code confers two or more equiprobable significations, we can hypothesize that theoretical discourse becomes postmodernist when it cites its sites. A theoretical proposition crosses the threshold of the postmodern when its very function, its claim to truth, is to mark off a place within an economy of (potentially) relevant propositions.

But it is high time to descend from apogee to perigee, to abandon synopsis for analysis. By examining particular instances of postmodern theory, we can work toward that secondary grammar, that metasyntactic code, which may allow us to reconcile citing with siting, locution with location. In order to stress how postmodernism, coordinated with some grammatical devices, can be reprogrammed to help account for its own discursive mechanisms, I shall cite fragments of discourse organized around the concept and figure of technics itself. Arguably, by factoring a number of representations of technology into the database on postmodernism, we can write a more powerful program for decoding postmodern discourse as, conversely, a technology of representation. Technology can be tracked as a negative effect or afterimage, an interference pattern emerging from an unstable latticework of conflicting theoretical discourses and figures, which are in turn situated in the field of postmodern culture at large. At the same time, the concept and figure of technology help flush out from the artifice of a single monolithic label—*Theory*—the generic instabilities that structure the specifically postmodern project of theoretical analysis. Indeed, as we shall see, the instability of the genre(s) of theoretical discourse effectively transforms the very will to truth—by tradition the stimulus, aim, and medium of all theory—into the somewhat less exalted task of acquiring competence in secondary grammar. To situate truth in its postmodern environs is to master or internalize rules for the fragmentation and recombination of texts (cf. Toulmin 1982), and this space of conceptuality is opened and limited by a global intertext.

5. Representations of Technology

In order to get a better fix on postmodern representations of technology, however, let us start by positioning those representations within an overarching framework of socioaesthetic inquiry. Engineered by Walter Benjamin and other members of the Frankfurt School, the framework at issue has sought to locate the criterion for aesthetic value in the relation between two different sets of production techniques: (i) a set of techniques internal to or coeval with the aesthetic object and necessary for its construction and inner organization and (ii) a set of techniques external to and imposed on the aesthetic object, techniques that are necessary only for the dissemination of the artifact for (mass) consumption. In *Dialectic of Enlightenment* (1988 [1944]), Max Horkheimer and Theodor Adorno insist on a positive correlation between aesthetic value and the differentiation of internal from external techniques. By contrast, Benjamin assigns a negative aesthetic value to the dissociation of i and ii. For Benjamin, it is only by coordinating the inner organization of the aesthetic artifact with techniques for its distribution within the public sphere—in short, it is only by politicizing art—that we can avoid that aestheticization of politics which Benjamin famously characterizes as fascistic toward the end of his essay "The Work of Art in the Age of Mechanical Reproduction" (1969 [1936]). The texts cited below, as fragments of postmodern theory, may be reassembled along Benjaminian lines, debatably; they install (information) technology at the heart of all aesthetic and, more generally, discursive practice.

For Horkheimer and Adorno, what the authors describe as the "Culture Industry" reinvests mechanically reproduced, postauratic art with noxious political energies. Not only does the Culture Industry supplant internal techniques of aesthetic production (those organic to art's "inner logic") with external techniques for its reproduction and distribution (Horkheimer and Adorno 1988 [1944]: 120ff.). Even more, Adorno in particular felt that, once such "external" or mass-production techniques become predominant, we eliminate the possibility of genuine or authentic art. Authentic art, for Adorno, depends on an antinomy between esoteric art forms and the grievous social conditions that cry out for immediate representation or thematization in art—conditions that paradoxically cannot be grasped, however, without the help of the esoteric art forms that seem oblivious and impervious to social evils (Adorno 1986a [1967]). Yet, in "The Author as Producer," Benjamin (1986 [1934]) invokes production techniques in attempts to get beyond just this (quasi-bourgeois) conception of art. Specifically, Benjamin launches a technology-based critique of the traditional distinction posed between the author (the art producer) and the audience (the art consumer). Benjamin devotes special care to an analysis of the formatting techniques used in the production of newspapers; his suggestion is that new information technologies have in turn altered the conditions of possibility for that subset of information that society previously coded as aesthetic. Newspapers no longer permit the kind of passive reception of data associated with revelation from divine, auratic, or otherwise authoritative sources.[13] Instead, the very formatting of newspapers presupposes a set of interpretive activities—selection, connection, subordination, apposition—necessary for the production of any (fragment of) knowledge about the world. A mosaic of headlines, accounts, captions, cartoons, numerical figures, etc., the newspaper represents a matrix of items whose recombinations determine the amount and kind of information a given reader will, in conjunction with this matrix of signals, produce.

In its form and functioning, postmodern theory reproduces and intensifies the fleeting, impatient glance of Benjamin's collaborative newspaper reader. It grounds (the production of) truth not in the painstaking labor of definition, not in the careful inspection and tabulation of data, but in the rapid dispersion and regrouping of textual fragments across a shifting surface of information— or, rather, to use a more electronic idiom, in the momentary disposition of data on a screen without inherent memory. We can now try to access, through a series of such screens, the citational codes to which we can apply the label *genres*. The genres of current theoretical discourse are based in turn on a set of metasyntactic codes required to facilitate postmodern (tele)communication.

6. Generic Interface

Take Gilles Deleuze and Félix Guattari's *Anti-Oedipus* (1983 [1972]). In this text, technology functions primarily as a metaphor; the metaphor of the machine structures the entire text. The authors' metaphoricization of the machine, furthermore, tends to overdetermine the conceptual role that they attribute to technology as such. By contrast, in a number of texts that thematize technics—in particular, *Of Grammatology* (1974 [1967]) and "Freud and the Scene of Writing" (1978a [1966])—Derrida adopts a different strategy for talking about machines and technology. Whereas in *Anti-Oedipus* Deleuze and Guattari assimilate Karl Marx, Friedrich Nietzsche, and Sigmund Freud to the vast, portentous metaphorics of the machine, Derrida stresses how these multiple and various discourses are crucial for thinking the notion *technics* in the first place.

These initial distinctions between Deleuze and Guattari versus Derrida, however, should not be construed as an attempt to condemn or condone the theoretical projects at issue. Rather, the point is to determine how these texts participate in (the genres of) postmodern theory. My claim is that the texts under examination participate in different *theoretical genres;* hence, by comparing and contrasting the texts under study, we may be able to discern at their interface a secondary grammar—a metasyntax—for postmodern discourses at large.

6.1. Deleuze and Guattari's basic concern in *Anti-Oedipus,* of course, is to liberate psychoanalysis itself from the repressive, constrictive metaphorics of the Oedipus syndrome; this concern may explain, at least to some extent, why the metaphor of "desiring-machines," as well as of molar and molecular forms of production, assumes such a prominent place in *Anti-Oedipus* as a whole. Whereas Freud had turned the unconscious into a classical theater, complete with a family drama of incestuous tendencies and concomitant lifelong neuroses, Deleuze and Guattari wish to rethink, through their self-styled "schizoanalysis," the unconscious in terms of an industrial factory. For them, the unconscious, by means of connective syntheses ("and then"), disjunctive syntheses ("and ... or ... or"), and conjunctive syntheses ("so it's"), invests with various libidinal intensities the highly ramified territories of human experience in late capitalist society. Taking their cue from Jacques Lacan's "Some Reflections on the Ego" (1953), Deleuze and Guattari wish to revolutionize psychoanalysis in response to the technological revolution. This latter revolution, as Lacan remarks toward the end of his essay, has taught us to look at the human psyche as one more machine in the network of productive machines that constitute social as well as industrial organizations. But, whereas Lacan defines the human machine chiefly by virtue of its dysfunctionality, its tendency to break down and upset the general rhythms of industrial society, Deleuze and Guattari describe the human machine in terms of its often subterranean productive capacities, its secret and willy-nilly functionality. Thus, Deleuze and Guattari can situate even Nietzsche's madness within the overall dynamics of unconscious production. Examining Nietzsche's late, crazed letter to Jakob Burkhardt ("every name in history is I," etc.), Deleuze and Guattari (1983 [1972]: 86) locate such patent megalomania within the sphere of disjunctive syntheses, one of the main mechanisms by which schizophrenic desiring-machines produce.

To be sure, Deleuze and Guattari owe more to Nietzsche than simply a productive reading of his last, ostensibly insane letters. After all, their analysis of "the full body without organs" vis-à-vis the late capitalist inflation of the "socius" (another Lacanian borrowing) also derives from Nietzsche's conception of the Dionysian, the force or feeling of intoxication that tends to abolish barriers between what Deleuze and Guattari would no doubt characterize as "merely" neurotic individuals. Schizo-analysis in general suggests how our "flows" of desire are at once territorialized by the world axiomatic of late capitalism and deterritorialized by the way in which capitalism allows money to figure desire for anything and everything. Correlatively desire is at once constrained by the "gridwork" of capitalism and allowed to escape through its "meshes." The rhythmic contraction and expansion of desire through the figurative energies of money represents, doubtless, an alternative form of that contraction and expansion of the unconscious which Nietzsche located in the play between Apollo and Dionysus, respectively.

In any event, my persistent use of quotation marks in the preceding paragraph ("flows," "gridwork," "meshes") suggests the sheer metaphoric density of *Anti-Oedipus*. This density of metaphor originates from Marx's texts in particular, perhaps even more than from those of Freud, Nietzsche, or Lacan. The metaphorics of machines and production stems directly from Marx, although Deleuze and Guattari so contextualize the Marxian metaphors as to produce what can be deemed *theoretical* transformations and extensions of Marx's technological concepts. For Deleuze and Guattari, desiring-machines and socioeconomic machines in general function as different regimes, different orders of magnitude, in which the same basic processes of production operate. Furthermore, in a reversal of Marx's idea that we must extricate ourselves from our *Naturwüchsigkeit,* our embeddedness in nature, Deleuze and Guattari suggest that, because the production of desire is structurally analogous to the processes of production in nature itself, we can find no real difference between humans and nature in the first place. Both are simply moments in a general flow and ebb of productive energy. And, as for any properly Marxian diagnosis of capitalism, in a sense Deleuze and Guattari assume what Habermas, building on Marx, laboriously describes in *Legitimation Crisis* (1975 [1973]) as the process by which capitalism's own forces eventually turn against themselves and produce an alternative form of socioeconomic organization. Psychoanalysis, with its metaphysics of Oedipus, still allows capitalist structures to secure legitimation simply by displacing discontent onto a sort of collective family drama. By contrast, argue Deleuze and Guattari, schizo-analysis or "materialist psychiatry" identifies and stimulates flows of desire that mark the limit of capitalism. Ultimately deterritorialized by capitalism itself, such flows of desire undermine capitalism from within, in a manner and to an extent that Marx's (and Habermas's) diagnosis of a self-destructive capitalism only barely prefigures.

In general, Deleuze and Guattari's appropriation of Nietzsche, Freud, and Marx amounts, really, to a sort of "deterritorializing" metaphorization of those texts, a reinscription of those texts in alternative contexts that itself alters and extends the very implications of the texts at issue. In this sense, *Anti-Oedipus* functions via that process of infinite citation, interminable montage, of which Derrida gives an account in, for instance, "Signature Event Context" (1982c [1971]) and which Gregory Ulmer (1983) associates with new, postmodern technologies that as a rule operate by means of citation, collage, and montage— technologies such as video and television, for example (cf. Jameson 1987). It is quite significant in its own right, however, that I just cited Derrida as an example of someone who has explained the dynamics of citation at work in *Anti-Oedipus* since Derrida's texts are commonly grouped together with texts like *Anti-Oedipus* as instances or incarnations of a single, all-encompassing genre of postmodern (or "poststructuralist") theory. To reiterate: Derrida's texts stand to *Anti-Oedipus* as an analysis stands to a metaphorics of technology. By superimposing Derrida's posterior analytics on Deleuze and Guattari's anterior metaphorics—that is, by indicating ways in which Derrida's analyses of technology differently inflect the psychoanalytic and philosophical concepts on which *Anti-Oedipus* is based—we can produce an interference pattern, a generic interface, in which the secondary grammar of postmodernism perhaps starts to become visible.

6.2. In "Freud and the Scene of Writing," Derrida (1978a [1966]) discusses Freud's vacillation between various metaphors for the psychical apparatus, in writings that span all the way from Freud's *Project* (1895) to the "Note on the Mystic Writing Pad" (1925). Derrida describes Freud's own dissatisfaction with the various models that he developed for the phenomenon of pathbreaking (*Bahnung*), which involves a structure both of retention and of release, both a furrowing and an imperturbable virginity vis-à-vis the surface that both registers impressions and preserves memory traces. As Derrida notes, after trying out a variety of less successful models, Freud eventually settled on the *Wunder-block* as a model for the psychical apparatus. In this way, Freud proceeded by means of a "technological" discovery to make a "scientific" discovery. Here, perhaps, we should contrast Husserl's argument in *The Crisis of European Sciences* (1970 [1937–39]), in which Husserl provides a genetic analysis of how scientific *intuitions* are displaced and alienated over the course of time by those (numerical, instrumental, and other) "symbols" through which scientific *methods* (*techne*) first acquire operative force. In "Freud and the Scene of Writing," Derrida argues instead that a sort of technological symbol is what allows Freud to have his scientific intuition in the first place.

In turn, the dependence of Freud's theory of perception and memory on a technological device leads Derrida to ask, at the end of his essay, about the relation between the psychical apparatus in particular and apparatus in general. Throughout his analysis Derrida has made suggestive connections between machines and the issue of representation; now, in closing, he arrives at the conclusion that machines in fact mark that originary relation with death that constitutes all life, all experience, all awareness. This quite far-reaching conclusion strictly parallels Derrida's treatment of writing as *techne* in *Of Grammatology*. There, Derrida argues that, whereas writing has always been thought of as outside, as exterior to, as lower than the full presence of speech, the full presence of the voice to itself, etc., writing should instead be thought of as a sort of originary technics. Arche-writing, or writing as "spacing," represents for Derrida the possibility for consciousness to move in nonlinear ways, to hold things in reserve. (We should keep in mind here, perhaps, that Martin Heidegger 1977 [1955] had already linked modern technology with a world picture that makes nature itself into a "standing-reserve." For Heidegger, the idea of nature as a stockpile of resources is interlinked with a massive technological overdetermination of natural objects, via a process that Heidegger calls *Ge-stell*, or "inframing.") For Derrida, writing therefore functions not as a subsidiary technology that society spawns as a sort of excrudescence or outgrowth but rather as the condition of possibility for society itself, the condition of possibility for institution in general. As opposed to researchers like Josef Vachek (1964b [1939], 1964a [1948]), John Mountford (1969), and Reinhard Klockow (1980), who in various ways exploit the possibility of a science of writing, Derrida, continuing his earlier exegesis of Husserl, argues that science in general is parasitic on its own techniques of documentation. Before it can be hypostatized as an object of linguistic or more broadly scientific study, writing provides the condition of possibility for that infinite transmissibility of knowledge with which we equate science as such (1974 [1967]: 74–100).

In brief, *Of Grammatology* allows us to conceptualize technology not as a system of means adjusted to a correlative system of ends, as Jacques Ellul would have it in *The Technological Society* (1964 [1954]), but rather as a moment of that "intersubjective violence" which Derrida describes in discussing the work of Claude Lévi-Strauss and which constitutes or rather institutes civilization (1974 [1967]: 101ff.). Whereas, significantly enough, Marx's is not a privileged text in Derrida's analysis, Nietzsche's text is, precisely because in Derrida's view Nietzsche subverts the traditional hierarchical relation that installs writing as a means to the end of *logos*. For Derrida, Nietzsche reveals how the hierarchical relation between writing and *logos* is intimately bound up with an entire system of oppositions—concept versus image, nature versus culture, etc.—that allows us to think of technology as a sort of supplement to an originary reality or a meaning otherwise present to itself. The critique of Jean-Jacques Rousseau in *Of Grammatology* continues Derrida's attack on this traditional conception of writing as mere *techne*. As Derrida shows, not only does Rousseau have a *theory* of writing, according to which Rousseau, like Husserl after him, identifies writing (and indeed the arts and sciences in general) as a sign of decadence, but he also has an *experience* of writing, according to which writing as *techne* enables Rousseau to be present to himself "as he really is" (141ff.). Rousseau's experience of writing is that of an originary supplement, to invoke the Derridean paradox. Moreover, by suggesting how, in Rousseau's text, each notion of writing is in fact structurally dependent on the other, Derrida can reveal the inner contradiction at the heart of logocentrism. Technology thus becomes for Derrida not simply a concept but also a symptom of logocentrism and a key to its deconstruction.

To return, however, to the larger question concerning the importance of genre vis-à-vis postmodern theoretical discourse: It is no doubt possible to describe in Derridean terms the difference between the metaphoric density of *Anti-Oedipus*, on the one hand, and the less periphrastic strategies by means of which Derrida's texts thematize technology, on the other hand. Thus, we might say that only a logocentric view would devalue a text solely on the grounds that it proceeds by citational reinscriptions of apparently exogenous concepts, rather than by painstaking analysis, the careful elaboration of coherent arguments, the persistence of an integral thematic, and so on. To the contrary, just as we must recontextualize technology so that it ceases to be merely secondary or supplementary, we must conceptualize Deleuze and Guattari's and Derrida's texts so that *all* of them operate within the limits of a strictly theoretical discourse.

If we pursue this Derridean strategy to its limit, however, we must then reinterpret theoretical discourse itself as an interlocked configuration of heterogeneous genres in which, and by means of which, truth (knowledge, information, additional discourse) is continually (re)produced as an effect, a transform, of citational networks and relations.[14] To this extent, the generic instability of the postmodern theoretical text, the difficulty of placing it either within philosophy or within literature, art or science, is largely a technical difficulty. We can now begin to address that difficulty—or at least begin outlining an operator's manual—through the application of some (meta)syntactic devices.

7. Toward a Postmodern Trivium: Grammar, Logic, and Rhetoric Revisited

Arguably, theoretical discourse registers a specifically postmodern effect by underdetermining differences of truth-value between different modes of inference. Or, rather, it overdetermines the role of entailment relations, forcing us to change the way we talk about drawing inferences and conducting arguments. If to every proposition we affix the mark of its intertextual legacy, if we detect the sign of its participation within a host of citational networks, then the position of a given proposition within an inferential chain becomes, in effect, indeterminate. If a given claim is thought to be essentially citing and/or cited, then the claim can be said to entail or be implied by indefinitely many other such claims—in a sense that I can only begin to spell out here.

In logical analysis, of course, the relation of entailment has a very narrow scope: one statement is said to imply or entail another if and only if it cannot be the case that the first statement is true (its truth-value is 1) and the second statement false (its truth-value is 0). For example, "x is red" implies or entails "x is colored" (but not vice versa); the same goes for "y is human" and "y is mortal." Other forms of propositional coordination—analogy, allusion, connotation— are excluded from the domain of the strict inference procedures grouped under the heading *entailment*. In the classical scheme at least, these other modes of coordination are not amenable to treatment in truth-functional logic and so fall within the domain of poetry or, worse, metaphysics (as in Carnap 1937a [1934]: 281ff.).

Yet if we follow the postmodernist and posit citation as a necessary condition for discourse, it becomes difficult to draw along classical lines the distinction between strict implication and other ways of coordinating statements. Every textual fragment now occupies at least some discursive coordinates; we can define these sets of coordinates in a given instance by using the rules of secondary grammar, postmodern counterpart to the analytic geometry with which Descartes mapped the space of modernity. As already suggested, secondary grammar can be thought of as a device for modeling the relations between texts and bits of text by way of a higher-order syntax, which we only very loosely designate by the term *citation* and its cognates. In the framework of this second-order syntax, texts may be said to entail one another in many different ways— through reproduction, transposition, elaboration, compression, combination, segmentation, and so on. As a result, the conditions for successful inference, good argument, are loosened; inferring, now just the generation of one text from another, reduces to a family of quotational gestures. Hence the format of articles in, for example, present-day literary studies—articles that, more and more, argue by quoting properly from other articles, according to the rules of our (emergent) citational syntax.

We can put the matter this way. In the postmodern framework of secondary grammar, the relation of entailment no longer governs just that subset of statements whose forms of linkage fall under the scope of truth-functional logic. Rather, entailment in a weakened sense of the term now figures as a general, indeed necessary condition for every possible and actual (sequence of) proposition(s), vis-à-vis every other such (sequence of) proposition(s).[15] This wholesale trivialization of the notion of entailment is in itself significant; it confers special importance on the task of cataloging the various modes of, rather than prescribing what can be, valid inference. (To build on the work of Bruns 1982: 1–13, whereas the cataloging of modes of inference is a task essentially rhetorical in nature, the prescription of *valid* ways of inferring is perhaps the philosophical task par excellence.) Once citation is made a necessary condition for discourse, the constraints determining when one proposition entails another must be defined in tactical or rhetorical, rather than strictly logical, terms. As a result, theoretical discourse in general becomes telecommunicational in form and hyperspatial in situation, allowing only the provisional distinction of one claim, one (discursive) territory, from another. Indeterminately close and/or distant—and thus sharing the position of one's interlocutor in a global, telecommunicational network—the place of the postmodern proposition is both everywhere and nowhere, it seems.

But to follow the rhetorician in saying that every inference is provisional is merely to intensify the necessity of making inferences. This is what we might call the antinomy of postmodern theory. Caught in the network of my own citations, I have tried to circumvent the antinomy at issue by invoking the notion of genre, which also permits of tactical or rhetorical, but not logical or ontological, distinctions between modes of coordinating texts and text fragments. On the one hand, as discussed in my reading of Deleuze and Guattari versus Derrida, the citational mechanisms of postmodern theory arguably do not allow us to rank, according to theoretical productiveness or power, different arrangements of texts—analytic versus metaphoric arrangements, say. On the other hand, the various modes of arranging texts might nonetheless be grouped into classes of rhetorical or quasi-rhetorical figures.[16] We could then link up such figures with particular discursive genres, each genre in turn being marked by a specific theoretical effect, a particular effect of theory. Such cataloging (further data entry) lies beyond the scope of the present analysis; there is space only to set up some initial parameters. Specifically, we could isolate the subordination of certain texts under others according to hypotactic figures. These figures might be used collectively to define the discursive genre, the inferential pattern, that we term *definition* or, more loosely, *analysis.* Other genres might be typified by their reliance on paratactic figures. We could then more precisely define the discursive genres known as *exemplification, analogy,* or *evocation,* as the case may be.

In any event, postmodern theory asks us to redescribe ways of quoting as different citational systems; all the different systems function as truth-making machines, affording various modes and patterns of inference. Conceived as a secondary grammar, postmodernism itself marks just this framework or horizon of inferential tolerance. After all, facing what other horizon, standing in what other framework, could I cite so many bits of text over so short a period of time and not be dismissed out of hand before reaching so inconclusive a conclusion?

5. Modes of Meaning in Film

1. Film Theory, Psychoanalysis, and the Two Semiotics

As Teresa de Lauretis (1984) points out, recent film theory has developed, by and large, along two primary lines: the semiotic line and the psychoanalytic line (15ff.).[1] In the same place, de Lauretis also describes a division emergent within semiological inquiry itself. An earlier, "logico-mathematical" semiotics, basically exhausted by semioticians like Julia Kristeva, it seems, has given way to a different, more properly sociological (or perhaps sociolectical) semiotics (105, 167).[2] For de Lauretis, this second semiotics, which focuses on the production of meanings by codes that are in turn socially produced, can be detected already in C. S. Peirce—and there already in much more radical form than in, say, Umberto Eco's semiotic model(s) (158–86). By proposing a film-theoretical framework that reconciles what we might call (Peircean) sociosemiotics[3] with (Lacanian) psychoanalysis, de Lauretis eo ipso proposes to articulate the search for a viable theory of signification, on the one hand, with the search for a viable theory of the subject, on the other hand (160; cf. de Lauretis 1987: 1–30, 127–48).

Arguably, however, since Lacanian theories of the subject are inextricably linked with structuralist—that is to say, Saussurean—conceptions of language, since for Lacan subjectivity itself is a function of language as understood by structuralist linguistics in particular, de Lauretis can discount formalist or "logico-mathematical" semiotic models only until such time as she begins to model in Lacanian terms a (for her) equally crucial theory of the subject (1984: 37–69). More generally, if merely by a shift in emphasis one can talk about the material production as opposed to the formal structures of semiotic codes, it is a somewhat different proposition further to specify materially produced semiotic codes by appeal to Lacanian notions of subjectivity. Insofar as, for Lacan, the (social) production of meaning situates itself in turn on the instance of the subject—on the spectator of cinema, for example—it seems that we must then derive our sociosemiotics from what might be termed Lacan's *quasi-transcendental* conditions for subjectivity.[4] After all, the a priori structure of the Lacanian subject predetermines, at least to some extent, just what sorts of (Symbolic) materials will engender new codes, new meanings, new significations. Only to the degree that it is caught in the mesh of those metonymic (displacing) and metaphoric (condensing) principles which structure the unconscious, and only because it is bounded on either side by the structural limits of Imaginary and Real, can a given phenomenon for Lacan be accorded Symbolic status, ranged amid the set of socially generated semiotic codes and so deemed constitutive of the subject as such (Lacan 1968 [1956], 1977d [1949], 1977c [1953], 1977a [1957]; cf. Laplanche and Pontalis 1973 [1967]; Jameson 1977; and, on Lacan's aprioristic habits of argumentation generally, Heath 1981: 77ff.). At issue, then, is how to reconcile a sociosemiotic film theory, which perpetually resolves cinematic meaning back into the empirical conditions of its production, with a Lacanian theory of subjectivity, which locates the conditions of possibility for meaning in the supra-, extra-, or preempirical domain of the subject (more narrowly, the unconscious).[5]

Take "The Agency of the Letter in the Unconscious" (1977a [1957]). Here Lacan argues that

> reference to the experience of the community, or to the substance of [its] discourse, settles nothing. For this experience assumes its essential dimension in the tradition that this discourse itself establishes. This tradition long before the drama of history is inscribed in it, lays down the elementary structures of a culture. And these very structures reveal an ordering of possible exchanges which, even if unconscious, is inconceivable outside the permutations authorized by language. (148)

With its emphasis on the "ordering of possible exchanges" and on (linguistically) authorized permutations, the quoted passage engages in what, ever since Immanuel Kant's distinctions between empirical and transcendental unities of apperception (Kant 1965 [1781/1787]: "Transcendental Deduction (B)," B139, p. 157; cf. Lacan 1977a [1957]: 60), for example, and his contrast between constitutive and regulative principles in the "Analogies of Experience" (A178–80/B222–23, pp. 210–11), has been termed argument of a specifically transcendental nature. Like Kant, Lacan makes claims about conditions of possibility, arguing in connection with his model for the structure and functions of the unconscious, "not that [the model] is true, but that it must be assumed to be true if some sphere of thought or discourse, especially an indispensable sphere, is to be possible" (Lacey 1986: 244; cf. Stroud 1982). If along jointly Freudian and Lacanian lines we say that "the unconscious is that part of the concrete discourse, in so far as it is transindividual, [which] is not at the disposal of the subject in re-establishing the continuity of his conscious discourse" (Lacan 1977c [1953]: 49), and if with Lacan we modify the classical Freudian framework by positing that the unconscious itself is structured like a language (1977a [1957]: 147), then it follows that "language and its structure exist prior to the moment at which each subject at a certain point in his mental development makes his entry into it" (1977a [1957]: 147–48). Language and its structure determine beforehand the conditions of possibility for subjectivity; in turn, the structure of the subject predetermines whether, and how, we experience a given phenomenon as meaningful, as significant in the broadest sense of that term.

I return to the specifics of the Lacanian model, and its applications to film, in more detail below. The point to stress here is that, if de Lauretis, along with other sociosemioticians indebted to Lacan (e.g., Nichols 1981), fails to make completely explicit the functioning of quasi-transcendental rules in the social production of meaning, nonetheless we should refrain from rejecting, in principle and strictly on these grounds, the very notion of a sociosemiotic film theory. We should merely point out, rather, the de facto failure of sociosemiotic theories to describe in any exact way the social and more broadly contextual constraints placed on rules governing the design and interpretation of cinematic meaning(s). Indeed, the looseness of fit between the rules and the contexts at issue is specific only to a certain phase of film-theoretical inquiry—a phase dominated for too long, arguably, by a broadly Lacanian emphasis on subjectivity. My hypothesis is that we can work toward more interesting and productive film-theoretical models by thinking about relations between (i) just those formal features of (cinematic) meaning which de Lauretis prematurely and perhaps inconsistently discounts and (ii) what de Lauretis identifies as the broader, social dimensions of semiotic inquiry. But, beyond this, we should explore the grounds for making a stronger (i.e., more controversial) claim: namely, that frameworks for understanding film can gain in descriptive and explanatory adequacy (in the sense of those terms specified by Chomsky 1965: 25ff.) if we abandon, or at the very least redescribe, Lacanian psychoanalytic theories of the subject.

Along these lines, this chapter makes a case for the importance and usefulness to film theory of a particular class of philosophico-linguistic inquiry that, developed in tandem with modal logic and under the impress of analytic philosophy of language, has come to be known as model-theoretic or, alternatively, possible worlds semantics. In what follows, I shall explore how, model theoretically, meaning is conceived as a function, in the strict sense, from some possible world or another to the truth conditions defining a world that is stipulated to be actual within a particular frame of reference and for the purposes of a given analysis. Next, we shall see that, by synthesizing possible world semantics with film theory, we can analyze cinematic meaning into two sets of mechanisms: on the one hand, a set of formal (i.e., model-theoretically describable) semantic mechanisms; on the other hand, a set of pragmatic (i.e., contextual and ipso facto social) mechanisms. Thus, eliciting some important illustrative instances from Peter Greenaway's *The Cook, The Thief, His Wife and Her Lover* (1989), I shall discuss what a model-theoretic account of film might look like. Such an account might allow us to reframe Lacanian notions of the spectating subject as the limit of cinematic meaning; no longer would we speak of that subject as the merely sutured site of a fundamentally asignifying or asemantic desire.[6] Just by detranscendentalizing Lacan's desiring subject—just by resolving it back into the sets of possible worlds of which it is, under specific semantic and pragmatic constraints, merely a function—model-theoretic approaches to film may provide, as part of what we can call a broadly grammatical framework for understanding cultural production in general, a semantics of cinema in particular.

2. Model-Theoretic Semantics: Genealogy and Aims

The first task at hand, then, is to sketch the advantages of talking about meaning via the construct *possible worlds*.[7] Generally speaking, model-theoretic semantics can be described as a more or less sophisticated logico-epistemological apparatus for handling the basic distinction between meaning and reference— that distinction having been drawn explicitly at least since Gottlob Frege's seminal analysis of sense and reference (Frege 1969e [1892], 1970 [1892]). For Frege, of course, whereas a given term or proposition can have many meanings or *Sinne,* that term or proposition can have, by contrast, only one (definite) referent or *Bedeutung* (1970 [1892]: 58). The classic example used in this connection is what, in the genre of scientific discourse at least (cf. Lyotard 1988a [1983]: 32–58), we refer to as the planet Venus. Thus, although for Frege the terms *morning star* and *evening star* each evoke a different meaning, nonetheless both terms refer to one and the same entity, both capture one and the same referent— namely, the referent (i.e., the planet Venus) that can be denoted by recourse to a particular set of scientific parameters, including, for example, the referent's orbital characteristics, its position relative to other planets in the solar system, its atmospheric conditions, its mean temperature, etc. So far, so good. Yet problems with the Fregean schema begin to assert themselves vis-à-vis what Frege himself bracketed from the start as cases of "oblique" or "indirect" (*ungerade*) sense and reference.[8] We can more generally characterize the problem of indirectness or obliquity by invoking a particular set of contextual features that belong to a certain class of utterances (i.e., sentences-in-contexts) expressing certain kinds of propositions. The contextual features in question later came to be discussed under the heading *propositional attitudes*—specifically, attitudes such as believing, knowing, judging, and the like. (See, e.g., Hintikka 1962.)

Take a sentence like

(S) Alexia believes the morning star to be visible in the morning.

If now we substitute the meaning of the term *the morning star* in (S) with its (more or less precisely specifiable) referent *the planet Venus,* we do not necessarily obtain a modified version of (S) expressing a proposition whose truth-value remains unchanged over the course of our substitution. Thus, the sentence

(S′) Alexia believes the planet Venus to be visible in the morning

does not necessarily express a true proposition, even supposing that Alexia does in fact believe the morning star to be visible in the morning—even if, that is, (S) has a positive truth-value. Yet if, for Frege, we resort to the distinction between meaning and reference precisely in order to resolve ambiguities introduced by different meanings that over time and in certain contexts have sedimented around one and the same referent, and hence to determine under what conditions a given set of terms can be said to be bound to one another in a relation of identity or at least homoreferentiality (Frege 1970 [1892]: 56–57), indeed, if the meaning-reference distinction purportedly allows us to characterize the relation of synonymity in general (cf. Frege 1970 [1892]: 64), how are we supposed to account for the change of truth-values introduced by the transformation of (S) into (S′)? What have we done besides resolve one of the possible meanings designated by a term into that term's proper referent, the entity it demonstrably denotes? And if we cannot determine the conditions under which what Charles Morris (1938) called the "denotation" of a term can be interchanged with what Morris called its "designation," how, more generally, are we ever to specify the conditions under which something like reference to a particular referent has in fact (or even in all likelihood) been made?

Just this class of substitutionary problems prompted the development, by Rudolf Carnap (1947) and others, of the further, model-theoretic distinction between intensions and extensions. Extensionally considered, the term *the planet Venus* and the term *the morning star* are in fact interchangeable; the extensions of the terms are equivalent. Intensionally considered, however, the terms are not similarly interchangeable; more precisely, intensions are not interchangeable *salva veritate*—to invoke (part of) the Leibnizian locution (cited in full by Frege 1970 [1892]: 64). Instead, meanings or intensions are, in a sense that even now remains to be spelled out fully (cf. Hintikka 1989b), context sensitive. Less elliptically, whereas a term's extension, best definable in the framework of set theory (Lyons 1977: 1:154ff.), is just the set of entities that the term in question denotes, picks out, or refers to in the Fregean sense, by contrast the intension of a term, what we mean by the term when we use it, cannot be captured in set-theoretical but rather in specifically model-theoretic terms and in particular with the operators of modality (possibility, impossibility, necessity, etc.) around which model-theoretic notions have been constructed (cf. sec. 2.2). Thus, if terms and propositions can mean different things to different people at the same time or different things to the same person at different times, model theoretically we can account for this state of affairs as follows: whenever they are used, and in whatever context, the terms and propositions denote entities and states of affairs that obtain, have positive truth-value, in some possible world. To say that the sentence (S) "Alexia believes the morning star to be visible in the morning" has a certain meaning (i.e., intension) is to say that in some possible world W_1 (S) constitutes a proposition whose truth-value is positive in W_1. Likewise, to say that the sentence (S') "Alexia believes the planet Venus to be visible in the morning" has a certain meaning is to say that in some possible world W_2 (S') constitutes a proposition whose truth-value is positive in W_2. And so on.

Yet model-theoretic semantics has as its special task, furthermore, the determination of the congruence or fit between possible worlds and the world stipulated to be actual within a given frame of reference. The raison d'être of model-theoretic notions is to help us negotiate between entities and states of affairs obtaining in some possible world or another, on the one hand, and entities and states of affairs obtaining within an adopted frame of reference, a world deemed actual for the purposes of a given (semantic) analysis, on the other hand. Model-theoretic frameworks (ideally) do not just permit us to characterize and assort the different intensions evoked by the terms *morning star, evening star,* and *Venus;* moreover, if supplemented by certain pragmatic considerations, model-theoretic schemes allow us to relegate to merely possible worlds, and in contradistinction to the world(s) postulated to be actual, any number of entities or states of affairs picked out by every imaginable kind of meaning or intension (secs. *4* and *5;* cf. secs. *2.6* and *2.7* above). Put otherwise, since a given entity, state, or event means by virtue of the intensions that its interpreters assign to it, that entity, state, or event must be conceived as a modal structure. This structure—a structure that gets embedded into higher-order modal structures in the case of cinema—encompasses the set of intensional functions, the meanings, that allow us to map merely possible worlds into the world that counts as actual according to the frame of reference adopted and so distinguish possibility from actuality in the first place.

3. Lacanian Film Theory: Meaning and (Quasi-Transcendental) Subjectivity

We can further clarify the importance of the model-theoretic apparatus in this connection by going on to link that semantic framework to the interpretation of filmic meaning in particular. We shall in other words return to possible worlds semantics through the (necessary) detour of Lacan-inspired film theory. In such film theory, cinema signifies to the extent that its operations mirror those of the subject's (i.e., spectator's) unconscious; in each domain we find a matrix of signs both overdetermined (hyperdenotative), because of its indefinitely many semantic relations to similar signs, and at the same time virtualized (hyperconnotative), because of its syntactic position in an indefinitely long chain of different signs. In a model-theoretic approach to film, by contrast, films signify just insofar as they generate strings of modal operators, the scope of whose possible permutations is determined not by quasi-transcendental subjective principles but rather by sets of pragmatic constraints that we can characterize (arguably) without recourse to any theory of subjectivity in general. Or such at least is the lesson that, for example, Greenaway's film, as we shall see, begins to teach us.

For the moment, however, let us simply confirm that film theory, true to its structuralist descent, and in league with Lacanian psychoanalysis, has in the first place traditionally postulated two classes of semiotic phenomena in film, two modes in which films mean. According to the nomenclature adopted, the two classes of phenomena in question may be termed those of image and montage (Eisenstein 1957); film features *in absentia* and film features *in presentia* (Saussure 1959 [1916]; Hjelmslev 1969 [1943]); filmic selections and combinations or concurrent and concatenative cinematic features (Jakobson 1971c [1954]); frames and sequences (Metz 1974a [1968]); paradigmatic instances and syntagmatic strings (Metz 1974b); "spaces in the frame" and "spaces beyond the frame" (Heath 1981); "partial moments" and "supplemental significance" (Nichols 1981); instantaneous images and (transformational) movements (Deleuze 1986 [1983]); or cues and (textual) trajectories (Bordwell 1989). What we are concerned with here, in short, is the (already very well-documented) organization of cinematic signification along two axes and thus within two sets of coordinates. Most basically, we can say that, on the one hand, films consist, over time, in ordered series or syntagmatic chains of framed images; on the other hand, films consist, at any given time, of those framed or arrested images (shots) themselves. Early on, Christian Metz (1974a [1968]) described these latter, framed images as more or less arbitrary selections from indefinitely large sets of other possible images,[9] and David Bordwell has more recently and more cogently identified them as cues that activate or access entire, culturally articulated semantic fields (1989: 105–28).

But, second, for any Lacanian film-theoretical approach, the syntagmatic and paradigmatic axes of cinematic meaning, and the system of coordinates in which they situate a given shot, will in turn be grounded in, or at least posited as homologous with, the quasi-transcendental principles of organization of the subject's (the spectator's) unconscious. Granted, Lacan himself articulates the principles of semiotic organization, at least initially, in classically Saussurean terms. Lacan (1977a [1957]) describes how "the structure of the signifier is . . . that it should be articulated. This means that no matter where one starts to designate their reciprocal encroachments and increasing inclusions, these units are subjected to the double condition of being reducible to ultimate differential elements and of combining according to the laws of a closed order" (152). The first part of this double condition, says Lacan, bears on "the essentially localized structure of the signifier," whereas "with the second property of the signifier, that of combining according to the laws of a closed order, is affirmed the necessity of the topological substratum of which the term I ordinarily use, namely, the signifying chain, gives an approximate idea" (153). Thus, Lacan, still parsing the terms of signification according to relations *in presentia* and relations *in absentia*, can claim that "it is in the chain of the signifier that the meaning 'insists' but . . . none of its elements 'consists' in the signification of which it is at the moment capable" (153).

Yet since Lacan also holds that "what the psychoanalytic experience discovers in the unconscious is the whole structure of language" (1977a [1957]: 147), since

Lacan, following Freud, attests to the "agency in the dream of that same literal (or phonematic) structure in which the signifier is articulated and analyzed in discourse" (159), Lacan must accordingly attempt to reroute, through the condensing and displacing operations identified in Freud's *Traumdeutung,* and thence through subjectivity as such, the rules constitutive of signification proper (159ff.). Specifically, Lacan asserts that "*Verdichtung,* or 'condensation,' is the structure of the superimposition of the signifiers, which metaphor takes as its field," whereas, "in the case of *Verschiebung,* 'displacement,' the German term is closer to the idea of that veering off of signification that we see in metonymy" (1977a [1957]: 160). What distinguishes the condensing-metaphorizing and displacing-metonymizing mechanisms of the unconscious from their "homologous function in discourse"—that is, from the metaphors and metonymies made possible by the jointly paradigmatic and syntagmatic organization of discourse—reduces to relatively minimal constraints "imposed upon the signifying material" (i.e., Freud's *Rücksicht auf Darstellbarkeit,* or "considerations of representability") (160). Lacan makes one further claim in this connection. He suggests that the "mechanism of metaphor is the very mechanism by which the symptom, in the analytic sense, is determined" and, furthermore, that "the enigmas of desire . . . amount to no other derangement of instinct than that of being caught in the rails—eternally stretching forth towards the *desire for something else*—of metonymy" (166–67; for an account of the *evolution* of Lacan's idea of the symptom, however, see Žižek 1989: 71–75). Hence, "the symptom *is* a metaphor whether one likes it or not, as desire *is* a metonymy, however funny people may find the idea" (175). By a series of extensions and transpositions that one might be tempted to call metonymic, Lacan projects the structures of the subject into those of language, and vice versa; the result is two clusters of concepts pertaining simultaneously, and ambiguously, to the unconscious and to discourse: on the one hand, the cluster condensation/paradigm/metaphor/symptom; on the other hand, the cluster displacement/syntagm/metonymy/desire. These clusters determine the scope and limits of subjectivity as well as the phenomena (experiences, images, signs) that the subject could in principle deem meaningful.

The film theory inspired by Lacan incorporates, more or less critically and reflexively, the same two clusters of concepts, perpetuating the (quasi-)transcendental elements of the Lacanian model. True, Metz (1982 [1977]: 174–211) has commented at length on the logical and methodological perils of positing a strictly homologous relation between the psychical mechanism of condensation, the paradigmatic axis of language, and the figure of metaphor; subject to

Metz's strictures, too, are attempts to equate the syntagmatic features of language, the psychical mechanism of displacement, and the figure of metonymy. Nonetheless, as the subtitle of his own study suggests (*Psychoanalysis and the Cinema*), Metz continues to argue by analogy from the structures of the subject to the semiotic organization of film (235ff.). Likewise, Kaja Silverman (1983), who argues that "condensation is . . . no more symmetrical with metaphor and paradigm than is displacement with metonymy and syntagm" (100), retains the view that "the sets metaphor and metonymy and paradigm and syntagm can no more be divorced from subjectivity than can condensation and displacement" (194). Indeed, argumentation for what Silverman describes as the "imbrication of signification and subjectivity" (85)—argumentation for "the profound interconnections between linguistic semiotics and psychoanalysis, interconnections which result both from the fact that language can be activated through discourse, within which the subject figures centrally, and from the fact that subjectivity is itself a product of . . . signifying activities" (72)—has emerged as the dominant mode of film-theoretical research. Thus, Laura Mulvey's influential analysis "Visual Pleasure and Narrative Cinema" (1988 [1975]) begins with the assumption that "the fascination of film is reinforced by pre-existing patterns of fascination already at work within the individual subject and the social formations that have moulded him" (57). Similarly, Constance Penley (1989), arguing that "all the possible roles in the narrative are available to the subject. . . . the subject can and does adopt these positions . . . in accordance with the mobile patterns of his or her desire" (79–80), goes on to suggest that "the formulation of fantasy, which provides a complex and exhaustive account of *the staging and imaging of the subject and its desire,* is a model that very closely approximates the primary aims of [e.g., Jean Baudry's] apparatus theory: to describe not only the subject's desire for the filmic image and its reproduction, but also the structure of the fantasmatic relation to that image, including the subject's belief in its reality" (80). Likewise, Jacqueline Rose (1988 [1976–77]) has as her chief concern "the position of women in relation to paranoia taken both as a structure latent to the film system and also as a mechanism of neurosis . . . vehicled by the narrative of the film in question" (154). In general, just by grounding the structures of cinema in the structures of the subject, the film theory inspired by Lacan construes the spectating subject "as the condition of possibility of the perceived and hence as a kind of transcendental subject, which comes before every *there is*" (Metz 1982 [1977]: 49).

Arguably, however, working toward a more productive and interesting film theory depends on our working past the condensation/paradigm/metaphor/

symptom and displacement/syntagm/metonymy/desire clusters, together with the transcendental or quasi-transcendental argumentation to which reliance on those clusters commits us. Examining in just what sense films might be said to be organized by way of the psychoanalytic constructs *symptom* and *desire,* we shall discover in what follows that a model-theoretic approach to film can usefully redescribe elements of cinematic meaning entrusted to psychoanalytic theory up to now. Such theory attempts to bind in the quasi-transcendental nexus of subjectivity filmic features that can be more productively distributed, debatably, between semantic and pragmatic components of interpretation. These interpretive components mark off a domain of (grammatical) principles that, as Greenaway's film in particular shows us, cannot be located or localized in any particular place whatsoever, let alone in that region of signification in which Lacan seeks to sketch the topography of the unconscious (1977a [1957]: 163).

4. Modes of Meaning in *The Cook, The Thief, His Wife and Her Lover*

Consider, then, and at long last, *The Cook, The Thief, His Wife and Her Lover.* How are we to begin describing the semiotic operations of this film, the modes in which it means? As we shall see, Greenaway's film patently thematizes its own mechanisms for meaning, with all the self-reflexive panache of high postmodern kitsch.[10] For the time being, however, let us try to separate, at least analytically, the deployment from the thematization of modes of meaning in the film. To be given the Lacanian imprimatur, remember, our analysis of the film must unfold within the condensing/paradigmatic/metaphoric dimension of overdetermined symptoms, on the one hand, and the syntagmatic/metonymic dimension of displaced and thereby virtualized desire, on the other hand.

4.1. Thus, we might begin by grouping sets of images into paradigmatically related symptoms. Take, for example, the yelping and incessant dogs that, along with an entire set of similarly sedimented images, condense around the sloping, windswept, and desolate car park, symptomizing in all their layered accretion that brutal naturalism that condenses also around the odious thief himself, Albert Spica. (Indeed, just as it condenses in its imagistic categories, or rather multiply denotes, the starkly naturalistic environment of the car park, on a still smaller scale the film mobilizes around the thief's very name the overdetermination of its constituent phonemes: "speaker," in the cook's French pronunciation—and throughout the film Albert is in fact continually speaking as well as not letting others speak; "spic," if an ethnic slur is brought to bear on the thief's swarthy appearance; "despicable," if we base our symptomatology on the ethical instance.) All the while beating Georgina in furious if comic impotence, Albert at one point runs over one of the dogs in the car park with what appears to be a large-model, 1970s-vintage American automobile. Here, presumably, we witness in the mangled and convulsing dog a further overdetermination of that category of outdoor images which, among other such categories, condenses along the axis of simultaneity. This category of images as a whole symptomizes the same (anti)technology of pure force embodied in part by Spica's car and by what he does in and with that car. And—to broach the second of our Lacanian principles of signification—the film syntagmatically links these paradigms of anticultural brutality to another, particularly overdetermined nexus of images: those of the raw, rotting, maggot-infested meat decomposing in the trucks just outside Le Hollandaise restaurant, inside of which, by dialectical contrast, multiple cultural technologies all center themselves on cooking. For Claude Lévi-Strauss (1969 [1964]), of course, the cooked is the sine qua non of culture as such.

In fact, as we proceed with our Lacanian (psycho)analysis, it is just this syntagmatic relation of difference—this being-related by juxtaposition, contrast, or opposition—that binds the cinematic condensations into an indefinitely extended chain whose links convey but also defer and virtualize desire. That desire, let us keep in mind, is ambiguous between film and spectator since it is constituted in the first place by the subject's position along, its suturing onto, the chain of contrasting symptoms introduced within the film. When therefore Georgina finds herself attracted to the plain, brown-suited Michael, whose lackluster appearance and humdrum demeanor contrast markedly with the outrageous attire that Albert (it seems) forces Georgina herself to wear; when, furthermore, Albert's ascription of Jewishness to the "bookkeeping" Michael overdetermines even more the condensation of symptoms that set Michael apart in syntagmatic contrast to Georgina, and when, again syntagmatically speaking, Georgina and Michael's kitchen trysts are set over against the scenes of bellowing, boarishness, and ribaldry carried out by Albert and his associates in the restaurant proper, we are to assume in each case that desire just *is* this chain of differentially defined traits, symptoms, and sites. Defined precisely by what it is not, desire can define, can mean, nothing in particular, but rather only mark an effect of differences of meaning. In turn, these differential chains thread themselves through the film along routes prescribed by the quasi-transcendental principles of meaning that we, good Lacanians that we are,

locate in the structure of subjectivity, of spectating, as such. In order to understand what the film means, we must look to the paradigmatic categories and
syntagmatic schemata that for Lacan, in classically Kantian fashion, determine
what can possibly be for some subject somewhere and at some time a (cinematic) phenomenon to begin with.

4.2. Yet if we now begin to factor into our account the way Greenaway's film
thematizes its own principles of signification, its own modes of meaning, we
start to see how the film at the same time invites us to bring into play a model-
theoretic framework for its interpretation. This latter framework obviates, or at
least inverts, the particular class of transcendental argument to which we have
just appealed in deference to Lacan. Instead of asking us to account for cinematic meaning by recourse to the conditions of possibility for the (spectating)
subject, the film suggests that we must view particular subjects as nodes in a
network comprising strategies for signification—strategies that films, among
other semiotic artifacts, both generate and comment on (see sec. 6.2 below).

Arguably, Greenaway's film as a whole sets signification into play within an
economy of possible worlds. Indeed, the film introduces an entire range of
possible worlds—or rather an (indefinitely large) set of frames of reference in
which those possible worlds could under certain conditions be stipulated as
actual. These frames of reference, if we set aside those of the book depository[11]
and the hospital, are what we might term *possible instances* of the more global
situation marked by the restaurant, Le Hollandaise. As the film also shows,
however, the restaurant in turn is nothing over and above the local instances—
that is, the meanings—it accommodates under different sets of (pragmatic)
constraints.

We have, besides the various segments of the car park outside, a segmentation of what might be called the kitchen domain, for example, into many
possible smaller frames of reference: for example, the hosing-off area just inside
the door, which functions much as the airlock does in the genre of science
fiction films. (This hosing-off area, which seals the always difficult passage
between possible worlds, is reduplicated in the book depository, where too, as
Michael tells Georgina, there are "a bathroom, a kitchen, and an extraordinary
view," reproducing in miniature and with all the earmarks of a *mise en abyme*
the entire layout of Le Hollandaise.) We also have the pot-washing region,
cross-referenced to that particular region of aesthetic production occupied by
the singing boy; the plucking, sauce-testing, and slicing areas; the china- and
pheasant-storage areas; and the frozen plenitude of the meat locker. Then we
have the field of the restaurant proper, often set as a whole over against the set of

kitchen worlds by a modulation in the soundtrack, which shifts from the a cappella or rather Gregorian austerity of the singing dishwasher in his stark industrial setting to the sound of rich orchestral strings in the lavishly furnished dining room. In the dining room itself a host of frames of reference situate themselves, wherever there is a table, group, occasion, and socialty—at least until such time as Albert violently imposes his world on, and either homogenizes or eliminates, everyone else's. Then too we have the set of bathroom frames, often set off from those of the dining room by another modulation in the soundtrack, this time from the lush resonance of strings to the quiet clarity of horns. The bathroom as a whole is further segmented into the narrow and furtive corridor (another airlock) connecting it to the dining room; the spacious blinding white territory housing mirrors (still more frames of reference), sinks, and urinals; and the subset of bathroom frames corresponding to each enclosed stall. In one of these minimal stall frames of course, Michael and Georgina first try, wordlessly and in absolute terror, to construct their own deprivileged or minority world, gradually insinuating their alternative perspective, at five-minute intervals, between the gaps in the totalitarian structure of Albert's master frame.

To be sure, our list of the referential frames staked out over the course of the film is as yet far from complete. (Remember here that, as Michael tells Georgina at one point, when things are quiet at his bookshop Michael falls back on a *stock-taking* job, cataloging French history.) But it should be evident by now that the film confines itself, on the whole, to the domain of Le Hollandaise precisely in order to highlight how even a single place houses, at least *in potentia,* an untold plurality of places, every global domain an indefinite series of microdomains. Panning leisurely from the car park through the kitchen and dining room territories on into the bathroom regions and then back again, the camera invites us to register an entire universe of possible places where, under other circumstances, guided by other scripts, we might otherwise be inclined to see merely a restaurant, a kitchen, a bathroom. Greenaway's film thereby portrays, in self-reflexive fashion, that virtualization of one place into many possible places by means of which films in general are accorded semantic pertinence to begin with. For cinema represents, in both senses of that term, the provisional and more or less wholesale annexation of possible worlds to the world(s) we deem actual according to our own particular frames of reference. At once indicating and issuing from what Thomas Pavel (1986) would term "salient" as opposed to "flat" ontologies, films both produce and represent ontological structures marked by complexly stratified systems of possibility (see sec. *6.1*

below). We enter these salient structures not just through the modal mechanisms of cinema, however, but also, as model-theoretic frameworks teach us,
whenever we try to produce or interpret meanings in the world(s) that, for very
many better or worse reasons, we deem our own.

Indeed, Greenaway's film thematizes precisely these pragmatic considerations—these better or worse reasons for designating a given thing, state, or
event as (partly) constitutive of some world or another—at the same time that
the film represents the proliferation of many competing frames of reference in
contexts that might otherwise and all too easily be thought of as single, monolithic. The film, chiefly through its representation of Albert Spica himself,
suggests, again in self-reflexive fashion, that not all the many microdomains
situating themselves on the global domain of Le Hollandaise are equally possible at a given time and under a given set of conditions. In fact, as the film's
representation of Albert implies, the pragmatic constraints delimiting the scope
of modal operators—specifically, the operator of possibility—are essentially
violent in nature.

Which worlds are possible when, how, and to what extent: these are matters
determined by, to put it most broadly, the relations of force between the various
competing frames of reference. Such relations of force dictate the violent disruption or even abolishment of some worlds by others. Albert's wealth and
physical power, for example, enable him to interrupt kitchen operations at any
moment; terrorize sous chefs, sauce stirrers, and dishwashers alike; upset pan
racks, smash jugs of milk, and so on—in what amounts to a series of cosmic
temper tantrums, thrown as if by some latter-day Zeus petulently eradicating
whole worlds at whim. In general, Albert cannot tolerate what we might term
the semantic polyfunctionality—and the ontological saliency—of a world on
whose very modal complexity, however, his own status as a hypothetical entity,
a cinematic construct, in turn depends. Albert at one point reproves Michael
for thinking it possible to read while eating, informing him that "this is a dining
room, not a library"; at another point Albert announces to those around him
that no dancing is to be allowed in the restaurant. And, if Albert breaks up other
dinner parties in order to clear a more expansively homogeneous place for his
band of thieves or else just for the sheer pleasure of violent action, conversely
Albert is incensed when Georgina brings up, in front of Michael and the other
guests, intimate details about her miscarriages, thus intermixing discourse belonging to the private and the public domains. Albert, it seems, must set the
terms on which various possible frames of reference are to be arranged and
hierarchicalized. Indeed, by brutalizing and murdering Michael, Albert not

only disrupts but utterly destroys that weak, fugitive frame of reference, that fragile and tentative world, which Georgina and her lover are powerless to maintain amid the neoclassical pillars and encyclopedic possibilities of the book depository. Suffocating the supine and bloodied bookkeeper with the pages of a book on the Terror of the French Revolution, Albert and his associates likewise try violently to extinguish the heterogeneity of perspective, the modal multiplicity, that no really terroristic politics, no repressive or mono-functionalist ontology, can permit.

5. Contexts and the Scope of Possibility

We can recapitulate the foregoing observations on Greenaway's film—observations assembled up to now in largely serendipitous fashion—by situating the film more squarely in the context of model-theoretic semantics. When we talk about the film's meaning in this connection, we need to keep in mind that, because of its highly self-reflexive nature, the film both means and thematizes how it is that films, among other such semiotic phenomena, can in general have meaning. Having made this (provisional) distinction between levels of semantic functioning in order to minimize ambiguity in our application of the model-theoretic schema, we can then say that, at any given time t_n, Greenaway's film means precisely by projecting an (indefinitely large) domain of intensions—a set of meanings corresponding to the entities, events, and states of affairs obtaining in any number of possible worlds—into the range of truth conditions defining the world(s) stipulated to be actual at t_n. This stipulation of actuality at t_n vis-à-vis a given possible world depends on the particular frame of reference that corresponds to t_n; and the particular frame of reference adopted at t_n necessarily competes with and excludes, as long as time is postulated to be linear and irreversible, those referential frames adopted at, say, t_{n-1} or t_{n+1}. (For a characterization of such adopted frames of reference as "model worlds," see sec. 2.6 above.) Thus—and the film as we have already discussed thematizes this very point—the meaning that one assigns to a given object, event, or situation in Le Hollandaise depends on the frame of reference in which one stands at any given time.

For example, for the restaurant staff at time t_n the kitchen means an economy of tools and functions, a familiar assemblage of interlocked operations, coordinated with a set of simultaneously aesthetic and monetary aims. For lovers stealing a few moments together under the very nose of a tyrannous husband at t_n, by contrast, the kitchen means the cover and anonymity afforded by the bustle of unconcerned cooks; the sanctuary of clutter and closets; the sound-deadening presence of slain, well-fed pheasants hanging from the ceiling. But, for the cuckolded husband at t_n, just about to begin smashing his way through the storage rooms in search of his unfaithful wife and her lover, the kitchen means an aggravating congeries of obscuring supplies and alien apparatus—an undifferentiated space full of unimportant objects in which the only state of affairs interesting enough for Albert to assign it a positive or negative truth-value is the state of affairs bearing on the exact location of his errant wife. What the film represents, what it thematizes, is just this competition and, moreover, incompatibility of frames of reference vis-à-vis one and the same (ontological) instance. That instance may correspond to the relatively large set of entities, states, and events that one recognizes, in various ways, as comprising the kitchen; or the instance in question may correspond to the relatively small set with which one is concerned, again in various ways, when it comes to a single bathroom stall. What remain constant, however, are the asymmetrical relations of force that result in—*and signify*—the domination of a particular frame of reference over other such frames attempting to situate themselves around the instance at issue.[12]

Granted, these relations of force between different frames of reference may themselves be differently inscribed, given alternative meaning, in the frames variously adopted. Thus, on the one hand, although it is structurally impossible for Georgina and Michael's frame of reference in the bathroom stall to coincide with that of the raging Albert, their frame of reference is in fact premised on this very noncoincidence of referential frames in general. Theirs is a bid to bring into being what in the dominant frame of reference counts as a merely possible world; their attempt to make the world mean otherwise than it does therefore roots itself in the merely fitful, partial ruin of a master frame that prescribes a different, properly antagonistic actuality. On the other hand, Albert's frame of reference is such that, in every case, he strives absolutely to reduce every other frame of reference to his own.[13] Albert thereby tries to dictate the scope of possibility itself, by enforcing what a given thing can mean, what possible worlds a thing's meaning might (partly) map into the world *he* deems actual. Albert will not allow the bathroom stall to mean, for example, an actual as opposed to a merely possible refuge for Georgina and Michael. It is worth emphasizing, however, that, even in frames of reference *not* premised on their domination over all other such frames, constraints of the sort represented by Albert's violent egotism, his referential monomania as it were, are always operative. Like Albert in particular, pragmatic constraints in general delimit the nature and scope of the meanings that can be assigned to anything at any given moment.

To this extent Albert merely figures with special force and intensity the pragmatic constraints that operate without exception in our every attempt either to mean something or to determine what something means. More specifically, by dictating what frame of reference is dominant or foregrounded at what moment and under what conditions, constraints of the sort figured by Albert delimit the scope of possibility itself by situating intensions in particular contexts—contexts that cannot be reduced to the formal (semantic) mechanisms captured in model-theoretic schemes (cf. sec. 2.7). Abstracted from such pragmatic constraints, all frames of reference would become equally prominent, and, as a result, no single world could be stipulated as actual but would rather take its place among an indefinitely large number of equally (and hence indeterminately) actual worlds. Effectively, the scope of possibility, extended to cover the domain of actuality itself, would become infinite. In recognizing that the scope of modal operators is always delimited by contexts, however, we return to the question with which we began: namely, how is it that rules governing filmic form are bound together with social contexts in the production and interpretation of cinematic meaning? We have perhaps pursued the form and functioning of Greenaway's film long enough to begin sketching how a model-theoretic approach—supplemented by some pragmatic considerations—allows us to frame at least a provisional response to our guiding question about cinematic rules and contexts and to do so without recourse to Lacanian theories of subjectivity as such.

6. (Filmic) Models for Meaning

To start characterizing in general terms how films mean is to begin specifying what might be called rules for well-formed strings of modal operators. On the well-formedness of such strings depends a modal structure that can be partitioned, at a given time and within a given frame of reference, between actuality and possibility. On this partitioning of modal structures depends, in turn, the very notion of a world—of *some* world or another. For a world is by definition nothing more than a structure or system of partitioned modalities (cf. Ryan 1991: 109–23). If all states of affairs were equally and simultaneously possible in a certain frame of reference, then there could be no such thing as a meaning or intension in that frame. Meaning just is a function from possible worlds to some world stipulated to be actual, so, without the differentiation of possible from actual states of affairs, all worlds whatsoever, and hence no world in particular, would be possible. By the same token, films mean precisely because they too partition our world(s) into more or less richly differentiated modal structures. Yet—and this is the crucial point—films create such modal structures on more than one level; or, rather, films mark the embedding of those structures one within another. Films *represent* the competition between frames of reference and their contexts, all the while competing with and partially dislodging the frame of reference in which we interpret the film, for, while participating in cinema, we partition the virtual and the actual differently than we do before or after we concern ourselves with a given filmic frame.

6.1. Thus, with respect to the modal structures created by cinema, the relations of force between frames of reference can be expressed as rules operative at two levels or, more precisely, within two different dimensions of semiosis: (i) the dimension centering on the formation and transformation of filmic form and (ii) the dimension centering on how films function in contexts. Some highly reflexive films, such as Greenaway's, encode information about ii through features pertaining to i. Hence, the film asks us not to be like Albert Spica in viewing *this very film;* we are not to delimit, in any overrestrictive way, the frames of reference that might conceivably be adopted for interpretation of the film; we are at least to entertain, despite prior stipulations of actuality, the possibility of *these* possible worlds. Encoding principles for the (trans)formation of indeterminately possible into provisionally actual worlds, *The Cook, The Thief, His Wife and Her Lover* means just by representing the situation of frames of reference in contexts that determine the relations of force between those frames, some of which include frames in contexts that we (might conceivably) call our own. The film thereby compels us to reevaluate why some of our frames of reference are foregrounded or largely dominant, others backgrounded or mostly incipient, and how changes of context might produce different relations of dominance and latency in connection with those frames.

This is not to say that only reflexive films such as Greenaway's are susceptible of description in model-theoretic terms. Although for reasons of space my discussion has been confined to Greenaway's film in particular, it would not be overly difficult, I believe, to extend to cinema in general (aspects of) the analysis developed here. Films as such constantly pose, are constituted by, questions about frames of reference: that is, who is looking at what (whom) from where, for how long, when, and for what reason? Films ask, and always only momentarily answer, these sorts of questions by providing more or less determinate values for the variables *who, what,* and *when* vis-à-vis frames of reference.

Indeed, the various genres of filmic art (melodrama, comedy, adventure, etc.) might be usefully redescribed via their relation to the technical features of film production—blocking, camera placement, focalization, shot duration, and so on—that account for the relative ease or difficulty of assigning values to the variables just listed. Collectively these technical features give point to the essential question for filmic design *and* interpretation: which (whose) frame of reference does the film foreground or construct as dominant? Self-reflexive films like Greenaway's, it is true, highlight their ongoing construction of dominant and latent frames, adhering to the metaconstructive logic of postmodernism generally (see secs. *4.4* and *4.7* above). Yet frames of reference are arguably an essential ingredient of filmic (among other) modes of representation; all films engage in a (more or less easily reconstructible) partitioning of the virtual and the actual through (more or less pronounced) techniques for framing. In fact, the less obvious the status of a filmic frame of reference *as* such a frame, the more likely that the film is trafficking in what can be called concealed hypotheticality (Herman 1994a)—that is, suppressed or occluded virtuality—by means of which merely possible states of affairs pass themselves off as actual, as factual. By multiplying frames of reference and highlighting even the most fugitive of possible worlds, Greenaway's film produces just the opposite effect, forcing us to situate the actual in contexts always subject to change.

From the model-theoretic perspective, of course, questions about meaning in general center themselves on the issue of what intensional functions, what meanings, are to project what possible worlds into which world stipulated to be actual in what frame of reference when. One might therefore venture that, if Georgina and Michael must battle it out with Albert in a struggle over whose world is really to exist, their struggle merely figures in particularly macroscopic fashion the semantic status of a term like *justice*, say. *Justice*, too, marks a more or less explicit struggle between frames of reference—or, rather, a contest between those frames' relations of force—to map different possible worlds, different configurations of possibility and actuality, into the world that in one of those frames is stipulated as the properly existent world (cf. Lyotard 1988a [1983]). To adapt the terminology of Jurij Lotman and Boris Uspenskij (1986 [1971]), however, cultural artifacts like movies and narratives function as "secondary modeling systems" rooted in the primary modeling system afforded by language itself. The question remains whether, in commenting on modes of meaning at the primary level, specifically filmic modeling systems can be distinguished from other secondary systems by the technical features (modulations in the soundtrack, fade-ins, shot/reverse shot pairs, etc.) only some of which have been discussed here. At issue are particular technical devices used in the service of meaning in the filmic medium, which models how we—standing now in this, now in that frame of reference—come to bestow meaning on things in general.

6.2. My larger point, however, is that we need not ground in any general theory of subjectivity either the semantic mechanisms of cinema or the ways in which those mechanisms comment, in turn, on the semantic profile of the primary modeling system, that is, language. The contrary view, given impetus by Lacan and (post-)Lacanians, derives from the assumption that the dependence of the subject on the structures of signification results in a reciprocal and symmetrical dependence of signification on the subject (cf. Silverman 1983: 85). But the two orders of dependence can be deemed symmetrical only if we assume beforehand the descriptive and explanatory adequacy of Lacan's two conceptual clusters—that is, condensation/paradigm/metaphor/symptom and displacement/syntagm/metonymy/desire—and only if we make similar assumptions about the quasi-transcendental modes of analysis of which those clusters are, ambiguously, at once a premise and a result. Using Greenaway's film as a case study, we have discovered ample reason *not* to make these sorts of assumptions. On the contrary, the analysis suggests that what film theorists and others typically call the subject—or, for that matter, the unconscious—can be usefully redescribed in model-theoretic terms. Besides accounting for modes of meaning in film by appeal to frames-in-contexts, possible worlds semantics may allow us to account for subjectivity itself as a particular configuration, or rather a range of possible configurations, of the virtual and the actual.

Symptom, condensation: names for the conflict between multiple frames of reference whose relations of force contextual constraints have not yet determined—multiple frames indefinitely situating themselves around one and the same entity, state or event. *Desire, displacement:* names for the process of such contextual determination itself. By means of that (ongoing) process, one frame of reference, provisionally foregrounded, brings under the scope of mere possibility those states and events whose more or less insuperable inactuality produces the effect we call desire. As the modal mechanisms of cinema themselves suggest, the subject effect, like the effect we term meaning, cannot be talked about in isolation from the frame of reference in which it manifests itself. The subject just is an operator that, within a particular frame of reference, helps generate that class of modal structures which we call worlds. Thus, to say that the cinema is the latest and best in a long line of technologies for staging the operations of the unconscious (cf. Penley 1989: 15–23) is to start speaking in bad metaphors. A more productive film-theoretical vocabulary might run something like this: films encode strategies for meaning to which we as (communicating) subjects regularly resort and on which the filmic modeling system gives us new perspectives, generating in turn new strategies for communication, new modes of meaning. Model-theoretic frameworks may be particularly helpful in illuminating the complicated, and circular, relation between universal grammar and filmic form.

To recapitulate: *The Cook, The Thief, His Wife and Her Lover* teaches us that what has gone by the name of the subject may be reconstrued as yet another (semiotic) site and occasion for the construction, conflict, and embedding of worlds. The location of that site, the time of that occasion, follows from, rather than accounts for, the (always emergent) relations of force between frames-in-contexts. The afterimage of the last frame of reference adopted, and the foreshadowing of indefinitely many other frames yet to come, the subject is in effect just as globally situated, just as divisible into microdomains, as Greenaway's Le Hollandaise. Its principles of constitution and functioning form part of a grammar predicated not on a specific language but rather on the possibilities and limits of communication, of signification, generally. The semantics of film pertain to the same general grammar. But discussion of this higher-order grammar—a theoretical enterprise as old as the λόγος itself—must be continued in another place, situated in another frame of reference.

Notes

Introduction: The Project of Universal Grammar

I am indebted to James Phelan and Jon Thompson for invaluable help during the revision and reconceptualization of earlier drafts of this introduction.

1   Under the title *Narratology after Structuralism: New Directions in Narrative Theory* (in preparation). Fragments of this study have been published as Herman (1994a, 1994b, 1994e).

2   In recent years researchers as diverse as Seymour Chatman (1990), Dorrit Cohn (1981), Marcel Cornis-Pope (1992), Didier Coste (1989), Lubomír Doležel (1989, 1990), Monika Fludernik (1993a, 1993b), Uri Margolin (1986), Wallace Martin (1986), Thomas Pavel (1985b, 1986), James Phelan (1989), Arkady Plotnitsky (1993), Gerald Prince (1983a, 1992a), Marie-Laure Ryan (1991), and the authors collected in Ann Fehn, Ingeborg Hoesterey and Maria Tartar's *Neverending Stories: Toward a Critical Narratology* (1992) have sought to develop new conceptual resources for narrative theory. Not all these studies inform my investigation to the same degree; but, as we shall see, I am indebted to some of the studies for specific ideas and to others for inspiration.

3   This book does not directly address the question of what specific historical and material conditions produced, around the turn of the century, the reinvigoration of (the ideal of) universal grammar. One contributing factor, however, may have been the advent of telecommunicational technologies such as the electronic telegraph in the mid-nineteenth century— technologies that generated interest in a universal code for communication (see chap. 4, n. 10).

Furthermore, for discussion of the theory of universal grammar as interpreted by Chomsky in particular, see section *4.1.* below; as we shall see, Chomsky's is a somewhat narrower interpretation of universal grammar than that developed by language theorists down the ages.

4   In calling for a specifically *linguistic* enrichment of narrative theory, this study seconds Rimmon-Kenan's (1989: 159) claim that (with some important exceptions) narratologists have historically "underplayed the role of language" itself in analyzing narrative units and structures. In the same connection, see Fludernik's (1993b: 743ff.) account of the way ideas drawn from linguistic pragmatics can usefully supplement classical narratological methods and concepts.

5   Here I borrow the language of Foucault (1972 [1969]): "Whenever one can describe, between a number of statements, . . . a system of dispersion, whenever, between objects, types of

statement, concepts, or thematic choices, one can define a regularity (an order, correlations, positions and functionings, transformations), we will say, for the sake of convenience, that we are dealing with a *discursive formation*—thus avoiding words that are already overladen with conditions and consequences, and in any case inadequate to the task of designating such a dispersion, such as 'science,' 'ideology,' 'theory,' or 'domain of objectivity' " (39). Furthermore, Foucault (1973 [1966]) defines *episteme* as "the general system of thought whose network, in its positivity, renders an interplay of simultaneous and apparently contradictory opinions possible. It is this network that defines the conditions that make a controversy or a problem possible, and that bears the historicity of knowledge" (75). For some preliminary distinctions between the categories *modernism* and *postmodernism*, see Herman (1991b).

6   As Prince (1987) remarks, words such as *narrator, narrate, narrative,* etc. are related to *gnarus*, "a Latin word meaning 'knowing,' 'expert,' 'acquainted with,' and deriving from the Indo-European root *gnâ* ('to know')" (39).

7   Note that, taken together, definitions 4 and 6 included under the *OED*'s entry for *grammar* display the same double profit of grammar—grammar construed as object and grammar construed as method—featured in the present study: "The phenomena which form the subject-matter of grammar; the system of inflexions and syntactical usages characteristic of a language" (definition 4); "the fundamental principles or rules of an art or science" (definition 6). The status of grammar as jointly model and data, method and object, invites comparisons between grammatical theory and aspects of postclassical physics.

8   However, Curtius (1953 [1948]) argues that, as a transitional period between antiquity and the Middle Ages, the Hellenistic era already marks the beginning of the split between grammar and literary theory: "From the unity of philosophy there emerge the separate branches of learning: grammar, rhetoric, philology, history of literature" (147).

9   Admittedly, significant differences of nuance and emphasis have sedimented around grammars variously termed *speculative, rational, general, universal,* and *philosophical* (on speculative grammar, see Thomas of Erfurt 1972 [ca. 1300–1310] and Bursill-Hall 1971; on rational, Gardies 1985 [1975]; on general, Arnauld and Lancelot 1972 [1660] and Arnauld and Nicole 1972 [1662]; on universal, Chomsky 1966a, Aarsleff 1982; and on philosophical, Wittgenstein 1974 and Descombes 1986 [1983]). For the sake of descriptive convenience, however, I use the various designations of grammars of higher order as if they were in fact interchangeable with *universal grammar*. Sometimes, in attempts to avoid monotony, I use the term *higher-order grammar* as a synonym for *universal grammar*. Another alternative might be Plett's (1985: 87ff.) term *Sekundärgrammatik* (secondary grammar) as discussed in chap. 4 below.

10 In this connection, see Ferriani (1987) for an account of how C. S. Peirce also draws on the idea of speculative grammar in characterizing "the parts of speech fundamental to the construction of a proposition" (151)—as opposed to those occurring within a sentence of a given (natural) language (see also chap. 4, n. 12, and sec. 4.7 below).

11 Both *subreption* and *surreptitious* derive from the Latin *subrepo*, "to creep under, steal into."
    In the section of the *Critique of Pure Reason* (1965 [1781/1787]) devoted to the "Transcendental Dialectic," e.g., Kant talks about "concepts of reason" that "contain the unconditioned," remarking that, "if these concepts possess objective validity, they may be called *conceptus ratiocinati* (rightly inferred concepts); if, however, they have no such validity, they have *surreptiously obtained recognition* through having at least an illusory appearance of being

inferences, and may be called *conceptus ratiocinantes* (pseudo-rational concepts)" (A311/B368, p. 309; my emphasis). Earlier, Kant had commented at length on "the fallacy of subreption" in his *Inaugural Dissertation* (1770). See Herman (1991a: 18ff.).

12 By contrast, in Leibniz's *New Essays on Human Understanding* (published posthumously in 1765), during a discussion of how "particles [i.e., prepositions, adverbs, and conjunctions] are all marks of the action of the mind" (bk. 3, chap. 7; Leibniz 1981 [1765]: 330), Leibniz cites examples from the French, German, English, and Hebrew. Working within the language-theoretical tradition stretching from the ancient Greeks through the Modistae on into "Cartesian linguistics" (Chomsky 1966a; see sec. 5.1. below), Leibniz has one of the discussants, Theophilus, remark, "I really believe that languages are the best mirror of the human mind, and that a precise analysis of the significations of words would tell us more than anything else about the operations of the understanding" (334).

13 In support of Chomsky's interpretation, cf. this passage from Arnauld and Lancelot's *Grammaire générale et raisonnée* (1972 [1660]): "Les cas et les Prepositions avoient esté inventez pour le mesme usage, qui est marquer les rapports que les choses ont les unes aux autres" (83).

14 Ullmann (1957), however, makes an important distinction between deductive and inductive variants of universal grammar. As Ullmann notes the stress on universal or general grammars has long been prominent in philology: "At the pre-scientific stage of language study, it had assumed a deductive and aprioristic form, only too often influenced by the overriding prestige of Latin" (258). By contrast, Wilhelm von Humboldt, whose work stimulated the development of historical and comparative linguistics in the nineteenth century, "advocated the production of an inductive general grammar based on the conception of different languages," as "opposed to the conception of [the older] deductive universal grammars" (258; cf. Doležel 1990: 64–77).

15 An example might help. The string *is ninety-three million miles away* functions as a first-order predicate modifying *the sun* in (S) "The sun is ninety-three million miles away." The very same linguistic string, however, functions as a second-order predicate in (S′) "'The sun is ninety-three million miles away' is a proposition subject to verification." Gardies's point is that in natural language contexts we find both sorts of predicates but no grammatical markers that would allow us to rank the predicates according to type—without appeal to language users' intuitions. Instead, in such contexts we must rely on surrounding expressions, the circumstances of utterance, and so on in order to differentiate between first-, second-, . . . , *n*-order predicates.

16 This conclusion has not always been so obvious. Thus, in *La Logique* (1792) and *La Langue des calculs* (1798), Étienne Bonnot de Condillac attempted to characterize language itself as a "méthode analytique." Accordingly, as Raffaele Simone (1987) points out, in Condillac "a long-standing view of the function of language is deliberately abandoned: language is not made for communication, it is rather an essential tool for analysing our thought and for reducing it into discrete segments" (69).

However, in some notes dictated to G. E. Moore in 1914, Ludwig Wittgenstein seems to suggest that what Gardies describes as the universality of natural language(s) itself serves functions that may be deemed logical: "An illogical language would be one in which, e.g., you could put an event into a hole. . . . Thus a language which can express everything mirrors certain properties of the world by these properties which it must have; and logical so-called propositions [show] *in a systematic way* these properties" (1961 [1914–16]: 107).

17   However, an early definition of *generative grammar* given by Chomsky suggests affiliations between the generative enterprise and the language-theoretical tradition discussed in previous sections. According to a definition framed in 1964, a generative grammar is "a device (or procedure) which assigns structural descriptions to sentences in a perfectly explicit manner, *formulated independently of any particular language*" (quoted in Lyons 1991: 188; my emphasis; cf. Stassen 1985; Foley and Van Valin 1984).

18   However, as discussed below (secs. *1.7.4ff.*), Chomsky's early, so-called standard theory of transformational generative grammar does use transformational rules to map logico-semantic properties of sentences (i.e., their underlying organization or deep structure) into the phonetic properties and overt phrasing of those sentences (i.e., their superficial organization or surface structure). To this extent, there may be grounds for construing transformational grammar, at least in its early incarnations, as yet another attempt to model a material calculus.

19   In the same connection, note that two of the founders of modern symbolic logic, Bertrand Russell and Louis Couturat, based their pathbreaking logical researches on prior assessments of Leibniz's contributions to logical analysis. In the case of Russell, *A Critical Exposition of the Philosophy of Leibniz* (1900) preceded both his *Principles of Mathematics* (1903) and also his and Whitehead's monumental *Principia mathematica* (1910–13). Meanwhile, Couturat (1901, 1903) preceded that author's *L'Algèbre de la logique* (1905) and *Les Principes des mathématiques* (1905).

20   The figure of the alphabet that Leibniz uses here may derive in part from a similar figure developed earlier by Arnauld and Nicole, in their *Logique* of 1662: "L'arrangement de nos diverses connoissances est libre comme celuy des lettres d'une Imprimerie, chacun a droit d'en former differens ordres selon son besoin" (Arnauld and Nicole 1972 [1662]: 23).

21   Compare this remark of Frege's, cited by Hermanns (1977): "Mein Zweck ein anderer als Booles war. Ich wollte nicht eine abstracte Logik in Formeln darstellen, sondern einen Inhalt durch geschriebene Zeichen in genauerer und übersichtlicherer Weise zum Ausdruck bringen, als es durch Worte möglich ist. Ich wollte in der That nicht einen blossen '*calculus ratiocinator*,' sondern eine '*lingua characterica*' im leibnizschen Sinne schaffen, wobei ich jene schlussfolgernde Rechnung immerhin als einen nothwendigen Bestandtheil einer Begriffsschrift anerkenne" (25).

22   Hence Frege's work is the modern-day source for ideal language philosophy (as opposed to ordinary language philosophy): i.e., philosophical analysis based on the assumption that we must "construct an alternative language (one whose undefined descriptive terms refer only to objects of direct acquaintance, whose logic is extensional, etc.) in order to prevent the possibility of formulating . . . the traditional problems of philosophy" (Rorty 1970: 12). As Patzig (1969) puts it, Frege's work on the foundations of arithmetic convinced Frege of the unsuitability of ordinary language for logical analysis: "Die Umgangssprache zur Wiedergabe der hier auftretenden feineren logischen Strukturen ungeeignet ist, und so zur geglückten Konstruktion einer logischen Kunstsprache, danach schrittweise zu weitausgreifenden Untersuchungen über das Verhältnis von Sprache und Wirklichkeit sowie über das Verhältnis der Logik zur Erkenntnistheorie und Psychologie" (7; cf. 9–10).

23   Thus, Frege later compares the development of an adequate conceptual notation to *technological* developments crucial for the advancement of the various special sciences: "Zur Eforschung

der Naturgesetze dienen die physikalischen Apparate; diese können nur durch eine fortge-shrittene Technik hervorgebracht werden, welche wieder auf der Kenntnis der Naturgesetze fußt" (97). See chap. 4 below.

24 As discussed in sec. 2.3 below (cf. sec. 5.2), whereas semantic theorists use the term *extension* when they are interested in the logic of referring expressions—i.e., what those expressions pick out in the world and, concomitantly, what logical inferences the expressions themselves entail and/or disallow—researchers use *intension* (*Inhalt*) to designate the semantic properties or contents attaching to terms and propositions in a given context of use.

25 Compare here another text of Leibniz's, quoted by Derrida (1974 [1967]): "The characteristic economizes on the spirit and the imagination, whose expense must always be husbanded. . . . *Characteristic* . . . teaches us the secret of stabilizing reasoning, and of obliging it to leave visible marks on the paper in a little volume, to be examined at leisure: finally, it makes us reason at little cost, putting characters in place of things in order to ease the imagination" (78).

26 This early distinction between grammatical rules for well-formed expressions and (logical) rules for correct judgment—a distinction that, as we have seen, is already implicit in Frege's justification of his *Begriffsschrift*—persists throughout Husserl's later writings, notably the fourth *Logical Investigation* and *Formal and Transcendental Logic* (1969 [1929]). (For a discussion of the importance of Husserl's distinction between grammar and logic for subsequent language theory, see sec. 1.6.2 below.) Compare also Heidegger (1978 [1915]: 339).

27 For the moment, we can adopt as a working definition of *narrative* itself the definition proposed by Prince: "Narrative may be defined (and usually is defined) as the representation of real or fictive events and situations in a time sequence" (1980: 49; cf. Prince 1973, 1982, 1987). However, chap. 1 explores whether twentieth-century narrative form may itself impose restrictions of scope on Prince's definition, along with related definitions (see sec. 1.8.2).

28 Compare Foucault's (1973 [1966]) characterization of general grammar itself: "It would be nonsense to see ['that new epistemological domain that the Classical age called "general grammar"'] as purely and simply the application of a logic to the theory of language. But it would be equally nonsensical to attempt to interpret it as a sort of prefiguration of a linguistics. . . . Its [general grammar's] proper object is . . . neither thought nor any individual language, but *discourse,* understood as a sequence of verbal signs" (83).

29 See Barbara Herrnstein Smith (1980) for arguments that the *fabula-sjužet* distinction is grounded in Platonistic assumptions—most blatantly, in the assumption that an abstract and quasi-noumenal story "is independent of any of its versions, independent of any surface manifestation or expression in any material form, mode, or medium" (216). For Smith, the more or less pronounced Platonism of narrative theory robs narratology of explanatory resources it would otherwise have at its disposal (221ff.). For counterarguments, see Prince (in press). Smith bases much of her critique on Seymour Chatman's (1978) skillful and influential reformulation of the *fabula-sjužet* distinction as that between story and discourse, respectively.

30 Note that, in this nearly thirty-year-old essay, Barth (1977b [1966]: 83, n. 2) cites Zellig Harris (1952) as a proponent of the new linguistics of discourse. It would take quite some time, however, before narrative theorists began to recognize the importance of discourse analysis for narratological research. See van Dijk (1985), Tolliver (1990), Herman (1994b), and sec. 1.8 below.

31   As early as 1966, however, Barthes remarked that "language never ceases to accompany discourse, holding up to it the mirror of its own structure—does not literature, particularly today, make a language of the very conditions for language?" (1977b [1966]: 85).

32   More recently, the question of where to draw the boundary between semantics and pragmatics became a somewhat controversial matter (cf. Herman 1994b). Generally, however, linguists think of semantics as the study of sentences and pragmatics as the study of utterances; thus, whereas semantics studies truth-conditional aspects of meaning (i.e., meanings that derive from the logico-semantic content of those expressions), pragmatics studies non-truth-conditional aspects of meaning (i.e., meanings that derive not from semantic content but rather from the contexts in which the sentences are uttered). In addition to chaps. 2 and 3 below, see Brown and Yule (1983: 19–26), Fasold (1990: 119ff.), Gazdar (1979: 89ff.), Herman (1994b: sec. 3), Levinson (1983: 18–21), and Prince (1988: 166–67).

1   The Modeling of Syntactic Structures: "Sirens," Schönberg, and the Acceptations of Syntax

1   See, e.g., Peter Galison's important article "Aufbau/Bauhaus" (1990), which shows how the effort to develop constructional systems links the logical positivism of the Vienna Circle with the architectural modernism of the Bauhaus groups. As Galison puts it, "Carnap, Neurath and others singled out modern architecture as the cultural movement with which they most identified. . . . Both enterprises sought to instantiate a modernism emphasizing what I will call 'transparent construction,' a manifest building up from simple elements of all higher forms that would, by virtue of the systematic constructional program itself, guarantee the exclusion of the decorative, mystical, or metaphysical" (710; cf. 723, 727). For more on Carnap's construction theory in particular, see sec. 6.4 below.

2   As Ellmann (1982) notes, Georges Borach has (somewhat awkwardly) transcribed a conversation he had with Joyce in 1919, at which time Joyce said this about "Sirens": "A big job. I wrote this chapter with the technical resources of music. It is a fugue with all musical notations: *piano, forte, rollentando,* and so on. . . . Since exploring the resources and artifices of music and employing them in this chapter, I haven't cared for music any more. I, the great friend of music, can no longer listen to it. I see through all the tricks and can't enjoy it any more" (459).

3   As Ferrer puts it, "At the beginning of the episode, a mass of material ('the overture') is fed into the text like data into a computer, or like highly concentrated nutriments into a digestive system. Then, through a long and thorough process of transformation, this inert matter is assimilated. . . . At the other end of the *tract,* expulsion takes place: the chapter actually finishes with an anal evacuation, Bloom's fart" (1986: 70). For further discussion of the idea that "Sirens" is computational in form, see sec. 6.7 below.

4   In 1936, Eugene Jolas wrote, "When the beginnings of this new age are seen in perspective, it will be found that the disintegration of words, and their subsequent reconstruction on other planes, constitute some of the most important acts of our epoch" (1974 [1936]: 79).

5   The links between modern music and philosophico-linguistic discourse have not been studied, it seems, as carefully as the topic warrants. Adorno (1973 [1948]), e.g., confines to one rather conjectural note remarks concerning Vienna as the birthplace of both Schönberg's music and logical positivism (68, n. 24). Janik and Toulmin (1973) make only a superfi-

cial comparison "between Schönberg's *Harmonielehre* and Whitehead and Russell's *Principia Mathematica* . . . as compendious expositions of a new logic" (107).

6   Only an interpretation of this sort allows us to resolve what appears to be a paradox in Curtius's presentation. On the one hand, Curtius labels Joyce's musical experimentation in "Sirens" "fragwürdig" because words used as verbal motifs do not have the same effect as musical motifs, in that the latter are intelligible in and of themselves (1954 [1929]: 312). On the other hand, however, Curtius suggests that, insofar as every passage, sentence, and sentence fragment in *Ulysses* can be understood only in relation to another, analogous segment of the text, Joyce's production reveals its "Verwandschaft . . . mit der Musik" (313).

7   Hermanns (1977) points out that Frege, e.g., explicitly likened his *Begriffsschrift* or conceptual notation to Leibniz's ideal of a *Characteristica Universalis* (26; cf. Husserl 1984 [1913]: 301ff.). Likewise Chomsky (1966a) traces his linguistic model back to notions of universal grammar already operative in the Port-Royal *Grammar* and *Logic*. See the introduction above.

8   Schönberg (1984a [1941]: 244).

9   Ellmann (1982) does remark that, while Joyce and his family lived in Zürich during the First World War, they moved into a flat part of which was occupied by "Philipp Jarnach, secretary and assistant Kapellmeister to Ferruccio Busoni, the celebrated composer, pianist and conductor." Yet Ellmann downplays the possibility of any real interest on Joyce's part in late-nineteenth-, early-twentieth-century revolutions in musical forms and concepts. Thus, although "Joyce theoretically was interested in modern music, . . . Donizetti and Bellini—for Jarnach, out of date—were the composers he wished to discuss. Joyce went to Busoni's concerts, but poked fun again and again at what he called 'Orchesterbetriebe' (orchestral goings-on)" (409). Contrast the account offered by Luening, presented later in this section.

10 As Janik and Toulmin (1973) suggest, Edward Hanslick's very popular *On the Beautiful in Music* (originally published in 1854) did much to initiate the modern, anti-Romantic critique of programmatic music. For Hanslick, "The central question was whether music was 'self-sufficient'—that is, merely a coherent assemblage of sounds, and a language unto itself—or whether it was essential for it to express ideas or feelings—that is to symbolize something other than the musical" (Janik and Toulmin 1973: 103). But see Adams (1977) on the antiprogrammatic use to which a quasi-Wagnerian technique could be put by Joyce. Thus, reading *Ulysses* "[demands] precisely that [the reader] not be caught up in the present of a scene, but allow the remote use of a phrase or theme to resonate in [his or her] mind like an intellectual dipthong" (9). For details on Joyce's own (evolving) attitude toward Wagner, see Mahaffey (1988b).

11 Throughout I shall cite "Sirens" by line number—as found in "the Gabler edition" (Joyce 1986 [1922])—alone. When referring to other episodes, the citations will include a line number prefixed by the number of the episode in which the line occurs: e.g., 5.102 would refer to line 102 of the fifth episode, "The Lotus Eaters." Further, when citing lines and segments of lines included in the introductory section of the episode, I shall retain the original punctuation marks (especially in the case of periods) in order to indicate Joyce's disruptions of stylistic and more particularly syntactic norms.

12 Compare, too, 1190ff.: "Cowley, he stuns himself with it: a kind of drunkenness. Better give way only half the way the way of a man with a maid. Instance enthusiasts. All ears. Not lose a demisemiquaver. Eyes shut. Head nodding in time. Dotty. You daren't budge. Thinking

strictly prohibited. Always talking shop. Fiddlefaddle about notes." Also, Richie Goulding at one point says that "*Sonnambula*" is the "[m]ost beautiful tenor air ever written" (610).

13   Note that by privileging form over medium—by foregrounding what Hjelmslev (1969 [1943]: 10, 16ff.) called "system" over what he described as "process"—Bloom merely inverts the other customers' tendency to conflate the verbal medium of "The Croppy Boy" with its musicality as such. Thus, the contrast between Bloom's and the other Dubliners' views on music anticipates the critical response to the episode. That response, too, has oscillated between emphasizing and trivializing the particular phonic medium—language—according to whose constraints "Sirens" itself unfolds (see the previous section). Bloom reverses his own antiphonic judgment, however, in contemplating the nature of "Musemathematics": "Numbers it is. All music when you come to think. . . . But suppose you said it like: Martha, seven times nine minus x is thirtyfive thousand. Fall quite flat. It's on account of the sounds it is" (830, 835–37).

14   In a letter to the author dated 29 December 1992, however, Mr. Luening remarks that "Joyce's knowledge of Schoenberg . . . was rather limited, although I am sure he had discussed his works with Jarnach." Mr. Luening continues, "When Joyce was in Paris, he discussed with George Antheil, the American composer, the possibility of writing an electronic opera based on 'Cyclops.' The idea of electronic sound production has been mentioned as a possibility of expanding the musical language in [Busoni's] "Sketch of a New Aesthetic." . . . Perhaps Joyce also discussed serial music with Antheil, in Paris. Schoenberg's first sketches seem to come from around March of 1920 but of course, thinking about twelve-tone and serial music goes back to Hauer and his followers, and discussions were in the air in Joyce's day in Zurich." I am grateful to Mr. Luening for permission to quote from his letter and to Michael Seidel for helping me get in touch with Mr. Luening.

15   "Kaleidoskopisches Durcheinanderschütteln von zwölf Halbtönen in der Dreispiegelkammer des Geschmacks, der Empfindung und der Intention: das Wesen der heutigen Harmonie" 'Kaleidoscopic jolting into confusion of twelve half tones in the three-mirrored chamber of taste, impression, and intention: the essence of today's harmony' (Busoni n.d. [1906]: 42). Compare the image of the kaleidoscope that Adorno uses in his brilliant *Philosophy of Modern Music* (1973 [1948]): "While the colors of Schoenberg's orchestration in his later works illuminate the compositional structure . . . these colors themselves are prevented from composing. The result is a dazzlingly hermetic sound with unrelentingly changing lights and shadows, bearing a certain similarity to a highly complicated machine, which remains firmly fixed in one place in spite of the dizzying movement of all its parts" (89).

16   On the notion of strings—a notion that will become increasingly important as we go on—see Nagel and Newman's (1958) exposition: "The first step in the construction of an absolute proof, as [the German mathematician David] Hilbert conceived the matter, is the *complete formalization* of a deductive system. . . . The purpose of this procedure is to construct a system of signs (called a 'calculus') which conceals nothing and which has in it only that which we explicitly put into it. The postulates and theorems of a completely formalized system are 'strings' (or finitely long sequences) of meaningless marks, constructed according to rules for combining the elementary signs of the system into larger wholes. Moreover, when a system has been completely formalized, the derivation of theorems from postulates is nothing more than the transformation (pursuant to rule) of one set of such 'strings' into another set of 'strings'" (26–27; cf. Hofstadter 1979: 33–34; Hermanns 1977: 19ff.; and see sec. 6 below).

17   On syntagm and paradigm, see Saussure (1959 [1916]: 122ff.), Ducrot and Todorov (1979 [1972]: 106–11), and Benveniste (1971 [1966]: 20–21, 101–2).

18   Thus, Schönberg's compositional theory merits comparison with Jakobson's (1960) famous definition of the poetic function of language—language's set toward the message as such: "What is the empirical linguistic criterion of the poetic function? . . . *The poetic function projects the principle of equivalence from the axis of selection into the axis of combination.* Equivalence is promoted to the constitutive device of the sequence" (358). Compare, too, that "Streben nach Simultaneität" 'striving after simultaneity' which the Austrian polymath Hermann Broch describes as the essential project of modern *Dichtung* or literary art in general and of Joycean narrative as the paradigm for *Dichtung* in its modern setting (1975 [1936]: 73ff.). Significantly, Broch was at one point a student of Carnap's.

19   My use of the terms *competence, structural description,* and *deviation* is meant to suggest the analogy, discussed in somewhat greater detail in sec. 7.4ff., between Schönberg's compositional principles and Noam Chomsky's account of grammatical rules. To anticipate: as early as *The Logical Structure of Linguistic Theory* (1975 [1955]), Chomsky had argued that linguistic theory is "concerned with three fundamental and closely related concepts: language, grammar, and structure. A language L is understood to be a set (in general infinite) of finite strings of symbols drawn from a finite 'alphabet.' The alphabet of primitive symbols is determined by general linguistic theory, in particular, by universal phonetics, which specifies the minimal elements available for any human language and provides some conditions on their choice and combination. A grammar of L is a system of rules that specifies the set of sentences of L and assigns to each sentence a structural description. The structural description of a sentence S constitutes, in principle, a full account of the elements of S and their organization" (5; cf., e.g., Chomsky 1966b [1957]: 13–14; Chomsky 1965: 3).

20   Adorno says as much, arguably, when he writes that Schönberg "extirpated 'meaning' insofar as meaning, in the tradition of Viennese classicism, lays claim to being present purely in the context of the technical structure. Structure as such is to be correct rather than meaningful. The question which twelve-tone music asks of the composer is not how musical meaning is to be organized, but rather, how organization is to become meaningful" (1973 [1948]: 67).

21   For relevant (nonmusicological) characterizations of the notion *motif,* see, among others, Bremond (1982: 139–41), Daemmrich and Daemmrich (1987: 187–91), Doležel (1972), and Tomaševskij (1965 [1925]: 68).

22   Compare Hjelmslev (1969 [1943]): "The relation between the parts of the textual process . . . is manifested in time but is not itself defined by time" (126; cf. van Fraassen 1991: 25ff.).

23   Compare Topia's (1984) characterization: "In each insertion [of an element into what we might call Joyce's formal matrices] the whole series of possible actualizations proceeding from a single initial pattern looms up potentially behind each text present on the page. This virtual multiplicity points both towards the infinity of repertory and paradigm and towards the infinity of products, versions and variations of the same matrix" (122).

24   As manifest in what we might call Roland Barthes's (1977b [1966]) suppression of the semantic in favor of the syntactic dimensions of narrative—a suppression determined at least in part by the suppression of the referent in Barthes's original linguistic paradigm: Ferdinand de Saussure's *Course in General Linguistics* (1959 [1913]; cf. Avni 1990; Prince 1991).

25   The same superimposition is evident in *"Blumenlied"* (844), a term combining singing

(breath) and blooms. Another possible association is that between *Bloom* and the Greek term ἄνθος, meaning "flower" or, more figuratively, "the bloom or flower of a given thing." Hence the word *anthology*.

26   Note, too, that the chain of transformations linking "Bloom" with "greaseabloom" (180) and then "Seabloom, greaseabloom" (1285) points ahead to the "Ithaca" episode, in which the "hydrophobe" (17.237) tendencies of Stephen Dedalus stand in marked contrast to Bloom's appreciation of the aqueous (17.183ff.). Also, the associations of flowers (B/blooms) with intoxication invoke the "Nausicaa" episode, in which the associations at issue are overlaid with further associations of sentimentality and nostalgia (see, e.g., 13.332–37).

27   On anaphora in the context of linguistic theories of government binding and (long-distance) coordination, see Sells's *Lectures on Contemporary Syntactic Theories* (1985: 164ff.; cf. van Dijk 1972: 59ff.; Ducrot and Todorov 1979 [1972]: 281–85; Webber 1979). On the contrast between categorematic and syncategorematic meanings, see Husserl (1984 [1913]: 314ff.); this is a contrast that Husserl himself refers back to the distinction between autosemantic terms (terms independently meaningful) and synsemantic terms (terms meaningful by virtue of their relations to other terms). That distinction, in turn, had been elaborated by Anton Marty (1918 [1893], 1976 [1908]) along lines set out by Franz Brentano (1973 [1874]), and it constitutes a linguistic corollary to the distinction between independent and dependent meanings (*pieces* vs. *moments*) developed by Husserl in his fourth *Logical Investigation*.

28   Gifford and Seidman gloss the latter part of lines 309–10 as follows: " 'Bloom smiled quick go. Afternoon.' But 'qui' suggests a pun on the Latin and French word for 'who' " (1988: 298).

29   I here use *deduction* in the broad sense indicated by the term's Latin derivation—from *deduco*, "to bring or lead down," "to trace downward," "to draw out, to spin out"—rather than the more technical and restricted sense attaching to *deduction* in logical usage, according to which only those propositions strictly entailed by other propositions can be deduced from the latter propositions (e.g., "*X* is mortal" can be deduced from "*X* is a cat," but not vice versa; see sec. 4.7.).

30   Note that Joyce explicitly mentions Jørgensen (or "Jargonsen") in the "Ricorso" section of *Finnegans Wake* (Joyce 1939: 621.22). See Herman (in press a).

31   For more on the importance of Husserl's groundbreaking distinction between nonsense and absurdity, see Bar-Hillel (1977 [1957]), Edie (1977 [1972]), Gardies (1985 [1975]), and Mulligan (1985).

32   We must therefore take *cum grano salis* Edie's claim that, in contrast to Carnap, "from the beginning to the end, Husserl was concerned, not with artificially constructed 'ideal' languages or the use of algorithms to define some independent mathematical system which could, in some extended sense, be called 'language,' but with *natural language itself*" (1977 [1972]: 139, n. 5). Edie's subsequent discussion (140–42) itself seems to contradict the claim just quoted.

33   Husserl later distinguished more particularly between "analytic" and "material" countersense. Material countersense arises when a noncontradictory *form* of inference, which indicates merely a certain range of possible judgments that could in principle be adopted with respect to a given ("material") state of affairs, happens in fact to yield an inadequate judgment in the case at hand. See Husserl (1969 [1929]: sec. 19, p. 65); cf. Edie (1977 [1972]: 139, n. 4).

34   Note that Marty (1918 [1893]) had already pointed out the dangers in trying to establish a

transparent and isomorphic relation between the facts of language and the categories of logic. In particular, if we construe syntax as what permits us both to be able to say anything at all and to know a priori whether the statement we have produced could follow from or else warrant other assertions, then we commit what Marty called the "rape of language" (*Vergewaltigung der Sprache*) by logic (62). In more modern parlance, problems of the kind identified by Marty involve confusion between prescriptivist and descriptivist ideals in the study of language.

35   Interpretation of the (syntactic) structures of specific languages as the conditions of possibility for linguistic structure as such—or, alternatively, interpretation of particular grammatical features as signs of what Husserl called "das Grammatische selbst" 'the grammatical itself' (1969 [1929]: sec. 22, pp. 70–71; cf. Edie 1977 [1972])—is particularly evident in Carnap's peculiar use of disjunctive *or* in the following italicized sentence from *The Logical Syntax of Language*: "*As soon as logic is formulated in an exact manner, it turns out to be nothing other than the syntax either of a particular language* or *of languages in general*" (1937a [1934]: sec. 62, p. 233; my emphasis).

36   Thus, equating the terms "Wahrheitskriterium," "Verifikationsmethode," and "Sinn," Carnap writes, "In dieser Weise wird jedes Wort der Sprache auf andere Wörter und schließlich auf die in sog. 'Beobachtungssätzen' oder 'Protokollsätzen' vorkommenden Wörter zurückgeführt. Durch diese Zurückführung erhält das Wort seine Bedeutung" (1975 [1931]: 152).

37   Chomsky mentions that, while engaged in preparatory research for *The Logical Structure of Linguistic Theory*, he was "particularly impressed by Nelson Goodman's work on constructional systems" in *The Structure of Appearance*, which appeared in 1951 (Chomsky 1975 [1955]: 33; cf. 39; 51–52, nn. 57–59; Chomsky 1966b [1957]: 14, n. 1). Goodman modeled his work, in turn, on Carnap's.

38   In fact, pursuing the chemical analogy established by Russell and Whitehead in *Principia mathematica*, Carnap further subdivides transformation rules into those which generate "molecular" and those which produce "generalized" compound sentences through concatenations of primitive or "atomic" sentences. Whereas for Carnap molecular sentences derive from extensional sentential connections such as negation and disjunction, generalized sentences derive from intensional sentential connections such as strict implication and modal functions (1937b: 15–16). (Logical) syntax, in short, becomes a means of drawing up the periodic table of the expressible as such. Compare Chomsky and Miller (1963): "In order to specify a language precisely, we must state some principle that separates the sequences of atomic elements that form sentences from those that do not" (283).

39   Compare Carnap's (1937a [1934]) remark concerning David Hilbert's metamathematical researches: "Hilbert was the first to treat mathematics as a calculus in the strict sense—i.e. to lay down a system of rules having mathematical formulae for their objects. This theory he called *metamathematics*. . . . Metamathematics is . . . the syntax of the mathematical language" (sec. 2, p. 9; cf. Carnap 1979 [1935]: 40; Hjelmslev (1969 [1943]: 110; Nagel and Newman 1958: 26ff.; Jørgensen 1932: passim).

40   Compare too Carnap's definition in "Foundations of Logic and Mathematics" (1971 [1938]): "We call the formal theory of an object-language, formulated in the metalanguage, the *syntax* of the object-language (or the logical syntax, whenever it seems necessary to distinguish this theory from that part of linguistics which is known as syntax but which usually is not restricted to formal terms)" (158; cf. 146; Carnap 1963: 53). Chomsky (1955: 39), however, shows

how the notion of "formal" used by Carnap in the sentence just quoted does not, of itself, allow us to demarcate linguistic from logical analysis.

41   Following Chomsky (1955), however, we might argue the reverse: i.e., that the formalization of a language represents an infinite restriction in scope vis-à-vis unformalized languages, insofar as formal languages cannot serve as idealized versions of the incalculably richer and more complicated natural languages.

42   Here I shall very briefly allude to another field of cultural production—the visual arts—in which the (proto-)computational model of input → operation → output became a principle of construction, and indeed a formal ideal, around the same time Joyce composed "Sirens." In particular, consider Duchamp's efforts to establish a pictorial syntax, as described by Thierry de Duve (1991). Duve argues that, in general, Duchamp attempted, "not to make color speak in its immanence à la Kandinsky, but to establish a code of colors that would make each hue correspond to a particular grammatical relation" (134). To take a specific example: "Each color of which, in the left hand side of [Duchamp's] *Tu m'*, samples are lined up in an infinite perspective perhaps encodes one of the grammatical relations by means of which the right-hand side composes 'sentences' that present themselves as mysterious multicolored ribbons, attached to the *Standard Stoppages,* which [to quote Duchamp himself] 'must be thought of as the letters of the new alphabet' " (134; cf. 83, 130–34).

43   The relevant (and often-cited) passage is the one in which Derrida, referring back to his own earliest writings on Husserl's late works, strikingly contrasts the Husserlian with the Joycean paradigm for "grasp[ing] a pure historicity." Husserl "proposes to render language as transparent as possible, univocal, limited to that which, by being transmittable or able to be placed in tradition, thereby constitutes the only condition of a possible historicity" and hence "resist[s] the Joycean overload and condensation" for the sake of "a reading, and the work's legacy." By contrast, the Joyce of *Finnegans Wake* "repeats and mobilizes and babelizes the (asymptotic) totality of the equivocal, he makes this his theme and his operation, he tries to make outcrop, with the greatest possible synchrony, at great speed, the greatest power of the meanings buried in each syllabic fragment, subject each atom of writing to fission in order to overload the unconscious with the whole memory of man: mythologies, religion, philosophies, sciences, psychoanalysis, literatures" (1984: 149).

44   In Greimas's later formulation: "All grammars, in a more or less explicit way, have two components: a morphology and a syntax. The morphology has a taxonomic nature and its terms are interdefining. The syntax consists of a set of operational rules or way of manipulating the terms provided by the morphology" (1987 [1969]: 67). Note that Greimas, himself heavily indebted to Hjelmslev's glossematics (see the next paragraph), in turn exercised a profound influence on early attempts to formulate narrative grammars, particularly Todorov's (1969) attempt. See sec. 8 below.

45   However, Joyce's use of abbreviation, truncation, and condensation as the signature, the *differentia specifica,* of thought processes does recall positivistic psychological theories developed around the same time that "Sirens" was composed. Consider the work of the philosopher and erstwhile physicist Ernst Mach. Mach—what you get if you cross Herbert Spencer with William James—imported quasi-Darwinian as well as pragmatist notions into psychology and epistemology, arguing that forms of reasoning and aids to thinking "survive" only to the extent that they *facilitate* thought (Mach 1902 [1886]). This is precisely the sort of

argument in contradistinction to which Šklovskij (1965 [1917]) developed his concept of art as defamiliarization—as the nonfacilitation of thought.

46   Compare a later passage:

> Pray for him, prayed the bass of Dollard. You who hear in peace. Breathe a prayer, drop a tear, good men, good people. He was the croppy boy.
>
> Scaring eavesdropping boots croppy bootsboy Bloom in the Ormond hallway heard the growls and roars of bravo, fat backslapping, their boots all treading, boots not the boots the boy. (1139–44; cf. 756–60)

47   Compare lines 473–76:

> —God, do you remember? Ben bulky Dollard said, turning from the punished keyboard. And by Japers I had no wedding garment.
>
> They laughed all three. He had no wed. All trio laughed. No wedding garment.

48   The hour brings particular anguish because it is also the hour that Bloom first met Molly, as Bloom recounts via pathetically deformed syntax: "Singing. *Waiting* she sang. I turned her music. Full voice of perfume of what perfume does your lilactrees. Bosom I saw, both full, throat warbling. First I saw. She thanked me. Why did she me? Fate. Spanishy eyes. Under a peartree alone patio *this hour* in old madrid one side in shadow Dolores shedolores. At me. Luring. Ah, alluring" (730–34; my emphasis on "this hour").

49   Compare, in this connection, Gérard Genette's remarks about Proust's "handling of inner speech," which shows throughout "an aversion to what Dujardin calls the mental 'hodge-podge,' 'thought in a dawning state,' represented by an infraverbal flux reduced to the 'syntactic minimum.'" Inner speech in Proust is thus "never the speech of a supposedly alogical depth, even the depth of dream, but is only the means of representing, by a sort of transitory and borderline *misunderstanding,* the gulf between two logics, each as distinct as the other" (1980 [1972]: 180–81).

50   We need to keep in mind, however, that this *form* of the argument about deep structure (and hence the gist of the following subsections) pertains to Chomsky's early or "standard" theory of transformational generative grammar (cf. Chomsky 1965), as opposed to the later "extended standard theory" (Chomsky 1977; Radford 1981) or, for that matter, Chomsky's still later theory of government and binding (cf. Chomsky 1980, 1981; Cook 1988; Horrocks 1987: 55–162; and the following note). I shall not explore here how Joyce's narrative form relates to the full gamut of (Chomsky's and others') theories of transformational generative grammar; instead, I focus on elements of the so-called standard theory that help contextualize formal features of "Sirens" and that Joyce's text in turn helps contextualize. The possibility for further contextualization is left open.

51   Chomsky offers a more sophisticated account of all these notions in *Rules and Representations* (1980). He retains the "fundamental idea . . . that surface structures are formed through the interaction of at least two distinct types of rules: base rules, which generate abstract phrase structure representations; and transformational rules, which move elements and otherwise rearrange structures to give the surface structures" (144). In contrast to earlier models, however, Chomsky now asserts "that it is, in fact, S-structures rather than D-structures that are directly associated with logical form" (147). More explicitly: "The rules relating surface structure and logical form should be 'factored' into several components, including base rules . . . and at least two kinds of rules of interpretation, those that map abstract structures (S-

structures) to surface structure and those that map abstract structures (again, S-structures) to LF [logical form]" (153–54). As Robins (1989) points out, Chomsky developed the "D" and "S" nomenclature "to avoid any suggestion of profundity on the one part or of superficiality on the other" (288). For discussion of analogous concerns in the context of narrative form in "Sirens," cf. secs. *7.4.3, 7.4.4,* and *8.1.2* below.

52   Van Dijk (1985) makes a similar point, although in a somewhat different context.

53   For an important consolidation and extension of the research tradition grounded in Propp's *Morphology,* see Doležel (1972). For a recent reconsideration of the actantial model, see also Coste (1989: 134–63). As Coste notes (135), Greimas borrowed the term *actant* itself from Lucien Tesnière's *Eléments de syntaxe structurale* (1959).

54   Compare Prince (1973): "Different combinational patterns of simple stories produce different kinds of complex stories," according to whether the type of combinatorial mechanism exploited is that of conjoining, alternation, or embedding (72). Prince (1980) later redescribes these combinatorial mechanisms as generalized transformations (55–57; cf. Prince 1982: 88, 90–92).

   Note that, in the present context, I use the terms *formation rules* and *transformation rules* in the sense specified by Husserl and then Carnap and Tarski, as described in secs. *6–6.4* above. Todorov himself does not use these locutions; I invoke them chiefly to suggest the (insufficiently recognized) precedent for narrative syntax in the earlier project of logical syntax.

2   Semantic Dimensions: Objects and Models in Kafka's *Der Prozeß*

1   For a particularly useful survey of such proposals, see Prince (in press). Prince's account informs the discussion of Lévi-Strauss that follows.

2   Ruth Ronen (Ronen 1990: 280–88; Ronen 1994: 47–107), for her part, has argued that the concept *possible worlds* cannot be mapped directly into the concept *fictional worlds* without extensive, and sometimes misleading, modifications of possible worlds semantics itself. Although I find Ronen's arguments problematic on several counts, the argument put forth here does not stand or fall with Ronen's claims. The present chapter does not seek to develop an understanding of Kafka's fictional world(s) via possible worlds semantics; rather, my purpose is to uncover (historico-conceptual) connections between Kafka's fictional techniques and the ideas informing possible worlds frameworks themselves.

3   For groundbreaking analysis of the semantic properties of Kafka's texts, see the seminal articles by Doležel (1979, 1983, 1984). Indeed, the present chapter can be viewed as an extended meditation on *why* the philosophico-linguistic tools chosen by Doležel are particularly useful for analysis of *Der Prozeß* and of other texts whose formal features affiliate them with Kafka's narrative. As in chap. 1, my argument here is that Kafka's text (and texts like it) not only invites semantic inquiry such as Doležel's but also helps generate new models for the very sort of inquiry that Doležel helped pioneer.

4   I borrow the term *object-theoretical* (*gegenstandstheoretisch*) itself from Meinong (1971 [1904]), Mally (1912), and Husserl (1979f [1894], 1981b [1910–11]), among others. Thus, the discourses pertaining to object theory are broader in scope than what we have come to call phenomenological discourse, which forms only one subset of object-theoretical discourse. In any event, it should already be apparent that I do not use the term *objectivity* and its cognates in their

customary sense; *objectivity* does not denote, here, an attitude, quality, or value opposed to an attitude, quality, or value associated with the term *subjectivity*. Rather, in the sense of the term captured by the philosophical term of art *Gegenständlichkeit, objectivity* bears on the constitution of and criteria for objects (entities, things) as such (cf. Cairns 1973; and secs. *4.2ff*. below).

Furthermore, *object theory,* as the term is used here, should not be confused with what today's computer programmers variously designate as object-oriented conceptual modeling (Dillon and Tan 1993), object-oriented programming (Pinson and Wiener 1991), and logic and object programming (McCabe 1992). In such contexts, objects are conceived differently than they are in the earlier object-theoretical discourse inspired by Brentano's analysis of intentional objects. A typical modern definition: "An object is an entity that contains both the attributes that describe the state of a real-world object and the actions that are associated with the real-world object" (Dillon and Tan 1993: 30). Still, insofar as intentional objects are historically and conceptually interlinked with *intensions* (sec. *4.0*), and insofar as both logic programming (McCabe 1992: 7, 199) and object-oriented conceptual modeling (Dillon and Tan 1993: 95) make use of intensions and other model-theoretic ideas, there may be grounds for positing at least a distant, highly mediated connection between the old and the new object theories. For more on the possibilities and limits of classical object theory itself, see Chisholm (1973), Herman (1993d), Parsons (1980), Routley and Routley (1973), Ryle (1972), and secs. *4ff.* below.

5   When special attention to the wording of Kafka's text seems warranted, I cite (and provide my own translations of) the German-language version of *Der Prozeß* (i.e., Kafka 1986 [1925]). Otherwise, I cite the English-language version of the text (i.e., Kafka 1956 [1925]), more or less minimally modifying the translation where my own sense of fidelity to the text differs from that of the translators. All such modifications are duly noted.

6   More precisely, throughout *Der Prozeß* Kafka exploits sentential adverbs, modal auxiliaries, *as if* constructions, and other grammatical forms that function as so-called evidentials (Chafe and Nichols 1986): i.e., as forms pertaining to the large repertoire of grammatical devices by means of which languages typically encode knowledge, or rather degrees of certainty with respect to what is known. See secs. *6.3.2ff.* below; cf. Herman (1994a).

7   For an important early statement of the distinction between intensional and extensional definitions, see Rudolf Carnap's (1969 [1928]) contrast between "a property description of a domain [that] indicates the properties of the individual objects of that domain" and "a relation description [that] indicates merely the relations between the objects" (sec. 25, p. 43; cf. Carnap 1947). Compare, also, C. I. Lewis and C. H. Langford's influential *Symbolic Logic* (1932): "The laws governing the relations of concepts constitute the logic of the *connotation* or *intension* of terms; those governing the relations of classes constitute the logic of the *denotation* or *extension* of terms" (27).

8   But see Green's (1989) account of how "Kripke and Putnam provide a view of the way common nouns refer that avoids reference to properties. . . . In this view of things, it is important not to confuse the analysis of the name of a kind such as *fish* or *water,* with analysis of the kind itself, or with people's knowledge, beliefs, or understandings about that kind. The first is part of the study of language . . . ; the second belongs to biology, chemistry, mechanical engineering, or whatever; and the last is part of cognitive psychology . . . or anthropology" (43).

9   For more on the distinction between intentions and intensions, see Hintikka and Hintikka (1989: 183ff.).

10   Writing about the bureaucratic stratification of the Austro-Hungarian Empire, Menger (1985) suggests that a beloved "sport" of bureaucracies in general is the formation of "Unüber-sichtliche und versteinerte Hierarchien" that "führen zur Zersplitterung der Verantwortlich-keit 'ins Unendliche'" (337). Hence, both Brentano's and Kafka's hierarchies may bear quite complicated connections to the sociocultural milieu in which both writers lived and worked. I am grateful to Michael Burri for bringing Menger's informative text to my attention.

11   To quote Milan Kundera (1988 [1986]): "The world according to Kafka: the bureaucratized universe. The office not merely as one kind of social phenomenon among many but as the essence of the world" (48).

12   Compare Husserl (1970 [1913]): "Objects are certainly possible, that in fact lie beyond the phenomena accessible to any human consciousness" (*Investigation II,* sec. 40, p. 428). Exam-ples of such impossible or, as Meinong called them (1972 [1917]: 10–22), "defective" objects might include the objects that would satisfy the variables x, y, and z contained in the following sentences: "That relation according to which p and not-p are biconditionally true is "x"; "In the sentence I am currently enunciating *the sentence I am currently enunciating* had the sense y"; and "The rate of acceleration of the frame of reference in which I determine the length of this pencil, relative to the rates of acceleration of all other frames of reference in the universe (by virtue of which this pencil becomes in effect longer or shorter), is z."

13   Thus, in editing the posthumous 1924 edition of the *Psychology,* Oskar Kraus, like Husserl, Meinong, and Marty a student of Brentano's, appended a series of notes rewording the text of the earlier edition in light of the later Brentano's own later nominalistic turn. Kraus's notes represent a repeated and ex post facto denial of anything like immanent objectivity as objec-tivity per se; i.e., Kraus tries to fend off the realist interpretation that Brentano's own earlier conflation of terms like content (*Inhalt*) and object (*Objekt, Gegenstand*) had to some extent invited (cf. Brentano's own note to the 1911 ed., bk. 2, chap. 7, sec. 2, p. 202). Hence, Kraus's apparatus represents what might be called an extended attempt at nominalistic damage control (see secs. 4.3ff. below). Kasimierz Twardowski's (1894) effort to formulate more precise characterizations of the acts, objects, and contents of representations (*Vorstellungen*) was no doubt occasioned by the same terminological slippage that Kraus sought to correct after the fact (see Twardowski 1894; and Twardowski 1977 [1894], esp. secs. 1, 2, 6, 12).

14   For my understanding of some of the consequences of the nominalism-realism dispute, I am indebted to Putnam (1971: 9–43) and Quine (1960: 243–53).

15   For extensive documentation of Brentano's eventual "rejection of the unreal," see the materials collected in Brentano (1966).

16   Compare Brentano's appendix to the 1911 edition of the *Psychology:* "Aristotle is quite cor-rect . . . in saying that the 'That is so,' by which we indicate our agreement with a judgement means nothing but that the judgement is true, that truth has no being outside of the person judging; in other words, it exists *only* in that loose and improper sense, but not strictly and in reality" (app. 9, p. 292). Compare in this connection Brentano (1981b [1907–17]): "From the fact that we often think about something universal or indeterminate, it does not follow that, in the strict sense of the word, there *is* something universal or indeterminate" (22). Compare too

app. 15 in Brentano (1973 [1874]), "On the Term 'Being' in Its Loose Sense, Abstract Terms, and Entia Rationis" (330ff.).

17 For a recent restatement of this view in the context of talk about phenomenal objects, see Descombes (1986 [1983]): "An object of knowledge is the grammatical complement of a phrase equivalent to *I know that.* This verb can be completed only by a proposition. Grammatically speaking, an object that we know and can identify is the designation of a thing to which the knowing subject has a relation enabling him to know it or to know something of it" (129).

18 Similarly, as Juhos (1967) notes, the critique of metaphysics launched by Moritz Schlick, one of the prime movers of the Vienna Circle, is based on Schlick's view that metaphysics does not seek to know "the *relations* between magnitudes characterizing states of affairs but strives to obtain knowledge of the *content* of phenomena" (321; cf. Schlick 1979 [1925–36]).

19 I restrict the following discussion to the early (pre–*Ideas I*) texts of Husserl because of their relatively more explicit participation in surrounding philosophical discourse on objects, such explicit polemical engagement having reached its high point, perhaps, as early as (the first edition of) the *Logical Investigations* (1900–1901).

20 In using the term *situations* and its derivatives I have in mind Barwise's (1989) and Barwise and Perry's (1983) self-styled "situation semantics." Barwise and Perry (1983) characterize situations as "individuals having properties and standing in relations at various spatiotemporal locations" (7) and as comprising "both . . . static situations, called *states of affairs,* and more dynamic situations, called *events*" (50). Insofar as "a key tenet of situation semantics is [that] . . . the semantic content of a representation in general depends on its embedding circumstances" (Barwise 1989: 157), Barwise and Perry's model may have useful applications not only for the study of Kafkan objects but also for the analysis of meaning in narrative discourse generally. Although a more careful assessment of situation semantics will have to be reserved for a future study, cf. Barwise's (1989: 79–92) illuminating chapter on "Situations and Small Worlds," which contains a brief comparison and contrast between possible worlds semantics and situation semantics (82–83).

21 Note here my use of the term *objects* in both a narrow sense (objects = "entities") and a broader, more generic sense (objects = "entities, events, and situations"). What may look like terminological slippage is rather part of the argument to be conducted over the course of secs. 5–7 below: the argument, namely, that Kafka invariably figures objects as elements *embedded in* relations (including events) and situations.

22 Such considerations (and other considerations that follow) cast doubt on Ronen's (1994) claim that "in reality, as opposed to fiction, we assume that there are no gaps and that gaps in representation can be filled by reference to a complete, fully detailed and, at least in principle, available object. Incompleteness is thus the formal manifestation of a difference between reality and fiction, between an extraliterary real object and a fictional construction" (115). Kafka's text suggests, instead, that the very search for completeness of representations (fictional *or* factual) is fundamentally misguided because the frames of reference undergirding all representations are themselves necessarily incomplete. See below; secs. 5.4 and 5.5 and n. 26 below; and, for an account of fictional representation *not* premised on notions of completeness, Ryan's (1991: 13–30) discussion of "fictional recentering."

23 The novel itself encodes (ekphrastic) instructions for construing *Der Prozeß* as a text premised

on an aesthetics of desolation. Titorelli's landscape painting, e.g., "showed two stunted trees standing far apart from each other in darkish grass." Further, in the painting of the knight errant hanging on the wall of the cathedral, the knight is represented as "leaning on his sword, which was stuck into the bare ground, bare except for a stray blade of grass" (Kafka 1956 [1925]: 163, 205).

24 As Willett (1978: 105) notes in the same place, *Veshch* is a Russian word for "object" as well as the name of an art journal founded by Russian emigrants in Berlin in 1922.

25 Note the rich diversity of lexical meanings associated with the word *Lücke* itself, including "gap," "break," "breach," "opening," "space," "void," "cavity," "hole," "interstice," "lacuna," "deficit," and "hiatus."

26 In this respect, the structure of Kafkan objects warrants comparison with what Arkady Plotnitsky has characterized as the postulate of "the *radical* incompleteness of all possible descriptions" (Plotnitsky 1993: 13; cf. Plotnitsky 1994: 65–88) found in the quantum-mechanical models of Niels Bohr and also in the theory of general economy associated with Georges Bataille. Plotnitsky (1994: 196–202) situates Kurt Gödel's incompleteness theorem—i.e., the theorem that "a proof of the consistency of a formalized system (provided that it is rich enough to contain arithmetic) cannot be contained within the formalism of this system itself" (196; cf. sec. *1.6.6* above)—in the same complex of ideas.

27 For the (very truncated) account of model-theoretic semantics that follows, I am indebted to the following sources, among others: Ackermann (1967); Allwood, Andersson, and Dahl (1977 [1971]); Carnap (1947, 1952 [1950]); Cresswell (1992); Doležel (1979); Frawley (1992); Green (1989); Hintikka (1969); Hintikka and Hintikka (1989); Kalish (1967); Kripke (1980); Lyons (1977); Montague (1974); Partee (1989); Pavel (1986); and Ryan (1991, 1992). (For a discussion of model-theoretic semantics in the context of modes of meaning in film, see chap. 5 below.) Cresswell (1992) remarks that, strictly speaking, "a model-theoretic semantic theory comprises three parts. First comes a syntactic description of the linguistic items . . . of the language in question; this is without reference to meaning. Second comes a description of a class of (usually abstract) language-independent entities which are the meanings of expressions in different categories. Finally comes a function which assigns a meaning to each linguistic item in such a way that whole sentences will be correlated with entities which adequately represent their meaning in the language being described" (404). Note that, in this chapter, I focus only on the second and third, and mostly the third, of Cresswell's three components. However, for arguments against the explanatory adequacy of model theory and in favor of "attention-directing" models for reference, see Roberts (1993: 95ff.).

28 To use the suggestive term of Champigny (1986: sec. D8, p. 39).

29 In the light of concerns raised by Derrida (1978b [1966], 1982), I shall make every effort to use the terms *periphery* and *center* strategically, not in the spirit of an unreconstructed logocentrism.

30 Apropos of the earlier discussion, we should perhaps restate this sentence as follows: beliefs about (P) where $W_x < W_{1,001}$ are, by virtue of certain pragmatic constraints, so peripheral that the beliefs are not worth contesting. For this subset of beliefs about (P), therefore, we establish no truth-values, positive or negative, over the matching subset of possible worlds to which the beliefs are indexed by virtue of our model world W.

31 In this connection, note that there may be parallels between the proliferation of model worlds

in Kafka's novel and certain implications of the theory of relativity, developed in the years immediately preceding the composition of *Der Prozeß*. (Binder 1979: 286ff. notes that the theory of relativity was taught by Einstein himself at the University of Prague in 1911–12 and that, for a time, both Einstein and Kafka seem to have attended the biweekly philosophical meetings held at the Café Louvre; cf. sec. *5.0* above.) Compare Kafka's techniques with Grünbaum's (1967) characterization of relativistic versus nonrelativistic physical theories: "If a physical theory *T* claims that an attribute or relation of a physical event or object is the same in every reference system in which it is specified, then *T* can be said to regard the attribute or relation in question as 'invariant' or 'absolute' in virtue of thus being independent of the reference system. By the same token, attributes or relations of an event or thing are called 'covariant' or 'relative' in *T* if *T* asserts that they do not obtain alike with respect to all physical reference systems but depend on the particular systems" (133).

Note, furthermore, that aspects of Kafka's text may have quantum-mechanical implications. For example, in describing to Josef K. how, if one chooses the route of ostensible acquittal (*scheinbare Freisprechung*), one's case passes from higher to lower back to higher courts—oscillating (*pendelt*) now in greater, now in smaller movements or arcs—Titorelli remarks, "Diese Wege sind unberechenbar" 'These movements are incalculable' (Kafka 1986 [1925]: 136; cf. Hanson 1967; Plotnitsky 1994: 149–90).

32   In this respect, compare the semantic indeterminacy of Kafka's text with the second of the two main currents of twentieth-century narrative that Gerald Prince (1988a) describes—i.e., that current in which we find "a lack of hierarchical distinction between several narrative lines of development (all of the narrated is hypothetical, all of it becomes disnarrated)" (6–7). On the *fabula-sjužet* distinction, see sec. *0.6.1* above.

33   On alethic, epistemic, axiological, and deontic modalities, see Doležel (1976a), Frawley (1992: 384–435), and Ryan (1991: 109ff.).

34   The text as a whole is virtually scored with such disjunctive constructions. See, e.g., Kafka (1956 [1925]: 41, 66, 81, 125, 149, 187).

35   But, for discussion of how textual *you* in (certain) second-person narratives sometimes works to dissolve the distinction between primitive and nonprimitive contextual coordinates, see Herman (1994e: esp. sec. 4.5).

3   Toward a Metapragmatics of Represented Discourse: Prague School Functionalism and Woolf's *Between the Acts*

I should like to thank Bruno Bosteels, Michael Burri, James English, Gerald Prince, Cees J. van Rees, and Peter Steiner for fruitful discussions of earlier drafts, and partial drafts, of this chapter.

1   In contrast to Doležel (1973), who reserves the term *represented discourse* (RD) for discourse more or less ambiguous between the narrator's (DN) and a character's (DC) discourse, in this chapter I use *represented discourse* as a generic term spanning that continuum of discourse types which traditional typologies divide into direct discourse, indirect discourse, and free indirect discourse (cf. Bally 1912; Ullmann 1964: 94ff.; Page 1973: 24–50; McHale 1978; Prince 1987: 34–35). In contradistinction to direct discourse (" 'I'm having trouble writing,' said the student") and indirect discourse ("The student said that he was having trouble writing"), free

indirect discourse ("The student moped. He was having the damnedest time trying to write") in traditional models has "the grammatical traits of 'normal' indirect discourse, but it does not involve a tag clause . . . introducing and qualifying the represented utterances and thoughts. Furthermore, it manifests at least some of the features of a character presented directly, with a first person as opposed to a third person's discourse" (Prince 1987: 35). Here, under the cover term *represented discourse,* I discuss the total range of discourse phenomena typically segmented into direct, indirect, and free indirect discourse. At issue is any form of discourse that, through any number of grammatical, stylistic, or broadly contextual indices, satisfies the following double condition: (i) we have reason to believe that the discourse in question exceeds the scope of discourse bearing only on the states and events of the narrated or *fabula;* and (ii) we have reason to believe that the discourse bears instead (or additionally) on *descriptions,* given by one or more characters, of the states and events comprised by the *fabula.*

2   Studies that have particularly influenced my thinking about represented discourse include, in addition to those mentioned in the previous note, the following: Genette (1980 [1972]); Pascal (1977); McHale (1978); Prince (1978); Bal (1981); Brinton (1980); Fillmore (1981); Ron (1981); Rimmon-Kenan (1983); Banfield (1982, 1987); and Brooke-Rose (1990).

3   Notable exceptions to this censure include van Dijk (1975, 1977); Pratt (1977); Warning (1980); Ron (1981); Prince (1983a); Hutchison (1984); Adams (1985); Stetter (1985); and Brooke-Rose (1990). In general, however, represented discourse lies outside the scope of these investigations—excepting Ron's and Brooke-Rose's. However, Fludernik's monumental study *The Fictions of Language and the Languages of Fiction* (1993a) includes a very full account of prior research on reported speech and thought (24–71) and attempts a more precise characterization of FID (free indirect discourse) in particular, using state-of-the-art developments in language theory. Although all subsequent research on represented discourse will be indebted to Fludernik's book, the present chapter relies on a somewhat different strategy of argumentation, suggesting crucial links between the *genealogy* of linguistic pragmatics and twentieth-century literary experiments with discourse representation in narrative contexts.

4   Cohn goes on to justify her use of " 'narrated monologue' as an English equivalent for *style indirect libre* and *erlebte Rede*" by noting that "the French and German terms have generally designated not only the rendering of silent thought in narrated form, but also the analogous rendering of spoken discourse, which displays identical linguistic features" (1978: 109). By contrast, Cohn deliberately chooses "a term that excludes this analogous employment of the technique, because in a literary—rather than a strictly linguistic—perspective the narration of silent thoughts presents problems that are quite separate, and far more intricate and interesting than those presented by its more vocal twin" (109). Since my chief concern here is in fact the "vocal twin" of silent thoughts, I shall be extrapolating from Cohn's arguments, although not deviating, I hope, from the spirit of her argumentation.

5   Cohn's claim that "a sentence rendering a character's opinion can look every bit like a sentence relating a fictional fact" should be compared with McHale's (1978) formulation: "The basic grammatical characteristics of FID—absence of reporting verb of saying/thinking, back-shift of tenses, conversion of personal and possessive pronouns, etc.—do not by themselves guarantee its being unequivocally distinguished from neutral (diegetic) narration in which only the narrator's voice is present" (264; quoted in Ron 1981: 17, n. 2).

6   We can operate here under the assumption, now common, that Bakhtin and Vološinov were actually one and the same writer.

7   For remarks on the possible *logical* ramifications of a dialogic model like Bakhtin-Vološinov's, however, see Swearingen (1990); and chap. 4 below. At stake, specifically, are problems inherent in any attempt to use an intertextual model for analyzing statements and propositions expressed via sentences. Note that Bakhtin-Vološinov tends to circumvent such problems by working with very small and very large linguistic units—"the word," "speech," "discourse"—instead of focusing on an intermediate unit of discourse such as the sentence.

8   I use the term *metapragmatic* mainly in the second of the two senses specified by Verschueren (1987): "The term . . . may refer to the study of natural language phenomena which reflect an awareness of (aspects of) the pragmatic nature of linguistic (inter)action. . . . But it may also refer to (pragmatic or nonpragmatic) reflections on the practice of pragmatics itself" (3). By contrast, the essays contained in Verschueren's collection *Linguistic Action,* as well as the essays contained in Lucy's still more recent *Reflexive Language* (1993), are concerned with metapragmatics in the first sense—i.e., metapragmatic features of natural language contexts. However, the discussion of Woolf below (secs. 7ff.) may have consequences for metapragmatic analysis in *both* senses of the term.

9   All quotations from Virginia Woolf's *Between the Acts* are taken from Woolf (1941) and given by page number in the text.

10 If we isolate the last *two* sentences of the text, we see how the narrative itself thematizes the link between speaking and acting: "Then the curtain rose. They spoke" (219). Note the double sense of the performative at work here since Isa and Giles's speaking constitutes not only an action but also, as we learn earlier in the text, a familiar (a family) drama: "Isa was immobile, watching her husband. She could feel the Manresa in his wake. *She could hear in the dusk in their bedroom the usual explanation.* It made no difference; his infidelity—but hers did" (110; my emphasis).

To put the point more generally, Woolf's narrative unfolds in the space between the different domains of performativity—the different senses of performance, illocutionary, dramatic, etc.—comprised by the extension of the term *acts* itself. Thus, the text contains what can be construed as an ethical diagnosis of war—recall that Woolf composed the novel in 1939—as that irrational domain of pure performativity, action for action's sake, which subsists precisely in the absence of any sustained reflection on one's acts and their consequences, any reasoned consideration of behavioral norms: "raising his foot, he [Giles] stamped on [a snake unable to swallow a toad]. The mass crushed and slithered. The white canvas on his tennis shoes was bloodstained and sticky. But it was action. Action relieved him. He strode to the Barn, with blood on his shoes" (99).

11 In her introduction to Gerard Deledalle's *Charles S. Peirce,* Susan Petrilli makes the same sort of distinction but in different terms, highlighting areas of overlap between Peircean semiotics and Bakhtin's dialogic theories of discourse—in contradistinction to Saussure's "code semiotics" (Petrilli 1990: xii–xiii).

12 Peirce, of course, had the same high hopes for a general semiotics, as evident in Peirce (1955 [1897–1903]). See Greenlee (1973: 13–22) for an account of how "sign theory for Peirce takes the form of a general theory of meaning" (7).

13 In fact, with its emphasis on the expedience and provisionality of contexts, Prague School

functionalism bears a striking resemblance to the pragmatism from which Morris's pragmatics stems (see Morris 1938: 29–30). Compare, e.g., William James's analysis of "truth" as an aspect of the ongoing process of inquiry itself: "The truth of an idea is not a stagnant property inherent in it. Truth *happens* to an idea. It *becomes* true, is *made* true by events. Its verity *is* in fact an event, a process: the process namely of verifying itself, its veri-*fication*. Its validity is the process of its valid-*ation*" (1948 [1907]: 161).

14   My thanks to Jacqueline Henkel for reminding me about this extenuating circumstance.

15   In other respects, however, Èjchenbaum's (1971 [1926]) text does not fall victim to the Poetic Language Fallacy. Thus, in a formulation that sounds strikingly similar to Pratt's call for a "socially-based, use-oriented" approach to literary discourse, Èjchenbaum makes this statement: "The facts of art demonstrate that art's uniqueness consists not in the parts which enter into it but in their original *use*" (834).

16   By no means should we concede this point to Pratt without hesitation, especially if we take her to mean that interest in the "structural properties of literary utterances" excludes interest in the functional context of such utterances. As Steiner (1982) points out, already in his early (1921) text on Xlebnikov, Jakobson stresses the polyfunctionality of *all* utterances—whereby the "functional classification [of a given utterance] is not simply a matter of the presence or absence of a particular function, but of the hierarchy in the functions co-present" (199; cf. Steiner 1984: 200ff.). Thus, while still nominally a Formalist, Jakobson situates the property of literariness within a polyfunctional matrix that tends, from the start, to make properties parasitic on functions, the "structure" of utterances on their use. Furthermore, whereas both Holenstein and Steiner construe Jakubinskij as a sort of exemplary monofunctionalist, even Jakubinskij demonstrates, in a passage that Èjchenbaum (1971 [1926]: 832) and then Holenstein and Steiner isolate, what might be interpreted as (incipient) polyfunctionalist tendencies. Thus, in describing poetic as opposed to practical language, Jakubinskij refuses to make the distinction a difference in kind, arguing that "linguistic systems . . . in which the practical purpose is in the background (*although perhaps not entirely hidden*)" constitute poetic language (my emphasis; Steiner's translation: "linguistic systems . . . in which the practical aim retreats to the background" [1982: 198]; Holenstein's translation: "sprachliche Systeme . . . in denen das praktische Ziel zweitrangig wird (obschon es nicht ganz verschwindet)" [1979a: 11]).

17   Because they were formulated in 1929, the "Theses" thus predate the important and influential functional schema articulated by Karl Bühler in his *Sprachtheorie* (1934). It was, as Holenstein (1979a: 14) points out, Bühler's trichotomy of functions that Mukařovský, around 1938, synthesized with a fourth, "poetic" function to produce the polyfunctional schema that Jakobson later expanded to six. In any event, because the "Theses" do not articulate the polyfunctional stance that Mukařovský and Jakobson went on to develop, they can indeed give the impression that Prague School functionalism merely replicates, in different terms, the Formalist preoccupation with literariness.

18   Holenstein goes on to link Jakobson's functional schema with the contemporary interest in communication theory, which made possible the redescription of Saussure's *parole-langue* distinction as that of *message* vs. *code* (1979a: 15).

19   Compare Jameson (1972): "If . . . one abandons the idea of technique and purpose, and speaks simply of dominant and secondary elements or of a dominant constructional principle which

is simply 'the promotion of one group of factors at the expense of others' [a quote from Tynjanov] (or of the 'foregrounding' of one set of elements, a later but most expressive term developed by the Prague Circle), then at once a model is constructed which has all the advantages of Shklovskian doctrine and none of its drawbacks" (92).

20   Note that McHale (1978) makes similar remarks in his study of FID but argues for a multiplication of types around the base opposition diegetic/mimetic also discussed by Wayne Booth (1983), Gérard Genette (1980 [1972]), and Paul Hernadi (1972). Thus, McHale ranges discursive types along "a scale [stretching] from the 'purely' diegetic to the 'purely' mimetic" (1978: 258). As I shall go on to suggest, however, multiplying discourse types around the opposition context backgrounding/context foregrounding seems to involve us in fewer questionable assumptions than does McHale's typology. After all, the very distinction between mimesis and diegesis, ostension and description, is a difference in degree, not kind.

21   Other important precedents include Leech and Short (1981) and Short (1988).

22   I should like to express my gratitude here to the anonymous reviewer for *Poetics* who, in connection with an earlier draft of part of this chapter, made a number of invaluable suggestions regarding the presentation, and underlying concepts, of the typology that follows. In particular, the reviewer made the point that D_n and AD seem to be of a different order of discourse than the other types inventoried, insofar as the one "*constitutes* the narrator's speech act" and the other "*refers to* a speech act." Hence my arrangement of the initial, synoptic list.

23   Here and in subsequent passages isolated from the text, all emphases are mine and are intended to throw into relief discourse types found embedded in longer passages containing other discourse types as well.

24   Note how this instance of IM itself centers on the appropriateness of a particular utterance to a specific context. Note, furthermore, that IM, or the representation of a character's thought insofar as that thought is silently verbalized or rather in principle subject to verbalization, must be distinguished from represented *perception* (Brinton 1980). In *Between the Acts*, multiple semicolons concatenating a series of short clauses into a single sentence often serve as a marker of represented perception. Compare, e.g., "The scullery maid, before the plates came out, was cooling her cheeks by the lily pond. . . . A grain fell and spiralled down; a petal fell, filled and sank. At that the fleet of boat-shaped bodies [of fish] paused; poised; equipped; mailed; then with a waver of undulation off they flashed" (43–44; cf. 23, 34, 83, 156).

25   Note that PDD/TIM also occurs in Woolf's earlier novel *To the Lighthouse* (1927): "He [Mr. Carmichael] stood by her [Lily Briscoe] on the edge of the lawn. . . . 'They will have landed,' and she felt that she had been right. They had not needed to speak. They had been thinking the same things and he had answered her without her asking him anything" (208). The discourse type can be found, too, in William Faulkner's *As I Lay Dying* (1987 [1930]), in which Dewey Dell and Darl at one point speak "without words" (24).

26   Although I do not have space here to argue the point in detail or with properly statistical rigor, it seems to me that one of the fundamental structuring devices of the novel—one of the basic formal principles that accounts for its overall rhythm—is the trajectory traced by its constituent types of represented discourse. Specifically, we witness a progression that leads from a high concentration of DD and IM in the opening sections of the narrative, where individual characters are not yet overdetermined by impersonal "voices"; through increasingly more indefinite forms of represented discourse (including FID), with indefDD of type 1 giving way

to that of type 2 and indefID 1 yielding mutatis mutandis to indefID 2; back down through increasingly more definite forms of represented discourse, as once more the disembodied voices begin to anchor themselves in the specific group of characters with whose representation the novel begins.

4   Postmodernism as Secondary Grammar

My thanks to Arkady Plotnitsky for conversations and, in particular, questions that helped me recombine the texts cited—the arguments developed—in this chapter. I am also grateful to Meg Sachse for helpful comments and suggestions during revisions that produced an earlier version of the chapter. A first, working draft was delivered under the title "Technologies of Analysis in Postmodern Theory: Citational Systems and the Production of Truth" at the 1991 conference of the Society for Literature and Science in Montréal.

1   Note that, in his foreword to the English translation of *European Literature and the Latin Middle Ages* (1953 [1948]), Curtius uses a metaphor similar to the one that opens this chapter. In order to establish (partial) isomorphism between the two analogies, however, we must adjust for different stages of technological development: "Contemporary archeology has made surprising discoveries by means of aerial photography at great altitudes. . . . A person standing on the ground before a heap of ruins cannot see the whole that the aerial photograph reveals. But the next step is to enlarge the aerial photograph and compare it with a detailed map. There is a certain analogy to this procedure in the technique of literary investigation here employed" (ix).

2   Hence, *postmodernism* will here designate, according to context, an aesthetic and broadly cultural phenomenon (or set of phenomena) as well as the set of discourses *about* that phenomenon (or set of phenomena).

3   On the notion of syntax as a grammatical "device," see the early arguments by Noam Chomsky in *Syntactic Structures* (1966b [1957]): "Syntax is the study of the principles and processes by which sentences are constructed in particular languages. Syntactic investigation of a given language has as its goal the construction of a grammar that can be viewed as a device of some sort for producing the sentences of the language under analysis" (11). Later in *Syntactic Structures,* Chomsky remarks that syntactic analysis allows us to "study language as an instrument or a tool, attempting to describe its structure with no explicit reference to the way in which this instrument is put to use" (103; cf. Chomsky 1965: 32).

4   Herman (1991b) likewise tries to place, instead of outrace, the postmodern.

5   For a critique of the a- or even antipolitical terms adopted by Western academics in their recent attempts to define the postmodern, see Wicke (1987). Wicke suggests that recent descriptions of postmodernism have by and large romanticized, or at least irresponsibly decontextualized, the idea (or ideal) of information technology. For related arguments, although in the context of modernism instead of postmodernism, see Herf's (1984) account of early-twentieth-century Germany's "reactionary modernism." Originating around the turn of the century and then gathering force during the period of the Weimar Republic, this oxymoronically regressive modernism, argues Herf, eventually issued in German fascism's peculiar combination of romantic nationalism with the worship of technology for its own sake. For a radically different assessment of (the liberating effects of) information technologies vis-à-vis the discourses of postmodernism, however, see, e.g., Haraway (1985) and Porush (1985).

6   For a useful introduction to the current state of and future prospects for telecommunicational
     technologies, see the recent special issue of *Scientific American* (vol. 265, no. 3 [1991]): "Com-
     munications, Computers and Networks."

     For fuller discussions of Derrida's concept of writing, see, e.g., Goldberg (1990) and Pavel
     (1989), the latter of whom suggests, however, that Derrida's transcendentalization of writing
     results from a misunderstanding of a number of crucial notions in linguistics (43ff.). Bruns
     (1982) discusses the shift from manuscript to print culture (44–59), whereas Ulmer (1989) uses
     the grammatological model to characterize video vs. print culture. See also McHale (1992: 115–
     41) on the televisual saturation of Thomas Pynchon's *Vineland* and on the functions of
     television as a privileged model and/or metaphor of postmodernist culture at large.

7   Here, the German term for *tradition*, *Überlieferung* (*überliefert*, "to hand down" [a manu-
     script, say]) serves particularly well. Compare Bernet's preface to the German translation of
     Derrida's *Introduction* (1987).

8   In this connection, see Pfister's suggestion that, by hyperextending Bakhtin's concept of the
     essential dialogicity of texts, Kristeva produces a poststructuralist "concept of text in the sense
     of a general semiotics of culture [that] is so radically generalized, that finally everything, or at
     least every cultural system and every cultural structure, becomes a text" (1985: 7).

9   Bertolt Brecht deciphered this new, electrifying, and, as we might put it, trans-Euclidian
     geometry quite early on. In the 1932 essay "Der Rundfunk als Kommunikationsapparat" 'The
     Radio as Communications Apparatus,' Brecht presciently envisioned the transformation of
     merely passively received radio waves into "ein ungeheures Kanalsystem" 'a monstrous system
     of canals' for the active production and exchange of information via transmitting and/or
     receiving components within a massive communicational network (1967: 134ff.).

10   In this connection, cf. Niehoff's (1991) analysis of the telegraph. Niehoff comments on how the
     originally predominantly military applications of the telegraph were eventually disseminated
     through the increasing use of Morse code (ca. 1832–40), thereby producing a more globalized
     form of information technology (130ff.). Niehoff remarks that, for the first time, the electronic
     telegraph made possible "the transmission of information by means of relays spanning the
     entire world. Communication becomes global. Therewith, however, a universal, generally
     understandable, absolutely transparent code also becomes necessary. Morse's famous alphabet
     was part and parcel of the demand for a universal language, a demand which Comenius and
     Leibniz [too] had made" (131). See the introduction above, esp. sec. *0.5.1*.

11   For a useful survey and bibliography of accounts of intertextuality, see Hebel (1989), together
     with Pfister (1985). Other influential studies include Barthes (1974 [1970], 1977a [1971]), Culler
     (1981), Kristeva (1980, 1984 [1974]), and Riffaterre (1981, 1983, 1984). Furthermore, see Hoeste-
     rey (1988: 130ff.) for arguments that periodization in general depends on the more or less co-
     optative intertextual mechanisms—i.e., the "discursive encroachment" (*Diskursüberbegriff*)
     (142)—operative in particularly explicit fashion in the discourses of postmodern in particular.
     On the question of citation, see Morawski's (1970) classic analysis of the basic functions of
     quotation, Perri's examination of allusion (1978), and Klockow's (1980) ingenious study of the
     linguistics of quotation marks.

12   Compare Kraft's (1953 [1950]) account of the Vienna Circle's own distinction between a
     primary or "philological" and a secondary or "logical" grammar. Although the members of
     the Circle drew the primary-secondary distinction along somewhat different (i.e., Wittgen-

steinian) lines, their notion of logical grammar, like Plett's *Intertextualitätspoetik*, also attempts to give an account of the structure of the world itself. As Kraft puts it, "Pseudostatements are sentences which do not violate the grammatical rules in the philological sense and therefore look like genuine statements. . . . This shows that traditional, philological grammar is unsatisfactory. The customary classification of kinds of words into substantives, adjectives, verbs, etc. needs to be supplemented by further subdivisions of these classes into syntactic categories in accordance with the classes of entities designated by the words of those kinds: things or thing-properties or thing-relations, numbers or number-properties or number-relations etc." (33–34). The classic account of this distinction—i.e., logical vs. philological syntax—is of course Carnap's *The Logical Syntax of Language* (1937a [1934]). See sec. 1.6.4 above and n. 16 of the introduction.

13 As Benjamin puts it, *citing himself,* "In our writing," a left-wing author writes, "opposites that in happier periods fertilized one another have become insoluble antinomies. . . . The theatre of this literary confusion is the newspaper, its content 'subject-matter,' which denies itself any other form of organization than that imposed on it by the readers' impatience. . . . Hand in hand, therefore, with the indiscriminate assimilation of facts, goes the equally indiscriminate assimilation of readers who are instantly elevated to collaborators. . . . For as writing gains in breadth what it loses in depth, the conventional distinction between author and public, which is upheld by the bourgeois press, begins in the Soviet press [for example], to disappear. . . . Work itself has its turn to speak. And the account it gives of itself is part of the competence needed to perform it" (1986 [1934]: 224–25).

14 In this connection, consider how the development and use of citation indexes for scientific research parallel the rise of the discourses of postmodernism. Noting that the first annual edition of the *Science Citation Index* appeared in 1963, Eugene Garfield (1979) characterizes citations as "the formal explicit linkages between [scientific] papers that have particular points in common" and goes on to describe how "the use of these citations as indexing statements enables a citation index to provide a trail of information that follows the convoluted process of scientific development as it crosses disciplinary lines and moves back and forth in time" (xiii, 1, 5). Later, in the chapter "Mapping the Structure of Science," Garfield describes how inquiry into the (meta)syntactic relationships between citations, which provide "the basic units in the mosaic structure" of science (98), is what allows us to chart the migratory patterns of scientific concepts over time.

15 A similar globalization—and *eo ipso* trivialization—of entailment is already evident in Hjelmslev (1969 [1943]), who cites Jørgen Jørgensen in support of the view that "logical entailment between propositions seems to us merely another special case of linguistic implication" (91). See secs. 1.7ff. above.

16 For a comparable extension of the notion of (rhetorical) figures, cf. Ducrot and Todorov (1979 [1972]: 273ff.) and Todorov (1977 [1971]: 22, 256). Further, Curtius (1953 [1948]) remarks that, in ancient and medieval grammars, figures of speech were reckoned a part of grammar. In Greek grammars, e.g., "such forms of expression are called *schemata,* 'attitudes,' in Latin *figurae*" (44). Curtius goes on to note that "the cultural ideal of late Antiquity was rhetoric, of which poetry was a subdivision. The assimilation of philosophy to rhetoric is a product of neosophism" (210).

5   Modes of Meaning in Film

My thanks to James Morrison, Marie-Laure Ryan, and Evan P. Young for their insightful comments on earlier drafts of this chapter. An earlier version of the chapter was delivered under the title "Possible Worlds in *The Cook, The Thief, His Wife and Her Lover:* Greenaway, Lacan, and the Semantics of Desire" at the 1991 Conference on Literature, Film and the Humanities at Salisbury State University, Salisbury, Maryland.

1   As the progression of their titles alone suggests, the influential film studies of Christian Metz, in the trajectory that leads from *Film Language: A Semiotics of Cinema* (1974a [1968]) and *Language and Cinema* (1974b) to *The Imaginary Signifier: Psychoanalysis and the Cinema* (1982 [1977]), follow the semiological and psychoanalytic lines in turn. In contrast to de Lauretis, Stephen Heath (1981) omits explicit comment on the semiotic heritage of film theory, insisting that "cinema brings historical materialism and psychoanalysis together in such a way that the consideration of film begins from and constantly returns us to their conjuncture" (4). Yet Heath here registers more of a prescriptive research plan for film studies than a genealogy of previous or existing film-theoretical discourse. In any event, for both de Lauretis and Heath, psychoanalysis figures as a constant (or at least desideratum) in film-theoretical frameworks in general.

2   With de Lauretis's opposition between the "logico-mathematical" and the sociological semiotics, respectively, compare Herman Parret's (1983) discussion of the Saussurean-Hjelmslevian semiotic tradition, in which sign relations are dyadic or two termed (signifier and signified), as opposed to the Peircean semiotic tradition, in which sign relations are triadic or three termed (signifier, signified, interpretant) (23ff.). See sec. 3.4.1. above.

3   With this term I mean to invoke, in particular, Jean Alter's (1990) use of *sociosemiotics* to refer "not only to a general sociology of signs but also, and mainly, to the survey of social factors that determine historical changes in the function, nature, and meaning of particular sets of signs" (13).

4   In using the term *quasi-transcendental* I make deliberate reference to Habermas's attempt—introduced in Habermas (1971 [1968]: 301–17), e.g., but later abandoned—to outline a "universal pragmatics" of communicative behavior in general. Habermas (1976) tries to found on quasi-transcendental principles of rationality and communication "a non-nomological science of experience based on reconstructive types" (204ff.). (Later, in his *Theory of Communicative Action,* Habermas would shift from a Kantian emphasis on the quasi transcendental to what might be characterized as a neo-Gricean focus on communicative praxis as the hallmark of rationality itself. See Habermas 1984 [1981]: 1:8–42, 2:43–111; and cf. Herman 1994b.) My claim is that, partly because of his Saussurean inheritance, Lacan also argues (quasi) transcendentally, highlighting what he takes to be the *linguistic* conditions of possibility for subjectivity. Compare Kaja Silverman's remarks in this connection: "Another Lacanian tenet which informs [Benveniste's] *Problems in General Linguistics* is that subjectivity is entirely relational. . . . [Subjectivity] can only be induced by discourse, by the activation of a signifying system which pre-exists the individual, and which determines his or her cultural identity. . . . Benveniste's assertion that 'language is . . . the possibility of subjectivity' thus has firm grounding in Lacan's writings" (1983: 52; cf. 43–53, 149–93).

5   De Lauretis does point out some of the limitations of Lacan's model of the subject, insofar as Lacan's is a masculinist interpretation of subjectivity that articulates the subject "in processes (drive, desire, symbolization) which depend on the crucial instance of castration, and [which are] thus predicated exclusively on a male or masculine subject" (1984: 16; cf. de Lauretis 1987: 6). De Lauretis therefore criticizes the sexism but not what I would call the quasi transcendentalism of the Lacanian model—of which its sexism is perhaps just one of the more visible effects. Even when de Lauretis suggests that "in opposing the truth of the unconscious to the illusion of an always already-false consciousness, the general critical discourse based on psychoanalysis subscribes too easily, as Eco does, to the territorial distinction between subjective and social modes of signification" (180–81), de Lauretis for her part tends merely to collapse these modes of semiosis together under the rubric *construction* (see, e.g., 1987: 1–30). As a general interpretive principle, however, the notion of the social constructedness of all meaning itself presupposes, rather than accounts for, specific mechanisms for linking a given semiotic code with the particular set of contexts by which (presumably) the code in question is exhausted—i.e., the social contexts out of which the code at issue is (re)constructible. Note that, in a somewhat different setting, Deleuze and Guattari also evade the articulation of codes with contexts, to some degree at least. The authors tend to collapse codes and contexts together under the concept and figure of (at once social, subjective, and physical) machines and machinic flows (1983 [1972], 1987 [1980]; cf. sec. *4.6.1* above). For an illuminating discussion of Deleuze's work in film theory vis-à-vis Deleuze's other writings and the writings of Deleuze and Guattari, see Morrison (1992).

6   On the concept of *suture* in this context, see Miller (1977–78), Oudart (1977–78), and Heath (1981: esp. 13–15, 76–112). Silverman (1983) provides a concise definition: " 'Suture' is the name given to the procedures by which cinematic texts confer subjectivity upon their viewers" (195). See also Silverman's (1983: 206–15) careful and suggestive analysis of Hitchcock's *Psycho* in her chapter "Suture."

7   Here we shall be going back over territory already partly covered above, in chap. 2 (see in particular secs. *2.3, 2.6*, and *2.7*) but also refining and extending the previous characterization of the methods and aims of possible worlds semantics. As before, my presentation of the model-theoretic framework is indebted to the sources listed in n. 27 of chap. 2.

8   Before Frege, Franz Brentano (1973 [1874]) had made an analogous distinction between the primary (direct) and the secondary (indirect) objects of mental presentations or *Vorstellungen* (bk. 2, sec. 9, pp. 128ff.). Subsequently, in an appendix to the more nominalistic 1911 edition of his *Psychology*, and in terms closer to Frege's own, Brentano respecified this distinction as one between modes of (mental) reference *in recto* versus modes of reference *in obliquo* (272). See secs. *2.4.2* and *2.4.3* above.

9   Compare Lacan's remark (1977a [1957]) that "there is in effect no signifying chain that does not have, as if attached to the punctuation of each of its units, a whole articulation of relevant contexts suspended 'vertically,' as it were, from that point" (154).

10 For example, just after Michael and Georgina have begun speaking, in addition to making love, in the recesses of the kitchen, Michael says, "I once saw a film in which the main character didn't speak for the first half hour. . . . I was completely absorbed as to what would happen because anything was possible."

11 Here again we come face to face with what appears to be a *mise en abyme* since each book in

the depository contains (represents, constructs) many possible frames of reference, including, at least potentially or in a Borgesian scenario, one in which the states and events represented in the movie would be deemed actual.

12   Compare Nietzsche (1968b [1887]): "Whatever exists, having somehow come into being, is again and again reinterpreted to new ends, taken over, transformed, and redirected to some power superior to it; all events in the organic world are a subduing, a becoming master, and all subduing and becoming master involves a fresh interpretation, an adaptation through which any previous 'meaning' and 'purpose' are necessarily obscured or even obliterated" (essay 2, sec. 12, p. 513).

13   For arguments for the *essential* incompleteness of frames of reference, see secs. 2.5.4 and 2.5.5 above.

References

Aarsleff, Hans. 1982. *From Locke to Saussure: Essays on the Study of Language and Intellectual History* (Minneapolis: University of Minnesota Press).

Abraham, Gerald. 1979. *The Concise Oxford History of Music* (Oxford: Oxford University Press).

Ackermann, Robert. 1967. *Introduction to Many Valued Logics* (London: Routledge & Kegan Paul).

Adams, Jon-K. 1985. *Pragmatics and Fiction.* (Amsterdam: John Benjamins).

Adams, Robert Martin. 1977. *After Joyce: Studies in Fiction after "Ulysses"* (New York: Oxford University Press).

Adorno, Theodor. 1973 [1948]. *The Philosophy of Modern Music,* trans. Anne G. Mitchell and Wesley V. Blomster (New York: Seabury Press).

——. 1984 [1970]. *Aesthetic Theory,* trans. C. Lenhardt, ed. Gretel Adorno and Rolf Tiedemann (London: Routledge & Kegan Paul).

——. 1986a [1967]. "Cultural Criticism and Society," in *Prisms,* trans. Samuel M. Weber, 17–34 (Cambridge, Mass.: MIT Press).

——. 1986b [1967]. "Notes on Kafka," in *Prisms,* trans. Samuel M. Weber, 243–71 (Cambridge, Mass.: MIT Press).

Alexander, Peter. 1967. "Ernst Mach," in *The Encyclopedia of Philosophy,* vol. 5, ed. Paul Edwards, 115–19 (New York: Macmillan Publishing Co.).

Allén, Sture, ed. 1989. *Possible Worlds in Humanities, Arts and Sciences: Proceedings of the Nobel Symposium 65* (Berlin: Walter de Gruyter).

Allwood, Jens, Lars-Gunnar Andersson, and Östen Dahl. 1977 [1971]. *Logic in Linguistics* (Cambridge: Cambridge University Press).

Alter, Jean. 1990. *A Sociosemiotic Theory of Theatre* (Philadelphia: University of Pennsylvania Press).

Aristotle. 1938 [4th century B.C.E.]. *The Categories,* in Aristotle, *The Organon,* trans. Harold P. Cooke, 12–109 (Cambridge, Mass.: Harvard University Press).

Arnauld, Antoine, and Claude Lancelot. 1972 [1660]. *Grammaire générale et raisonnée* (Genève: Slatkine Reprints).

Arnauld, Antoine, and Pierre Nicole. 1972 [1662]. *La Logique ou l'art de penser* (Genève: Slatkine Reprints).

Attridge, Derek. 1986. "Joyce's Lipspeech: Syntax and the Subject in 'Sirens,' " in *James Joyce: The Centennial Symposium,* ed. Morris Beja, 59–65 (Urbana: University of Illinois Press).

Austin, J. L. 1962. *How to Do Things with Words* (New York: Oxford University Press).

——. 1963 [1940]. "The Meaning of a Word," in *Philosophy and Ordinary Language*, ed. Charles Caton, 1–22 (Urbana: University of Illinois Press).

Avni, Ora. 1990. *The Resistance of Reference: Linguistics, Philosophy and the Literary Text* (Baltimore: Johns Hopkins University Press).

Bakhtin, Mikhail. 1984 [1929]. *Problems of Dostoevsky's Poetics*, ed. and trans. Caryl Emerson (Minneapolis: University of Minnesota Press).

Bal, Mieke. 1981. "Notes on Narrative Embedding," *Poetics Today* 2, no. 2: 41–59.

——. 1991. *On Story-Telling: Essays in Narratology*, ed. David Jobling (Sonoma, Calif.: Polebridge Press).

Bally, Charles. 1912. "Le Style indirect libre en français moderne," *Germanisch-romanische Monatsschrift* 4:549–56, 597–606.

——. 1914. "Figures de pensée et formes linguistiques," *Germanisch-romanische Monatsschrift* 6:405–22, 456–70.

Banfield, Ann. 1982. *Unspeakable Sentences: Narration and Representation in the Language of Fiction* (Boston: Routledge & Kegan Paul).

——. 1987. "Describing the Unobserved: Events Grouped around an Empty Centre," in *The Linguistics of Writing: Arguments between Language and Literature*, ed. Nigel Fabb, Derek Attridge, Alan Durant, and Colin MacCabe, 265–85 (New York: Methuen).

Bar-Hillel, Yehoshua. 1954. "Indexical Expressions," *Mind* 63: 359–79.

——. 1977 [1957]. "Husserl's Conception of a Purely Logical Grammar," in Mohanty (1977: 128–36).

Barthes, Roland. 1974 [1970]. *S/Z*, trans. Richard Miller (New York: Hill & Wang).

——. 1977a [1971]. "From Work to Text," in *Image, Music, Text*, trans. Stephen Heath, 155–64 (New York: Hill & Wang).

——. 1977b [1966]. "Introduction to the Structural Analysis of Narratives," in *Image, Music, Text*, trans. Stephen Heath, 79–124 (New York: Hill & Wang).

——. 1985 [1964]. *Elements of Semiology*, trans. Annette Lavers and Colin Smith (New York: Hill & Wang).

Bartsch, Renate. 1987. *Norms of Language: Theoretical and Practical Aspects* (London: Longman).

Barwise, Jon. 1989. *The Situation in Logic* (Stanford, Calif.: Center for the Study of Language and Information and Stanford University Press).

Barwise, Jon, and John Perry. 1983. *Situations and Attitudes* (Cambridge, Mass.: MIT Press).

Beckett, Samuel. 1974 [1936]. "Dante . . . Bruno. Vico . . . Joyce," in *An Exagmination of James Joyce*, ed. Samuel Beckett, 1–22 (New York: Haskell House).

Behse, G. 1974. "Grammatik," in *Historisches Wörterbuch der Philosophie*, vol. 3, ed. Joachim Ritter, 846–60 (Basel/Stuttgart: Schwabe & Co.).

Benjamin, Walter. 1969 [1936]. "The Work of Art in the Age of Mechanical Reproduction," in *Illuminations*, ed. Hannah Arendt, trans. Harry Zohn, 217–51 (New York: Schocken Books).

——. 1986 [1934]. "The Author as Producer," in *Reflections*, ed. Peter Demetz, trans. Edmund Jephcott, 220–38 (New York: Schocken Books).

Bense, Max. 1952. *Die Theorie Kafkas* (Cologne: Kiepenheuer & Witsch).

Benveniste, Émile. 1971 [1966]. *Problems in General Linguistics*, trans. Mary Elizabeth Meek (Coral Gables, Fla.: University of Miami Press).

Bergmann, Hugo. 1908. *Untersuchungen zum Problem der Evidenz der inneren Wahrnehmung* (Halle: Max Niemeyer).

Bernet, Rudolf. 1987. "Vorwort zur deutschen Ausgabe," in Jacques Derrida, *Husserls Weg in die Geschichte am Leitfaden der Geometrie,* trans. Rüdiger Hentschel and Andreas Koop, 11–30 (Munich: Wilhelm Fink).

Binder, Hartmut, ed. 1979. *Kafka-Handbuch,* vol. 1 (Stuttgart: Alfred Kröner).

Bloomfield, Leonard. 1926. "A Set of Postulates for the Science of Language," *Language* 2:153–63.

———. 1933. *Language* (New York: Henry Holt).

———. 1936. "Language or Ideas?" *Language* 12:89–95.

———. 1971 [1939]. "Linguistic Aspects of Science," in *Foundations of the Unity of Science: Toward an International Encyclopedia of Unified Science,* vol. 1, ed. Otto Neurath, Rudolf Carnap, and Charles Morris, 216–77 (Chicago: University of Chicago Press).

Blumberg, Albert E. 1967. "Modern Logic," in *The Encyclopedia of Philosophy,* vol. 5, ed. Paul Edwards, 12–34 (New York: Macmillan Publishing Co.).

Booth, Wayne C. 1983. *The Rhetoric of Fiction,* 2d ed. (Chicago: University of Chicago Press).

Bordwell, David. 1989. *Making Meaning: Inference and Rhetoric in the Interpretation of Cinema* (Cambridge, Mass.: Harvard University Press).

Boyer, Carl B. 1968. *A History of Mathematics* (Princeton, N.J.: Princeton University Press).

Brantlinger, Patrick. 1990. "Mass Media and Culture in Fin-de-Siècle Europe," in *Fin de Siècle and Its Legacy,* ed. Mikulás Teich and Roy Porter, 98–114 (Cambridge: Cambridge University Press).

Brecht, Bertolt. 1967. *Schriften zur Literatur und Kunst I, 1920–32* (Frankfurt am Main: Suhrkamp Verlag).

Bremond, Claude. 1973. *Logique du récit* (Paris: Seuil).

———. 1980 [1966]. "The Logic of Narrative Possibilities," trans. Elaine D. Cancalon, *New Literary History* 11:387–411.

———. 1982. "A Critique of the Motif," in *French Literary Theory Today: A Reader,* ed. Tzvetan Todorov, trans. R. Carter, 125–46 (Cambridge: Cambridge University Press).

Brentano, Franz. 1930. *Wahrheit und Evidenz: Erkenntnistheoretische Abhandlungen und Briefe,* ed. Oskar Kraus (Leipzig: Felix Meiner, 1930).

———. 1966. *Die Abkehr vom Nichtrealen,* ed. Franziska Mayer-Hillebrand (Bern and Munich: A. Francke).

———. 1973 [1874]. *Psychology from an Empirical Standpoint,* ed. Linda L. McAlister, trans. Antos C. Rancurello et al. (London: Routledge & Kegan Paul).

———. 1981a [1929]. *Sensory and Noetic Consciousness,* ed. Oskar Kraus, English edition ed. Linda L. McAlister, trans. Margarete Schätte and Linda L. McAlister (London: Routledge & Kegan Paul).

———. 1981b [1907–17]. *The Theory of the Categories,* trans. Roderick Chisholm and Norbert Gutterman (The Hague: Martinus Nijhoff).

Brinton, Laurel. 1980. " 'Represented Perception': A Study in Narrative Style," *Poetics* 9:363–81.

Broch, Hermann. 1975 [1936]. "James Joyce und die Gegenwart," in *Schriften zur Literatur I: Kritik,* ed. Paul Michael Lützeler, 63–94 (Frankfurt am Main: Suhrkamp Verlag).

———. 1977 [1946]. "Über syntaktische und kognitive Einheiten," in *Kommentierte Werkausgabe,* vol. 10, pt. 2, ed. Paul Michael Lützeler, 247–99 (Frankfurt am Main: Surhkamp Verlag).

Brooke-Rose, Christine. 1990. "Ill Locutions," in *Narrative in Culture: The Uses of Storytelling in the Sciences, Philosophy and Literature,* ed. Christopher Nash, 154–71 (London: Routledge).

Brown, Gillian, and George Yule. 1983. *Discourse Analysis* (Cambridge: Cambridge University Press).

Bruns, Gerald L. 1982. *Inventions: Writing, Textuality and Understanding in Literary History* (New Haven, Conn.: Yale University Press).

Bühler, Karl. 1965 [1934]. *Sprachtheorie* (Stuttgart: Fischer).

Burkhardt, Hans. 1980. *Logik und Semiotik in der Philosophie von Leibniz* (Munich: Philosophia Verlag).

——. 1987. "The Leibnizian *Characteristica Universalis* as Link between Grammar and Logic," in Buzzetti and Ferriani (1987: 43–64).

Bursill-Hall, G. L. 1971. *Speculative Grammars of the Middle Ages* (The Hague: Mouton).

Busoni, Ferruccio. N.d. [1906]. *Entwurf einer neuen Ästhetik der Tonkunst,* 2d ed. (Leipzig: Insel-Verlag).

Buzzetti, Dino, and Maurizio Ferriani, eds. 1987. *Speculative Grammar, Universal Grammar and Philosophical Analysis of Language* (Amsterdam: John Benjamins).

Cairns, Dorion. 1973. *Guide for Translating Husserl* (The Hague: Martinus Nijhoff).

Capozzi, Mirella. 1987. "Kant on Logic, Language and Thought." In Buzzetti and Ferriani (1987: 97–148).

Carnap, Rudolf. 1937a [1934]. *The Logical Syntax of Language,* trans. Amethe Smeaton (London: Routledge & Kegan Paul).

——. 1937b. "Testability and Meaning," *Philosophy of Science* 3, no. 4:420ff.; 4, no. 1:3–40.

——. 1947. *Meaning and Necessity* (Chicago: University of Chicago Press).

——. 1952 [1950]. "Empiricism, Semantics and Ontology," in *Semantics and the Philosophy of Language,* ed. Leonard Linsky, 208–28 (Urbana: University of Illinois Press).

——. 1963. "Intellectual Autobiography," in *The Philosophy of Rudolf Carnap,* ed. Paul Arthur Schilpp, 12–83 (La Salle, Ill.: Open Court).

——. 1969 [1928]. *The Logical Structure of the World: Pseudoproblems in Philosophy,* trans. Rolf A. George (Berkeley: University of California Press).

——. 1971 [1938]. "Foundations of Logic and Mathematics," in *Foundations of the Unity of Science: Toward an International Encyclopedia of Unified Science,* vol. 1, ed. Otto Neurath, Rudolf Carnap, and Charles Morris, 139–213 (Chicago: University of Chicago Press).

——. 1975 [1931]. "Überwindung der Metaphysik durch die logische Analyse der Sprache," *Logischer Empirismus: Der Wiener Kreis,* ed. Hubert Schleichert, 149–71 (Munich: Wilhelm Fink).

——. 1979 [1935]. *Philosophy and Logical Syntax* (London: Kegan Paul; Trench, Trubner & Co.).

Caws, Peter. 1988. *Structuralism: The Art of the Intelligible* (Atlantic Highlands, N.J.: Humanities Press International).

Chafe, Wallace, and Johanna Nichols, eds. 1986. *Evidentiality: The Linguistic Coding of Epistemology* (Norwood, N.J.: Ablex Publishing Corp.).

Champigny, Robert. 1972. *Ontology of the Narrative* (The Hague: Mouton).

——. 1986. *Sense, Antisense, Nonsense* (Gainesville: University of Florida Press).

Chatman, Seymour. 1978. *Story and Discourse* (Ithaca, N.Y.: Cornell University Press).

——. 1990. *Coming to Terms: The Rhetoric of Narrative in Fiction and Film* (Ithaca, N.Y.: Cornell University Press).

Chisholm, Roderick M. 1967. "Intentionality," in *The Encyclopedia of Philosophy*, vol. 4, ed. Paul Edwards, 201–4 (New York: Macmillan Publishing Co.).

——. 1973. "Homeless Objects," *Revue Internationale de Philosophie* 27:207–23.

Chomsky, Noam. 1955. "Logical Syntax and Semantics: Their Linguistic Relevance," *Language* 31:36–45.

——. 1963. "Formal Properties of Grammars," in *Handbook of Mathematical Psychology*, vol. 2, ed. R. Duncan Luce, Robert R. Bush, and Eugene Galanter, 323–418 (New York: John Wiley & Sons).

——. 1964a. *Current Issues in Linguistic Theory* (The Hague: Mouton).

——. 1964b. "On the Notion 'Rule of Grammar,'" in *The Structure of Language: Readings in the Philosophy of Language*, ed. J. A. Fodor and J. J. Katz, 119–36 (Englewood Cliffs, N.J.: Prentice-Hall).

——. 1965. *Aspects of the Theory of Syntax* (Cambridge, Mass.: MIT Press).

——. 1966a. *Cartesian Linguistics* (New York: Harper & Row).

——. 1966b [1957]. *Syntactic Structures* (The Hague: Mouton).

——. 1975 [1955]. *The Logical Structure of Linguistic Theory* (New York: Plenum Press).

——. 1977. *Essays on Form and Interpretation* (Amsterdam: Elsevier North-Holland).

——. 1980. *Rules and Representations* (New York: Columbia University Press).

——. 1981. *Lectures on Government and Binding* (Dordrecht: Foris).

——. 1986. *Knowledge of Language: Its Nature, Origin, and Use* (New York: Praeger).

Chomsky, Noam, and George A. Miller. 1963. "Introduction to the Formal Analysis of Natural Languages," in *Handbook of Mathematical Psychology*, vol. 2, ed. R. Duncan Luce, Robert R. Bush, and Eugene Galanter, 269–321 (New York: John Wiley & Sons).

Church, Alonzo. 1950. "The Need for Abstract Entities in Semantic Analysis," *Proceedings of the American Academy of Arts and Sciences* 80: 100–112.

Cohn, Dorrit. 1978. *Transparent Minds: Narrative Modes for Presenting Consciousness* (Princeton, N.J.: Princeton University Press).

——. 1981. "The Encirclement of Narrative: On Franz Stanzel's *Theorie des Erzählens*," *Poetics Today* 2:157–82.

Cole, Peter, ed. 1981. *Radical Pragmatics* (New York: Academic Press).

Cook, V. J. 1988. *Chomsky's Universal Grammar* (Oxford: Basil Blackwell).

Copi, Irving M., and Robert W. Beard, eds. 1973. *Essays on Wittgenstein's "Tractatus"* (New York: Hafner Press).

Copleston, Frederick. 1962 [1950]. *A History of Philosophy*, vol. 2 (Garden City, N.Y.: Image Books).

Corngold, Stanley. 1973. *The Commentator's Despair: The Interpretation of Kafka's "Metamorphosis"* (Port Washington, N.Y.: Kennikat Press).

Cornis-Pope, Marcel. 1992. *Hermeneutic Desire and Critical Rewriting: Narrative Interpretation in the Wake of Poststructuralism* (New York: St. Martin's Press).

Coste, Didier. 1989. *Narrative as Communication* (Minneapolis: University of Minnesota Press).

Couturat, Louis. 1901. *La Logique de Leibniz* (Paris: Ancienne Librairie Germer Baillière).

——. 1903. *Opuscules et fragments inédits de Leibniz* (Paris: Ancienne Librairie Germer Baillière).

Cresswell, Maxwell J. 1992. "Truth-Conditional and Model-Theoretic Semantics," in *International Encyclopedia of Linguistics*, vol. 3, ed. William Bright, 404–6 (New York: Oxford University Press).

Culler, Jonathan. 1975. *Structuralist Poetics: Structuralism, Linguistics and the Study of Literature* (Ithaca, N.Y.: Cornell University Press).

——. 1981. "Presupposition and Intertextuality," in *The Pursuit of Signs: Semiotics, Literature, Deconstruction*, 100–118 (Ithaca, N.Y.: Cornell University Press).

Curtius, Ernst Robert. 1953 [1948]. *European Literature and the Latin Middle Ages*, trans. Willard R. Trask (New York: Pantheon Books).

——. 1954 [1929]. "James Joyce und sein Ulysses," in *Kritische Essays zur Europäischen Literatur*, 290–314 (Bern: A. Francke).

Daemmrich, Horst S., and Ingrid Daemmrich. 1987. *Themes and Motifs in Western Literature: A Handbook* (Tübingen: A. Francke).

Danto, Arthur. 1981. *The Transfiguration of the Commonplace: A Philosophy of Art* (Cambridge, Mass.: Harvard University Press).

Davidson, Donald. 1973–74. "On the Very Idea of a Conceptual Scheme," *Proceedings of the American Philosophical Association* 17:5–20.

de Lauretis, Teresa. 1984. *Alice Doesn't: Feminism, Semiotics, Cinema* (Bloomington: Indiana University Press).

——. 1987. *Technologies of Gender: Essays on Theory, Film, and Fiction* (Bloomington: Indiana University Press).

Deleuze, Gilles. 1986 [1983]. *Cinema 1: The Movement-Image*, trans. Hugh Tomlinson and Barbara Habberjam (Minneapolis: University of Minnesota Press).

Deleuze, Gilles, and Félix Guattari. 1983 [1972]. *Anti-Oedipus: Capitalism and Schizophrenia*, trans. Helen R. Lane, Robert Hurley, and Mark Seem (Minneapolis: University of Minnesota Press).

——. 1986 [1975]. *Kafka: Toward a Minor Literature*, trans. Dana Polan (Minneapolis: University of Minnesota Press).

——. 1987 [1980]. *A Thousand Plateaus: Capitalism and Schizophrenia*, trans. Brian Massumi (Minneapolis: University of Minnesota Press).

Derrida, Jacques. 1974 [1967]. *Of Grammatology*, trans. Gayatri Chakravorty Spivak (Baltimore: Johns Hopkins University Press).

——. 1978a [1967]. "Freud and the Scene of Writing," in Derrida (1978b: 196–231).

——. 1978b [1966]. *Writing and Difference*, trans. Alan Bass (Chicago: University of Chicago Press).

——. 1978c [1966]. "Structure, Sign and Play in the Discourse of the Human Sciences," in Derrida (1978: 278–93).

——. 1982a [1968]. "Différance," in Derrida (1982b: 1–27).

——. 1982b. *Margins of Philosophy*, trans. Alan Bass (Chicago: University of Chicago Press).

——. 1982c [1971]. "Signature Event Context," in Derrida (1982b: 309–30).

——. 1984. "Two Words for Joyce," in *Poststructuralist Joyce: Essays from the French*, ed. Derek Attridge and Daniel Ferrer, 145–59 (Cambridge: Cambridge University Press).

——. 1988a [1962]. *Edmund Husserl's "Origin of Geometry": An Introduction*, trans. John P. Leavey (Lincoln: University of Nebraska Press).

——. 1988b. *Limited Inc*, ed. Gerald Graff, trans. Samuel Weber and Jeffrey Mehlman (Evanston, Ill.: Northwestern University Press).

——. 1988c. "Ulysses Grammaphone: Hear Say Yes in Joyce," in *James Joyce: The Augmented Ninth*, ed. Bernard Bernstock, 27–75 (Syracuse, N.Y.: Syracuse University Press).

Descombes, Vincent. 1986 [1983]. *Objects of All Sorts: A Philosophical Grammar,* trans. Lorna Scott-Fox and Jeremy Harding (Baltimore: Johns Hopkins University Press and Basil Blackwell).

Dijk, Teun A. van. 1972. *Some Aspects of Text Grammars: A Study in Theoretical Linguistics and Poetics* (The Hague: Mouton).

———. 1975. "Action, Action Description, and Narrative," *New Literary History* 6, no. 2:273–94.

———. 1977. *Text and Context: Explorations in the Semantics and Pragmatics of Discourse* (London: Longman).

———. 1985. "Introduction: Discourse Analysis as a New Cross-Discipline," in *Handbook of Discourse Analysis,* vol. 3, ed. Teun A. van Dijk, 1–10 (Orlando, Fla.: Academic Press).

Dik, Simon C. 1978. *Functional Grammar* (Amsterdam: North-Holland Publishing Co.).

Dillon, Tharam, and Poh Lee Tan. 1993. *Object-Oriented Conceptual Modeling* (New York: Prentice-Hall).

Doležel, Lubomír. 1972. "From Motifemes to Motifs," *Poetics* 4:55–90.

———. 1973. *Narrative Modes in Czech Literature* (Toronto: University of Toronto Press).

———. 1976a. "Narrative Modalities," *Journal of Literary Semantics* 5:5–14.

———. 1976b. "Narrative Semantics," *PTL* 1:129–51.

———. 1979. "Extensional and Intensional Narrative Worlds," *Poetics* 8:193–211.

———. 1983. "Intensional Function, Invisible Worlds, and Franz Kafka," *Style* 17:120–41.

———. 1984. "Kafka's Fictional World," *Canadian Review of Comparative Literature/Revue Canadienne de Littérature Comparée* 11:61–83.

———. 1989. "Possible Worlds and Literary Fictions," in Allén (1989: 221–42).

———. 1990. *Occidental Poetics: Tradition and Progress* (Lincoln: University of Nebraska Press).

Ducrot, Oswald, and Tzvetan Todorov. 1979 [1972]. *Encyclopedic Dictionary of the Sciences of Language,* trans. Catherine Porter (Baltimore: Johns Hopkins University Press).

Duve, Thierry de. 1991. *Pictorial Nominalism: On Marcel Duchamp's Passage from Painting to the Readymade,* trans. Dana Polan and T. de Duve (Minneapolis: University of Minnesota Press).

Eco, Umberto. 1976. *A Theory of Semiotics* (Bloomington: Indiana University Press).

———. 1984. *Semiotics and the Philosophy of Language* (Bloomington: Indiana University Press).

———. 1987. "Semantics, Pragmatics, and Text Semiotics," in *The Pragmatic Perspective: Selected Papers from the 1985 International Pragmatics Conference,* ed. Jef Verschueren and Marcella Bertuccelli-Papi, 695–713 (Amsterdam: John Benjamins).

———. 1989. "Report on Session 3 [of Nobel Symposium 65]: Literature and Arts," in Allén (1989: 343–55).

Edie, James M. 1977 [1972]. "Husserl's Conception of 'the Grammatical' and Contemporary Linguistics," in Mohanty (1977: 137–61).

Eichelberger, Carl. 1986. " 'Words? Music? No: It's What's Behind': Verbal and Physical Transformations in 'Sirens,' " in *International Perspectives on James Joyce,* ed. Gottlieb Gaiser, 59–67 (Troy, N.Y.: Whitson Publishing Co.).

Einstein, Alfred. 1954 [1920]. *A Short History of Music,* 4th American ed., trans. Alfred Einstein (New York: Vintage Books).

Eisenstein, Sergej. 1957. *Film Form,* ed. and trans. Jay Leyda (New York: World Publishing Co.).

Èjchenbaum, Boris. 1971 [1926]. "Theory of the 'Formal Method,' " in *Critical Theory since Plato,* ed. Hazard Adams, 828–46 (San Diego: Harcourt Brace Jovanovich).

Eley, Lothar. 1973. "Afterword to Husserl, *Experience and Judgment:* Phenomenology and the Philosophy of Language," in Husserl (1973 [1939]: 399–429).

Eliot, T. S. 1975 [1923]. "*Ulysses,* Order, and Myth," in *Selected Prose of T. S. Eliot,* ed. Frank Kermode, 175–78 (New York: Farrar Straus Giroux).

Ellmann, Richard. 1977. *The Consciousness of Joyce* (London: Faber & Faber).

———. 1982. *James Joyce,* 2d ed. (New York: Oxford University Press).

Ellul, Jacques. 1964 [1954]. *The Technological Society,* trans. John Wilkinson (New York: Vintage Books).

Erzgräber, Willi. 1985. "James Joyces Ulysses—zur Konstruktion und Komposition eines modernen Romans," *Universitas* 40, no. 3:289–301.

Even-Zohar, Itamar. 1980. "Constraints of Realeme Insertability in Narrative," *Poetics Today* 13:65–74.

Fasold, Ralph. 1990. *Sociolinguistics of Language* (Cambridge: Basil Blackwell).

Faulkner, William. 1987 [1930]. *As I Lay Dying* (New York: Vintage Books).

Fehn, Ann, Ingeborg Hoesterey, and Maria Tatar, eds. 1992. *Neverending Stories: Toward a Critical Narratology* (Princeton, N.J.: Princeton University Press).

Ferrer, Daniel. 1986. "Echo or Narcissus?" in *James Joyce: The Centennial Symposium,* ed. Morris Beja, 70–75 (Urbana: University of Illinois Press).

Ferriani, Maurizio. 1987. "Peirce's Analysis of the Proposition: Grammatical and Logical Aspects," in Buzzetti and Ferriani (1987: 149–72).

Fillmore, Charles J. 1981. "Pragmatics and the Description of Discourse," in Cole (1981: 143–66).

Findlay, John. 1963 [1933]. *Meinong's Theory of Objects and Values,* 2d ed. (Oxford: Oxford University Press).

Fleischman, Suzanne. 1990. *Tense and Narrativity: From Medieval Performance to Modern Fiction* (Austin: University of Texas Press).

Fludernik, Monika. 1986. "Narrative and Its Development in *Ulysses,*" *Journal of Narrative Technique* 16, no. 1:15–40.

———. 1993a. *The Fictions of Language and the Languages of Fiction* (London: Routledge).

———. 1993b. "Narratology in Context," *Poetics Today* 14, no. 4:729–61.

Foley, William A., and Robert D. Van Valin Jr. 1984. *Functional Syntax and Universal Grammar* (Cambridge: Cambridge University Press).

Foucault, Michel. 1972 [1969]. *The Archeology of Knowledge,* trans. A. M. Sheridan Smith (New York: Pantheon Books).

———. 1973 [1966]. *The Order of Things* (New York: Vintage Books).

———. 1979 [1975]. *Discipline and Punish: The Birth of the Prison,* trans. Alan Sheridan (New York: Vintage Books).

Frank, Joseph. 1988 [1945]. "Spatial Form in Modern Literature," in *Essentials of the Theory of Fiction,* ed. Michael J. Hoffman and Patrick D. Murphy, 86–100 (Durham, N.C.: Duke University Press).

Frawley, William. 1992. *Linguistic Semantics* (Hillsdale, N.J.: Lawrence Erlbaum).

Frege, Gottlob. 1879. *Begriffsschrift, eine der arithmetischen nachgebildete formalsprache des reinen denkens* (Halle: L. Nebert).

———. 1969a. *Funktion, Begriff, Bedeutung: Fünf logische Studien,* 3d ed., ed. Günther Patzig (Göttingen: Vandenhoeck & Ruprecht).

———. 1969b [1891]. "Funktion und Begriff," in Frege (1969a: 18–39).

———. 1969c [1892]. "Über Begriff und Gegenstand," in Frege (1969a: 66–80).

———. 1969d [1882]. "Über die wissenschaftliche Berechtigung einer Begriffsschrift," in Frege (1969a: 91–97).

1060e [1892]. Über Sinn und Bedeutung," in Frege (1969a: 40–65).

1970 [1892]. "On Sense and Reference," trans. Max Black, in *Translations from the Philosophical Writings of Gottlob Frege,* ed. Peter Geach and Max Black, 56–78 (Oxford: Basil Blackwell).

Galison, Peter. 1990. "Aufbau/Bauhaus: Logical Positivism and Architectural Modernism," *Critical Inquiry* 16:709–52.

Gardies, Jean-Louis. 1985 [1975]. *Rational Grammar,* trans. Kevin Mulligan (Washington, D.C.: Catholic University of America Press).

Garfield, Eugene. 1979. *Citation Indexing: Its Theory and Application in Science, Technology, and Humanities* (New York: John Wiley & Sons).

Garvin, Paul L. 1954. Review of Louis Hjelmslev, *Prolegomena to a Theory of Language, Language* 30, no. 1:69–96.

Gazdar, Gerald. 1979. *Pragmatics: Implicature, Presupposition and Logical Form* (New York: Academic Press).

Genette, Gerard. 1980 [1972]. *Narrative Discourse,* trans. Jane E. Lewin (Ithaca, N.Y.: Cornell University Press).

Gifford, Don, with Robert J. Seidman. 1988. "*Ulysses*" *Annotated: Notes for James Joyce's "Ulysses,"* 2d ed. (Berkeley and Los Angeles: University of California Press).

Gilbert, Stuart. 1958 [1930]. *James Joyce's "Ulysses": A Study* (New York: Vintage Books).

Givón, Talmy. 1979. *On Understanding Grammar* (New York: Academic Press).

———. 1984. *Syntax: A Functional-Typological Introduction,* vol. 1 (Philadelphia: John Benjamins).

Gödel, Kurt. 1931. "Über formal unentscheidbare Sätze der Principia Mathematica und verwandter Systeme I," *Monatshefte für Mathematik und Physik* 38:173–98.

Goldberg, Jonathan. 1990. *Writing Matter: From the Hands of the English Renaissance* (Stanford, Calif.: Stanford University Press).

Green, Georgia A. 1989. *Pragmatics and Natural Language Understanding* (Hillsdale, N.J.: Lawrence Erlbaum).

Greenlee, Douglas. 1973. *Peirce's Concept of Sign* (The Hague: Mouton).

Greimas, Algirdas Julien. 1983 [1966]. *Structural Semantics,* trans. Daniele McDowell, Ronald Schleifer, and Alan Velie (Lincoln: University of Nebraska Press).

———. 1987 [1969]. "Elements of a Narrative Grammar," in *On Meaning: Selected Writings in Semiotic Theory,* trans. Paul J. Perron and Frank H. Collins, 63–83 (Minneapolis: University of Minnesota Press).

Greimas, Algirdas J., and François Rastier. 1987 [1968]. "The Interaction of Semiotic Constraints," in *On Meaning,* trans. Paul J. Perron and Frank H. Collins, 48–62 (Minneapolis: University of Minnesota Press).

Grice, Paul. 1989. *Studies in the Way of Words* (Cambridge, Mass.: Harvard University Press).

Grünbaum, Adolf. 1967. "[The] Philosophical Significance of Relativity Theory," in *The Encyclopedia of Philosophy,* vol. 7, ed. Paul Edwards, 133–40 (New York: Macmillan Publishing Co.).

Gurwitsch, Aron. 1977 [1950]. "Outlines of a Theory of 'Essentially Occasional Expressions,'" ed. Lester Embree, in Mohanty (1977: 112–27).

Haaparanta, Leila. 1988. "Frege and His German Contemporaries on Alethic Modalities," in *Modern Modalities: Studies of the History of Modal Theories from Medieval Nominalism to Logical Positivism*, ed. S. Knuuttila, 239–74 (Dordrecht: Kluwer Academic Publishers).

Habermas, Jürgen. 1971 [1968]. *Knowledge and Human Interests*, trans. Jeremy Shapiro (Boston: Beacon Press).

——. 1975 [1973]. *Legitimation Crisis*, trans. Thomas McCarthy (Boston: Beacon Press).

——. 1976. "Was heißt Universalpragmatik?" in *Sprachpragmatik und Philosophie*, ed. Karl-Otto Apel, 174–272 (Frankfurt am Main: Suhrkamp Verlag).

——. 1984 [1981]. *Theory of Communicative Action*, vols. 1 and 2, trans. Thomas McCarthy (Boston: Beacon Press).

Haller, Rudolf, ed. 1972. *Jenseits von Sein und Nichtsein: Beiträge zur Meinong-Forschung* (Graz: Akademische Druck & Verlaganstalt).

Halliday, M. A. K. 1961. "Categories of the Theory of Grammar," *Word* 17, no. 2:241–92.

Halliday, M. A. K., and Ruqaiya Hasan. 1976. *Cohesion in English* (London: Longman).

Hanson, Norwood Russell. 1967. "Philosophical Implications of Quantum Mechanics," in *The Encyclopedia of Philosophy*, vol. 7, ed. Paul Edwards, 41–49 (New York: Macmillan Publishing Co.).

Haraway, Donna. 1985. "A Manifesto for Cyborgs: Science, Technology, and Socialist Feminism in the 1980s," *Socialist Review* 15, nos. 79–84: 65–107.

Harris, Zellig. 1952. "Discourse Analysis," *Language* 28:1–30.

Hayman, David. 1985. "James Joyce, Paratactician," *Contemporary Literature* 26, no. 2:155–78.

Hayman, Ronald. 1982. *Kafka: A Biography* (New York: Oxford University Press).

Heath, Stephen. 1981. *Questions of Cinema* (Bloomington: Indiana University Press).

——. 1984. "Ambiviolences: Notes for Reading Joyce," in *Poststructuralist Joyce: Essays from the French*, ed. Derek Attridge and Daniel Ferrer, 31–68 (Cambridge: Cambridge University Press).

Hebel, Udo J., ed. 1989. *Intertextuality, Allusion, and Quotation: An International Bibliography of Critical Studies* (New York: Greenwood Press).

Heidegger, Martin. 1977 [1955]. "The Question concerning Technology," in *The Question concerning Technology and Other Essays*, trans. William Lovitt, 3–35 (New York: Harper & Row).

——. 1978 [1915]. *Die Kategorien- und Bedeutungslehre des Duns Scotus*, in *Gesamtausgabe*, 1:189–411 (Frankfurt am Main: Vittorio Klosterman).

Heidsieck, Arnold. 1984. "Kafka's Narrative Ontology," *Philosophy and Literature* 11:242–57.

——. 1986. "Logic and Ontology in Kafka's Fiction," *Germanic Review* 61:11–17.

——. 1989. "Physiological, Phenomenological and Linguistic Psychology in Kafka's Early Works," *German Quarterly* 62:489–500.

Heinekamp, Albert. 1976. "Sprache und Wirklichkeit bei Leibniz," in Parret (1976: 518–70).

Hendricks, William O. 1967. "On the Notion 'Beyond the Sentence,'" *Linguistics* 37:12–51.

Herf, Jeffrey. 1984. *Reactionary Modernism: Technology, Culture and Politics in Weimar and the Third Reich* (Cambridge: Cambridge University Press).

Herman, David. 1991a. "The Incoherence of Kant's Transcendental Dialectic: Specifying the Minimal Conditions for Dialectical Error," *Dialectica* 45, no. 1:1–29.

——. 1991b. "Modernism versus Postmodernism: Towards an Analytic Distinction," *Poetics Today* 12, no. 1:55–86.

——. 1991c. "Pragmatika, Prag-matika, meta-pragmatika: Kontexty pragmatických kontextů," *Česká Literatura* 3:220–41.

——. 1992a. "Meaning, Model-Theoretic Semantics and Model-Worlds," *Journal of Literary Semantics* 21, no. 1:55–73.

——. 1992b. "Pragmatics, Prague-matics, Metapragmatics: Contextualizing Pragmatic Contexts," *Neophilologus* 76:321–46.

——. 1993a. "Postmodernism as Secondary Grammar," *boundary 2* 20, no. 2:205–29.

——. 1993b. Review of Jean-François Lyotard, *Phenomenology, Sub-Stance* 70:112–16.

——. 1993c. "Towards a Pragmatics of Represented Discourse: Narrative, Speech and Context in Woolf's *Between the Acts*," *Poetics* 21:377–409.

——. 1993d. "*Ulysses* and Vacuous Pluralism," *Philosophy and Literature* 17, no. 1:65–76.

——. 1994a. "Hypothetical Focalization," *Narrative* 2, no. 3:230–53.

——. 1994b. "The Mutt and Jute Dialogue in Joyce's *Finnegans Wake:* Some Gricean Perspectives," *Style* 28, no. 2:219–41.

——. 1994c. "On the Semantic Status of Film: Subjectivity, Possible Worlds, Transcendental Semiotics," *Semiotica* 99, nos. 1–2:5–27.

——. 1994d. " 'Sirens' after Schönberg," *James Joyce Quarterly* 31, no. 4:473–94.

——. 1994e. "Textual *You* and Double Deixis in *A Pagan Place*," *Style*. 28, no. 3:378–410.

——. In press a. "Rethinking the Ricorso: Reflexivity and Recursion in *Finnegans Wake*," *Language and Style*.

——. In preparation. *Narratology after Structuralism: New Directions in Narrative Theory*.

Hermanns, Fritz. 1977. *Die Kalkülisierung der Grammatik: Philologische Untersuchungen zu Ursprung, Entwicklung und Erfolg der sprachwissenschaftlichen Theorien Noam Chomskys* (Heidelberg: Julius Groos).

Hernadi, Paul. 1972. "Dual Perspective: Free Indirect Discourse and Related Techniques," *Comparative Literature* 24, no. 1:32–43.

Hiebert, Erwin N. 1990. "The Transformations of Physics," in *Fin de Siècle and Its Legacy*, ed. Mikulás Teich and Roy Porter, 235–53 (Cambridge: Cambridge University Press).

Hintikka, Jaakko. 1962. *Knowledge and Belief: An Introduction to the Logic of the Two Notions* (Ithaca, N.Y.: Cornell University Press).

——. 1969. *Models for Modalities* (Dordrecht: D. Reidel).

——. 1989a. "Exploring Possible Worlds," in Allén (1989:52–73).

——. 1989b. "On Sense, Reference, and the Objects of Knowledge," in *The Logic of Epistemology and the Epistemology of Logic: Selected Essays*, ed. J. Hintikka and M. Hintikka, 45–62 (Dordrecht: Kluwer Academic Publishers).

Hintikka, Jaakko, and Merrill B. Hintikka, eds. 1989. *The Logic of Epistemology and the Epistemology of Logic* (Dordrecht: Kluwer Academic Publishers).

Hirst, R. J. 1967. "Phenomenalism," in *The Encyclopedia of Philosophy*, vol. 6, ed. Paul Edwards, 130–35 (New York: Macmillan Publishing Co.).

Hjelmslev, Louis. 1969 [1943]. *Prolegomena to a Theory of Language*, trans. Francis J. Whitfield (Madison: University of Wisconsin Press).

——. 1971a. *Essais linguistiques* (Paris: Minuit).

——. 1971b [1948]. "L'Analyse structurale du langage," in Hjelmslev (1971a: 34–41).

——. 1971c [1943]. "Langue et parole," in Hjelmslev (1971a: 77–89).

Hoesterey, Ingeborg. 1988. *Verschlungene Schriftzeichen: Intertextualität von Literatur und Kunst in der Moderne/Postmoderne* (Frankfurt am Main: Athenäum).

Hofstadter, Douglas R. 1979. *Gödel, Escher, Bach: An Eternal Golden Braid* (New York: Vintage Books).

Holenstein, Elmar. 1979a. "Einfuhrung: Von der Poesie und der Plurifunktionalität der Sprache," in *Roman Jakobson Poetik: Ausgewahlte Aufsatze, 1921–71*, ed. Elmar Holenstein, 7–60 (Frankfurt am Main: Suhrkamp Verlag).

——. 1979b. "Prague Structuralism—a Branch of the Phenomenological Movement," in *Language, Literature and Meaning I: Problems of Literary Theory*, ed. John Odmark, 71–97 (Amsterdam: John Benjamins).

Horkheimer, Max. 1972 [1968]. *Critical Theory: Selected Essays*, trans. Matthew J. O'Connell and others (New York: Herder & Herder).

——. 1974 [1967]. *Critique of Instrumental Reason*, trans. Matthew J. O'Connell and others (New York: Seabury Press).

Horkheimer, Max, and Theodor Adorno. 1988 [1944]. *Dialectic of Enlightenment*, trans. John Cumming (New York: Continuum).

Horrocks, Geoffrey. 1987. *Generative Grammar* (London: Longman).

Husserl, Edmund. 1939. *Erfahrung und Urteil: Untersuchungen zur Genealogie der Logik*, ed. Ludwig Landgrebe (Prague: Academia/Verlagsbuchhandlung).

——. 1969 [1929]. *Formal and Transcendental Logic*, trans. Dorion Cairns (The Hague: Martinus Nijhoff).

——. 1970 [1937–39]. *The Crisis of European Sciences: An Introduction to Phenomenological Philosophy*, trans. David Carr (Evanston, Ill.: Northwestern University Press).

——. 1970 [1913]. *Logical Investigations*, vols. 1 and 2, trans. J. N. Findlay (London: Routledge & Kegan Paul).

——. 1973 [1939]. *Experience and Judgment: Investigations in a Genealogy of Logic*, ed. Ludwig Landgrebe, trans. James S. Churchill and Karl Ameriks (Evanston, Ill.: Northwestern University Press).

——. 1979a [1890–1910]. *Aufsätze und Rezensionen (1890–1910)*, in *Husserliana*, vol. 22, ed. Bernhard Rang (The Hague: Martinus Nijhoff).

——. 1979b [1891]. "Beilage I: Aus Entwürfen Husserls zu seiner Schröder-Rezension," in Husserl (1979a [1890–1910]: 381–99).

——. 1979c [1910]. "Besprechung von A. Marty, *Untersuchungen zur Grundlegung der allgemeinen Grammatik und Sprachphilosophie*," in Husserl (1979a [1890–1910]: 261–65).

——. 1979d [1891]. "Besprechung von E. Schröder, *Vorlesungen über die Algebra der Logik (Exakte Logik)*," in Husserl (1979a [1890–1910]: 3–43).

——. 1979e [1891]. "Der Folgerungskalkül und die Inhaltslogik," in Husserl (1979a [1890–1910]: 44–66).

——. 1979f [1894]. "Intensionale Gegenstände," in Husserl (1979a [1890–1910]: 303–48).

——. 1981a [1887]. "On the Concept of Number: Psychological Analyses," trans. Dallas Willard, in *Shorter Works*, ed. Peter McCormick and Frederick A. Elliston, 92–119 (Notre Dame, Ind.: University of Notre Dame Press).

——. 1981b [1910–11]. "Philosophy as Rigorous Science," trans. Quentin Lauer, in *Shorter Works*, ed.

Peter McCormick and Frederick A. Elliston, 166–97 (Notre Dame, Ind.: University of Notre Dame Press).

——. 1984 [1913]. *Logische Untersuchungen,* in *Husserliana,* vol. 19, ed. Ursula Panzer (The Hague: Martinus Nijhoff).

Hutchison, Chris. 1984. "The Act of Narration: A Critical Survey of Some Speech-Act Theories of Narrative Discourse," *Journal of Literary Semantics* 13, no. 1:3–34.

Jakobson, Roman. 1960. "Closing Statement: Linguistics and Poetics," in *Style in Language,* ed. Thomas A. Sebeok, 350–77 (Cambridge, Mass.: MIT Press).

——. 1971a [1936]. "Die Arbeit der sogennanten 'Prager Schule,'" in *Selected Writings,* 2:547–50 (The Hague: Mouton).

——. 1971b [1935]. "The Dominant," in *Readings in Russian Poetics: Formalist and Structuralist Views,* ed. Ladislav Matejka and Krystyna Pomorska, 82–87 (Cambridge, Mass.: MIT Press).

——. 1971c [1966]. "Retrospect," in *Selected Writings,* 2:709–22 (The Hague: Mouton).

——. 1971d [1957]. "Shifters, Verbal Categories and the Russian Verb," in *Selected Writings,* 2:130–47 (The Hague: Mouton).

——. 1971e [1954]. "Two Aspects of Language and Two Types of Aphasic Disturbances," in *Selected Writings,* 2:239–59 (The Hague: Mouton).

James, William. 1948 [1907]. "Pragmatism's Conception of Truth," in *Essays in Pragmatism,* ed. Alburey Castell, 159–76 (New York: Hafner Publishing Co.).

Jameson, Fredric. 1972. *The Prison-House of Language: A Critical Account of Structuralism and Russian Formalism* (Princeton, N.J.: Princeton University Press).

——. 1977. "Imaginary and Symbolic in Lacan: Marxism, Psychoanalytic Criticism, and the Problem of the Subject," *Yale French Studies* 55/56:338–95.

——. 1981. *The Political Unconscious: Narrative as a Socially Symbolic Act* (Ithaca, N.Y.: Cornell University Press).

——. 1987. "Reading without Interpretation: Postmodernism and the Video Text," in *The Linguistics of Writing: Arguments between Language and Literature,* ed. Nigel Fabb, Derek Attridge, Alan Durant, and Colin MacCabe, 199–223 (New York: Methuen).

Jamme, Christoph, and Otto Pöggeler, eds. 1989. *Phänomenologie im Widerstreit: Zum 50. Todestag Edmund Husserls* (Frankfurt am Main: Suhrkamp Taschenbuch Verlag).

Janik, Allan, and Stephen Toulmin. 1973. *Wittgenstein's Vienna* (New York: Simon & Schuster).

Jespersen, Otto. 1965 [1924]. *The Philosophy of Grammar* (New York: W. W. Norton & Co.).

Jolas, Eugene. 1974 [1936]. "The Revolution of Language and James Joyce," in *An Exagmination of James Joyce,* ed. Samuel Beckett, 77–92 (New York: Haskell House).

Jørgensen, Jørgen. 1932. "Über die Ziele und Probleme der Logistik," *Erkenntnis* 3, no. 1:73–100.

——. 1939. "Reflexions on Language and Logic," *Journal of Unified Science* (*Erkenntnis*) 8, no. 4:218–28.

Joyce, James. 1939. *Finnegans Wake* (New York: Viking Penguin).

——. 1986 [1922]. *Ulysses,* ed. Hans Walter Gabler (New York: Random House).

Juhos, Béla. 1967. "Moritz Schlick," trans. Albert E. Blumberg, in *The Encyclopedia of Philosophy,* vol. 7, ed. Paul Edwards, 319–24 (New York: Macmillan Publishing Co.).

Kafka, Franz. 1956 [1925]. *The Trial,* trans. Willa Muir and Edwin Muir, rev. E. M. Butler (New York: Schocken Books).

——. 1986 [1925]. *Der Prozeß* (Frankfurt am Main: Fischer Taschenbuch Verlag).

Kalish, Donald. 1967. "Semantics," in *The Encyclopedia of Philosophy,* vol. 7, ed. Paul Edwards, 348–58 (New York: Macmillan Publishing Co.).

Kalsi, Marie-Luise Schubert. 1978. *Alexius Meinong: On Objects of Higher Order and Husserl's Phenomenology* (The Hague: Martinus Nijhoff).

Kant, Immanuel. 1965 [1781/1787]. *Critique of Pure Reason,* 1st and 2d (A and B) eds., trans. Norman Kemp Smith (New York: St. Martin's Press).

Karcevskij, Sergej. 1982 [1929]. "The Asymmetric Dualism of the Linguistic Sign," trans. Wendy Steiner, in Peter Steiner (1982: 47–54).

Katz, Jerrold J. 1972. *Semantic Theory* (New York: Harper & Row).

Kenner, Hugh. 1987a [1956]. *Dublin's Joyce* (New York: Columbia University Press).

——. 1987b [1980]. *Ulysses,* 2d ed. (Baltimore: Johns Hopkins University Press).

Kessler, Susanne. 1983. *Kafka: Poetik der sinnlichen Welt* (Stuttgart: J. B. Metzlersche).

Klockow, Reinhard. 1980. *Linguistik der Gänsfüßchen: Untersuchungen zum Gebrauch der Anführungszeichen im gegenwärtigen Deutsch* (Frankfurt am Main: Haag & Herchen).

Knobloch, Clemens. 1984. "Sprache und Denken bei Wundt, Paul und Marty," *Historiographica Linguistica* 11:413–48.

Körner, Stephan. 1960. *The Philosophy of Mathematics* (London: Hutchinson University Library).

Kraft, Victor. 1953 [1950]. *The Vienna Circle: The Origin of Neo-Positivism,* trans. Arthur Pap (New York: Philosophical Library).

Kripke, Saul A. 1980. *Naming and Necessity* (Cambridge, Mass.: Harvard University Press).

Kristeva, Julia. 1980. *Desire in Language: A Semiotic Approach to Literature and Art,* ed. Leon S. Roudiez, trans. Thomas Gora, Alice Jardine, and Leon Roudiez (New York: Columbia University Press).

——. 1984 [1974]. *Revolution in Poetic Language,* trans. Margaret Waller (New York: Columbia University Press).

Kuhn, Thomas. 1989. "Possible Worlds in History of Science," in Allén (1989: 9–32).

Kundera, Milan. 1988 [1986]. *The Art of the Novel,* trans. Linda Asher (New York: Grove Press).

Kurz, Gerhard. 1987. "Meinungen zur Schrift: Zur Exegeses der Legende 'Vor dem Gesetz' im Roman 'Der Prozeß,'" in *Frank Kafka und das Judentum,* ed. Karl Erich Grözinger et al., 209–23 (Frankfurt am Main: Athenäum).

——. 1989. "Nietzsche, Freud, Kafka," in *Reading Kafka: Prague, Politics and the Fin de Siecle,* ed. Mark Anderson, 128–48 (New York: Schocken Books).

Labov, William, and Joshua Waletzky. 1967. "Narrative Analysis: Oral Versions of Personal Experience," in *Essays on the Verbal and Visual Arts,* ed. June Helm, 12–44 (Seattle: University of Washington Press).

Lacan, Jacques. 1953. "Some Reflections on the Ego," *International Journal of Psycho-Analysis* 34:11–17.

——. 1968 [1956]. *The Language of the Self: The Function of Language in Psychoanalysis,* trans. Anthony Wilden (Baltimore: Johns Hopkins University Press).

——. 1977a [1957]. "The Agency of the Letter in the Unconscious, or Reason since Freud," in Lacan (1977b: 146–78).

——. 1977b. *Écrits: A Selection,* trans. Alan Sheridan (New York: W. W. Norton & Co.).

——. 1977c [1953]. "The Function and Field of Speech and Language in Psychoanalysis," in Lacan (1977b: 30–113).

———. 1977d [1949]. "The Mirror Stage as Formative of the Function of the I as Revealed in Psycho-analytic Experience," in Lacan (1977: 1–7).

Lacey, A. R. 1986. *A Dictionary of Philosophy*, 2d ed. (London: Routledge).

Laplanche, J., and J.-B. Pontalis. 1973 [1967]. *The Language of Psychoanalysis*, trans. Donald Nich-olson Smith (New York: W. W. Norton & Co.).

Lawrence, Karen. 1981. *The Odyssey of Style in "Ulysses"* (Princeton, N.J.: Princeton University Press).

Leech, Geoffrey. 1983. *Principles of Pragmatics* (London: Longman).

Leech, Geoffrey, and Michael Short. 1981. *Style in Fiction: A Linguistic Introduction to English Fictional Prose* (London: Longman).

Lees, Heath. 1984. "The Introduction to 'Sirens' and the *Fuga per Canonem*," *James Joyce Quarterly* 22, no. 1: 39–54.

Leibniz, Gottfried Wilhelm. 1973 [1683]. "On Universal Synthesis and Analysis, or the Art of Discovery and Judgment," in *Philosophical Writings*, ed. G. H. R. Parkinson, trans. Mary Morris and G. H. R. Parkinson, 10–17 (London: Dent).

———. 1981 [1765]. *New Essays on Human Understanding*, trans. and ed. Peter Remnant and Jonathan Bennett (Cambridge: Cambridge University Press).

Levinson, Stephen C. 1983. *Pragmatics* (Cambridge: Cambridge University Press).

Lévi-Strauss, Claude. 1963 [1958]. *Structural Anthropology*, trans. Claire Jacobson and Brooke G. Schoepf (New York: Basic Books).

———. 1969 [1964]. *The Raw and the Cooked*, trans. John Weightman and Doreen Weightman (New York: Harper & Row).

Lewis, C. I., and C. H. Langford. 1932. *Symbolic Logic* (New York: Century Press).

Lewis, David. 1973. *Counterfactuals* (Cambridge, Mass.: Harvard University Press).

Liddenfield, David. 1980. *The Transformation of Positivism: Alexius Meinong and European Thought, 1880–1920* (Berkeley and Los Angeles: University of California Press).

Lightfoot, David. 1988. "Syntactic Change," in *Linguistics: The Cambridge Survey*, vol. 1, ed. Freder-ick J. Newmeyer, 303–23 (Cambridge: Cambridge University Press).

———. 1992. "Formal Grammar," in *International Encyclopedia of Linguistics*, vol. 2, ed. William Bright, 17–21 (New York: Oxford University Press).

Lips, Marguerite. 1926. *Le Style indirect libre* (Paris: Payot).

Litz, A. Walton. 1961. *The Art of James Joyce: Method and Design in "Ulysses" and "Finnegans Wake"* (London: Oxford University Press).

Lotman, Jurij, and Boris Uspenskij. 1986 [1971]. "On the Semiotic Mechanism of Culture," trans. George Mihaychuk, in *Critical Theory Since 1965*, eds. Hazard Adams and Leroy Searle, 410–22 (Tallahassee: University Presses of Florida).

Lucy, John A., ed. 1993. *Reflexive Language: Reported Speech and Metapragmatics* (Cambridge: Cambridge University Press).

Luening, Otto. 1980. *Odyssey of An American Composer: The Autobiography of Otto Luening* (New York: Charles Scribner's Sons).

Luft, David S. 1980. *Robert Musil and the Crisis of European Culture, 1880–1942* (Berkeley and Los Angeles: University of California Press).

Lyons, John. 1970. *Noam Chomsky* (New York: Viking Press).

———. 1977. *Semantics*, vols. 1 and 2 (Cambridge: Cambridge University Press).

———. 1991. *Natural Language and Universal Grammar* (Cambridge: Cambridge University Press).

Lyotard, Jean-François. 1984 [1979]. *The Postmodern Condition: A Report on Knowledge,* trans. Geoff Bennington and Brian Massumi (Minneapolis: University of Minnesota Press).

———. 1988a [1983]. *The Differend,* trans. George Van Den Abbeele (Minneapolis: University of Minnesota Press).

———. 1988b. *Peregrinations: Law, Form, Event* (New York: Columbia University Press).

MacCabe, Colin. 1978. *James Joyce and the Revolution of the Word* (London: Macmillan Publishing Co.).

McCabe, Francis G. 1992. *Logic and Objects* (New York: Prentice-Hall).

McElroy, Joseph. 1987. *Plus* (New York: Carroll & Graff).

McGee, Patrick. 1988. *Paperspace: Style as Ideology in Joyce's "Ulysses"* (Lincoln: University of Nebraska Press).

Mach, Ernst. 1902 [1886]. *Die Analyse der Empfindungen und das Verhältnis des Physischen zum Psychischen,* 3d ed. (Jena: Gustav Fischer).

McHale, Brian. 1978. "Free Indirect Discourse: A Survey of Recent Accounts," *PTL* 3:249–88.

———. 1990. "Constructing (Post)Modernism: The Case of *Ulysses,*" *Style* 24, no. 1:1–21.

———. 1992. *Constructing Postmodernism* (London: Routledge).

Mahaffey, Vicki. 1988a. *Reauthorizing Joyce* (Cambridge: Cambridge University Press).

———. 1988b. "Wagner, Joyce and Revolution," *James Joyce Quarterly* 25, no. 2:237–47.

Mally, Ernst. 1912. *Gegenstandstheoretische Grundlagen der Logik und Logistik,* in *Zeitschrift für Philosophie und philosophischen Kritik,* vol. 148 (Leipzig: Johann Ambrosius Barth).

———. 1971 [1941–44]. *Logische Schriften,* ed. Karl Wolf and Paul Weingartner (Dordrecht: D. Reidel).

Marciszewski, Witold. 1988. "Towards Universal Grammars: Carnap's and Ajdukiewicz' Contributions," in *The Vienna Circle and the Lvov-Warsaw School,* ed. Klemens Szaniawski, 87–112 (Dordrecht: Kluwer Academic Publishers).

Margolin, Uri. 1984. "Narrative and Indexicality: A Tentative Framework," *Journal of Literary Semantics* 13, no. 3:181–204.

———. 1986. "Dispersing/Voiding the Subject: A Narratological Perspective," *Texte* 5/6:181–210.

———. 1991. "Structuralist Approaches to Character in Narrative: The State of the Art," *Semiotica* 75, no. 1–2:1–24.

Martin, Timothy, and Ruth Bauerle. 1992. "The Voice from the Prompt Box: Otto Luening Remembers James Joyce in Zurich," *Journal of Modern Literature* 17, no. 1:35–48.

Martin, Wallace. 1986. *Recent Theories of Narrative* (Ithaca, N.Y.: Cornell University Press).

Martínez-Bonati, Félix. 1981. *Fictive Discourse and the Structures of Literature: A Phenomenological Approach,* trans. Philip W. Silver (Ithaca, N.Y.: Cornell University Press).

Martinich, A. P., ed. 1990. *The Philosophy of Language,* 2d ed. (Oxford: Oxford University Press).

Marty, Anton. 1918 [1893]. "Über das Verhältnis von Grammatik und Logik," in *Gesammelte Schriften,* vol. 2, part 2, ed. Josef Eisenmeier et al., 59–99 (Halle: Max Niemeyer).

———. 1976 [1908]. *Untersuchungen zur Grundlegung der allgemeinen Grammatik und Sprachphilosophie* (Hildesheim: Georg Olms).

Matthews, P. H. 1981. *Syntax* (Cambridge: Cambridge University Press).

———. 1993. *Grammatical Theory in the United States from Bloomfield to Chomsky* (Cambridge: Cambridge University Press).

Meinong, Alexius. 1971 [1904]. "Über Gegenstandstheorie," in *Gesamtausgabe,* vol. 2, ed. Rudolf Haller et al., 481–530 (Graz: Akademische Druck- und Verlagsanstalt).

——. 1972 [1917]. *On Emotional Presentation*, trans. Marie-Luise Schubert Kalsi (Evanston, Ill.: Northwestern University Press).

——. 1977 [1902]. *Über Annahmen*, in *Gesamtausgabe*, vol. 4, ed. Rudolf Haller et al. (Graz: Akademische Druck- und Verlagsanstalt).

——. 1978 [1899]. "On Objects of Higher Order and Their Relationship to Internal Perception," trans. Marie-Luise Schubert Kalsi, in Kalsi (1978: 137–208).

Menger, Karl. 1985. *Beamte: Wirtschafts- und sozialgeschichtliche Aspekte des k. k. Beamtentums* (Vienna: Verlag der Österreichischen Akademie der Wissenschaften).

Metz, Christian. 1974a [1968]. *Film Language: A Semiotics of Cinema*, trans. Michael Taylor (New York: Oxford University Press).

——. 1974b. *Language and Cinema*, trans. Donna Jean Umriker-Sebeok (The Hague: Mouton).

——. 1982 [1977]. *The Imaginary Signifier: Psychoanalysis and the Cinema* (Bloomington: Indiana University Press).

Miles, David H. 1983. " 'Pleats, Pockets, Buckles, and Buttons': Kafka's New Literalism and the Poetics of the Fragment," in *Probleme der Moderne: Studien zur deutschen Literatur von Nietzsche bis Brecht*, ed. Benjamin Bennett el al., 331–42 (Tübingen: Max Niemeyer).

Miller, Jacques-Alain. 1977–78. "Suture (Elements of the Logic of the Signifier)," trans. Jacqueline Rose, *Screen* 18, no. 4:24–34.

Mohanty, J. N., ed. 1977. *Readings on Edmund Husserl's "Logical Investigations"* (The Hague: Martinus Nijhoff).

——. 1982. *Husserl and Frege* (Bloomington: Indiana University Press).

Montague, Richard. 1974. *Formal Philosophy: Selected Papers of Richard Montague*, ed. Richmond H. Thomason (New Haven, Conn.: Yale University Press).

Morawski, Stefan. 1970. "The Basic Functions of Quotation," in *Sign, Language, Culture*, ed. A. J. Greimas, R. Jakobson, et al., 690–705 (The Hague: Mouton).

Morris, Charles. 1938. *Foundations of the Theory of Signs* (Chicago: University of Chicago Press).

Morrison, James. 1992. "Deleuze and Film Semiotics," *Semiotica* 88, nos. 3/4:269–90.

Morscher, Edgar. 1972. "Von Bolzano zu Meinong: Zur Geschichte des logischen Realismus," in Haller (1972: 69–102).

Mountford, John. 1969. "Writing," in *Encyclopedia of Linguistics, Information and Control*, ed. A. R. Meetham and R. A. Hudson, 627–33 (Oxford: Pergamon Press).

Mukařovský, Jan. 1970 [1936]. *Aesthetic Function, Norm and Value as Social Facts*, trans. Mark E. Suino (Ann Arbor: University of Michigan Press).

——. 1976 [1936]. "Poetic Reference," in *Semiotics of Art: Prague School Contributions*, ed. and trans. Ladislav Matejka and Irwin R. Titnik, 155–63 (Cambridge, Mass.: MIT Press).

——. 1977 [1940]. "On Poetic Language," in *The Word and Verbal Art*, ed. and trans. John Burbank and Peter Steiner, 1–64 (New Haven, Conn.: Yale University Press).

——. 1978a [1937]. "The Aesthetic Norm," in *Structure, Sign, and Function*, ed. and trans. John Burbank and Peter Steiner, 49–56 (New Haven, Conn.: Yale University Press).

——. 1978b [1934]. "Art as a Semiotic Fact," in *Structure, Sign, and Function*, ed. and trans. John Burbank and Peter Steiner, 82–88 (New Haven, Conn.: Yale University Press).

——. 1978c [1937–38]. "On the Problem of Functions in Architecture," in *Structure, Sign, and Function*, ed. and trans. John Burbank and Peter Steiner, 236–50 (New Haven, Conn.: Yale University Press).

——. 1978d [1942]. "The Place of the Aesthetic Function among the Other Functions," in *Structure, Sign, and Function*, ed. and trans. John Burbank and Peter Steiner, 31–48 (New Haven, Conn.: Yale University Press).

Mulligan, Kevin. 1985. " 'Wie die Sachen sich zueinander verhalten': Inside and Outside the *Tractatus*," *Teoria* 2:145–74.

Mulvey, Laura. 1988 [1975]. "Visual Pleasure and Narrative Cinema," in Penley (1988: 57–68).

Nagel, Ernest, and James R. Newman. 1958. *Gödel's Proof* (New York: New York University Press).

Nägele, Rainer. 1980. "Modernism and Postmodernism: The Margins of Articulation," *Studies in Twentieth-Century Literature* 5, no. 1:5–25.

Neesen, Peter. 1972. *Vom Louvrezirkel zum Prozeß: Franz Kafka und die Psychologie Franz Brentanos* (Göhingen: Alfred Kümmerle).

Nichols, Bill. 1981. *Ideology and the Image: Social Representation in the Cinema and Other Media* (Bloomington: Indiana University Press).

Niehoff, Rainer. 1991. *Die Herrschaft des Textes: Zitattechnik als Sprachkritik in Georg Büchners Drama "Dantons Tod" unter Berücksichtigung der "Letzten Tage der Menschheit" von Karl Kraus* (Tübingen: Max Niemeyer).

Nietzsche, Friedrich. 1968a [1886]. *Beyond Good and Evil*, in *Basic Writings*, ed. and trans. Walter Kaufmann, 181–435 (New York: Modern Library).

——. 1968b [1887]. *On the Genealogy of Morals*, in *Basic Writings*, ed. and trans. Walter Kaufmann, 451–599 (New York: Modern Library).

Oblau, Gotthard. 1979. "Erkenntnis- und Kommunikationsfunktion der Sprache in Franz Kafkas 'Der Prozeß,' " in *Zu Franz Kafka*, ed. Gunter Heintz, 209–29 (Stuttgart: Klett-Cotta).

Oudart, Jean-Pierre. 1977–78. "Cinema and Suture," trans. Kari Hanet, *Screen* 18, no. 4:35–47.

Page, Norman. 1973. *Speech in the English Novel* (London: Longman).

Palmer, F. R. 1981. *Semantics*, 2d ed. (Cambridge: Cambridge University Press).

——. 1990. *Modality and the English Modals*, 2d ed. (London: Longman).

Parret, Herman. 1983. *Semiotics and Pragmatics: An Evaluative Comparison of Conceptual Frameworks* (Amsterdam: John Benjamins).

——, ed. 1976. *History of Linguistic Thought and Contemporary Linguistics* (Berlin: Walter de Gruyter).

Parsons, Terence. 1980. *Nonexistent Objects* (New Haven, Conn.: Yale University Press).

Partee, Barbara H. 1989. "Possible Worlds in Model-Theoretic Semantics: A Linguistic Perspective," in Allén (1989: 93–123).

Pascal, Roy. 1977. *The Dual Voice* (Manchester: Manchester University Press).

Patzig, Günther. 1969. "Vorwort," in Frege (1969a: 3–16).

Paul, Lothar. 1978. *Geschichte der Grammatik im Grundriß: Sprachdidaktik als angewandte Erkenntnistheorie und Wissenschaftskritik* (Weinheim and Basel: Beltz Verlag).

Pavel, Thomas. 1973. "Remarks on Narrative Grammars," *Poetics* 8:5–30.

——. 1976. *La Syntaxe narrative des tragedies de Corneilles* (Paris: Klincksieck).

——. 1985a. "Literary Narratives," in *Discourse and Literature*, ed. Teun A. van Dijk, 83–104 (Amsterdam: John Benjamins).

——. 1985b. *The Poetics of Plot: The Case of English Renaissance Drama* (Minneapolis: University of Minnesota Press).

——. 1986. *Fictional Worlds* (Cambridge, Mass.: Harvard University Press).

———. 1989. *The Feud of Language: A History of Structuralist Thought,* trans. Linda Jordan and Thomas G. Pavel (Cambridge: Basil Blackwell).

Peirce, C. S. 1955 [1897–1903]. "Logic as Semiotic: The Theory of Signs," in *Philosophical Writings of Peirce,* ed. Justus Buchler, 98–119 (New York: Dover Publishers).

———. 1982 [1865]. "Logic of the Sciences," in *Writings of Charles S. Peirce: A Chronological Edition,* vol. 1, ed. Max H. Fisch et al., 322–36 (Bloomington: Indiana University Press).

Penley, Constance. 1989. *Future of an Illusion: Film, Feminism, and Psychoanalysis* (Minneapolis: University of Minnesota Press).

———, ed. 1988. *Feminism and Film Theory* (New York: Routledge).

Perri, Carmela. 1978. "On Alluding," *Poetics* 7:289–307.

Petöfi, János S. 1990. "Language as a Written Medium: Text," in *An Encyclopedia of Language,* ed. N. E. Collinge, 207–43 (London: Routledge).

Petrilli, Susan. 1990. "On the Semiotics of Interpretation: Introduction," in Gérard Deledalle, *Charles S. Peirce: An Intellectual Biography,* trans. Susan Petrilli, xi–xxvii (Amsterdam: John Benjamins).

Pfister, Manfred. 1985. "Konzepte der Intertextualität," in *Intertextualität: Formen, Funktionen, anglistische Fallstudien,* ed. Ulrich Broich and Manfred Pfister, 1–30 (Tübingen: Max Niemeyer).

Phelan, James. 1981. *Worlds from Words: A Theory of Language in Fiction* (Chicago: University of Chicago Press).

———. 1989. *Reading People, Reading Plots: Character, Progression, and the Interpretation of Narrative* (Chicago: University of Chicago Press).

Picardi, Eva. 1987. "The Logics of Frege's Contemporaries, or 'der verderbliche Einbruch der Psychologie in die Logik,' " in Buzzetti and Ferriani (1987: 174–204).

Pinson, Lewis J., and Richard S. Wiener. 1991. *Objective-C: Object-Oriented Programming Techniques* (Reading, Mass.: Addison-Wesley Publishing Co.).

Plett, Heinrich. 1975. *Textwissenschaft und Textanalyse: Semiotik, Linguistik, Rhetorik* (Heidelberg: Quelle & Meyer).

———. 1985. "Sprachliche Konstituenten einer intertextuellen Poetik," in *Intertextualität: Formen, Funktionen, anglistische Fallstudien,* ed. Ulrich Broich and Manfred Pfister, 78–98 (Tübingen: Max Niemeyer).

Plotnitsky, Arkady. 1983. "The Razor's Edge: Parsimony, Proof, Power" (paper delivered at the World Congress of Aesthetics, Montréal, August).

———. 1987. "Interpretation, Interminability, Evaluation: From Nietzsche toward a General Economy," in *Life after Postmodernism: Essays on Value and Culture,* ed. John Fekete, 120–41 (New York: St. Martin's Press).

———. 1993. *Reconfigurations: Critical Theory and General Economy* (Gainesville: University Presses of Florida).

———. 1994. *Complementarity: Anti-Epistemology after Bohr and Derrida* (Durham, N.C.: Duke University Press).

Porush, David. 1985. *The Soft Machine: Cybernetic Fiction* (New York: Methuen).

Pratt, Mary Louise. 1977. *Toward a Speech Act Theory of Literary Discourse* (Bloomington: Indiana University Press).

———. 1986. "Ideology and Speech-Act Theory," *Poetics Today* 7, no. 1:59–73.

Prince, Ellen F. 1988. "Discourse Analysis: A Part of the Study of Linguistic Competence," in *Linguistics: The Cambridge Survey,* vol. 2, ed. Frederick J. Newmeyer, 164–82 (Cambridge: Cambridge University Press).

Prince, Gerald. 1973. *A Grammar of Stories* (The Hague: Mouton).

——. 1978. "Le Discours attributif et le récit," *Poetique* 35:305–13.

——. 1980. "Aspects of a Grammar of Narrative," *Poetics Today* 1, no. 3:49–63.

——. 1982. *Narratology: The Form and Functioning of Narrative* (Berlin: Mouton).

——. 1983a. "Narrative Pragmatics, Message, and Point," *Poetics* 12:527–36.

——. 1983b. "Worlds with Style," *Philosophy and Literature* 7:59–65.

——. 1987. *A Dictionary of Narratology* (Lincoln: University of Nebraska Press).

——. 1988a. "The Disnarrated," *Style* 22, no. 1:1–8.

——. 1988b. "Narratological Illustrations," *Semiotica* 68, nos. 3–4:355–66.

——. 1991. "Narratology, Narrative, and Meaning," *Poetics Today* 12, no. 3:543–52.

——. 1992a. *Narrative as Theme: Studies in French Fiction* (Lincoln: University of Nebraska Press).

——. 1992b. "Remodeling Narratology," *Semiotica* 90, nos. 3–4:259–66.

——. In press. "Narratology," in *A Cambridge History of Literary Criticism,* vol. 8 (Cambridge: Cambridge University Press).

Propp, Vladimir. 1968 [1928]. *Morphology of the Folktale,* 2d ed., trans. Laurence Scott, rev. Louis A. Wagner (Austin: University of Texas Press).

Putnam, Hilary. 1971. *Philosophy of Logic* (New York: Harper & Row).

——. 1981. *Reason, Truth and History* (Cambridge: Cambridge University Press).

Quine, Willard Van Orman. 1960. *Word and Object* (Cambridge, Mass.: MIT Press).

——. 1980. *From a Logical Point of View,* 2d ed. (Cambridge, Mass.: Harvard University Press).

Rabaté, Jean-Michel. 1986. "The Silence of the Sirens," in *James Joyce: The Centennial Symposium,* ed. Morris Beja, 82–88 (Urbana: University of Illinois Press).

——. 1991 [1984]. *James Joyce: Authorized Reader* (Baltimore: Johns Hopkins University Press).

Radford, Andrew. 1981. *Transformational Syntax: A Student's Guide to Chomsky's Extended Standard Theory* (Cambridge: Cambridge University Press).

Riffaterre, Michael. 1981. "Interpretation and Undecidability," *New Literary History* 12:227–42.

——. 1983. *Text Production,* trans. Teresa Lyons (New York: Columbia University Press).

——. 1984. "Intertextual Representation: On Mimesis as Interpretive Discourse," *Critical Inquiry* 11:141–62.

Rimmon-Kenan, Shlomith. 1983. *Narrative Fiction: Contemporary Poetics* (London: Methuen).

——. 1989. "How the Model Neglects the Medium: Linguistics, Language, and the Crisis of Narratology," *Journal of Narrative Technique* 19, no. 1:157–66.

Roberts, Lawrence D. 1993. *How Reference Works: Explanatory Models for Indexicals, Descriptions, and Opacity* (Albany: State University of New York Press).

Robertson, Ritchie. 1985. " 'Antizionismus, Zionismus': Kafka's Responses to Jewish Nationalism," in *Paths and Labyrinths,* ed. J. P. Stern and J. J. White, 25–42 (London: Institute of Germanic Studies).

Robins, R. H. 1951. *Ancient and Medieval Grammatical Theory in Europe* (Port Washington, N.Y.: Kennikat Press).

——. 1976. "Some Continuities and Discontinuities in the History of Linguistics," in Parret (1976: 13–31).

——. 1989. *General Linguistics*, 4th ed. (London: Longman).

Ron, Moshe. 1981. "Free Indirect Discourse, Mimetic Language Games and the Subject of Fiction," *Poetics Today* 2, no. 2:17–39.

Ronen, Ruth. 1990. "Possible Worlds in Literary Theory: A Game in Interdisciplinarity," *Semiotica* 80, nos. 3–4:277–97.

——. 1994. *Possible Worlds in Literary Theory* (Cambridge: Cambridge University Press).

Rorty, Richard. 1970. "Introduction: Metaphilosophical Difficulties of Linguistic Philosophy," in *The Linguistic Turn*, ed. Richard Rorty, 1–39 (Chicago: University of Chicago Press).

——. 1972. "Indeterminacy of Translation and of Truth," *Synthese* 23:443–62.

——. 1982. "The World Well Lost," in *Consequences of Pragmatism*, 3–18 (Minneapolis: University of Minnesota Press).

Rose, Jacqueline. 1988 [1976–77]. "Paranoia and the Film System," in Penley (1988: 141–58).

Routley, Richard, and Valerie Routley. 1973. "Rehabilitating Meinong's Theory of Objects," *Revue Internationale de Philosophie* 27:224–54.

Russell, Bertrand. 1900. *A Critical Exposition of the Philosophy of Logic* (Cambridge: Cambridge University Press).

——. 1905. "On Denoting," *Mind* 14:480–93.

Ruthrof, Horst. 1984. "The Problem of Inferred Modality in Narrative," *Journal of Literary Semantics* 13, no. 2:97–108.

Ryan, Marie-Laure. 1991. *Possible Worlds, Artificial Intelligence, and Narrative Theory* (Bloomington: Indiana University Press).

——. 1992. "Possible Worlds in Recent Literary Theory," *Style* 26, no. 4:528–53.

Ryle, Gilbert. 1972. "Intentionality-Theory and the Nature of Thinking," in *Jenseits von Sein und Nichtsein: Beiträge zur Meinong Forschung*, ed. Rudolf Haller, 1–18 (Graz: Akademische Druck- und Verlaganstalt).

Saleemi, Anjum P. 1992. *Universal Grammar and Language Learnability* (Cambridge: Cambridge University Press).

Salus, Peter H. 1976. "Universal Grammar, 1000–1850," in Parret (1976: 85–101).

Saussure, Ferdinand de. 1959 [1916]. *Course in General Linguistics*, ed. Charles Bally, Albert Sechehaye, and Albert Riedlinger, trans. Wade Baskin (New York: McGraw-Hill).

Schiffrin, Deborah. 1987. *Discourse Markers* (Cambridge: Cambridge University Press).

——. 1990. "The Principle of Intersubjectivity in Communication and Conversation," *Semiotica* 8, nos. 1–2:121–51.

Schlick, Moritz. 1979 [1925–36]. *Philosophical Papers*, vol. 2, ed. Henk L. Mulder and Barbara F. B. Van de Velde-Schlick, trans. Peter Heath et al. (Dordrecht: D. Reidel).

——. 1984c [1923]. "Twelve-Tone Composition," in *Style and Idea: Selected Writings of Arnold Schoenberg*, ed. Leonard Stein, trans. Leo Black, 207–8 (London: Faber & Faber).

Schönberg, Arnold. 1984a [1941]. "Composition with Twelve Tones (I)," in *Style and Idea: Selected Writings of Arnold Schoenberg*, ed. Leonard Stein, trans. Leo Black, 214–45 (London: Faber & Faber).

——. 1984b [1941]. "Composition with Twelve Tones (II)," in *Style and Idea: Selected Writings of Arnold Schoenberg*, ed. Leonard Stein, trans. Leo Black, 245–49 (London: Faber & Faber).

Searle, John. 1969. *Speech Acts: An Essay in the Philosophy of Language* (Cambridge: Cambridge University Press).

——. 1991 [1975]. "Indirect Speech Acts," in *Pragmatics: A Reader*, ed. Steven Davis, 265–77 (New York: Oxford University Press).

Sells, Peter. 1985. *Lectures on Contemporary Syntactic Theories* (Stanford, Calif.: Center for the Study of Language and Information).

Short, Michael. 1988. "Speech Presentation, the Novel and the Press," in *The Taming of the Text: Explorations in Language, Literature and Culture*, ed. Willie van Peer, 61–81 (London: Routledge).

Silverman, Kaja. 1983. *The Subject of Semiotics* (New York: Oxford University Press).

Simone, Raffaele. 1987. "Languages as *Méthodes Analytiques* in Condillac," in Buzzetti and Ferriani (1987: 65–74).

Šklovskij, Viktor. 1965 [1917]. "Art as Technique," in *Russian Formalist Criticism*, ed. Lee T. Lemon and Marion J. Reis, 3–24 (Lincoln: University of Nebraska Press).

Smith, Barbara Herrnstein. 1980. "Narrative Versions, Narrative Theories," *Critical Inquiry 7*, no. 1:213–36.

Smith, Barry. 1987. "Husserl, Language, and the Ontology of the Act," in Buzzetti and Ferriani (1987: 205–27).

Smith, Neil, and Deirdre Wilson. 1979. *Modern Linguistics: The Results of Chomsky's Revolution* (Bloomington: Indiana University Press).

Sözer, Önay. 1989. "Die Idealität der Bedeutung in den Vorlesungen Husserls über Bedeuntungslehre (1908)," in Jamme and Pöggeler (1989: 121–40).

Sperber, Dan, and Deirdre Wilson. 1986. *Relevance: Communication and Cognition* (Cambridge, Mass., and Oxford: Harvard University Press and Basil Blackwell).

Spiegelberg, Herbert. 1960. *The Phenomenological Movement: A Historical Introduction* (The Hague: Martinus Nijhoff).

Stassen, Leon. 1985. *Comparison and Universal Grammar* (Oxford: Basil Blackwell).

Steiner, Peter. 1984. *Russian Formalism: A Metapoetics* (Ithaca, N.Y.: Cornell University Press).

——. 1990. "Gustav Špet and the Prague School: Conceptual Frames for the Study of Language," in *Semantic Analysis of Literary Texts*, ed. Eric de Haard, Thomas Langerak, and Willem G. Weststeijn, 553–62 (Amsterdam: Elsevier Science Publishers).

——, ed. 1982. *The Prague School: Selected Writings, 1929–46*, trans. John Burbank, Peter Steiner, et al. (Austin: University of Texas Press).

Stetter, Christian. 1985. "Pragmatik, Kompetenz, Öffentlichkeit," in *Romanistik Integrativ: Festschrift für Wolfgang Pollak*, ed. Wolfgang Bandhauer and Robert Tanzmeister, 547–64 (Vienna: Wilhelm Braunmüller).

Stroud, Barry. 1982. "Transcendental Arguments," in *Kant on Pure Reason*, ed. Ralph C. Walker, 117–31 (Oxford: Oxford University Press).

Swearingen, C. Jan. 1990. "Dialogue and Dialectic: The Logic of Conversation and the Interpretation of Logic," in *The Interpretation of Dialogue*, ed. Tullio Maranhao, 47–68 (Chicago: University of Chicago Press).

Tarski, Alfred. 1990 [1944]. "The Semantic Conception of Truth and the Foundations of Semantics," in *The Philosophy of Language*, ed. A. P. Martinich, 48–71 (Oxford: Oxford University Press).

Tesnière, Lucien. 1959. *Eléments de syntaxe structurale* (Paris: Klincksieck).

Thomas of Erfurt. 1972 [ca. 1300–1310]. *Grammativa Speculativa*, trans. G. L. Bursill-Hall (London: Longman).

Thompson, Michael. 1979. *Rubbish Theory: The Creation and Destruction of Value* (Oxford: Oxford University Press).

Todorov, Tzvetan. 1969. *Grammaire du "Décaméron"* (The Hague: Mouton).

——. 1977 [1971]. *The Poetics of Prose,* trans. Richard Howard (Ithaca, N.Y.: Cornell University Press).

——. 1981 [1968]. *Introduction to Poetics,* trans. Richard Howard (Minneapolis: University of Minnesota Press).

Tolliver, Joyce. 1990. "Discourse Analysis and the Interpretation of Literary Narrative," *Style* 24, no. 2:266–83.

Tomaševskij, Boris. 1965 [1925]. "Thematics," in *Russian Formalist Criticism: Four Essays,* ed. and trans. Lee T. Lemon and Marion J. Reis, 61–98 (Lincoln: University of Nebraska Press).

Topia, André. 1984. "The Matrix and the Echo: Intertextuality in *Ulysses,*" in *Poststructuralist Joyce: Essays from the French,* ed. Derek Attridge and Daniel Ferrer, 103–25 (Cambridge: Cambridge University Press).

——. 1986. " 'Sirens': The Emblematic Vibration," in *James Joyce: The Centennial Symposium,* ed. Morris Beja, 76–81 (Urbana: University of Illinois Press).

Toulmin, Stephen. 1958. *The Uses of Argument* (Cambridge: Cambridge University Press).

——. 1982. "The Construal of Reality: Criticism in Modern and Postmodern Science," *Critical Inquiry* 9:93–111.

Twardowski, Kasimierz. 1894. *Zur Lehre vom Inhalt und Gegenstand der Vorstellungen* (Vienna: Alfred Holder).

——. 1977 [1894]. *On the Content and Object of Presentations,* trans. R. Grossman (The Hague: Martinus Nijhoff).

Tynjanov, Jurji, and Roman Jakobson. 1971 [1928]. "Problems in the Study of Literature and Language," trans. Hebert Eagle, in *Readings in Russian Poetics: Formalist and Structuralist Views,* ed. Ladislav Matejka and Krystyna Pomorska, 79–81 (Cambridge, Mass.: MIT Press).

Ullmann, Stephen. 1957. *The Principles of Semantics,* 2d ed. (London: Basil Blackwell and Mott).

——. 1964. *Style in the French Novel,* 2d ed. (Oxford: Basil Blackwell).

Ulmer, Gregory. 1983. "The Object of Post-Criticism," in *The Anti-Aesthetic: Essays on Postmodern Culture,* ed. Hal Foster, 83–110 (Port Townsend, Wash.: Bay Press).

——. 1989. *Teletheory: Grammatology in the Age of Video* (New York: Routledge).

Vachek, Josef. 1964a [1948]. "Written Language and Printed Language," in *A Prague School Reader in Linguistics,* ed. Josef Vachek, 453–60 (Bloomington: Indiana University Press).

——. 1964b [1939]. "Zum Problem der geschriebenen Sprache," in *A Prague School Reader in Linguistics,* ed. Josef Vachek, 441–52 (Bloomington: Indiana University Press).

Vaihinger, Hans. 1913. *Die Philosophie des als ob,* 2d ed. (Berlin: Reuther & Reichard).

van Frassen, Bastiaan C. 1991. "Time in Physical and Narrative Structure," in *Chronotypes: The Construction of Time,* ed. John Bender and David E. Wellbery, 19–37 (Stanford, Calif.: Stanford University Press).

Verschueren, Jef. 1985. Review of Geoffrey N. Leech, *Principles of Pragmatics,* and Stephen Levinson, *Pragmatics, Journal of Linguistics* 21, no. 2:459–70.

——. 1987. "Metapragmatics and Universals of Linguistic Action," in *Linguistic Action: Some Empirical-Conceptual Studies,* ed. Jef Verschueren, 125–10 (Norwood, N.J.: Ablex Publishing Corp.).

Vološinov, V. N. 1973 [1929]. *Marxism and the Philosophy of Language,* trans. Ladislav Matejka and
    I. R. Titunik (New York: Seminar Press).

Von Wright, G. H. 1949. *Form and Content in Logic* (Cambridge: Cambridge University Press).

Waggenbach, Klaus. 1958. *Franz Kafka: Eine Biographie seiner Jugend, 1883–1912* (Bern: A. Francke).

Walker, Jeremy D. B. 1965. *A Study of Frege* (Ithaca, N.Y.: Cornell University Press).

Walton, Kendall. 1990. *Mimesis as Make-Believe: On the Foundations of the Representational Arts*
    (Cambridge, Mass.: Harvard University Press).

Warning, Rainer. 1980. "Staged Discourse: Remarks on the Pragmatics of Fiction," *Dispositio* 5, nos.
    13–14:35–54.

Webber, Bonnie Lynn. 1979. *A Formal Approach to Discourse Anaphora* (New York: Garland).

Weber, Ingegorg. 1986. "Die Sprache des Scweigens in Virginia Woolfs Roman *Between the Acts,*" in
    Theorie und Praxis im Erzählen des 19. und 20. Jahrhunderts, ed. Winfried Herget et al., 141–52
    (Tübingen: Gunter Narr).

Welton, Donn. 1989. "Verbindende Namen—Verbundene Gegenstände: Frege und Husserl über
    Bedeutung," in Jamme and Pöggeler (1989: 141–91).

Whorf, Benjamin L. 1956. *Language, Thought, and Reality,* ed. John B. Carroll (Cambridge, Mass.:
    MIT Press).

Wicke, Jennifer. 1987. "Postmodernism: The Perfume of Information," *Yale Journal of Criticism*
    1:145–60.

Willett, John. 1978. *The New Sobriety, 1917–1933: Art and Politics in the Weimar Period* (Hampshire:
    Thames & Hudson).

Wittgenstein, Ludwig. 1958 [1933–35]. *The Blue and the Brown Books: Preliminary Studies for the
    "Philosophical Investigations"* (New York: Harper & Row).

——. 1961 [1914–16]. *Notebooks,* ed. G. H. von Wright and G. E. M. Anscombe, trans. G. E. M.
    Anscombe (New York: Harper & Row).

——. 1969. *Philosophical Investigations,* ed. G. H. von Wright and G. E. M. Anscombe, trans. G. E.
    M. Anscombe, 3d ed. (New York: Macmillan Publishing Co.).

——. 1973 [1929]. "Some Remarks on Logical Form," in Copi and Beard (1973: 31–37).

——. 1974. *Philosophical Grammar,* ed. Rush Rhees, trans. Anthony Kenny (Berkeley: University of
    California Press).

——. 1986 [1922]. *Tractatus Logico-Philosophicus,* trans. C. K. Ogden (London: Routledge & Kegan
    Paul).

Wolf, Karl. 1972. "Der Bedeutungswandel von 'Gegenstand' in der Schule Meinongs," in Haller
    (1972: 63–68).

Woolf, Virginia. 1927. *To the Lighthouse* (London: Harcourt Brace Jovanovich).

——. 1941. *Between the Acts* (Orlando, Fla.: Harcourt Brace Jovanovich).

Zacchi, Romana. 1986. "Discourse Types, Discourse Objects in *Ulysses,*" in *Myriadminded Man:
    Jottings on Joyce,* ed. Rosa Maria Bosinelli, Paola Pugliatti, and Romana Zacchi, 185–93 (Bolo-
    gna: Cooperative Libraria Universitaria Editrice Bologna).

Žižek, Slavoj. 1989. *The Sublime Object of Ideology* (London: Verso).

Index

Prague School, 140–41; polyfunctionalist theories of, 141–42, 155, 161–68
Pratt, Mary Louise, 158–64
Prince, Gerald, 92, 93
Propp, Vladimir, 89, 95
Prozeß, Der: bureaucratization in, 107, 240 n.10; frames of reference in, 120–21, 123–24, 127, 129, 136; internal focalization in, 99, 100, 119; metasemantic form of, 134–38; modal operators in, 117, 130–36; object-theoretical aspects of, 105–24; and possible worlds semantics, 124–38. *See also* Model worlds; Object theory; Possible worlds semantics; Semantic indeterminacy

Quine, Willard Van Orman, 11, 103, 104–105

Realemes, 117–18, 121
Referential opacity, 103
Represented discourse: in narrative, 139, 243–44 n.1; in *Between the Acts,* 150–54, 171–81. See also *Between the Acts;* Free indirect discourse
Rimmon-Kenan, Shlomith, 31–32
Ronen, Ruth, 238 n.2, 241 n.22
Rubbish theory, 120
Ryan, Marie-Laure, 89

Schönberg, Arnold, 46–49
Semantic indeterminacy: and the issue of context, 136–38, 218–20; and the problem of interpretation, 130; radical varieties of, 129–38; trivial varieties of, 128–29
Semantics, 96–97, 102–105, 124–31; as distinguished from pragmatics, 230 n.31. *See also* Model worlds; Possible worlds semantics; *Prozeß, Der*
"Sirens": vis-à-vis actantial paradigms, 56–57, 89–93; anacoluthon in, 79; and axiomatic/

constructional systems, 59–60, 64–71; and Chomsky on deep and surface structure, 82–86; and computational technologies, 71–72; and logical calculi, 67–69; and the logic of puns, 76; and logico-grammatical syntax, 60–71; melodic and harmonic dimensions of, 50; and morpho-syntactic features of English, 54–58, 75–82; and narrative syntax, 88–93; and the nature of narrative, 51; onomatopoeia in, 77; and paratactic structure, 81–82; polyphonic form in, 49–53; and the relationship between music and language, 39–42
Steiner, Peter, 159, 246 n.16
Syntagmatic and paradigmatic relations, 47, 51, 52, 209–15
Syntax, 1–2, 59–88, 190–93; of narrative, 38–39, 88–93. *See also* "Sirens"

Tarski, Alfred, 59–60, 64, 69–70
Thomas Aquinas, Saint, 173
Thompson, Michael, 120
Todorov, Tzvetan, 1, 9–10, 29–30, 90–91
Transformational generative grammar, 237 n.50, 237–38 n.51
Twelve-tone row, 46–48, 54

Universal grammar: Chomsky's theory of, 17–18; vis-à-vis narrative grammar, 28–32, 88; as material calculus, 30–31; as object and method of description, 4, 226 n.7
Unsinn and *Widersinn:* Husserl's distinction between, 61–63

Vološinov, V. N., 146–49

Whorf, Benjamin Lee, 11
Wittgenstein, Ludwig, 64–65

David Herman is Associate Professor of English at
Purdue University.

Library of Congress Cataloging-in-Publication Data
Herman, David
Universal grammar and narrative form / David Herman.
p.   cm. — (Sound and meaning)
Includes bibliographical references and index.
ISBN 0-8223-1656-0 (alk. paper). — ISBN 0-8223-1668-4 (alk. paper : pbk.)
1. English fiction—20th century—History and criticism—Theory,
etc. 2. Woolf, Virginia, 1882–1941—Technique. 3. Joyce, James,
1882–1941—Technique. 4. Kafka, Franz, 1883–1924—Technique.
5. Grammar, Comparative and general. 6. Narration (Rhetoric)
7. Fiction—Technique. 8. Literary form. I. Title. II. Series.
PR826.H47   1995
801'.953'09041—dc20   95-6223